Based on the massive Institute of Race Relations Report, *Colour and Citizenship*, this present study brings the story down to the end of 1969.

The original report's crucial conclusion retains its stark significance; the arrival of large numbers of immigrants into these islands has but heightened problems already existing, tensions already at work in our society. In short, urban decay, the frustrating limitations of our medical and educational services, new kinds of working conditions appearing and old ones disappearing under the impact of technological change, above all, the ever-growing gulf between the very rich and the very poor, may have been exacerbated but were certainly not imported by the immigrants. They are problems fundamental to our present British way of life. *Colour, Citizenship and British Society* puts many records straight.

NICHOLAS DEAKIN WITH BRIAN COHEN AND JULIA MCNEAL

Colour, Citizenship and British Society

based on the Institute of Race Relations Report

with a foreword by E. J. B. Rose, editor of the original report

Panther Modern Society

Colour and Citizenship: An Institute of Race Relations report by E. J. B. Rose and associates, first published by Oxford University Press 1969.

Colour, Citizenship and British Society based on the Institute of Race Relations report, first published by Panther Books 1970
Copyright © Institute of Race Relations 1970

Printed in Great Britain by Cox & Wyman Ltd., London, Reading and Fakenham and published by Panther Books, 3 Upper James Street, London, W.1.

Contents

CONTENTS

7

Editor's Note

The present volume is a substantially abridged and up-dated version of the report *Colour and Citizenship*, which was published in July 1969. In making the changes necessary for this edition we have tried wherever possible to be faithful to the style, presentation and interpretation in the longer work: where significant changes have been made there is an indication in the text. We have also taken this opportunity to correct the too numerous misprints and small slips that appear in the longer volume and are explained – but not excused – by the haste with which that work was produced. In general, we have tried to follow the ground plan of the original volume. In cases where the pressure on space generated by the drastic nature of the abridgement has proved too great (the present volume is less than half the length of the original work) we have preferred to omit altogether rather than carry condensation to the point of destroying the flow of the argument. In some instances we have referred the reader back to the longer volume for substantiating evidence or detailed exposition of complex points.

In detail, the relationship between the present volume and the longer report is as follows:

Chapter 1 of the present volume draws on chapters 2 and 3 of the original, new chapter 2 on old chapter 5, new chapter 3 on old chapters 6, 7 and 8, new chapter 4 on old chapters 9 to 14 and 30, new chapter 5 on old chapters 15, 16, 26, 27 and 29, new chapter 6 on old chapter 17, new chapter 7 on old chapter 18, new chapter 8 on old chapters 19 and 31, new chapter 9 on old chapter 20, new chapter 10 on old chapter 21. New chapter 11 is based on old chapters 23–25 and new chapter 12 on the first part of old chapter 28. New chapter 13 is based on old chapter 29 and new chapter 14 is substantially revised. Old chapters 1, 4, 22 and the second part of chapter 28, together with the Appendices, have been wholly omitted.

One chapter requires special mention – the section on the survey of attitudes conducted by Dr. Mark Abrams (chapter 12 in the present volume). In cutting this chapter we have been very conscious that it was the section which has attracted most comment and discussion. In the abridgement, with which Dr. Abrams was good enough to help us, we have tried to avoid unnecessary changes of emphasis while making the cuts necessary to bring the chapter down to length. However, there are a few additional amendments intended to help clarify some points in the original version. In particular, there is a slight shift of emphasis in the presentation of the prejudice-tolerance scale which formed a part of Dr. Abrams' analysis; we have chosen on this occasion to consider these findings more from the perspective of the extent of prejudice than in relation to the presence of tolerance. A copy of the questionnaire used in the original investigation is lodged in the Institute of Race Relations' Library, where it can be seen on request. Readers interested in following the debate on the original chapter are referred to the articles cited in the text.

Finally, a word about those involved in the present work. Like the Forth Bridge, this report has sometimes seemed to need endless repainting in order to remain in service. Several of my colleagues, like myself, have been perched on this particular structure continuously for a matter of two years. Despite this, they have somehow managed to preserve an appetite for the job and the commitment without which work in this field is meaningless. Brian Cohen (who is responsible for chapters 3, 4 and 8 in the present version) and Julia Gaitskell, now Julia McNeal (who rewrote chapters 7 and 11) have been involved in this work from the beginning. I'm glad to have the chance here of recording my lasting gratitude to them for their contribution at all stages in the operation. They have been helped in the present work by Margot Levy (who rewrote chapters 9 and 10) and Alan Marsh, who produced the new version of chapter 12. I was responsible for the remainder of the rewriting.

Several of those who contributed to the longer report were

kind enough to help us with revision of their work. I have already referred to Dr. Abrams, who was most helpful; Mr. Paul Ward himself undertook the abridgement of the second half of chapter 9 and Professor Maurice Peston was kind enough to review the revision of his material, as was Mr. Badr Dahya. Mrs. Valerie Jackson (now Mrs. Herr) commented copiously and constructively on the revision of her material on the censuses. Astrid Joseph was responsible for the endless task of retyping drafts and kept her cool throughout. We are very grateful to her and to Margaret John, who helped her.

Mrs. Elizabeth (Burney) Parker read the whole text and made valuable proposals for amendments. Jim Rose (who was Director of the Survey of Race Relations) which benevolently over the dismemberment of the volume that bears his name and contributed helpful suggestions, together with the introduction that follows. Our associates at the Institute of Race Relations – who will forgive us if we do not single out individuals – also provided assistance. Finally, it is a pleasure to be able to thank our publishers in this paperback edition, John Boothe and William Miller, who were everything editors should be.

The families of those involved were, as usual, the unsung heroes; to them go our particular thanks.

Nicholas Deakin

Joint Unit for Minority and Policy Research,
London,
January 1970

Foreword

This book is an abridgement of *Colour and Citizenship* which appeared in July 1969. The first edition sold out within two months and has since been reprinted; but it runs to over 800 pages and there is clearly a need for a shorter version which will bring to the general reader the findings and proposals of the original report without burdening him with the mass of supporting evidence. The report was fortunate in the amount of attention which it received but for our findings to make their full contribution to the development of race relations in this country they must reach a wider audience.

Colour and Citizenship was itself the outcome of a five-year survey of race relations in Britain which I was invited to direct for the Institute of Race Relations. Very little was known in 1963 about the coloured immigrant communities and how they were adapting themselves to this country; still less was known about the reactions of the British to their presence. The survey was to assemble a body of knowledge and it was to aim at practical results. We would commission a number of independent research studies and we would write an overall report in which we would put forward our recommendations for policy.

Philip Mason, the Director of the Institute who conceived the idea of the survey and the Nuffield Foundation who generously agreed to finance it, found a precedent in the great study of the Negro in America which Gunnar Myrdal, a Swedish economist, had undertaken twenty-five years earlier. They hoped that something of the kind might be done in Britain, at a much earlier stage while the situation was still fluid and before attitudes hardened.

Myrdal's influence continued to operate when we began to

make the plan for our study. For he had seen that in the United States the Negro problem was in reality the white man's problem and that it was the white man's behaviour towards the Negro which had created and perpetuated the problem. It was one of the strengths of his study that he focused his attention on American society at large, both because this was where power resided and because he assumed that the Negro's problem existed and was modified by the forces operating in the larger American society. Twenty-five years later this was also to be the conclusion of the National Advisory Commission on Civil Disorders (the Kerner Commission), which was appointed by President Johnson following the riots which took place in the summer of 1967.

In the United States the problem was a familiar one and attitudes and positions were largely fixed. We were to consider a very recent phenomenon, the presence of coloured immigrants who had been in England for less than ten years; and yet it seemed to us that Myrdal's approach was in many ways also appropriate for us. It is true that he found an enormous literature on the Negro, while little was known about our immigrant communities: we should certainly need to commission separate studies of these groups. But whatever the influences of their origins and cultures on their adaptation to our society, the behaviour of the British would in the end be decisive and so the main focus of our inquiry was on the response of the British. British society and British policies would be the subject of inquiry at least as much as the immigrant communities. Our study would have to be concerned with the social life of the nation.

The pivot of Myrdal's analysis was his perception of an inner contradiction between the American Creed, the profession of faith in the equality and the right to liberty of all Americans enshrined in the Declaration of Independence, and the American practice of according unequal treatment to one section of the population. He perceived that this contradiction between belief and practice posed an acute moral problem for white Americans, which he called *An American Dilemma*.

Could we assume a British dilemma? Could we postulate that there might be a moral conflict between the British ideals of fair play and of equality before the law, on one side, and possible discrimination against groups of citizens distinguished by the colour of their skin, on the other? Great Britain too had owned slaves and had freed them, but her slaves had lived 3,000 miles away across the seas. When 100 years after emancipation their descendants came here to seek a living, they came as immigrants and it might therefore be assumed that because they were immigrants they would not be on the conscience of the country in the way that the Negro had for generations been on the conscience of Americans. There might however be some feeling of obligation towards these immigrants because they were members of the Commonwealth, but this would have less force if there were different attitudes towards the coloured Commonwealth and the white Dominions.

Underlying these assumptions, that immigrants despite the possession of a common citizenship would not be felt to have a a claim to equal treatment, there lay yet a further assumption about the importance of colour in determining the response of the British. This assumption was crucial and ran counter to prevailing theory. The ideas that had held the field were first, that in our class-conscious society colour is seen as a facet of class and a coloured man is perceived as occupying a position at the bottom of the class spectrum; this was the so-called colour-class theory. Another school held that colour should be equated with foreignness and that the coloured man is perceived as a stranger whose colour makes him appear more strange than other foreigners. He is in fact the archetypal stranger. On either of these theories the coloured immigrant would find barriers erected against him which would spring from class-consciousness or from xenophobia: but it is implicit in both theories that these barriers can be overcome as coloured people rise in the social scale or become familiar with British norms of behaviour and adopt them. Both theories had much force, but we felt that neither could wholly account for a phenomenon familiar elsewhere. European immigrants to the United States had overcome barriers of this kind where Negroes had failed to do so. This phenomenon was due not to any inherent incapacity on the part of the black minority deriving from purely racial criteria (the notion that such criteria have any objective existence is now virtually extinct), but to the effects of discrimination past and present on the part of the white majority and to the progressively narrowing opportunities for those without skills in a changing economic situation. Without wanting to draw too close a parallel between the two situations, we could not exclude the possibility that something similar might occur here.

We therefore took the decision to concentrate on the factor of colour in most of the commissioned research. Our discussions with those social scientists who agreed to undertake research for us, convinced us that we must break away from the focus of an immigrant-host relationship and turn instead to a study of the relationships between groups within a society in which one of the groups was distinguished by the factor of colour. We felt that we must consider the possibility that colour generates a response which cannot be satisfactorily explained in terms of class or the fact of strangeness.

These then were some of the assumptions with which we began the survey. They would have to be tested against the evidence and in a rapidly developing situation they were also to be tested by events which took place during the course of our study. We were not conducting research in a vacuum. The situation which we were studying was changing all the time.

The landmarks in this short period include the 1964 General Election in which the issues of race and immigration for the first time played an important part and threw the Labour Party on to the defensive. Then, within a year, the Labour Government issued a White Paper which imposed further restriction on immigration. 1965 also saw the passing into law of the first Race Relations Act and the creation of the Race Relations Board. The political temperature then appeared to be lowered during the next two years, until the arrival of the several thousand Asians from Kenya, entitled to entry as citizens of the U.K. and Colonies, revived the agitation about numbers entering the country. This led the Government early in 1968 to break its pledge to these citizens and to change the rules governing their entry, an action that was doubly dishonourable, both because it distinguished between citizens on the grounds of their colour and because it repudiated a solemn obligation. The confidence of coloured immigrants already in this country was shaken; it was not long before they were deeply disturbed by Mr. Enoch Powell's Birmingham speech and the expression of prejudice which followed in some parts of the country. The passing in the same month of the second Race Relations Act outlawing discrimination in employment and housing was overshadowed by these events.

It was at this point, that we decided to abandon our original intention and to produce a summary report of our findings. Within the original plan of the survey, we had commissioned or assisted eighteen major and twenty minor research projects. The timetable for the survey envisaged the individual projects being completed – and in many cases published – before we produced our final report. By the spring of 1968 it became clear that this original concept of a final study based on completed research covering the whole field would not materialize, nor would it satisfy current requirements. We therefore decided as a matter of urgency to produce a report which would draw on the findings of the various research projects and make this information available while it was fresh and relevant.

Although the report owed its form to the changing political circumstances which led us to accelerate its production, the structure closely followed the original plan which was devised at the outset of the survey. The report and this abridgement falls into four main divisions. First, there is an account of the British society which the coloured immigrants were to enter. This is followed by a description of the sending societies, the history of the migrations and their development within this country. The central section deals with the interaction of the native British and the immigrant communities. This is a study of challenge and response. Finally we assess the implications of our findings and make our recommendations.

The report was the product of a number of hands but nearly half of it was written by Nicholas Deakin who was assistant director of the survey throughout its five years. It is most appropriate that he should have prepared this abridgement which will, we hope, bring the analysis and findings of *Colour and Citizenship* to a wide audience.

E. J. B. Rose

London,
January 1970

Chapter One

After the Liberal Hour

It was the late Adlai Stevenson who first formulated the doctrine of 'the Liberal Hour'. This is the moment when public men of all shades of opinion, from radical to conservative, accept the necessity of a movement in policy on a social problem issue, in the liberal direction. For race relations in Britain the liberal hour has already passed. It lasted at most two years. 1968, the year in which it ended, was what the French call *année zéro* for those who believe there are solutions to be found to problems arising from interracial contact and that the way to achieve them is through the traditional devices of discussion, bargaining, and legislation.

One characteristic of the liberal hour, while it lasts, is that response to idealistic themes is general, even among those who normally reject an appeal to them as impractical or emotionally dishonest. At least four such themes can be distinguished in the appeal to action on race relations. First, a belief that the claim of ethnic groups, suffering disabilities deriving from colour, to a greater share in the rights and benefits enjoyed by white majorities is a natural subject for sympathy and concern. ('Am I not a man and a brother?') Secondly, the view that the significance of those issues transcends purely national interests and must be considered in a broader perspective. Thirdly, the Christian view of the overriding importance of the brotherhood of man has often been seen as important; so finally, has the straightforward belief that human suffering, whatever its cause, urgently demands alleviation through formal intervention by the state.

Once, all these themes could evoke a clear response. Some of them have deep roots in our culture and, severally or together, provide the momentum for such diverse episodes as the anti-slavery movement, the response of the Non-conformist conscience to the exploitation of Africa, and the radical critique of imperialism. Two years ago, they commanded sufficient sympathy to underpin Roy Jenkins' attempt to translate liberal attitudes into practice. Now, even the relevance of the last is questioned. Honourable men shrug their shoulders and turn aside from a situation whose implications in terms of human misery are better known than ever before. The international perspective has for some time past provided mounting evidence of the apparent inevitability of racial conflict, vastly magnified by the electronic revolution which brings televised violence from all quarters of the globe to every sitting-room. The image projected by this process is of mankind threatened with an apocalyptic rendezvous at some future super-Detroit. At the same time, there has been a progressive process of disillusionment, with the Commonwealth and with black Africa: for a country struggling with apparently intractable domestic problems, the easiest moral to draw is that we should opt out of our residual responsibilities.

But disillusion has gone further than this. There are now those who cannot by any stretch of the imagination be dismissed as racialist, who begin to wonder if the whole problem can be most effectively eliminated by exporting it. The appeal from the sufferings of minorities is stood on its head to provide support for the thesis that the liberal least of all men can accept — that if a problem is out of sight it can be out of mind as well.

A Rubicon was finally crossed in the spring of 1968. This was when the British Government decided, on grounds which were quite openly those of expediency rather than principle, that it could no longer accept responsibility for certain of its citizens because of the colour of their skins. Unlike the Dutch, we were not prepared to accept the responsibility for winding up our past imperial role. At that moment, the liberal rhetoric with which ministers clothed their policies finally ceased to convince. The credibility gap opened; and through it walked those who defined their objective in terms of 'realism'. That is to say, the wholesale rejection of all idealism in favour of a calculation based solely on what are perceived as British interests.

In this atmosphere, the British dilemma first identified by the American sociologist Clarence Senior – the tension between the ethic of fairness embedded in our culture and system of law and the failure to live up to those standards in practice – has never been easier to resolve, because the relevance of the ethic to this particular situation is no longer accepted.

The implication for this book is that appeals to idealism are no longer in order. Any proposals for the amelioration of relationships between minorities and majority – and this book is intended principally as a constructive contribution towards policy making in this field – must be justified in purely practical terms. That is, they must be seen to have an application to the real problems of the adjustment process, and relate to the short run as well as the long term, the backstreets as well as Whitehall.

In adopting this approach there are two preliminary issues which we would like to resolve. First, that in rejecting the liberal's approach from ideology, we do not wish to be understood to be rejecting the liberals. The English, as George Orwell once pointed out, take a peculiar pleasure in detecting hypocrisy, which has been elevated in our culture almost to the status of a Deadly Sin. But whatever the cultural imperatives, nothing can excuse the disgraceful way in which the liberals are now being treated, particularly by those who at the height of the liberal hour subscribed most fervently to the liberal orthodoxy – in other words, 'fair-weather liberals'. The fact that the means that liberals have chosen to adopt in this situation – occasionally, it is true, the sherry glass, more often the letter, the pamphlet, or the open meeting – were pitifully inadequate and too soon abandoned is not ultimately their fault. The failure of the rhetoric cut the ground from under their feet. Unlike their critics, at least they tried – even if they did not understand.

Nor do we accept the nihilism that has replaced liberalism as the fashionable orthodoxy. The twin doctrines of the necessity of violence and the impossibility of any solution short of sweeping all the pieces off the board and setting the game up afresh now command very wide support, and find strange bed-fellows among the believers. Although parallel events in other multi-racial societies are important, we do not accept that they are decisive evidence of the inevitability of violent conflict. For, ultimately, the determining element in deciding the future of race relations in Britain is the character of British society and the manner in which it responds to the stresses set up during the process of adaptation and change. To the extent that our society and its values are unique, so will the response be unique. And, in our view, there are still good grounds for arguing that present difficulties can be resolved without compromising either the cultural integrity of our society or the values and principles which animate it.

Moreover, all studies of minorities must logically imply a concern with the majority. No analysis which takes as its starting point the notion of 'immigrant problem' can be complete; for what is at stake is essentially the outcome not of a unique encounter but of another in a long series of disputes about who belongs within our society. But it is not only the question of the right of entry into this society that needs to be resolved: there is also the question of the terms on which acceptance is obtained. A group may enter another society through migration — that is, from the outside in the strictly geographical sense. It may then adjust itself so completely to its new surroundings that it merges into the host society and loses its separate identity. This can conveniently be labelled 'assimilation'; it is a process usually involving inter-marriage and likely to take generations to complete. To say of a group that it has assimilating tendencies argues a willingness to adopt the culture of the majority and to become identified with it. The concept has recently fallen into disrepute: it tends to involve patronage on the part of the majority and insecurity on the part of the minority. Nevertheless, there are many instances of full assimilation, of groups as well as of individuals in Britain. Perhaps the most notable example are the Huguenots who can be separately identified only by name.

And then there is integration. This is a term almost entirely emptied of meaning by repetition, in the course of which a whole range of different meanings have become attached to it. In fact, integration – as it has recently been employed by those social scientists who are students of race relations – denotes a process whereby a minority group, while retaining its own culture and religion, adapts itself to and is accepted as a permanent part of the majority society in all external aspects of association. This form of integration – in the sense of a part being integrated into the whole while retaining its separate identity – is sometimes called cultural pluralism or, simply, pluralism and, as the name implies, it involves the co-existence and mutual tolerance of several cultures within one society. Integration in this sense may be a final phase or may lead on to assimilation. It was in this sense that Roy Jenkins, in his attempts to define goals for policy, defined integration as 'not a flattening process of assimilation but as equal opportunity accompanied by cultural diversity, in an atmosphere of mutual tolerance.'[1] That this formula is not merely an elegant abstraction but a practical reflection of the diversity that already exists in our society can be simply illustrated from the experience of other immigrant groups which have been accepted into the wider circle of British society but still constitute distinct identities that can easily be identified – the Irish, the Jews, the post-war European migration (the most intensive this country has ever experienced).

To reach the state of pluralism achieved by these earlier migrations may take one or more generations. In the early stages of an economic migration, where the newcomer is struggling to establish himself, the process of adaptation may be slow and the degree the minimum required to obtain employment and shelter. This may in turn be met by the minimum amount of acceptance. This *modus vivendi* between host and immigrant has been termed 'accommodation'. When the newcomers begin to adapt themselves to the roles required of them in order to obtain employment and access to the social services, they are able to retain, rebuild or re-orient their own patterns and values. This process will differ as between groups that are potentially self-segregating, integrating or assimilating. Once begun it is not by any means irreversible. The process may be retarded, halted or even set into reverse by hostility. The pace at which it proceeds will differ for different groups and will not be uniform for all the members of the group.

The pattern eventually assumed by the relationship between minorities and the majority society (of which they have eventually come to form part) will be governed to a large extent by the values held in common in that society. The problem is to pin down the significance of these values and to establish their relevance. Attempts to chart the assumption with which the ordinary citizen approaches those problems that face him have generally revealed a number of misty pre-conceptions whose substance dissolves on closer analysis. Or alternatively, investigators find that values whose significance has been taken for granted, like the American Creed – the pivot of Gunnar Myrdal's analysis of the American situation[2] – have only intermittent and sometimes distant relevance for some citizens. For these reasons we have preferred to employ a concept which has a concrete reference through its function of binding society together – the concept of citizenship. It is this term that we intend to explore a little further, as a means of placing our analysis in perspective.

Definitions of citizenship are simple enough to produce: they are part of a lawyer's stock-in-trade. But the term citizenship, as we propose to employ it here, also implies something broader – the nexus that in any State links society and the individual. In other words, we conceive of citizenship more in the terms in which classical political philosophers discussed it and less in relation to practical issues of citizenship and nationality law, like the right to a passport. Not that this is a purely technical matter, as William Joyce (who was hanged for possessing one) and British citizens in East Africa (who found theirs devalued overnight) discovered.

The key issue in assessing the real significance of citizenship in the broader sense is the terms on which the rights conferred by the relationship between State and citizen are guaranteed, and the manner and extent of access to them. And the best case which, more than any other, helps to resolve this issue is that of the individual who falls into one of the various groups classed as outsiders and the processes through which he has to pass to obtain these rights and then to exercise them.

The minority with which we are concerned here, coloured immigrants from the Commonwealth, originally came to this country equipped with the status of 'citizen of the United Kingdom and Colonies'; the latent rights attached to that citizenship sprang to life, so to speak, at the moment of their entry. The discrepancy between this ideal concept, in law, and reality, in terms of the social situation, caused a reaction to take place. We deal with the political aspects of this reaction later; but one of its implications is important here. For, in its extreme form, this takes the form of asserting that neither the newcomers nor their descendants can ever become full members of society because of the presence of the visible factor of colour. And this in turn evokes the response on the part of the minority that membership of a society in which distinctions of this kind are drawn is no longer desirable. Since the countries from which the minorities originally came have obtained independence, this response takes the form of stressing a separate status based on citizenship of those countries.

Both these reactions are as unrealistic as the original doctrine of the indivisible citizenship linking metropolitan country and colony – a lawyer's attempt to give substance to the fading shadow of the imperial connection. What is called, in a famous definition of nationality, the 'connection of existence, interests and sentiments' does exist in a limited form from the outset – for example, in common economic interests. But the relationship is a dynamic one. It will develop over time to the substance of full citizenship, if underpinned from the start by unimpeded access to the rights and acceptance of the duties secured by citizenship in the legal definition. In this process of evolution to full citizenship differences of colour should not constitute an insuperable obstacle any more than differences of class or foreign birth have done in the past. Still more important, the elimination of cultural or religious differences is not a pre-condition of such citizenship, which should involve the unfettered enjoyment of social rights and the opportunity for full participation in public affairs. With the descendants of the newcomers the two concepts should converge and the rights deriving from birth in this country be fully exercised.

To speak of the majority, who are equally important parties to this whole process, as a homogeneous entity is in many ways seriously misleading. The structure of our society derives much of its character from a dialectical process: a constant series of challenges produces responses, and their resolution determines where the boundary lines are drawn and who is included. Some of those challenges have come from groups now unquestioningly accepted as forming an integral part of society on an equal basis – most significantly of all, the working class, whose struggle for political equality has been one of the major themes of British politics in the first half of the 20th century. To telescope the argument absurdly, the historical evidence suggests that a marked degree of adaptability exists in the British social and political system which has produced flexible responses to the successive claims. Each group of claimants has been in turn effectively incorporated and the system modified to legitimate the process. With the result that, in Bonham's frequently quoted phrase, post-war British politics have been until the sixties 'almost wholly innocent of those issues which cross the class lines in other lands, for example race, nationality, religion, town and country interest, regional interest or the conflict between authoritarian and parliamentary methods'.[3]

An important element in these modifications has been the development of a new series of structures – the apparatus of planning and centralized provision of welfare services – which has cemented the process of inclusion. Asa Briggs, looking back at the Welfare State, in historical perspective, points not only to the structural changes reflected in this process but also to a basic change of attitude in which the key concept is one of fairness and tolerance and sympathy towards poverty and replacing the idea that to be poor is to have committed a social crime punishable by starvation or formal deprivation of rights in the work house. Unemployment is seen increasingly as a misfortune for which, like other contingencies, it is the duty of the state to provide.

Yet beneath an apparently placid surface sharp differences persist. Class distinctions, though they are the main determining factor in political loyalties, do not provoke outright conflict: a certain measure of inequality based on social distinctions is generally accepted as valid. But these differences have an additional consequence in generating widely differing attitudes towards the outside world. This is not to imply that there are no responses held in common which can be described as distinctively British. On closer examination a series of tenaciously held beliefs can be glimpsed, widely diffused among all classes, which can be translated into action under the stimulus of exceptional events – for example, the appearance of a substantial group of new-comers or (to take more extreme cases) by natural disaster or national emergency. Some of these beliefs are favourable to newcomers and can in the right circumstances produce favourable responses. Ideas of fairness, for example; respect for law and the acceptance of the legitimacy of authority; and the rejection of violence. Others militate against their acceptance. Most of these are bound up with a rejection of outsiders; either directly – the xenophobia most foreign ob-servers have found among the English, especially in the urban working class – or indirectly in a shrinking away from contact with strangers. One side of this coin is the retreat into the private world of the contracting family unit: the other is the selfish lack of concern for those with whom no human contact has been established. In these circum-stances the coloured newcomers' strangeness may be sufficient to ensure their rejection: or the link that many Englishmen make between colour and their social status may bring down upon them the chilly response that the class-conscious English preserve for their visible inferiors.

Many of these ideas are explored by George Orwell in his essay *England, your England*, in which he claims, half seriously, to find the Englishman's national characteristics summed-up in the seaside postcard:

> Their old-fashioned outlook, their guarded snobberies, their mixture of bawdiness and hypocrisy, their extreme gentleness, their deeply moral attitude to life, all are mirrored here.[4]

Geoffrey Gorer has added to this picture, in his study of English character,[5] the acceptance of authority incarnated in the policeman as a key feature in the development of that character, and a detailed exposition of the pattern of re-straints the English impose on themselves. Taken together, these seem to us still to provide the clearest explanation of the attitudes and behaviour of Englishmen of a certain gen-eration, especially in the 'traditional' working class. But it needs to be modified in the light of various developments since the second world war. One such development is the changing position of this country in relation to the outside world, perhaps most clearly reflected in the abandonment of the imperial role. Orwell refers in his essay to the habitual hypocrisy of the Englishman, who totally ignores the significance of the Empire in his evaluation of the state of the nation; and he half-answers himself by referring to the working classes' inability to grasp that the Empire even existed. What we have said so far is open to the same reproach; it is clear that – quite apart from its economic consequences – the experience of imperialism permanently marked and affected the attitudes of generations of Englishmen of the upper and middle classes – perhaps especially the latter, in confidence trick by which the lesser breeds were kept within the law. But this has been to a surprising extent a passing phenomenon, a question of generations; the direct influence of imperialism seems to have been remarkably transitory.

The second important modifying factor has been the rapid social changes brought about by the wider diffusion of prosperity since the war, and the establishment of the Welfare State. Mark Abrams, in his analysis of these changes, describes Britain at the beginning of the fifties as still bearing 'the stubborn imprints of the nineteenth century'.[6] The most important amenities of life were in short supply; housing in particular, and restricted educational opportunities and limited access to the consumer durables which were yet to become part of the citizen's common expectations (only 11% of house-holders owned a washing machine in 1952, 10% a car, 9% a television set, and 5% a refrigerator). Leisure activities were virtually identical to those that had flourished in the thirties. By contrast, in the early sixties, sixteen million young people born after the death of Hitler confronted the twelve and a half million whose experience stretches back to before the first world war. Educational opportunities have expanded substantially and with it opportunities for social mobility. Housing conditions have also improved and alongside this improvement there has been a sharp increase in home ownership. The comparative figures for consumer durables in 1963 were 85% owning television, 52% a washing-machine, 37% a refrigerator, and 40% a car.

Tastes have changed; foreign travel is a common-place and the availability of cheap and well-designed clothes has meant that a visual identification by class is wholly no longer possible.

The other side of the coin is the growing disparity between the prosperous majority and the minority who have been left behind as standards rise. Fissures have opened not only between rich and poor but in relation to age and to stages in the family life cycle. Geographical segregation has become an increasingly common phenomenon; to those trapped in the shrinking private rented sector, with rising rents and poor facilities, their underprivileged black neighbours trapped in the same sticky web are simultaneously perpetual symbols of their deprivation and potential scapegoats. In these ways, the movement has been not towards homogeneity but away from it: in this situation, a uniform response towards newcomers is less likely than a fragmented one. This fragmentation may help or hinder mutual adjustment between black and white. Common poverty can produce either the incentive to bridge gaps and the resolution to solve problems held in common, or the excuse to set up scapegoats for them. In either case the arrival of the newcomer shows up the weaknesses in the structure of society and it is in this sense – if no other – that he deserves attention, as a focus for the Condition of England question for this generation.

REFERENCES

1. Address given by the Home Secretary on 23rd May, 1966 to a meeting of the voluntary liaison committees (London, N.C.C.I., 1966).
2. G. Myrdal, *An American Dilemma* (New York: Harper 1944).
3. J. Bonham, *The Middle Class Vote* (London, Faber and Faber 1954).
4. George Orwell, *England, Your England and Other Essays* (London, Secker & Warburg, 1953).
5. G. Gorer, *Exploring English Character* (London, Cresset Press, 1955).
6. Mark Abrams, *The Newspaper Reading Public of To-morrow* (London, Odhams Press, 1964), p. 8.

Chapter Two

The Sending Societies and the Beginning of the Migration

Immigration is no novelty, so far as Britain is concerned: in the last 500 years a wide variety of people have come to settle here. But their variety pales to the sameness of a monochrome print when they are compared with the immigrants from the tropical Commonwealth who have arrived here in the last twenty years. The differences between the latter are as great as the distances that separate their homelands. Yet the label of Commonwealth immigrant that has been attached to them, and which for most people is synonymous with colour, has tended to mask these differences and to disguise the nature of the influences that play upon them and affect the quality of their response to their environment as they settle in a new country.

THE MIGRATIONS FROM THE WEST INDIES AND GUYANA

By far the largest of the migrations has come from the West Indies and Guyana. Jamaica contributes rather more than half this number and the remainder was drawn from a group of islands nearly 1,000 miles to the east, which extend in an arc from the Virgins to Trinidad. The distance between Jamaica and the Eastern Caribbean is often maintained by the immigrants, for the small islanders have their own patriotisms which are rooted in their nurture and their history. Generally, the men, women and children who have come to Britain in the last twenty years were brought up within a British culture, were taught in English-speaking schools by teachers with English middle-class values. The English taught in the schools was very different from the English spoken in the home and in some of the islands it was virtually a second language. But in their schools West Indian children were taught from English textbooks about the

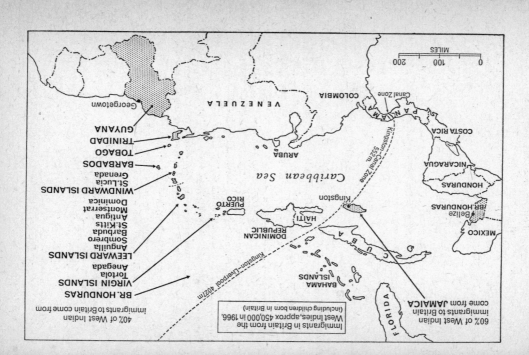

60% of West Indian immigrants to Britain come from JAMAICA

40% of West Indian immigrants to Britain come from

Immigrants in Britain from the West Indies, approx 450,000 in 1966, (including children born in Britain)

BR. HONDURAS
VIRGIN ISLANDS
Anegada
Tortola
LEEWARD ISLANDS
Anguilla
Sombrero
Barbuda
St.Kitts
Antigua
Montserrat
Dominica
WINDWARD ISLANDS
St.Lucia
Grenada
BARBADOS
TOBAGO
TRINIDAD
GUYANA

Georgetown

V E N E Z U E L A

COLOMBIA

Canal Zone
Kingston—Canal Zone 552m

P A N A M A

COSTA RICA

NICARAGUA

HONDURAS

Belize
/BR HONDURAS

MEXICO

ARUBA

Caribbean Sea

PUERTO RICO

DOMINICAN REPUBLIC

HAITI

Kingston

C U B A

Kingston—Liverpool 4021m

BAHAMA ISLANDS

FLORIDA

MILES
0   100   200

history of the Mother Country and learned as loyal subjects of the Crown to sing 'Rule Britannia' and 'God Save the King'. Their African origins had been overlaid by this colonial culture.

The influence of Christianity has also been of very great importance. Church attendance is high: all the major denominations flourish, along with less orthodox forms like the Pentecostal sects, which now make up the third largest group in Jamaica.[1]

The opportunities for education vary greatly with the comparative wealth or poverty of the islands. The level of literacy is highest in Barbados; in most of the islands less than one in ten of the adult population has gone beyond an elementary education. However, this kind of statistic can be misleading, as in some of the islands, for example in Jamaica, there are many all-age schools which provide elementary education up to the age of 15. While levels of education vary between islands, there are also great contrasts within the islands between the town and country schools. Until recently, secondary education has been available mainly for the middle classes who could pay for it, but this is no longer the case in the larger islands where free places, grants, and competitive entry have opened opportunities to a much wider field. Many of the secondary schools have a high standard but teachers are burdened with large classes.[2]

Slavery has left a permanent mark on all the island societies. For example, there are sharp differences that arise from the variations in the supply of land available to emancipated slaves. Then there is the persisting importance of varieties of colour and class relationships. In the plural societies of Trinidad and Guyana the position of the Creole has been more dominant than in Jamaica, where society has been stratified along a colour spectrum. Barbados provides a further contrast, where the close patron-client relationship has brought the advantage of a high level of education which paternalism bestowed and has made the Barbadian more of an Englishman in his attitudes to law and authority than probably any of the other West Indian islanders. It has also left a more clear-cut division between white and black than in other islands.

The legacy of slavery also remains in its effect on the

family system and on the way society is stratified. Few slaves were allowed to marry and it was made impossible for a man to assume the responsibilities of the head of a family as he had no legal rights or duties towards his child. Women found in concubinage an escape from hardship and a hope for their children, who were often treated with affection by their planter fathers, and might even obtain their freedom.

Today, West Indian family life still bears traces of slavery, in a very high illegitimacy rate and the instability of many unions. Among peasants and the urban working classes it is common to marry late, generally when the woman is past child-bearing age and when there is enough economic security to undertake the obligations of a legal union. Young girls have early sexual experience and remain at home after the birth of the first child, which is often left in the care of mother or sisters. A girl is likely to have borne one or two children before she leaves home and sets up a more or less stable union, but if this breaks down she returns to her family. By the time they are 30 most women are living in stable unions, sometimes called common law marriages. The irresponsibility of the father is part of the legacy of slavery: although a man will support the children of earlier unions while he is living with their mother, few men contribute to the care of their children once a union is broken. With so much instability the man's authority passes to the woman, and the role of the mother and the grandmother is by far the strongest in the West Indian family system.[3] The fact that women from an early age are used to managing their own lives and to leaving their children to the care of others explains the presence of so many women in the early years of the West Indian migration to Britain. Very often they came on their own to earn money for the support of their children, who were left in the care of the grandmothers.

While the proportion of women in the West Indian migration was high, men were in the majority throughout the period of uncontrolled entry. There seems no doubt that in the early stages the migration contained a very high proportion of skilled men, far higher than in the West Indian population as a whole. This high level of skills was maintained throughout the 1950s. As late as 1962 there were still more Jamaicans coming to England from Kingston and St.

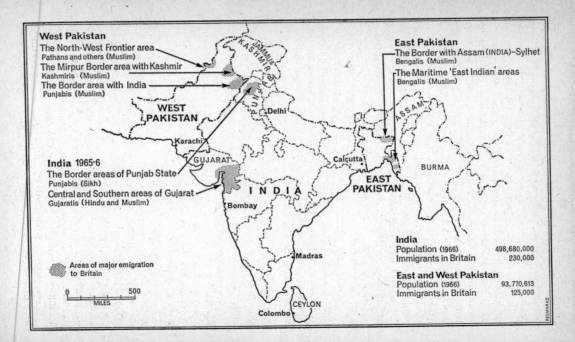

West Pakistan
The North-West Frontier area
Pathans and others (Muslim)
The Mirpur Border area with Kashmir
Kashmiris (Muslim)
The Border area with India
Punjabis (Muslim)

WEST PAKISTAN

KASHMIR

JAMMU

PUNJAB

Delhi

Karachi

GUJARAT

India 1965-6
The Border areas of Punjab State
Punjabis (Sikh)
Central and Southern areas of Gujarat
Gujaratis (Hindu and Muslim)

INDIA

Bombay

East Pakistan
The Border with Assam (INDIA)–Sylhet
Bengalis (Muslim)
The Maritime 'East Indian' areas
Bengalis (Muslim)

ASSAM

Calcutta

BURMA

EAST PAKISTAN

Madras

Areas of major emigration to Britain

0   500
MILES

CEYLON

Colombo

India
Population (1966)   498,680,000
Immigrants in Britain   230,000

East and West Pakistan
Population (1966)   93,770,613
Immigrants in Britain   125,000

Andrew than from the rural parishes, and half of them, according to Francis, had had some form of vocational training.[4]

In fact, in each of a series of studies a majority of men emigrating to Britain from the West Indies are shown to have been skilled or semi-skilled workers.[5] This does not mean that a skilled worker in, for example, Jamaica, has the same training and expertise as a skilled man in the same trade in Britain, but it does mean that on the whole those who migrated were successful in their own societies. Only a small number were drawn from the ranks of the unemployed: for example, the Economist Intelligence Unit Survey in 1961 found that only 12% of a sample of 603 West Indians had been unemployed before leaving the West Indies.

The majority of the women migrating were also part of the labour force. For example, Francis found that 69.5% of women were part of the labour force. The main occupations among women migrants were dressmaking and domestic or personal service work: but there were also a minority of non-manual workers, for example, 630 clerical workers, 210 teachers and 162 nurses, in his sample.

THE MIGRATIONS FROM INDIA AND PAKISTAN

One of the most striking features of the migrations from both India and Pakistan is the limited extent of the areas from which they originate. Emigration has been confined to the Punjab and Gujarat in India and to half a dozen areas in the two wings of Pakistan.

The Sikhs, who constitute four-fifths of the Indian migration to Britain,[7] come mainly from two districts in Eastern Punjab, Jullundur and Hoshiarpur, in an area known as the Doaba. The Sikhs are perhaps the most mobile people in the whole of India and have contributed nearly one-quarter of the Indian armed forces. They are great wanderers and in the last hundred years have settled far afield. They are frontiersmen and pioneers: they opened up the Western Punjab when the British built a canal system towards the end of the last century, and turned these arid tracts into rich wheat-producing farmland. But they were not to enjoy them for long; in 1947, after the partition of India, they and the Hindus were driven out of their farms across the new frontier.

In the exchange of populations over four million refugees flooded into the Eastern Punjab where they took over the generally smaller and sometimes poorer Muslim holdings.[8] The migrations had their effect throughout East Punjab as all land-holdings were reduced by legislation to a ceiling of thirty acres.[9] As there is no system of primogeniture among the Sikhs the land becomes fragmented through inheritance and the migrations after Partition greatly added to the already existing pressure of population on the land. Jullundur district, where one-quarter of all land-holdings are less than one acre, has the highest percentage of uneconomic land-holdings and also the highest population density in the Punjab.[10]

It is, therefore, not surprising that the villages and towns of this area should have been the most fruitful source of the migration to Britain. In some of the villages visited in 1965 more than one in ten of the inhabitants had gone and more hoped to follow, and remittances from relatives in England have brought great improvements to the land and to the villages.[11]

It is the joint family that determined the pattern of Sikh migration and enabled sons, and in some cases the father, to leave their wives and children to the shelter and security of the family home. It is common for a husband to remain abroad for many years, returning occasionally to his wife, only to leave again after a year or so, when he may take one of his sons with him.[12] This pattern began to be broken when control of immigration was seen to be imminent in Britain: and it was from 1958 onwards that the Sikhs began to bring their wives and families to this country.

Throughout the first centuries of their existence the Sikhs were a minority that had to fight against great odds to survive. Their faith began as a reform movement within Hinduism under the rule of Muslim emperors. The founder Guru Nanak (1469-1539), preached the oneness of God and the equality of all men, and thus the movement was one of dissent not only from the ritualism and idolatry of the Hindu religion, but also against the burden of caste which imposes a social hierarchy ordained from birth. Initiates have names with the suffix Singh, must swear to observe the five K's, namely to wear their hair and beard unshorn (*Kesh*), to wear a comb (*Kangha*), a pair of shorts (*Kachha*), a steel bangle on the wrist (*Kara*) and to carry a sword (*Kirpan*). This observance is still the mark of a religious Sikh and the wearing of long hair plays a very important part in the co-hesion of the Sikh community in the Punjab as it serves to mark them off as a separate religious community.

Although the gurus who succeeded Guru Nanak set their faces resolutely against caste, Sikhism has not suc-ceeded in breaking the system which is still of great import-ance in the choice of a partner in marriage. Yet it has been modified and weakened with time, and the rigid concept of pollution has disappeared. Jat peasant proprietors probably form the majority in the Sikh emigration to Britain. Some craftsmen have emigrated to East Africa and many more sought their fortune in Britain. Most of the other castes are also represented in the emigration including some former untouchables.[13]

Another fundamental change is the gradual breaking up of the joint family which, for all the economic security it affords, has many disadvantages, particularly for women. Emigration is contributing to this change as with increasing prosperity from remittances women begin to assert their in-dependence.

The village schools are simple structures with few class-rooms, but for most of the year lessons are taken out of doors. Primary education is free and in theory compulsory. A child enters at 5 and passes by examination to the middle school from 11 years upward, leaving at 14. English is taught in the last year of the primary school, but because of the very low pay there is a shortage of qualified teachers.

Not all the Punjabis who have come to England are Sikhs, but the number of Hindus is comparatively small. Travelling across the sea involves ritual impurity and this may still in-hibit some Hindus from migrating, but it does not seem to have proved an obstacle to the Hindus of Gujarat, the second area in India from which immigrants have come to this country. Gujaratis, like the Sikhs, have a long tradition of migration and for centuries have been trading with East Africa where they settled to become the traders and mer-chants of the country. The Hindus from Gujarat who have settled in England belong mainly to the agricultural castes and the remainder are usually village craftsmen. Pressure on the land and unemployment have been the motive forces behind the emigration, which was drawn mainly from the central and southern parts of Gujurat.[14]

The Gujaratis who have emigrated appear to be a highly literate group. Desai did not come across one illiterate Gujarati in five years, and all the 191 men in his sample had had a high school education, while sixteen had been to a university. In fact, there was always a significant minority of educated and professional people among the post-war Indian migrants.

Gujaratis and Punjabis are of different ethnic origin and, while both their languages are Sanskritic, they are mutually unintelligible, though simple Hindi which is connected with both might serve as a medium of communication. The two main elements in the Indian emigration are thus separated by custom, and in most cases by religion, and can probably best communicate with one another through the medium of English.

The two wings of Pakistan are separated by more than 1,000 miles and except at the official level and among businessmen there is very little communication between them. Migrants from East and West Pakistan have little in common except their religion and some sense of belonging to the same nation. Language is as great a barrier as distance, for although Urdu has been made an additional language, it has not gained much currency in East Pakistan, where Bengali is the mother tongue, and is understood only by an educated minority in the Western wing, not by the majority of the migrants, who speak various dialects of Punjabi.

It is from the hill districts in both wings of the country, from Mirpur in the west and Sylhet in the east, that most of the Pakistanis have come to Britain. Poor soil which yields a bare subsistence drove many farmers' sons to the towns in search of employment; others took service in the Merchant Navy in the days of British rule and later settled in port towns in England and Wales.

The district of Mirpur was formerly part of the State of Jammu and Kashmir, and since 1947 it has been one of the three districts of Azad ('Free') Kashmir held by Pakistan. Under the maharajas' rule the whole area was 'shamefully neglected' and contained hardly any schools.[15] Partition and independence have brought changes particularly in the spread of primary education, but there is a limit to progress in this developing country; unemployment is high and the per capita income is as low as £30 per annum.

Most of the emigrants from Mirpur came from families connected with the land, whether as small peasant proprietors or landless labourers. It is villagers working on the land who also comprise the majority of the Campbellpuris, who form another large group from West Pakistan.[16] Among the East Pakistanis in Britain Sylhetis predominate, but fairly large numbers have also come from the port town of Chittagong and from Comilla.

There are no detailed analyses of the occupations of Pakistanis prior to emigration, but a sample of 300 West Pakistanis examined by Dahya showed that two-thirds had been helping to farm their family lands and of the rest nearly one-half had been in the Armed Forces or Merchant Navy and so presumably originated from the villages.[17] There is an urban-educated middle class in the emigration but it has always been a very small fraction of the whole.

The poverty of Pakistan is reflected in the low literacy rate (15%) and the poor provision of schools: little money is spent on primary education, teachers are very poorly paid and not always well qualified.[18] School attendance is irregular for many parents cannot afford to buy the slates and textbooks, which are not provided by the state, and there is a temptation to use the children to supplement the family income. Very few children enter secondary school and less than half stay to the age of 15.

All Muslims acknowledge five imperative religious duties: the profession of faith ('there is but one God, Mohammed is his prophet'), daily prayers, alms-giving, fasting during the month of Ramadan, and pilgrimage to Mecca. These are the pillars of Islam and to these most Muslims add a dietary prohibition against eating the pig and drinking alcohol. But Islam is more than a set of ritual acts and a body of religious belief. Like Judaism it is a way of life in which there is no separation between the spiritual and the temporal. Law and social organization form an inseparable whole, governing not only religious practice and morality but social relationships, diet and hygiene, and those areas of conduct which in Western Society are regulated by secular law and the civil authority.

In their early phases migrations are predominantly male, but the imbalance between the sexes in the Pakistani emigration and the preponderance of boys among the children brought over to all-male households was determined by the cultural patterns in a Muslim community, the seclusion of women and their subordination within the home.

The Pakistani family consists of a man, his wife, his unmarried sons and daughters, and his married sons and their wives and children. In this extended family, authority is vested in the father and passes on his death to his eldest son. From the age of puberty all girls are secluded from men who are not related; this seclusion is far more rigidly enforced among the Sylhetis than in either Mirpur or Campbellpur and accounts for the very small numbers of wives who have come from East Pakistan. When a woman marries, she enters her husband's family as a subordinate and an outsider; she subordinates her will not only to her husband and his father but also to her husband's mother. The pre-eminence of the male is reflected not only in his authority within the family but in the early separation of boys from girls inside the home. Women never eat with their husbands – but after they have served their meals. Men spend their leisure not with their wives but in the company of other men. This close relationship with their male kin and with other villagers is carried through into the emigration to England, and influences the pattern of settlement in this country.

REFERENCES

1. Clifford Hill gives the following figures for the West Indies, including British Guiana. Anglicans 897,000, Roman Catholics (who are in the majority in Trinidad and Tobago, and the Leeward and Windward Islands), 808,000, Baptists 156,000, Methodists 156,000, Congregationalists 30,000, Presbyterians 30,000. After the Anglicans and Roman Catholics the largest number, 390,000, are listed under Other

Denominations, which embrace a number of Christian sects unknown in England (*West Indian Migrants and the London Churches*, London, Oxford University Press, for Institute of Race Relations, 1963). By far the largest are those who claim affiliation to the Church of God, a Pentecostal Sect which has in recent years attracted a great many believers, particularly in Jamaica, where at the 1960 Census it had become the third largest of the Churches (O. G. Francis, *The People of Modern Jamaica*, Kingston, Department of Statistics, 1963).

2. G. W. Roberts and N. Abdulah, 'Some Observations on the Educational Position of the Caribbean', *Social and Economic Studies* (Vol. XIV, no. 1, March, 1965).

3. M. G. Smith, introduction to *My Mother Who Fathered Me* (2nd ed.) by E. Clarke.

4. O. G. Francis, 'The Characteristics of Emigrants just prior to changes in British Commonwealth Immigration Policies'.

5. See, for example, G. W. Roberts & D. O. Mills, 'Study of External Migration Affairs, Jamaica 1953–55' *Social & Economic Studies* (VIII, 2, Supplement 1958): Ruth Glass, *The Newcomers* (London: Allen & Unwin for the Centre for Urban Studies, 1960), Francis (op. cit.) and G. E. Cumper, 'Working Class Emigration from Barbados to the U.K., October 1955' (*Social & Economic Studies*, VI, 1, 1957).

6. Economist Intelligence Unit, *Studies on Immigration from the Commonwealth*, 1. *Basic Statistics* (London, E.I.U., 1961).

7. R. Desai, *Indian Immigrants in Britain* (London, Oxford University Press, for Institute of Race Relations, 1963).

8. Khushwant Singh, *A History of the Sikhs*, Vol. 2, 1839–1964 (Princeton, Princeton U.P., 1966), p. 234, gives the following figures: 4,351,477 Hindus and Sikhs came from the N.W. Frontier Province and West Punjab against 4,286,755 Muslims who left East Punjab. The Hindus and Sikhs left behind 6.7 million acres of the best agricultural land; the Muslims of East Punjab left behind 4.7 million acres of comparatively poor soil.

9. K. Singh, op. cit., p. 285. The immigrations were not the sole reason for the ceiling which was also meant to break up the Zamindari estates.

10. G. S. Aurora, *The New Frontiersmen* (Popular Prakashan, Bombay, 1967).

11. From the village of Jandiala (population 10,000) 1,000 were said to be in the United Kingdom. In the neighbouring village of Samrai, one mile away 700 out of the 7,000 had gone.

12. Some typical cases from the village of Kala Singa, population 6,500: a teacher, J. S., has forty relatives in the U.K. His

father emigrated to England 25 years ago and ran a clothing business in Nottingham. Now he is retired and has an income of £12 a week from the rent of a house which he has bought. He left behind in the joint family two brothers, two sisters and his mother. Among J. S.'s forty relatives is an uncle with five children who lives in Dudley. He and two of his sons work in a factory and have a Hillman car. One son is married and has a daughter. There is a second uncle in Dudley with four sons there. One son is married and his wife is waiting to join him. The second son had married two months previously in the village. His father and mother came over for the wedding. This son will build a home in the village in which his mother will live and also the widow of the fifth brother and another sister-in-law. He also has four more cousins in Dudley, of whom one had just returned to marry and bring his wife back to England. Out of these forty relatives none got married in the U.K. but all returned to find their wives in the Punjab.

13. In the village of Mehru the writer heard of a Harijan who had gone to England and had prospered. His wife was building a beautiful home and had given 100 rupees to the Defence Fund during the short war between India and Pakistan. In most villages there is a quarter reserved for untouchables, generally outside the wall, easily distinguished by the very poor quality of their mud huts.

In a sample of eighty families taken in Southall, Narindar Uberoi found that occupation in India had been farming (25), military and police service (11), small business (8), carpentry (5), and other skilled crafts (5). There were twelve students in the sample and the rest had been in unskilled manual work or unemployed.

14. Desai, op. cit., pp. 13, 14.
15. L. F. Rushbrook Williams, *The State of Pakistan* (rev. ed) (London, Faber, 1955) p. 90.
16. Dahya estimated in 1965 that of 10,500 West Pakistanis in Bradford, 5,400 were Mirpuris and 3,000 Campbellpuris. These groups all have a rural background. He also estimated that 1,800 came from the largest cities ('Study of Pakistanis in Bradford', for Institute's 'Survey of Race Relations in Britain', 1968).
17. Of the remainder of the sample the largest number were: clerical (21), semi-skilled (9), teachers (8), and railway workers (5).
18. John Goodall in *New Backgrounds* edited by R. Oakley (Oxford University Press, for Institute of Race Relations,

1968) gives the following statistics. The average salary for primary school teachers is £4 10s. per month in East Pakistan and £7 10s. in West Pakistan. For every 100 children enrolled in class I only fifteen in East and thirty-eight in West Pakistan survive to class V. Only 20% of 11-year-olds go to secondary school and of these less than half remain in school up to the age of 15.

Chapter Three

How the Migration Developed

ORIGINS

We begin our account of the development of the migration with the second world war, although this was not the first occasion on which the British confronted coloured new-comers in any numbers. Troops from all of the Empire were stationed in Britain during the war; in particular, 7,000 West Indians enlisted in the Royal Air Force and were stationed in the United Kingdom. Other West Indians were recruited, as skilled craftsmen, to work during the war in factories. The success of this scheme, which was carefully planned and supervised by the Ministry of Labour, and for which Mr. (now Lord) Learie Constantine acted as welfare officer, had a good deal to do with subsequent development of immi-gration to Britain from the West Indies. Although initial difficulties were encountered in persuading employees to accept West Indian workers and in providing accommoda-tion, both problems were eventually overcome. Most of the workers concerned went back to the West Indies when the scheme was wound up in 1947, but the unfavourable em-ployment conditions they encountered there caused quite a number to consider returning to Britain. The experience of the Royal Air Force contingent, who had mostly been re-turned to the West Indies on demobilization, was similar.

The first indication of the new migration came in June 1948 when the former German pleasure cruiser, the *Empire Windrush*, which had been chartered to take European mi-grants out to Latin America, called on return at Kingston. Enterprising advertising and acute shortage of passenger transport to Great Britain ensured that the liner was booked to capacity. The *Empire Windrush* was followed in due course by the *Orbita*, with 108 passengers, and the *Georgic*.

However, total migration from the West Indies at this stage was very small and, until 1951, never reached a figure of 1,000 in any year.

The United States had been the main receiver of Jamaican immigrants or migrant workers. But after the war, the passage of the McCarran-Walter Act in 1952 restricted migration to the United States from Jamaica to 100 a year. Britain then became the only major industrial country open to large-scale migration from the West Indies and reports of easily obtainable jobs induced others to migrate. By 1954, migration to Britain from the West Indies – and in particular, from Jamaica – began to assume numerically significant proportions, and increased rapidly until it reached its first plateau in 1956. From 1955 onwards the Home Office maintained records of all arrivals and departures of Commonwealth travellers.

The migration from the Caribbean was characterized from the start by a high proportion of women, a low incidence of return migration, and its responsiveness to labour demand in Britain. But no effort was made, with one exception, to match employment vacancies with the supply of migrant labour available before the process of migration got under way. This is the sharpest of the many contrasts between the Commonwealth immigrants and those recruited under the European Volunteer Worker scheme. The exception was the direct arrangements made by the Barbadian Immigrants Liaison Service with the London Transport Executive (from 1956) and the British Hotels and Restaurants Association for the recruitment of labour in Barbados.

Towards the end of 1955 the British economy went into a period of recession and as labour demand fell, migration from the Caribbean declined. In 1960 with rising labour demand and fear of control it leapt to a new peak and continued to rise throughout 1961. In the eighteen months from 1961 to mid-1962, net arrivals amounted to 98,000 persons from the Caribbean.

It is impossible to give a firm date for the start of the migration of Sikhs from the Punjab to Britain after the war. But from the early 1950s pioneer settlers from India and Pakistan who had prospered in British industry began to send for their kinsmen and fellow villagers. Usually the migrant had a contact or sponsor in Britain who could arrange his housing and employment, and often contributed to his fare to Britain.

Travel agents also began to be active at an early stage in the ports and the large towns, and within a few years were operating in country towns as well. The scale of operations of the travel agents was one reason why Indian and Pakistani migration was able to attain the high levels it reached in 1961 and the first half of 1962.

The agencies also helped intending migrants to evade the restrictions imposed by their own governments, at the request of Britain, to discourage emigration. The various systems of control, which included checks on the issue of passports and monetary deposits, tended to work in an arbitrary and unsatisfactory way. The various illegal practices employed by the travel agents to get their clients to Britain developed essentially as a black market to get round restrictions imposed at first not by Britain but by their home governments. The practices continued in 1962 when the British controls took effect, but their heyday was over in 1964 when the issue of C vouchers for unskilled workers ended.

In one outstanding case, restrictions on the issue of passports to Britain were reversed. In 1961, when control looked to be imminent, the Pakistani Government withdrew restrictions and promoted the migration of 5,000 people to Britain. This was intended to help some of the Mirpuri families due to be dispossessed by the construction of a dam at Mangla, but also included some people not affected by the dam project.

The proportion of women among the Indian and Pakistani migrants was much lower than that among the West Indians. A study in Southall in the late 1950s estimated that the proportion of women in the Sikh community there was as low as 4%.[1] The threat of control caused many more Sikhs to bring their wives to England after 1960 but among the Pakistanis there were very few women indeed before 1962. In Bradford, one of the main areas of Pakistani settlement, the 1961 Census revealed 3,376 men and only eighty-one women. The Pakistanis who arrived between 1959 and 1962 and who constituted the majority of the immigrant population were mostly young and unmarried. Their predecessors who came in the middle fifties, sponsored by former seamen, were somewhat older and the majority were married. It is these men who have brought over their wives since 1962.

To put this immigration into perspective we need to look at the evidence of the two censuses taken at the beginning and towards the end of the period. At the 1951 census the coloured population born overseas was hardly more than 75,000, amounting to only 1.7 persons per 1,000 of the population. In 1961 it amounted to 7.3 persons per 1,000 of the population. But the increase was not so great in absolute terms as the public debate might have suggested. Citizens of the Irish Republic remained in 1961, as in 1951, the largest of the ethnic minorities in Britain. Within the intercensal period the absolute increase among the Irish was still larger than the number of West Indians arriving in the same ten years. The number of aliens was also greater in both years than the coloured population.

IMMIGRATION CONTROL: SOME UNINTENDED CONSEQUENCES

The passing of the Commonwealth Immigrants Act of 1962 radically changed the pattern of migration from the Commonwealth. The first effect of the Act predated its passing and even its introduction as a Bill into Parliament. Until 1960 the migration to Britain was regulated by conditions in the labour market in Britain. The main source of the immigration to Britain until the end of 1960 was from the West Indies. Ceri Peach in his important study has shown that labour demand in Britain had a decisive influence on the level and composition of the arrivals from the West Indies.[2] It will be seen from Figure 1 that when labour demand rose in Britain the arrivals increased and when labour demand fell arrivals decreased. When migration rose the proportion of men in the migration also rose, as labour demand has greater effect on male migration than on women and children. However, the expectation of control led to a dramatic increase in the numbers entering from 1960 onwards. The sharp rise in the rate of West Indian migration in 1961 and 1962 was for the first time against the economic indicators. Similarly, fear of control caused even greater increases in the Indian and Pakistani migration, which did not become substantial until 1961. In 1961, net inward migration from India increased fourfold and from Pakistan tenfold over the previous year. Before 1961 the migration from India and Pakistan fluctuated at a fairly low level. As late as 1959 the net inward flow from both countries combined was only 3,800. The changing pattern and balance of the migration is

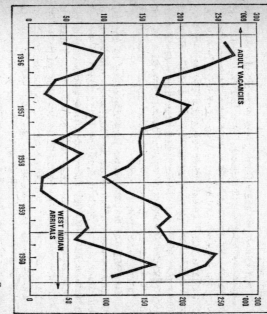

Figure 1. Quarterly figures of employment vacancies and West Indian arrivals, 1956–1960.

Source:
G. C. K. Peach, *West Indian Migration to Britain*, Table 18 ('Adult vacancies figures from Ministry of Labour, 'West Indian arrivals' from Migrant Services Division).

shown in Table 1. It will be seen that well over half the Indians and approximately three-quarters of the Pakistanis who arrived in Britain before control arrived in the 18-month period January 1961 to June 1962. By contrast, only just over a third of the West Indians arrived in this period.

The introduction of control and the political agitation that led to it distorted the pattern of migration and induced many people to migrate, at an economically difficult time, who would possibly not otherwise have migrated. The paradoxical conclusion is that the proponents of control created the very situation that they most feared by inducing a far higher rate of migration than had occurred before: in eighteen months the net inflow was almost as great as that of the previous six years. This massive increase was to compound the real problems which lay within the United Kingdom, not at the gates.

If the Commonwealth Immigrants Act initially failed in its objective of limiting numbers even before it came into force, its effects since control have also not been exactly what its proposers had intended. The numbers of immigrants from India and Pakistan, those whom the Government were most anxious to restrict, has remained substantially higher in every year since control than it had been in any year before 1961. But the advocates of control have registered a success in the decline in the number of West Indian immigrants since the introduction of control.

The 1962 Act and the subsequent tightening of control has had a number of consequences for the composition of the migration, not all of them intended. The balance of the migration since July 1962 has shifted in a number of ways: from the Caribbean to India and Pakistan (see Table 1), from the economically active to the economically inactive, from men to women, from adults to children and within the small numbers of men still entering from the unskilled to the professionally qualified.

Half the total West Indian immigration took place before 1960, and there has been a sharp decline since the introduction of controls. Exactly the reverse is true of immigration from India and Pakistan. Two-thirds of the total number of Indians and over half the Pakistanis have arrived in the period since control.

These differences can be explained by the nature of the controls and the composition of the migration before control. The 1962 Act permitted the dependants of persons already resident in Britain to enter freely but imposed on adults intending to work in Britain a system of regulation based on employment vouchers issued by the Ministry of Labour (as it then was). There were three categories of voucher: for those who had specific jobs to come to (A), for those who possessed special skills or qualifications (B), and for unskilled workers without definite prospects of employment (C). Overall priority was given to the A and B categories, and the C group applications were dealt with on a 'first come first served' basis; special consideration was given

Table 1: NET INWARD MIGRATION FROM INDIA, PAKISTAN AND THE WEST INDIES, 1955–68.

	India	Pakistan	Jamaica	Rest of Caribbean	Total
1955-60	33,070	17,120	96,180	65,270	211,640
1961–30th June, 1962	42,800	50,170	62,450	35,640	191,060
1st July, 1962–December 68	124,260	78,670	32,700	31,310	266,940
Total:	200,130	145,960	191,330	132,220	669,640

Sources: for 1955–30 June 1962, Home Office; for 1st July, 1962–68 Commonwealth Immigrants Act 1962, Statistics.

to those who had served with the armed forces in the second world war or later. In the White Paper issued in 1965 it was announced that category C vouchers would be discontinued; but in fact the Ministry had ceased to issue them from the previous August. In all 40,000 C vouchers were issued and nearly three-quarters went to India and Pakistan compared with only 10 per cent to the West Indies.

The West Indies received an even smaller proportion of the B vouchers for special skills (1% of the total) compared to 74% allocated to India and Pakistan. The only remaining means of entry for West Indians was through the 'A' vouchers for those with jobs to come to – especially for those Barbadians entering the direct recruitment schemes referred to previously.

The number of vouchers issued in all categories decreased sharply after the 1965 White Paper. The White Paper set a limit of 8,500 vouchers issued per year (with 1,000 reserved for Malta) and gave preference to applicants for B vouchers. The number of voucher holders actually arriving in Britain in the years since the White Paper has in fact been considerably less than 8,500 (Table 2.) By 1968 the number of new entrants holding vouchers from all the Commonwealth was less than 5,000; approximately half were B voucher holders. The B voucher system has been increasingly used to recruit highly qualified personnel from the Commonwealth to Britain. This policy was made explicit by the Minister of Labour in 1968. New regulations gearing the issue of vouchers to British labour needs came into force on the 1st June 1968. Oscar Gish has shown that B vouchers issued to doctors increased from 42% of the total in January–May 1968 to 71% in the period June–December 1968.[3] The overwhelming majority of these vouchers go to Indians and Pakistanis.

Table 2 shows that migration since control has been mainly made up of dependants. From the outset more dependants than voucher holders entered from the West Indies; by 1964 there were more than twice as many dependants from India and Pakistan than voucher holders. Indeed by 1967 over 90% of all Commonwealth immigrants were dependants. As we have already explained, dependants of persons already resident in Britain were exempted from control by the 1962 Act, which defined dependants as wives, children under 18 and elderly parents with additional small categories for other relatives, where it could be shown that their well-being depended upon renewed residence with a Commonwealth citizen in Britain. This definition of dependant status and eligibility to enter has been narrowed and tightened a number of times since 1962. In the 1965 White Paper the Government allowed – as a 'concession' – 16-18-year-olds to be admitted as dependant children at the discretion of immigration officers. The Commonwealth Immigrants Act 1968 and the Immigration Appeals Act 1968 required children to travel in the company of one parent (who is a Commonwealth citizen) at least. All dependants are also required to obtain an Entry Certificate from a British High Commission in their country of origin. In addition to these specific limitations, successive revisions

Table 2: COMMONWEALTH CITIZENS ARRIVING IN THE U.K. JULY 1962–DECEMBER 1968
DISTRIBUTION OF VOUCHER HOLDERS AND DEPENDANTS

		India		Pakistan		West Indies		Total Commonwealth	
		Voucher Holders	Dependants	Voucher Holders	Dependants	Voucher Holders	Dependants	Voucher Holders	Dependants
July–									
Dec.	1962	646	1,565	391	505	1,600	3,730	5,120	8,830
	1963	8,366	6,616	13,526	3,304	2,077	7,896	30,130	26,230
	1964	3,828	8,770	3,296	7,046	2,635	11,461	14,705	37,460
	1965	3,794	12,798	2,520	6,763	2,987	11,147	12,880	41,210
	1966	2,433	13,357	721	9,319	628	9,878	5,460	42,030
	1967	2,175	15,822	754	17,506	630	11,211	4,980	52,810
	1968	1,864	13,718	672	12,535	507	6,230	4,691	48,650*
	Total:	23,106	72,646	21,880	56,978	11,064	61,553	77,966	257,220

* Includes 4,771 United Kingdom passport holders from East Africa not included in previous figures.
Source: Commonwealth Immigrants Act 1962 statistics.

of the Home Office standing instruction to immigration officers have tightened the application of existing rules. For example, formal legal evidence is required of a dependant's relationship with his sponsor, together with medical evidence of age. There are also additional powers to impose health checks.

The continuing tightening of the conditions for the entry of dependants was partly a response to fears that the number of dependants was limitless. There was also over publicized anxiety about evasion, avoidance and illegal immigration inflating the figures. But the changing patterns among new arrivals had less to do with these fears – and the administrative responses to them, after 1965 – than with the demographic structure of the migrant communities. As the immigrants who had arrived in the period 1961–63 settled down they were joined by members of their families. Thus a Home Office study showed that 51% of West Indians and 41% of Indian and Pakistani dependants arriving at selected times in 1968 were joining heads of households who had migrated in 1963 or earlier.[4] The numbers of Asian dependants were much higher than those from the Caribbean because a much higher proportion of women had migrated from the Caribbean before control. From 1963 onwards, the number of West Indian women arriving dropped while from January 1965 the numbers of Indian women entering began to stabilize. Only among Pakistanis did the number of female dependants entering rise steadily until 1968, when they also began to fall. The biggest group of dependants were children; their numbers showed a steady increase nearly every year for all three groups, although the West Indian figures showed signs of levelling off after 1964. As dependants became an increasing proportion of new immigrants, so children became a larger proportion of dependants.

Eversley and Sukdeo[5] in a study published in 1969 attempted to calculate the maximum number of dependants who were likely to enter this country to join those heads of households who had arrived before December 1967. They calculated that the maximum number of dependants likely to enter was under 250,000 – of whom the largest number would be from Pakistan (nearly 100,000). The majority of families from the Caribbean were nearly complete; Pakistani settlement contained the lowest proportion of complete families. Eversley and Sukdeo excluded future voucher holders from their calculations but estimated that each voucher holder has approximately 2½ dependants. They thought it likely that a large number of the latest arrivals, especially professional men, would stay only for a few years.

Since their study was completed the statistics that are available would seem to be bearing out their main predictions. For example, their statement that the rate of entry of dependants would shortly start to decline receives some support from the 1968 figures, and preliminary figures for the first six months of 1969 show a further decline on 1968 figures.[6]

Immigration control seems to have changed the migration, especially in the case of Asians, from one primarily composed of worker migrants to one which increasingly consists of families coming for settlement. Control accelerated any tendencies that there were among the Asian communities to bring over their families and inhibited the original practice of one member of a family replacing another after a number of years in Britain. Because of fears that re-entry would be difficult control also inhibited many returning migrants from staying for long periods in their countries of origin. For West Indians increasing control and fears of further control have also accelerated the process of full family units being reunited in Britain. Generally, for both Asians and West Indians, complete families have been less likely to consider return than single males or females. Thus the ultimate paradox of the Commonwealth Immigrants Acts has been that by progressively closing the door to new entries it has given an impetus to the permanent settlement of migrants and their families.

REFERENCES

1. G. S. Aurora, *The New Frontiersmen*, (Bombay, Popular Prakashan, 1967).

2. G. C. K. Peach, *West Indian Migration to Britain* (London, Oxford University Press, for Institute of Race Relations, 1968); also Peach, 'West Indian Migration to Britain: the Economic Factors', *Race* (Vol. VII, no. 1, July 1965).

3. Oscar Gish, *Britain and the Immigrant Doctor* (Institute of Race Relations Briefing Paper, London 1969).

4. Report of the Select Committee on Race Relations and Immigration, Vol. IV, pp. 3–5. H.M.S.O., 1969.

5. D. Eversley and F. Sukdeo, *The Dependants of the Coloured Commonwealth Population of England and Wales* (Institute of Race Relations Special Series, 1969).

6. Further information on migration became available after this chapter was written which showed that there had been a further decline in the number of dependants entering in 1969. In a written answer on the February 1970, House of Commons, Vol. 795, Mr. Callaghan stated that 36,557 Commonwealth citizens of whom 29,454 were dependants were admitted for settlement in 1969. This meant that there had been a decline of approximately one-third in all entries, including dependants, which confirms the prediction of D. Eversley and F. Sukdeo. Preliminary figures released by the Home Office for January 1970 show a further decrease in entries of slightly more than 20% compared with January 1969.

Figures for holders of U.K. passports brought under control in the Commonwealth Immigrants Act 1968 – mainly Asians from East Africa – show that 6,249 (including 4,771 dependants) entered in 1969 compared to 6,043 (including 4,366 dependants) from March–December 1968. Preliminary figures for January 1970 show a further decline in January 1970 compared to January 1969 of approximately one-third.

Chapter Four

The Evidence of the Census

Unfortunately, accurate, factual information is rarely a feature of current discussions on race relations in Britain. In an attempt to remedy this deficiency this chapter presents a statistical profile of the main coloured communities and sets this profile against that of the total population. By far the most important source of information that will be used for this purpose is the 1966 10% sample census; we shall use this to assess the number and distribution of coloured people but also their demographic characteristics and situation in housing and employment. An additional source of information is the 1961 census, which makes it possible to give some indication of change over time. Finally, we shall also utilize survey data to estimate incomes and expenditure.

Before proceeding it is necessary to discuss certain weaknesses in census data and to explain how we have attempted to overcome them for this analysis. One difficulty is that the census classifies persons by birthplace and not by race or colour. Thus if we attempt to indicate colour by birthplace certain problems appear. The two most important 'problem' groups are the 'white Indians' and the 'black British'. 'White Indians' are persons born in India and Pakistan of European (usually English) descent, and it is estimated that there were approximately 74,000 in England and Wales in 1966. Since 'white Indians' constituted nearly one-third of the census enumerated Indian population in 1966 it is clearly important to exclude them from the analysis wherever possible; this has been attempted throughout this chapter except in the section relating to employment. The precision with which this exclusion can be made has limitations, it is true, but such an editing process provides a more accurate picture of the coloured Indian population. The 'black British' are coloured people born in Britain who are recorded in the census as born in the United Kingdom. However, as the overwhelming majority are children still living with their parents, it is possible to adjust estimates to include them.

Another source of weakness in census data is the under-enumeration which occurs in even the most carefully conducted censuses. Essentially it is difficult to make contact with those whose housing conditions and working hours are unorthodox. It is clear that some immigrant groups were substantially under-enumerated in the 1966 10% sample census. Using immigration data we have attempted to correct this under-enumeration in order to obtain estimates of total numbers. What we cannot say is how far the non-enumerated population differs from the enumerated population except to suggest that they probably live in worse housing conditions, have lower employment status and include a higher proportion of single persons. Thus both the housing and employment profiles presented here are probably biased in favour of the longer and better established migrants.[1]

Despite weaknesses, the census does provide valuable material on demographic, economic, and social conditions, providing comprehensive coverage of many topics which are central to much social research. We are able to ask a series of questions of the whole population, or of parts of it; the census enables comparison of separate groups within the whole. In particular we are able to compare coloured immigrants with white migrant groups, the Irish and Cypriots, as well as with the population born in the United Kingdom.

NUMBERS

As we have shown, the precise number of coloured people currently resident in Britain is difficult to estimate. The 1966 census provides a basic starting point but, as we have already indicated, three different types of adjustment to this data are necessary. First, it is necessary to exclude 'white Indians'; second, to allow for under-enumeration; and, third, to include coloured children born in this country. After these adjustments the coloured population in England and Wales in April 1966 was estimated at approximately 924,000. This estimate includes people born in

the Far East but excludes those born in East or South
Africa, Cyprus and Malta.[2]

Table 3 shows the component parts of this estimate. The

Table 3. TOTAL ESTIMATED COLOURED POPULATION RESIDENT
IN ENGLAND AND WALES, 1966 CENSUS, BY COUNTRY OF
ORIGIN.

Area of origin	Born overseas	Born in the United Kingdom	Total
India*	180,400	43,200	223,600
Pakistan*	109,600	10,100	119,700
Ceylon	12,900	3,200	16,100
Jamaica	188,100	85,700	273,800
Rest of Caribbean	129,800	50,500	180,300
British West Africa†	43,100	7,600	50,700
Far East‡	47,000	13,000	60,000
Total	710,900	213,300	924,200

* excluding white Indians and Pakistanis
† Gambia, Ghana, Nigeria and Sierra Leone
‡ Far East includes Hong Kong, Malaya and Singapore

Source: *Colour and Citizenship*, Table 10.2

total of 924,200 consists of 710,900 Commonwealth immigrants including children born abroad and 213,300 children
born in this country. Within the total population the Jamaicans form the single largest group, about 30%; *in toto* the
West Indians (49%) are more important than the Indians and
Pakistanis together. The number of children born in the
U.K. is particularly large in West Indian households. Using
these figures as a base-line Valerie Jackson has estimated
that the total population for the seven groups listed in Table
3 in mid-1968 was 1,113,000. Updating this estimate to mid-
1969 gives a total of 1,185,000.

The future size of the coloured population has been the
subject of considerable debate. Estimating future numbers is
a complex task. Mrs. Jackson has prepared projections to
1986 for the five major coloured immigrant groups (Jamaicans, Rest of Caribbeans, Indians, Pakistanis and West
Africans). These projections are based on assumptions about
birth and death rates likely to occur to immigrants already in

the United Kingdom, and on possible flows of new entrants, either dependants of current residents, or new primary migrants. She has assumed that death rates of coloured persons will be like those obtaining in the population at large, but two possible levels of fertility have been considered. *High fertility projections* assume that immigrant fertility rates are twice those applying to English women at all ages; *low fertility projections* assume that under the age of twenty-five immigrant women have English fertility rates, but over that age rates will be twice those applying to English women.[3] Some coloured children will be born to white mothers, a feature which is very difficult to estimate. For the purposes of this calculation it has been assumed that for every ten babies born to a coloured mother there will be one coloured baby born to a white mother. Eversley and Sukdeo in their work on coloured Commonwealth dependants[4] estimated that approximately 250,000 dependants were still eligible for entry into Britain in 1968; but Mrs. Jackson has suggested that nearly 100,000 of them would not actually arrive. The projections have used these results, which indicate that most dependants would come from India and Pakistan. Some new labour vouchers will be issued; it is assumed that the current rate of new issues will be maintained and that the majority will be granted to Indians. A final assumption in these projections is that there will be no return migration.

The five population groups considered contained 848,000 persons at April 1966. On the low fertility projection an increase to 2,074,000 persons in 1986 is expected and on the high fertility projection to 2,373,000 persons – that is approximately 14% greater. This increase between 1966 and 1986 is summarized in Table 4 and the predicted totals at intermediate dates are shown for the low fertility model.

It must be recognized that all attempts to predict future population growth are hazardous and it has been the fate of many such projections to be proved wrong within a fairly short time. It is for this reason that both a high and low fertility projection has been offered. Evidence of current fertility from Birmingham and Notting Hill suggests that the lower fertility model is more likely to be achieved; similarly the assumption of no return migration gives a strong upward bias. In general, it seems likelier that these estimates will prove too high rather than too low. Obviously changes in immigration law or rates of intermarriage in the period up to 1986 could also drastically alter the projection in either direction. However, the lower estimate of between 2 and 2¼ million in 1986 does seem reasonable. This number would constitute very roughly 4% of the total population of the country depending on the future pattern of growth of the total population.

Table 4. ESTIMATED FUTURE POPULATIONS, FIVE MAJOR IMMIGRANT GROUPS 1971–86.

Country of origin	1966*	1971†	1976†	1981†	1986†	1986‡
India	223,600	377,000	510,000	579,000	768,000	890,000
Pakistan	119,700	211,000	290,000	306,000	408,000	485,000
Jamaica	273,700	343,000	383,000	411,000	474,000	529,000
Rest of Caribbean	180,300	229,000	265,000	293,000	341,000	375,000
West Africa	50,700	68,000	74,000	80,000	83,000	94,000
Totals:	848,000	1,228,000	1,522,000	1,669,000	2,074,000	2,373,000

* see Table 3
† Low fertility projection
‡ High fertility projection

Source: *Colour and Citizenship*, Table 30.1

One final caveat must be made about all projections of this nature. Very simply, our definitions of coloured or who is coloured are based on what are or are believed to be social realities of our time. Social realities change over time and to assume that the definitions of colour or the relevance of colour will remain the same in 1986 as in 1969 may be needlessly pessimistic.

DISTRIBUTION AND CONCENTRATION

Commonwealth immigrants are mainly found in the conurbations of England and Wales – predominantly in London and the West Midlands. Table 5 sets out percentage distributions which enable us to locate major concentrations and their significance. 70% of the three major immigrant populations (West Indian, Indian and Pakistani) to which this analysis is confined, were resident in the six conurbations of England and Wales in 1966, areas which contained only 35% of the population at large. There is considerable regional variation. Tyneside, South East Lancashire and Merseyside contain less than their pro-rata share of immigrants; Greater London and the Midlands contain 59% of the immigrants listed here, but only 21% of the total population. Ethnic variations are also present; West Indians are over-concentrated in the London area, while Pakistanis are almost evenly divided between London, the West Midlands and West Yorkshire.

Table 5. DISTRIBUTION OF MAIN COLOURED COMMONWEALTH IMMIGRANT GROUPS IN ENGLAND AND WALES, 1966

	India*	Pakistan	West Indies	India, Pakistan, W. Indies combined	Total Population
Number in England & Wales	163,800	73,140	267,910	504,850	47,135,510
Conurbation	%	%	%	%	%
Tyneside	0.9	0.8	0.1	0.5	1.8
West Yorkshire	5.6	17.3	3.1	6.0	3.6
S.E. Lancashire	3.7	7.0	4.0	4.3	5.1
Merseyside	0.9	0.6	0.6	0.7	2.8
West Midlands	14.9	19.3	13.4	14.7	5.0
Greater London	33.9	22.0	56.7	44.3	16.3
Six Conurbations combined	60.0	67.0	77.9	70.5	34.6
Rest of England and Wales	40.0	32.9	22.1	29.5	65.4

* excluding white Indians

Source: 1966 10% Sample Census

At local authority level concentration was greater in London than anywhere else. In the whole country there were only six local authority areas in which 5% or more of the total population were born in the Caribbean, India and Pakistan. All were London boroughs – Brent 7.4%, Hackney 7.1%, Lambeth 6.7%, Haringey 5.6%, Islington 5.4%

and Hammersmith 5·4%. In another fourteen areas including five London boroughs the concentration of these three immigrant groups exceeded 4%. It seems very unlikely, even allowing for considerable under-enumeration and children born in this country, that there were more than two or three local authority areas (all in London) where more than one in every ten persons was coloured at the time of the 1966 census.

Even within local authority areas such work as has been done suggests that beliefs about all-coloured areas are exaggerated. An examination of ward data for Greater London showed that the highest single concentration of immigrants from the entire New Commonwealth was 31% in Northcote Ward, Ealing.[5] In seven other London wards concentrations reached 20% or more, but excluding persons born in Cyprus and Malta reduces the number of wards to two. Thus even allowing for under-enumeration and children born in England, only one ward in London has anything which might approach a coloured majority. It is true that almost without exception census figures are considered extreme under-estimates by local authority officials. However, the higher estimates – derived mainly from observation – are usually shown to be far more inaccurate than the census when it is possible to validate estimates against some third objective measure. Thus a recent survey in Northcote Ward found that half the households surveyed in the ward were predominantly Indian ward.[6] A number of other area studies in London have also shown that numbers are much lower than generally believed; similar beliefs are found in an industrial setting.[7]

While attention is usually directed at concentrations of immigrants it is necessary to examine the overall pattern of their dispersal and how this affects the total population. In 1961 over half the enumeration districts* of Birmingham had no West Indians present.[8] On the other hand 30% of West Indians in Birmingham were in enumeration districts where they comprised 15% or more of the population. Doherty in his examination of London wards in 1966 showed that 60% of the G.L.C. population lived in wards with less

An enumeration district contains about 200 households.

than 1% West Indian population. Conversely, 20% of the West Indians of London were in wards where they comprised more than 10% of the population.[9] If Doherty had been able to consider enumeration districts, which are much smaller, the contrast between areas with no West Indians and areas with many would have been considerably greater. However, he was able to show that within the G.L.C. area West Indians were concentrated to a greater extent and were more spatially segregated than any other immigrant group in London. This confirms Valerie Jackson's conclusion that West Indians were more concentrated than either Indians or Pakistanis in England and Wales.[10]

THE DEMOGRAPHIC SCENE

Nearly all migrations are characterized by an excess of males and a preponderance of young adults. The immigration from the Commonwealth to Britain has been no exception, although we have shown in the last chapter that the Commonwealth Immigrants Act has reduced and is continuing to reduce the excess of males. Indeed, since control the excess proportion of males in all coloured immigrant communities has been declining and this decline has been accelerated with increasing immigration control. Some indication of the changing sex structure can be obtained from Table 6. The recent sharp increase in the proportion of women entering is to some extent masked by the period between the 1961 census and mid-1962 when a very large number of male immigrants entered. Despite this, for one main group – the West Indians – more women than men arrived between 1961 and 1966.

The very different sex ratios among distinct immigrant groups are indicative of the widely differing problems which these groups encounter. The problems faced by the overwhelmingly male Pakistani communities are obviously very different from those of the West Indians who have a balanced sex ratio. It should also be noted that even within groups there are quite large differences in sex ratios in different areas. These reflect, among other things, the economic structure of the different areas, the status of jobs which members of the immigrant groups have obtained and the length of time the community has been established in the area. All the immigrant groups show higher proportions of women in London than elsewhere.

The proportion of immigrant women (fifteen years and over) who are married has increased for all the main coloured immigrant groups between 1961 and 1966; by 1966 a slightly greater proportion of them were married than females in the total population. Census data does not indicate whether a married person is living with their spouse but for immigrant women this seems eminently likely. For males the situation

Table 6. NUMBER OF MALES PER 1,000 FEMALES AMONG IMMIGRANTS, 1961 AND 1966

Area of Origin	England and Wales			London Conurbation 1966	West Midlands Conurbation 1966	West Yorkshire Conurbation 1966
	At 1961	Arrivals 1961–1966	At 1966			
India*	1,568	1,373	1,479	1,520	1,644	1,640
Pakistan†	5,380	3,541	4,231	2,890	9,451	5,394
Jamaica	1,258	773	1,066	983	1,181	1,356
Rest of Caribbean	1,264	809	1,026	1,048	1,181	1,145
British W. Africa	1,949	1,452	1,614	1,572	—	—
All coloured	1,548	1,279	1,384	1,230	1,754	4,418
Cyprus	1,273	1,016	1,191	1,182	1,484	—
Total population	937	—	940	916	979	949

* Excluding White Indians
† Excluding White Pakistanis

Source: Colour and Citizenship, Table 11.1

is far more confusing, since many immigrants (especially Indians and Pakistanis) have left their wives in their country of origin. However, one can infer from the data that the proportion of immigrant men living with their wives has increased considerably between 1961 and 1966. For West Indians this proportion is probably not much lower than in the total population; in contrast we estimate that only 15% of the total Pakistani males could have had a Pakistani wife in this country in 1966.

The dominant feature of the age structure of every immigrant group is youth. Migrants have universally been drawn from the younger age groups, particularly under thirty years. Continued rejuvenation has occurred through further migration and births. Immigration control has shifted the balance of migration to dependants, particularly children. Since the original migrants were concentrated in the younger, child-bearing ages many coloured children have been born in this country. While the average age of initial migrants was young in comparison with a normal adult population, the addition of children from these two sources has more than offset the normal ageing process. Thus between 1961 and 1966 the average age of coloured residents in England and Wales has fallen slightly. Comparative age structures for different migrant groups, constructed to include both migrants and children born here, are shown in Table 7; figures relate to the Greater London and West Midlands conurbations in 1966. Nearly 40% of all West Indians were under fifteen years of age, compared with 23% in the population at large. In strong contrast, few immigrants were over forty-five years of age; the main coloured groups have between 8% and 11% in this category, compared with 38% in the total population.

Table 7. COMPARATIVE AGE STRUCTURE OF DIFFERENT IMMIGRANT GROUPS 1966 CENSUS, GREATER LONDON AND WEST MIDLANDS CONURBATIONS BY PERCENTAGE.

Age (years)	India*	Pakistan	Jamaica	Rest of Caribbean	British West Africa	Cyprus	Total Population
0–14	33	24	40	39	23	35	23
15–24	16	15	11	12	16	18	14
25–44	40	51	41	41	59	34	25
45+	11	10	8	8	2	13	38

* Excluding white Indians

Source: 1966 Census

In view of this age structure, a high rate of natural increase is to be expected; but fertility rates which make direct comparison between immigrant and English women of the same age are difficult to obtain. Using 1961 census data, Jean Thompson of the General Register Office has examined the fertility of comparable marriage durations.[11] Using births in the year before the census she found higher fertility rates among immigrants than in the total population, for comparable marriage durations. The highest excess occurred among Irish women, who in their second year of marriage had 40% higher fertility than those born in England and Wales. Rates for the coloured immigrant groups were about 20% higher at this stage, though differentials tended to narrow with increased marriage duration.

Valerie Jackson has examined the ratio of children under five years of age to married women fifteen to forty-four years old.[12] This method biases the immigrant fertility figure upwards and this does show a significant excess fertility in all immigrant groups at 1966. In the West Midlands fertility rates were consistently higher than those in London for all main immigrant groups and the total population. In both areas the Asian rate was about 40% higher and the West Indian about 60% higher than the English rate. However, immigrant fertility rates were much lower than would be expected on the basis of birth-rates in the West Indies and India.

Evidence from Birmingham, where births to non-European parents are separately recorded, shows a progressive decline in the number of births to West Indians in each year since 1963.[13] The number of births in 1967 was 25% lower than the peak figure in 1963. If the adult West Indian population has increased by immigration over this period then the crude birth-rate has fallen further. This suggests a greater use of family planning in response to a new environment. However, it is not possible to establish exactly what the final fertility of immigrant women will be until we can examine their whole reproductive span.

An examination of family structure for the main immigrant groups in the Greater London and West Midland conurbations confirms previous findings. Households with English-born heads are more likely to be without children compared to immigrant (other than Pakistani and African) households. Where there are children the average number in families is greatest for immigrant-headed households – especially Irish and West Indians. Finally the proportion of larger families, i.e. with three or more children, is greater for immigrants and largest of all for the Irish.

HOUSING

Our analysis of immigrant housing conditions is based on census data for the Greater London and West Midlands conurbations, which covers about 60% of the main coloured groups. Since the total housing stock varies in composition from region to region we cannot use this information to make general inferences. Many results stem in part from the type of housing which is available in these two study areas, but we are able to illustrate distinctly different patterns which result from different types of housing pressure and availability.

The most useful single indicator of housing conditions is housing density measured by the number of persons per room. Table 8 shows persons per room in the London and West Midlands conurbations. The five major coloured immigrant groups and Cypriots are listed and can be compared with a residual category formed by excluding these six immigrant groups from the total population of each conurbation. A consistent wide differential is immediately evident. All immigrant groups are living at close to one person per room in comparison with only about 0.6 persons per room in the rest of the population. There is little variation within immigrant communities and the situation is remarkably similar in London and the West Midlands.

Higher housing density among the immigrant groups stems from two factors; first, more people per household and secondly less space per household. The larger household size is due to age structure differences. Immigrants are predominantly young, and have children in their families. There are few two-person families where the children have left home. Additionally, economic pressures and the responsibilities to the extended family draw extra members into the household. Consequently, immigrant households are 30% larger than average in the London conurbation, and 57% larger in the West Midlands. In both conurbations the larger

English families can be traced to the suburbs, but there is no similar tendency among immigrants.

Space is a second limiting feature. On average an immigrant household has 1.4 less rooms than an English one in London and just about one less room in Birmingham; immigrant households therefore have 29% less space than the English in the London area and 18% less in the West Midlands. Hence we can state that in the West Midlands household size is the major cause of high density, while in London blame must be equally shared between household size and the number of rooms available.

Table 8. PERSONS PER ROOM, LONDON AND WEST MIDLANDS CONURBATIONS, 1966.

Area of Residence *†	India*	India†	Pakistan†	Jamaica	Rest of Caribbean	West Africa	British Coloured Immigrants	All plus Cyprus	Total Population	Total Population less 6 Immigrant groups
London Conurbation	0.80	0.93	1.07	1.14	1.10		1.05	0.94		0.57
W.Midlands Conurbation	1.06	1.13	1.09	1.09	1.08	1.00	1.10	1.01		0.58

* Not adjusted for white Indians
† Adjusted for white Indians or Pakistanis

Source: Colour and Citizenship, Table 12.1 (adapted)

Extremes of housing density are illustrated in Table 9 by the high proportion of immigrants living at more than one person per room. In both conurbations about 12% of the non-immigrant population lives at this density, compared with 50% to 60% for coloured immigrants. The distribution within this high density category is also instructive. Only 25% of English residents in this high density group are living at more than 1.5 persons per room; in the immigrant groups over half of the high density residents (and this means nearly

Table 9. PERCENTAGE OF PERSONS LIVING AT MORE THAN ONE, AND MORE THAN ONE AND A HALF PERSONS PER ROOM (P.P.R.), LONDON AND WEST MIDLANDS CONURBATIONS, 1966 CENSUS.

Area of residence	All coloured immigrants			English		
	More than 1 p.p.r.	More than 1.5 p.p.r.	More than 1 p.p.r.	More than 1.5 p.p.r.	More than 1 p.p.r.	More than 1.5 p.p.r.
London Conurbation	51.5	27.7	11.1	2.8		
West Midlands Conurbation	57.4	30.0	12.3	2.9		

Source: *Colour and Citizenship*, p. 128 (adapted)

30% of the total population) live at this extreme level of overcrowding.

Sharing a dwelling with other families is a difficulty that immigrants often face. Shared dwellings are usually smaller, and in terms of quality less advantageous; all immigrant groups in both areas have much higher proportions of households sharing accommodation. In London over 70% of coloured immigrant households are sharing, compared with 22% of English households. The contrast in the West Midlands is more extreme, with coloured immigrants being nearly ten times more likely to share accommodation than the rest of the population (41% compared with 4.2%). Additionally, sharers live at higher densities than non-sharers. But sharing and non-sharing immigrants live at higher densities than the rest of the population.

For sharers, apart from the disadvantage of less space per person, there are also the very considerable handicaps of sharing basic facilities. Thus a quarter of coloured households in London and just under a third in the West Midlands share cooking facilities; these figures compare with 2% in London and the West Midlands among non-coloured households. Generally, coloured immigrants are much more likely to be sharing a W.C. and a bath than the rest of the population, and sharing is greater in London than in the West Midlands.

Success in the housing market may be measured through an analysis of housing tenure. Table 10 indicates that the major differences between coloured immigrants and the rest of the population are in renting from a local authority and renting furnished accommodation. Coloured immigrants are poorly represented in local authority housing and very greatly over-represented in furnished rented accommodation. Of the four main types of housing tenure furnished renting is usually the least advantageous for the occupier. It is more expensive, there is less security of tenure and often amenities are of a very poor standard.

Table 10. HOUSING TENURE, BY HOUSEHOLDS, LONDON AND WEST MIDLANDS CONURBATIONS, 1966.

Area of Residence	Owner-occupiers		Renting from a local authority		Renting unfurnished		Renting furnished	
	All coloured immigrants	All English	All coloured immigrants	All English	All coloured immigrants	All English	All coloured immigrants	All English
London Conurbation	32.6	38.9	4.2	22.3	18.1	29.0	43.6	7.3
W. Midlands Conurbation	59.4	41.1	7.7	39.1	9.4	14.6	21.2	2.6

Source: *Colour and Citizenship*, p. 133 (adapted)

The extent to which coloured immigrants have moved into owner-occupation is significant considering the areas in which immigrant settlement has occurred. In selected inner-London and West Midland areas immigrant owner-occupancy was nearly twice that of the rest of the population.[14] This high proportion in owner-occupation reflects not only the preference of many immigrants for property-owning but also the extreme difficulties they face in obtaining accommodation in the other preferred sectors of the housing market – renting unfurnished and renting from a local authority.

Assessment of the change in the general housing situation of coloured immigrants between the 1961 and 1966 censuses is complicated by changes in the definition of a room. These changes had the effect of including in the 1966 census kitchens, used for cooking only, which were excluded in the 1961 census. So while overcrowding among immigrant groups in seven inner London metropolitan boroughs (1961 boundaries) appears to have declined between 1961 and 1966 this decline is in fact almost entirely the result of this change of definition. It is possible to apply a crude correction factor to allow for this change in definition and when this is used it can be seen that there appears to have been no significant decline in the proportion of coloured immigrants living at more than 1.5 persons per room (Table 11). Over half the West Indian population in these seven inner London boroughs were living at more than 1.5 persons per room in 1961 and in 1966 (using 1961 definitions). Overcrowding in the English population which started from a very much lower level (8%) in 1961 declined to 5% in 1966 (using 1961 definitions).[15]

During the period 1961 to 1966, sharing has increased for all immigrant groups. The proportion of coloured immigrant households sharing in these inner London boroughs rose from 74% to 79%, but it also rose for English households from 30% to 39%. Access to housing amenities such as a bath and exclusive use of a W.C. improved for everybody except Pakistanis in the five-year period. West Indians and Indians both showed increases in the proportion who were owner-occupiers and renting unfurnished. Renting from a local authority had also increased but at a much slower rate than for either the English or Irish householders.

Between 1961 and 1966 the main coloured immigrant groups showed very little overall improvement in their housing conditions. While access to household facilities improved and there was movement out of the least advantageous sector of the housing market (renting furnished), their level of over-crowding remained very high and the proportion sharing showed a slight increase. In contrast the period has been one of improvement for English residents of these boroughs and, while comparisons are difficult, it would seem that the coloured immigrants were being left even further behind as the general level of housing amenity has risen.

Table 11. CHANGES IN HOUSING DENSITY AND SHARING IN SEVEN LONDON BOROUGHS 1961 TO 1966

	Percentage of the population at more than one and a half persons per room		Percentage of households sharing accommodation	
	1961	1966 (1966 Basis)	1966 (1961 Basis)* 1961	1966
India and Pakistan	25	22	32	53	59
Jamaica	53	34	47	76	82
Rest of Caribbean	63	43	59	82	84
All Coloured	52	36	50	74	79
Ireland	32	18	27	50	60
Cyprus	41	24	36	51	62
England	8	3	5	30	39

Sources: 1961: R. B. Davison in *Black British*
1966: *Colour and Citizenship* (Table 12.9 amended)

* The census definition of a room changed between 1961 and 1966, but for purposes of comparison we have made a correction in this column. For details of the correction see ref. 15 at the end of this chapter.

EMPLOYMENT

In this section the employment position of coloured immigrants in the Greater London and West Midlands conurbations is examined. As for housing the situation nationally is not necessarily the same as in these two areas, especially as the employment position in the two conurbations differ. Unlike the previous sections of this chapter, we have not been able to exclude the white Indians from this analysis as a result of difficulty in estimating their activity rates and general employment position. However, as we know that their occupational distribution is heavily weighted towards the higher status end of the employment scale, the distributions given for Indians should probably be adjusted downwards. The extent of this correction is not clear but it is greater for London than the West Midlands, where there are far fewer 'white Indians'.

All the male immigrant groups, except the West Africans, have higher proportions of their population (15 years and over) economically active* than the population as a whole. This is because the proportion of retired persons in the immigrant groups is far lower than in the total population. All groups also have higher rates of economic activity in the West Midlands than in Greater London; due mainly to the large student population in London reducing the proportion economically active. West Indian women have substantially higher rates of economic activity (67%) than the total population (49%). Indian and Pakistani women have economic activity rates fairly similar to the total population in London (16%). This difference is partly due to the presence of 'white Indians' discussed above, but there are a number of reports that suggest that Asian women in London are much more likely to be economically active than those living in the Midlands.

The overwhelming majority of immigrants in employment are found in the rank and file of the employed population and have not achieved promotion. In the West Midlands less than 2% of males born in the Caribbean (compared to 20% of the total population) were self-employed, managers, foremen or professionals. The status of West Indians in London is marginally higher but immigrants are rarely in those positions where they can take the crucial decisions about economic life. All immigrant groups (except Cypriots) are heavily under-represented in all positions of power and authority compared to the total population. The position of Cypriots in London is exceptional: nearly a fifth of the males are self-employed and it is interesting to speculate how and why this particular immigrant community has been able to take this entrepreneurial route. None of the other communities has as yet managed on anything approaching this

* Persons are defined as economically active if they are in employment or if they are seeking employment.

scale to employ this classic expedient for new immigrants, although there are signs that certain Asian groups are moving into the entrepreneurial activities. The Cypriots have typically moved into those industries which require comparatively little capital such as clothing, catering and small shop-keeping.

The occupational distribution of male immigrant groups in London shows a fairly wide spread with considerable diversity between different immigrant groups. There are no overwhelming concentrations (except possibly for Cypriots) of any immigrant group in any occupation (Table 12). The pattern for males in the West Midlands shows greater concentration and fewer differences between each immigrant group. Over one-fifth of the males of each immigrant group are labourers and this rises to over half for Pakistanis, most of whom work in engineering and allied trades. Asian-born men in London are well represented in clerical and professional jobs and have low numbers in labouring jobs; the reverse occurs in the West Midlands.

Comparing the occupational distribution of immigrants to the population as a whole, certain major differences appear. For men in London, the greatest over-representation is for Cypriots in service occupations and West Indians as labourers. Africans and Indians are over-represented and West Indians under-represented in clerical and professional occupations. West Indians are also over-represented as wood-workers and transport and communications workers. In the West Midlands, there was a very large over-representation of all male groups, especially Pakistanis, as labourers. The other major over-representation was of Indians as furnace, forge, foundry and rolling mill workers.

Few West Indian women in either conurbation are in clerical jobs compared to the total population or to Indian women in London. The biggest concentrations of West Indian women are in service jobs in London and in the engineering trades in the West Midlands. They are also heavily over-represented as nurses. In London, two out of every three Cypriot women are clothing workers, by far the heaviest concentration of any group.

An examination of the numbers in each immigrant group in 'white-collar' or 'white-blouse' jobs presents the reverse

Table 12. DISTRIBUTION IN MAJOR OCCUPATIONS FOR SELECTED BIRTHPLACE GROUPS BY PERCENTAGE, BY SEX, 1966.

(a) Males – Greater London conurbation

	India	Pakistan	Jamaica	Rest of Caribbean	All Caribbean	British West Africa	Cyprus	Total population
Number economically active	36,530	9,440	30,710	30,240	63,950	8,480	18,700	2,468,300
Selected occupations								
VII. Engineering and allied trades workers n.e.c.*	13.7	11.0	17.4	15.4	16.4	12.1	9.1	12.6
XVIII. Labourers n.e.c.	6.0	5.9	20.7	15.1	18.1	7.5	4.7	6.0
XIX. Transport and communications workers	7.6	5.8	12.4	18.3	15.2	10.7	3.2	10.1
XXI. Clerical workers	17.9	12.9	1.9	5.6	3.6	21.8	3.3	11.3
XXIII. Service, sport, and recreation workers	5.1	3.2	3.6	6.5	5.0	6.6	33.9	7.6
XXV. Professional, technical workers, artists	18.1	12.3	1.6	4.7	3.0	17.5	3.6	11.0

* 'n.e.c.' after an occupational description means 'not elsewhere classified'.

Table 12—*contd.*

	India	Pakistan	Jamaica	All Caribbean	Total population
(b) Males – West Midlands conurbation					
Number economically active	12,630	11,470	13,530	16,910	777,490
Selected occupations					
V. Furnace, forge, foundry, rolling mill workers	15.9	5.7	8.6	7.8	4.3
VII. Engineering and allied trades workers n.e.c.	19.2	22.3	25.3	25.7	28.3
XVIII. Labourers n.e.c.	26.6	53.1	22.9	22.5	7.8
110. *Labourers n.e.c. in engineering and allied trades**	9.9	37.4	11.8	11.9	3.6
XIX. Transport and communication	4.9	1.1	9.8	10.3	6.3

* Unit groups (identified by 3-digit code numbers) are sub-divisions of the occupation order (identified by roman numerals) directly above them.

Table 12—*contd.*

	India	Jamaica	Rest of Caribbean	All Caribbean	British West Africa	Cyprus	Total population
			(c) *Females – Greater London conurbation*				
Number economically active	16,220	23,510	20,340	45,850	5,150	8,170	1,611,140
Selected occupations							
XI. Clothing workers	2.7	15.6	10.8	13.4	7.6	64.5	4.7
XXI. Clerical workers	45.5	7.5	13.4	10.2	21.4	8.1	35.7
XXIII. Service, sport, and recreation workers	9.9	27.9	22.2	25.3	17.5	13.6	21.4
XXV. Professional, technical workers, artists	18.6	13.5	22.0	17.4	19.0	1.8	10.4
183. *Nurses*	*1.0*	*12.8*	*14.3*	*13.5*	*13.4*	*0.5*	*3.9*

Table 12—*contd*.

	Jamaica	All Caribbean	Total population
(d) Females – West Midlands conurbation			
Number economically active	7,720	9,670	447,110
Selected occupations			
VII. Engineering and allied trades workers n.e.c.	39.5	37.8	15.0
XXIII. Service, sport, and recreation workers	14.2	14.5	20.4
XXV. Professional, technical workers, artists	15.9	16.4	7.4
183. *Nurses*	15.8	16.3	2.7

Source: *Colour and Citizenship*, Table 13.3 (adapted).

side of the coin. From Table 13 it can be seen that West Indians in both conurbations and Asians in the West Midlands are very much under-represented in white-collar jobs (i.e. clerical, sales, administrative and professional jobs). Thus while over a third of males in the total population in London and a quarter in the West Midlands were in these jobs, under 5% of Jamaicans in London and about $2\frac{1}{2}\%$ of all West Indians in the West Midlands were in these jobs. Similarly, for women 43% of the total population in the West Midlands, but only 4% of the West Indian population were in white-blouse jobs. (It should be noted that we have excluded nurses from this comparison in order to highlight a position which might otherwise be masked by their inclusion.)

Table 13. PERCENTAGE OF POPULATION ECONOMICALLY ACTIVE IN WHITE-COLLAR* OCCUPATIONS.

| | Males | | | | Females† | | | |
| | Greater London Conurbation | | West Midlands Conurbation | | Greater London Conurbation | | West Midlands Conurbation | |
	1961	1966	1961	1966	1961	1966	1961	1966
India	50.2	45.3	—	12.1	66.8	70.0	—	—
Pakistan	34.5	32.0	—	3.2	—	—	—	—
Jamaica	4.8	4.5	—	1.7	7.5	9.7	—	3.3
Rest of Caribbean	11.9	11.8	—	—	15.1	22.7	—	—
All Caribbean	8.0	7.8	—	2.6	10.6	15.6	—	3.8
Total Population	35.8	36.9	—	24.8	51.1	53.4	—	42.6

Notes: * White-collar occupations include clerical workers, sales workers, administrators and managers and professional, technical workers, artists.
† Female data exclude nurses.

Source: Colour and Citizenship, Tables 13.5 and 13.6

So far we have looked only at one moment in time and to assess change we need to examine 1961 employment data as well, which unfortunately is available only for London. Between 1961 and 1966 the percentage of men in the total population in white-collar jobs increased but all immigrant groups showed a drop in the proportion of males in these jobs (Table 13). This decrease was greatest for the Indians and least for the West Indians. For women, all groups, including the total population, showed increases in the percentage in white-blouse occupations between 1961 and 1966. As for other occupations, West Indian men became slightly more concentrated and over-represented as wood-workers, transport workers, and engineering workers – but in labouring there was a decline in concentration and in over-representation. The concentration of West Indian women in nursing also declined between 1961 and 1966.

Another viewpoint from which the employment of immigrants can be examined is through the industries in which they work. As for occupation, their industrial distribution differs not only from the total population but between the different immigrant groups. Generally in both conurbations higher proportions of immigrants of both sexes are working in manufacturing industry and lower proportions in services than the total population. Transport and communications employed over a fifth of West Indians in London but only a tenth in the West Midlands. In the West Midlands well over half of the Indians and Pakistanis are in the metal manufacture and metal goods industries compared with less than a quarter of the total population. About a quarter of West Indian women are employed in the medical and dental services but more are employed in the West Midlands in the metal goods and manufacturing industries. Finally, it should be noted that all the immigrant groups, male and female in both conurbations, were under-represented compared to the total population in the distributive trades.

To complete our profile of immigrant employment it is necessary to look at those who cannot find work – the unemployed. Unlike the other topics we have discussed in this chapter, regularly collected national data are available on the number of registered unemployed. In 1963, when data on its present basis was first collected, Commonwealth males comprised over 4% of all unemployed and females over 6%. In absolute terms and as a percentage of the total, immigrant unemployment fell steadily until the end of 1966. With the increasing unemployment of winter 1966–67, the number of Commonwealth immigrants unemployed rose sharply as did their proportion of the total unemployed. Since the beginning of 1968, however, immigrant unemployment has been slowly dropping. By mid-1969 immigrant males comprised about 2% of all unemployed and females 3%.

Generally, changes in the numbers of immigrant unemployed are in the same direction and the movement has the same timing as for the total population. However, as total unemployment rises, the proportion of immigrants among the total unemployed also rises which means that in times of rising unemployment Commonwealth immigrants tend to be harder hit than the general population. This is not of course entirely unexpected from the earlier analysis of occupations.

In broad terms the position of immigrant groups differs not only from the total population but also between themselves. Occupationally and industrially, coloured immigrants are not a homogeneous group; the situations of Indians, Pakistanis and West Indians must be considered separately. Furthermore, within immigrant groups there are wide differences in job achievement between different areas and it is generally higher in London than the West Midlands. Nevertheless, in neither conurbation have immigrant groups achieved anything like a comparable position to that of the rest of the population. Immigrants are less well-represented than the total population in those jobs usually considered most desirable, and are over-represented in those jobs considered most undesirable. No direct information from the census is available on whether this is due to lack of skills on the part of immigrants or resistance by the local population. An indicator that the achieved position of immigrants in the labour force is not solely due to their lack of abilities is the peculiar position of West Indian women. For example, in the West Midlands there are four times as many West Indian nurses as 'white-blouse' workers, but for the total population there are sixteen times as many white-blouse workers as nurses. While the reasons for these extreme differences are complex, it seems that employer resistance to West Indian women in white-blouse jobs is partly responsible. Employer resistance almost certainly also applies to West Indian men and to the other immigrant groups and is a contributory factor to their low level of employment achievement compared with the total population.

Finally, the concentration of coloured immigrants in

certain sections of employment and their absence in others, coupled with the fact that there has been little or no change between 1961 and 1966, gives most cause for concern. If this pattern continues into the 1970s, then the assessment that the situation is still fluid and has not hardened into a rigid class-colour or caste-colour structure may well be over-optimistic. The basic problem should not, however, be seen in those sectors of employment that have over-concentrations of coloured immigrants, but in those that have few. It is in the occupations and industries where the coloured immigrant is rare or absent that the answers to concentration, lack of achievement, and frustration are to be found.

INCOME AND EXPENDITURE

There are no national data on the household income and expenditure of immigrants and the 1966 census contained no questions on these subjects. The Family Expenditure Survey does not give information in its national survey by birth-place or some similar criterion. Therefore to complete our statistical profile of the different immigrant groups, we will summarize A. H. Vanags' comparison of Robert Radburn's survey of immigrant households in Birmingham in 1966–67 with the Family Expenditure Survey for 1966.[16] As the sample of immigrant households was only drawn from Birmingham, it cannot be claimed that the results have national validity, but there seems no reason to think that there are very wide divergencies between this sample and that of other immigrant groups in the conurbations and large cities.

As would be expected, the sample of immigrants contained hardly any retired persons and there was a heavy concentration of manual workers. The average size of households in the sample was similar to that of the total population but this average masked the fact that immigrant households were usually either one-person or large (5 plus persons) households. Pakistani households were exceptional in that nearly two-thirds of them were one-person. Examining average household size by length of time the head of household had spent in this country showed that for pre-1959 arrivals it was 3.59, 5.43 and 2.67 in 1966–67 for West Indians, Indians and Pakistanis respectively: for arrivals after 1962, the average size was 1.80, 2.20 and 1.30. These differences in household size and length of time in the U.K. make direct comparisons of income difficult but an attempt is made to summarize them in Table 14.

It can be seen from this that household income rises with length of time in this country but this increase is least for West Indians. However, the increase of household size over time does mean there is no rise in income *per capita* over time. From Table 14 it will be seen that the household incomes of the immigrants is generally lower than that of the total population. On a *per capita* basis Indians and West Indians are worse off than the total population, but Pakistanis, although they have a low household income, are better off, due to the high number of one-person households. These comparisons, it should be stressed, are approximate due to the different demographic characteristics of the different groups.

No direct evidence on the earnings of immigrants compared to white workers was obtained from the Birmingham survey. A survey in Nottingham suggested that coloured workers earn less than their white counterparts, and this difference may arise because coloured workers are less frequently offered overtime.[17] A survey in Lambeth also found a discrepancy in average earnings between white and coloured manual workers and the difference was greatest for skilled workers.[18]

The most important single item in the budgets of most households is housing and we have some information on this from the Birmingham survey. Nearly 60% or more of households in the sample in each immigrant group are renting accommodation. However, if only the pre-1959 arrivals are examined, then this proportion renting falls to 46% for West Indians and 33% for Indians while the proportions in owner-occupation increase. The pattern of tenure also changes with level of income and this is shown in Table 15.

At low incomes, the proportion of owner-occupiers is larger among the general population than among the immigrants. For all four groups the proportion of owner-occupiers naturally rises as income rises, but for the immigrants it rises much faster, so that in all cases the proportion of

Table 14. HOUSEHOLD INCOME OF IMMIGRANTS IN BIRMINGHAM BY DATE OF ARRIVAL IN U.K. COMPARED TO INCOME OF TOTAL POPULATION OF U.K.

Date of arrival in U.K. of head of household:	West Indian			Indian			Pakistani			Total population	
	−1959	1959–62	1962–	−1959	1959–62	1962–	−1959	1959–62	1962–	U.K. as a whole	U.K. manual workers
	%	%	%	%	%	%	%	%	%	%	%
Up to £17	30	38	33	13	25	43	30	54	72	35	23
£17–£23	31	32	40	29	39	37	48	34	24	20	27
£23 and more	39	31	27	58	36	21	23	12	4	45	50
Average income	£23 2s.	£20 7s.	£20 10s.	£29 14s.	£22 0s.	£20 12s.	£21 1s.	£17 12s.	£14 8s.	£23 10s.	£24 3s.
Average household size	3.59	3.21	1.80	5.43	3.23	2.20	2.67	1.78	1.30	3.03	3.43
Workers per household	1.69	1.39	1.1	1.62	1.2	1.18	1.1	1.03	1.0	1.36	1.75

Source: *Colour and Citizenship*, Tables 14.5 and 14.3.

Table 15. TYPE OF ACCOMMODATION BY HOUSEHOLD INCOME.

	Total population			West Indian			Indian			Pakistani		
	−£17	£17–£23	£23+	−£17	£17–£23	£23+	−£17	£17–£23	£23+	−£17	£17–£23	£23+
	%	%	%	%	%	%	%	%	%	%	%	%
Rented	63	56	44	82	66	30	81	71	43	85	70	40
Owner-occupied	32	40	53	18	34	70	19	29	57	15	30	60
Rent free	5	3	3									

Source: *Colour and Citizenship*, Table 14.7.

owner-occupiers among those with incomes in excess of £23 is larger than for the general population. For West Indians, the rise in the proportion of owner-occupiers is particularly sharp. Little information was obtained on the cost of buying houses in the Birmingham study but information from other studies suggests that repayment periods are often shorter and interest rates sometimes higher for coloured buyers.

All the immigrant groups in the Birmingham study paid more rent on average than the general population. In large part this was due to the very heavy concentration of immigrants in the furnished sector where rents are higher. Additionally, immigrants would generally be paying more for unfurnished accommodation because their tenancies on average have been established more recently when rents have been rising. However, the immigrants tended to pay more the longer they had been here and it would seem that the growth in household size and thus the demand for extra housing space offsets the influences which might lead to less rent being paid with longer residence. Two studies which provide additional detail are the Lambeth survey and the Notting Hill Housing Survey Interim Report.[19] The Lambeth study showed that at all levels of income, white families paid less rent than coloured families and both studies clearly showed that at all levels of rent paid, the quality of housing which coloured families obtained was generally inferior to that of the whites.

The Birmingham survey also obtained information on the household expenditure, savings, and remittances of the immigrants. It is not possible to say how reliable the data are, since they are based on what respondents said they spent and saved, rather than upon written records. The median levels of household expenditure for West Indians, Indians, and Pakistanis, respectively, were £9–£10, £11, and £7–8, which is a pattern roughly in keeping with the relative sizes of the households of the three groups. For Indians and Pakistanis, household expenditure increased with the length of time they had been here, but did not do so for the West Indians. Since expenditure tends to reflect income, this appears to be a corollary of the fact that their household incomes did not increase very much with time. However, as the size of West Indian households did increase with time, just as it did for the others, it seems that they became relatively worse off the longer they had been here.

The information on savings and remittances suggests that the proportion of income saved by the immigrants is relatively high. Remittances were considered separately from savings so that the total weekly savings is the sum of the two items. Weekly savings for West Indians, Indians and Pakistanis were respectively: £4 1s 0d, £4 9s 0d, and £4 17s 0d. On average, £1 7s 0d, £1 7s 0d, and £2 5s 0d was sent to their home country. It was also found that while the level of remittances fell with the length of time here for Indians this was not so for West Indians and Pakistanis. Standardizing for income and only looking at those immigrant households with incomes between £17 and £23, it was found that the proportion of total income saved or remitted, was 16.5% for West Indians, 18% for Indians and 26% for Pakistanis. This compares with just over 5% of net income saved by the U.K. population.

THE EVIDENCE OF THE CENSUS

As we have seen, the 1966 10% sample is capable of providing information on a number of questions regarding the situation of coloured Commonwealth immigrants and their children in Britain. Much of this information directly contradicts many of the myths that are current in political and social debate. In 1966, the coloured population was less than 1 million or just under 2% of the population. Due to its age structure, the rate of growth of the coloured population will be faster than that of the total population but there is nothing very startling about the fertility rates of coloured immigrant women – they are no higher than those of the Irish.

The Commonwealth immigrant in the 1950s and 1960s came to the great urban centres and the majority live in the great cities, especially London. The widespread belief that it is the West Midlands and Yorkshire that have 'suffered most' from an 'overwhelming' influx of coloured immigrants is incorrect. Apart from the doubtfulness of the proposition that 'numbers are the essence' all the highest concentrations in the country are in fact in the London boroughs. Even here nothing approaching an all-black ghetto exists. But the converse, the 'all-white ghetto', does exist.

The cities and towns where the coloured immigrants have found work have often been those towns which because of their attraction for labour have severe housing shortages. The coloured immigrants have found themselves living in overcrowded circumstances, sharing facilities and receiving poor value for high rent in the declining inner-city or twilight areas of these cities. The coloured worker has not yet been able to break through in any number to the white-collar jobs and his job opportunities are limited in certain industries. Despite beliefs to the contrary, few immigrants are unemployed: there is a higher proportion in employment than in the rest of the adult population.

These are some broad conclusions that can be drawn from this picture that the census provides of the situation in 1966. It shows how far we must travel to reach a society with equality of achievement. The fact that we failed to narrow the gap significantly between 1961 and 1966 in either the housing conditions of minorities or in their employment circumstances shows how long and difficult the journey towards equality will be.[20]

REFERENCES

1. For a much fuller discussion of the quality of census data and also of the methods used to adjust errors due to the presence of 'White Indians', the absence of coloured children born in the U.K. and under-enumeration in the 1966 census, see Valerie Jackson in *Colour and Citizenship*, Chapter 9 (pp. 93–95) and Appendices III, 3 (pp. 769–75) and III, 4 (p. 779).

2. The steps in the calculation of this estimate are given by Valerie Jackson in *Colour and Citizenship*, Chapter 10 (pp. 96–100) and Appendix III, 4 (pp. 776–79).

3. The full method of calculation is given by Valerie Jackson in *Colour and Citizenship*, Chapter 30 (pp. 629–38) and Appendix VII, 1 (pp. 795–96).

4. D. Eversley and F. Sukdeo, *The Dependants of the Coloured Commonwealth Population of England and Wales* (London I.R.R. Special Series), 1969.

5. Joe Doherty, 'The Distribution and Concentration of Immigrants in London', *Race Today*, Vol. 1, No. 8 (Dec. 1969).

6. *Children in Southall*, Report of survey carried out in Northcote Ward, Southall, 21st–27th August, 1968, by volunteers from the Grail Centre, Southall Indian Workers Asso-

ciation, in association with London Council of Social Services, 1969.

7. An excellent illustration of the tendency to over-estimate numbers is reported in the annual report of the Race Relations Board for 1968–69. (H.M.S.O, London, 1969), pp. 67–68. The British Overseas Airways Corporation invited 170 of their general apprentices and senior trainees to estimate the number of coloured workers in B.O.A.C, U.K., and 60% of them estimated in the region of 2,500. In fact there were 924.

8. Ceri Peach, *West Indian Migration to Britain* (London, O.U.P. for I.R.R., 1968), p. 88. See also Ruth Glass and John Westergaard, *London's Housing Needs* (Centre for Urban Studies, London, 1965) for a similar analysis of London.

9. Joe Doherty, op. cit.

10. *Colour and Citizenship*, p. 103.

11. Jean Thompson, 'Differential Fertility among immigrants to England and Wales and some implications for population projections' in *The Journal of Biosocial Science* (Supplement No. 1, July 1969).

12. V. Jackson in *Colour and Citizenship*, Chapter 11, pp. 112–16.

13. Statistics from Public Health Department, Birmingham.

14. *Colour and Citizenship*, pp. 133–34.

15. The boroughs were Battersea, Camberwell, Deptford, Hackney, Lambeth, Paddington and Stoke Newington (1961 metropolitan boroughs). These boroughs were selected for study by R. B. Davison, *Black British* (London, O.U.P. for the I.R.R. 1966). The effect of the change in definition of a room from 1961 to 1966 was to reduce the number of people in 1966 living at more than 1.5 person per room in these 7 boroughs from 97,290 (1961 definition) to 69,530 (1966 definition). The effect of this change in definition was proportionately more important for non-sharing households (29,550–16,300) than for sharing households (67,740–53,230). To estimate over-crowding at 1.5 person per room from the 1966 definition two correction factors have been used – for sharing households (1.28) and for non-sharing households (1.81). It should however be noted that these correction factors are general factors for the total population of these 7 boroughs and it can only be an approximation in converting overcrowding figures for specific-birthplace groups.

16. For further details see Chapter 14 by A. H. Vanags in *Colour and Citizenship*. The survey of the income and expenditure of immigrant households was carried out by Robert Radburn in Birmingham using West Indian, Indian, and Pakistani

interviewers. The responses were derived from a quota sampling of areas identified as being settled by immigrants. The sample contained 302 West Indian, 311 Indian, and 307 Pakistani households. Of these, the heads of household of 126 West Indian, 70 Indian, and 84 Pakistani households arrived in this country before 1st January 1959; 146, 115, and 149 respectively, arrived between that date and 31 December 1962, and of the remainder, 30 West Indians, 126 Indians and 74 Pakistanis arrived after 1962. The West Indians and Indians were interviewed partly between December 1966 and February 1967 and partly between August and September 1967. This means that the figures which are in money terms may be slightly inflated when compared with the Family Expenditure Survey for 1966. However, no significant difference was found in the results for the two dates, so the information has been compounded. The Pakistani house-information was interviewed between October 1966 and February 1967.

17. F. J. Bayliss and J. E. Coates, 'West Indians at Work in Nottingham', *Race*, Vol. VII, no. 2 (October 1965).

18. Survey of housing occupancy commissioned by Lambeth Borough Council from Research Services Limited in 1966, and quoted by Elizabeth Burney in *Housing on Trial* (London, O.U.P.; for Institute of Race Relations, 1967).

19. Ibid., and Notting Hill Housing Survey Interim Report (Notting Hill Housing Service, London, 1969).

20. Since this chapter was written, the Registrar General's *Quarterly Return for England and Wales*, 3rd Quarter 1969 (London, HMSO 1970) has been published giving details of live births by the birth-place of parents. This shows that 11.8% of the births in the second and third quarters of 1969 were to overseas born mothers – 3.2% were to mothers born in Eire, 5.8% to mothers born in the New Common-wealth and 2.8% to mothers born in other countries, of which Europe and the U.S. were most important. The figures in the *Quarterly Return* are not inconsistent with any of the estimates in this chapter. The projections given on page 60 appear to need no amendment; if anything, the low fertility projections are still more likely to be correct. Additionally, the figures show that over half the immigrant mothers giving birth are white – and that, despite popular belief, the highest concentrations of coloured immigrants are in London and not in the West Midlands or Yorkshire. In short, the main implications of the Registrar General's *Quarterly Return* are political rather than demographic.

Chapter Five

Policies and Practices

We shall be concerned in this chapter with the policies and practices devised within our own society and their effect on the processes of adjustment and inter-penetration which took place between the newcomers and their new surroundings. In the previous chapter, we considered the situation of the migrants and its development over time: the policies and decisions taken during this period and the manner in which they were implemented were major factors in determining the evolution of that situation. The content of these decisions, their scope, and the manner in which they were taken depended to a substantial extent on factors external to the migration itself. Weaknesses in the existing system of government, although their significance varied in detail from one situation to another, have had a pervasive effect on the evolution of policy on race relations.

However, despite the deficiencies in the system, new policy issues which call for remedial action usually pass through a series of processes: discussion, consultation, debate, legislation, and finally administrative action. In the case with which we are concerned these processes were unusually slow in taking place. For ministers and civil servants had accepted a proposition which had been defined contemporaneously with the migration and whose significance had increased alongside its numerical growth. This was that the principal aim of policy should be to preserve the equality of status of the newcomer. The point of reference for this doctrine lay not in administration practice but the law. That is, the law conceived of as the quintessence of colour blindness. Equality before the law served as a symbol of the community's intent; the words of Mr. Justice Salmon passing sentence on youths convicted of participation in the disturbance of 1958 in Notting Hill achieved something of the status of a sacred text:

You are a minute and insignificant section of the population who have brought shame on the whole nation with horror, you lived and have filled the whole nation with horror, indignation and disgust. Everyone, irrespective of the colour of their skin, is entitled to walk through our streets with their heads erect and free from fear. This is a right which these courts will always unfailingly uphold.[1]

But the role of the law in this situation was limited by the concept of the place of law in society held both by the judiciary and the executive. To both, the notion that the law might guarantee not only civic rights but social rights through legislation against racial discrimination was quite unacceptable. The law's function was symbolic.

The doctrine of equality by proclamation, confined in practice to the assurance of legal rights, has far reaching consequences: it was for ten years the backcloth against which all policy decisions were taken. An additional major cause of the failure and missed opportunities in this field stems from the decision arising from this doctrine to allow the existing local services to take the strain. For, in practice, the link between centre and periphery is one of the weakest points in our system of government. Local authorities have been entrusted with a vastly increased range of responsibilities in the social welfare legislation passed since the war, and although government departments determine the broad lines of policy, the methods of supervision employed leave a wide area of discretion to the local authorities. On issues of detail, Whitehall must cajole rather than control. And the capacity of local authorities to execute policy on any complex or controversial issue is in turn often limited.

Such action as was taken during the fifties was therefore severely restricted; the form that it took tended to be determined by the capacity of local government officers – as defined by their training and attitudes – to handle specific problems as they arose. Not surprisingly, their response tended to be tentative in style and unpredictable in its consequences.

This process of groping towards *ad hoc* solutions was true

of the local agencies of central government as of the departments of local government. But gradually a process of feedback to the centre began to take place. Although the official position remained unchanged until long after the scope of the difficulties rendered its absurdity self-evident, the informal swopping of experiences between local authorities and individuals and the demonstration function of certain activities eroded it in practice. The legitimacy of action directed specifically to needs deriving from the presence of coloured minorities in Britain slowly became accepted. The first attempt to give coherent expression to this new orthodoxy was the Prime Minister's White Paper of 1965, *Immigration From the Commonwealth*.[2] Our review of policy turns on the axis of the White Paper, which stands out as the first systematic review of policy or attempt to define remedies. It falls into two main parts: a section, Part II, dealing with immigration policy, and a second, Part III (which we have already briefly discussed) covers departmental proposals and the creation of a new agency to deal with problems of integration. The first provoked immediate dispute. What was proposed was, first of all, a reduction to 8,500 in the rate of employment vouchers issued, including a special allowance of 1,000 vouchers for Malta; entry of unskilled workers was to be abolished; 'strict tests of eligibility' were to be applied to the entry of dependants; powers of medical examination extending to dependants were to be sought; and, finally, new powers were to be sought to combat evasion, including an extension of the Home Secretary's power to repatriate. The proposals in Part II of the White Paper attracted widespread criticism on the well-justified grounds that there was an invasion of civil liberties involved in the provisions for deportation and some aspects of the proposals on dependants. Furthermore, despite the elaborate consultations that had taken place, the solutions reached, and in particular the selection of the number of employment vouchers to be issued, seemed arbitrary. But perhaps the most potent case for the resistance of Labour supporters to the proposal had less to do with their content than with the manner in which they were presented and the psychological shock administered to their beliefs about the party. Here was clear evidence that the party of the Commonwealth, faced with an admittedly difficult situation, had taken the same line as its predecessor. In the *Economist*'s telling phrase, they had 'pinched the Tories' white trousers'.[3]

The novelty lies in Part III of the White Paper, which deals with policies for integration and the devising of special measures to deal with the problems that had arisen. These represent a new departure stemming at least in part from the appointment of a co-ordinating Minister. That the structures eventually proved inadequate is less important than the fact that they could at last be contemplated without self-conscious references to the dangers of unequal treatment. The White Paper has other deficiencies. It lacks a point of reference in the realities of the situation, as a result of a failure to undertake effective gathering of information. Roy Jenkins was able to make this deficiency good during his term at the Home Office by setting in train processes that led up to the P.E.P. investigation into the extent of discrimination.[4] His attempt at a concerted programme is so important that we have dealt with it as a separate section within this chapter. In the following chapters we deal with the evolution of policy and practice in a number of particularly significant areas. Despite the discontinuities produced by the fact that local authorities possess different powers in different fields and by variations from one situation to another, these studies should be seen as running parallel and affecting the general evolution of practice at local authority level. At the end of the period we are considering, a recognition of responsibility on the part of central government finally takes place and there is a belated readiness to consider the problems of the areas of immigrant settlement as a whole. The concrete evidence of this acceptance of responsibility lies in the Urban Programme with which the section on the evolution of policy closes.

The influence of public opinion, both as projected through the mass media and reflected in the opinion polls, grew throughout this period, and its relevance was eventually recognized and then exaggerated. But we reserve our discussion of the content and changes in attitudes until a later section. There has, of course, been a missing term in the whole discussion to date – the immigrant and his perception of the situation. This omission faithfully reflects the role of the immigrant as patient, not agent, during the evolution of the debate that was determining the position he would occupy in our society. His response to this situation and its consequences will be the subject of a separate chapter later in this book.

THE DECLINE AND FALL OF LAISSEZ-FAIRE

One of the major obstacles confronting anyone proposing to discuss official policy on immigration and race relations in the period leading up to the Labour Government's White Paper of 1965 is the widespread belief that no such thing existed. This is a view common to all shades of opinion: it is one of the main themes of Paul Foot's devastating polemic;[5] Enoch Powell employs it as the cornerstone of his jeremiads on national negligence.[6] Politicians nearer the centre of the spectrum have repeated it; Henry Brooke, who as a senior minister in the fifties was as closely concerned as anyone with these questions, told the House of Lords in 1966 that:

> If only these problems had been thought out in advance, and if only action had been taken in the 1950s to keep the pace of immigration at a rate which the country could successfully absorb, without risk of over-heating the points of friction ... we should have far more cause to be proud of the way this country grew to be a multi-racial society.[7]

He repeated these strictures with even greater emphasis in 1969.

Similarly, Lord Gardiner, Lord Chancellor in the incoming Wilson Administration, told the House in the previous year that in his view:

> The actions, or rather the inaction, of the last two administrations means that neither our children nor their children will ever see the England which we have been used to seeing, because for good or ill England has become a multi-racial society.

And this was chiefly because:

> Just as until 1962 we had no real national plan about immigration, so we had no national plan as to how those

who were here were to be integrated or assimilated into the population.[8]

In fact, constructive steps were taken at the outset by the Colonial Office – some inherited from the provision made during the second world war to meet the needs of newcomers from the Colonies. In the years immediately after the arrival of the first substantial group of West Indians in the *Empire Windrush* in June 1948, this machinery provided a cushion against immediate problems generated for the immigrants. But with the progress of the Colonies towards independence, emphasis was increasingly placed on the equal status of Colonial and Commonwealth citizens and the undesirability of any measures that singled them out for special attention. Independence also opened up the possibility that newly independent governments might take responsibility for their own nationals in the U.K. – a prospect confirmed when the recommendations of the Senior-Manley mission dispatched to Britain by the Jamaican Government resulted in the creation of the British Caribbean Welfare Service.[9] Responsibility for migration passed from the Colonial Office to the Home Office and the conclusion was reached by the British Government in 1955 that no control over entry was necessary.[10]

At a time when little public concern was felt about immigration and the flow of newcomers seemed to have settled down to an acceptable level, the incentive for central government to take further action was not great. Members of Parliament who felt differently were a small and politically isolated minority. This apparently calm situation was ruffled by two significant developments. First, the appearance of a substantial number of immigrants from India and Pakistan whose position differed substantially from that of the West Indians provoked considerable alarm in the Home Office. However, the British Government was able to negotiate agreements with the Indian and Pakistani Governments who agreed in mid-1958 to take steps to curb the migration.[11] But no sooner was this problem apparently resolved than an altogether more serious one arose.

The disturbances which took place in Nottingham and Notting Dale in August and September 1958 blew away the complacency with which the subject was still clothed and left the Government's lack of policy indecently exposed. Reactions within the Government were mixed. A small faction wished to introduce immediate control over immigration, but the majority view was that bilateralism, which was apparently working adequately with the Indians and Pakistanis, should be extended to the West Indians. But neither Norman Manley nor the ministers of the West Indies Federal Government were prepared to accept any responsibility for such a solution. A compromise decision was taken, which consisted of employing the machinery of bilateral consultation to introduce deportation provisions for Commonwealth or colonial citizens involved in serious crime. This line was duly adopted for the Home Secretary's speech to a concerned audience at the Conservative Party Conference, who passed by a substantial majority a motion calling for control; most members thought that his speech meant legislation in the following session. As for the rest, Government spokesmen could refer critics to the sonorous words of Mr. Justice Salmon, sentencing the nine youths convicted for assault during the disturbances.

Outside Whitehall the disturbances had a further important result, in that they pushed the Opposition into a position of outright resistance to the control of immigration. Both Hugh Gaitskell and Jo Grimond were initially inclined to favour the deportation of convicted criminals, but in the debates at the end of the year, the spokesmen for the Labour party nailed their party's colours firmly to the mast by opposing control in any foreseeable circumstances.

One extra-Parliamentary organization which had been as surprised as anyone by the events in Notting Hill was Sir Oswald Mosley's Union Movement, formed largely from the wreckage of the pre-war British Union of Fascists and a scattering of post-war recruits. Early in 1959 Mosley announced his intention to contest the North Kensington seat at the forthcoming general election, his platform epitomized in the statement, 'we are going to treat these people fairly but we are going to send them home'. Evidence soon began to suggest that Mosley was gaining ground, and when a West Indian carpenter, Kelso Cochrane, was stabbed to death in the same area by an unknown assailant in May, the danger of further disturbances forced the Government to make another lengthy self-exculpatory statement. 'I am satisfied', the Home Secretary told the House of Commons in June, 'from consultations which I have had with my colleagues mainly concerned and from consultations which have taken place with local authorities, voluntary bodies, the official welfare organizations, and the police that everything possible is being done and that every effort will continue to be made in areas where there is a large coloured population to encourage their effective integration into the community.'[12] And further than that, with a general election imminent, the Government was not prepared to go.

As the election approached the subject began to sink below the political horizon, and Mosley's failure at the polls, where he obtained less than 3,000 votes and lost his deposit for the first time in his career, added a sour smell of failure to the generally squalid impression made by the way in which he had presented his case.[13] This setback for explicit opposition to continued uncontrolled immigration, coupled with the handsome majority obtained by the Government at the election, gave it the last of a series of breathing spaces. The fact that it failed to use it to any effect, either by taking the plunge and adopting control, or by devising positive policies with a degree of direct central intervention, is ultimately bound up with the new departure on colonial policy introduced by Iain Macleod when he succeeded Alan Lennox-Boyd as Colonial Secretary at the beginning of the new Parliament. This effectively pre-empted the Opposition's position and shifted the centre of gravity of policy sharply to the left. The keynote oration of this period was the Prime Minister's 'wind of change' speech in Capetown in February 1960 (perhaps more radical in style than content), and one of its major symbolic acts was the decision to allow South Africa to leave the Commonwealth in the following spring. Both reflect the diminishing significance attached in official policy to the position of the white man in Africa, and in this realignment, a significant element was a countervailing belief in the importance of the black man in the new dispensation for the Commonwealth. As the Colonial Secretary saw it, the introduction of control over West Indian immigration at a time when the Federation of the West Indies was at last getting on its feet and preparing for independence would be a substantial setback for this limb of his policy.

But while the tide was running powerfully in one direction in colonial policy, another current of opinion within the Conservative Party had begun to run with increasing strength. As a result of the general election, a group of Members from the Birmingham area, several of them newly-elected, had come together to launch a systematic campaign for the introduction of controls. These members could claim direct constituency experience of the difficulties associated with immigration – a claim which, for reasons of electoral geography, was previously mainly confined to Labour members. Of the problems themselves there could be no longer any serious argument, although the basic causes of the difficulties remained in dispute; the housing situation in particular now demanded some form of action and the Ministry of Housing was being strongly pressed by local authorities, particularly Birmingham. But perhaps most significant, these members were claiming that the view they were putting forward was representative of public opinion at large. In this claim they were assisted by the setting up in the Birmingham area of a lobbying organization, the Birmingham Immigration Control Association. This association brought together in the simulacrum of a mass organization a number of local figures who had been campaigning for some years, with the assistance of extensive publicity from the press, for the control of immigration. This now became a demand for a complete stop for five years. The B.I.C.A. campaign in Birmingham and the West Midlands was that it provided the Birmingham Conservative members with a means of demonstrating, in a way that polls could never do, that public opinion was aroused on the issue. And those local members who disagreed with the campaign, particularly Sir Edward Boyle, were made to feel the weight of the people's displeasure.

The confluence of these two tides began to produce rough water for ministers very early in the new Parliament. The difficulty was sharpened by the substantial rise in the migration from the West Indies in 1959 and 1960; and in August 1960 the Colonial Secretary made a further attempt to persuade the Jamaican Government to restrict the number of emigrants through passport limitations – the figure of 15,000 per annum was mentioned. Almost equally disturbing was the patent erosion of the bilateral agreements between the British Government and the Indian and Pakistani Governments, brought about by systematic forgery of passports and evasion of control by racketeers manipulating the migration for profit. As a result, the Home Secretary decided that the question of the mechanics of control should be thoroughly re-examined by an inter-departmental standing committee. Their report came down in favour of a system of control based on the availability of employment and incorporating checks on health and criminal record.

This move provoked a strong reaction within Whitehall from the Commonwealth and Colonial Offices. The affront to the susceptibilities of territories shortly to become independent, it was argued, would be insupportable. The Treasury was anxious about the prospect of losing a beneficial supply of extra labour for an economy in a state of expansion. The political arguments cut both ways: as *The Times* pointed out, was it seemly for a Home Secretary with a liberal reputation like Butler's to capitulate to pressure of this kind?

In the circumstances, it was decided to make one more attempt at a bilateral solution. The Prime Minister himself paid a visit to the West Indies as part of a trip which included Washington and Ottawa. The results were disappointing. And after a further bout of hesitation, the Government reluctantly decided to take the plunge. The decisive factors in determining the introduction of legislation in the autumn of 1961 were two: first, the decision of the Jamaican electorate in September not to consent to their country's participation in the Federation. Secondly, the Prime Minister's decision to move Iain Macleod from the Colonial Office to the leadership of the House of Commons removed, as one paper put it, 'the main obstacle'. The plans proposed at the beginning of the year by the Home Office and the Ministry of Labour could be put into effect without further delay. R. A. Butler, in a speech of exquisite ambiguity, made the fact that control was impending clear to the Conservative party conference.

The conflict that followed over the passage of the Commonwealth Immigrants Bill was to a very striking degree a symbolic one; the issue of control was debated by reference to its impact on the Commonwealth. It is true that Labour, in their reasoned amendment to Second Reading, stressed the irrelevance of the measure and immediate needs in areas of settlement, but this line of criticism was not developed at any length (except briefly, at a later stage, by Marcus Lipton): moral indignation about post-imperial obligations was more effective in shaking the ranks of Tuscany.

The achievements of the Labour party, in modifying a Bill whose provisions – based on a system of entry on employment vouchers – were by subsequent standards mild, were detailed at length by Eric Fletcher in his speech on Third Reading in March 1962. These were: early renewal (in 1963), easier entry for residents, a broader definition of students and dependants, the institution of entry certificates, and the publication of instructions to immigration officers. The degree to which these achievements did not represent a total success was reflected in the melancholy winding up speech by Denis Healey, who carefully reserved the Labour position on renewal of the legislation, and by the Opposition's poor showing in the vote that followed. But at the time, the damage to the Conservative party looked quite extensive. Abstentions and outright opposition in several sections of the party had been frequent. Ministers, who had 'hated the necessity for the Bill', stressed that it represented 'control rather than a stop', and accepted the need for frequent review of the situation, were anxious to forget the episode. Control was duly introduced, with comparatively little difficulty, at the end of June, and a new advisory Committee – the Commonwealth Immigrants Advisory Council (C.I.A.C.) – set up as a result of proposals made during the passage of the Bill – was left to review the situation in a nightwatchman role. Virtually unnoticed, the Migrant Services Division of the West Indian Federal High Commission, the chief prop of the welfare system, was broken up, and the Colonial Office's co-ordinating committee slipped quietly into oblivion.

For a brief period it seemed as if the Labour party might be prepared to try to fill the vacuum. But the energies of radicals were diverted to a prolonged campaign to keep first

Colin Jordan, then Oswald Mosley, off the streets; 'punch up politics' and petition campaigns for legislation against incitement to racial hatred (in which the major Jewish organizations made one of their rare interventions in this field) served as a surrogate for direct involvement in race relations. In Parliament, hostility was canalized into a campaign against the incoming Home Secretary, Henry Brooke, for a series of decisions on the deportation of Commonwealth citizens and aliens. The attention of the Labour movement itself was increasingly diverted by the approaching prospect of power.

In January 1963 Hugh Gaitskell died, universally regretted, and in his first major speech as leader Harold Wilson committed the party to the support of Fenner Brockway's Racial Discrimination Bill, which incorporated provisions on racial incitement. There was nothing in this to foreshadow the drastic modification to the party's line which took place during the year. Indeed, evidence during the spring and summer from by-elections suggested that the issue was no longer salient. The only shadow on proceedings was cast by a cloud no bigger than a man's hand at Smethwick, where the Conservative achievement in winning a seat against one of the strongest of all municipal election swings reflected the diversion of the energies, objectives, and personnel of the local immigration control association into the local Conservative party.

Nor was there any evidence of concern on the part of the Government. Control itself, in the Government view, required no further debate: action had been taken. The C.I.A.C. had already produced one report;[14] oversight of the situation was in reliable hands, and voluntary efforts were making headway in local situations.

In this atmosphere, might not the Labour party have a responsibility to avoid any controversial commitment that would jeopardize a long awaited election victory? With this in mind and informal soundings by the whips suggesting anxiety in the constituencies, the Shadow Cabinet met to consider their line in the debate on the renewal of the Act. After acrimonious debate a solution was found: bilateral controls. This was duly put forward by Wilson in a debate that revealed considerable disarray in the Labour ranks.

Henry Brooke had no difficulty in disposing of the argument for the further consultation with the Commonwealth which Wilson offered as a price for unopposed renewal; the Opposition were forced to divide the House.

For the Conservatives, the opportunity was too good to miss. Control had, after all, been introduced by the Conservative Government as a deliberate act of policy. Beside this, the reports of the C.I.A.C. and their recommendations for action were of marginal significance. Henry Brooke had told the Commons in November 1963 that he would not want to suggest that all those 300,000 applicants awaiting vouchers would have necessarily entered the country if controls had not existed. By July 1964 he was implying the opposite in the House, and by September the claim that their entry had been averted was official party policy.

Certain Conservatives were prepared to push the matter further. In July, a meeting of the Birmingham group of members, under the chairmanship of Geoffrey Lloyd, made the case for a full-blooded campaign based on a contrast between stringent Conservative controls and Opposition laxity. However, the Birmingham initiative failed to carry the Conservative party. This was fortunate for the Labour party who were in serious difficulties over the problem of devising a solid plank for the election manifesto. With infinite pains a package was put together: bilateral controls, the Brockway Bill, and aid to areas affected by immigration. With the subject raised more and more frequently in Wilson's whistle-stop tours, and the developing Conservative strategy of referring to the numbers they had kept out (now putatively swollen to a million, by the Prime Minister in Birmingham and Bradford), a clear statement became impossible to avoid. Wilson provided a substitute of a kind, with some off-the-cuff remarks, at a mass meeting in the Bull Ring at Birmingham, and a few copies were hastily run off in Transport House; but these, and the confused variety of statements by individual candidates, did not correct the impression of a party increasingly on the defensive on this issue.

It was in this posture that the new Labour Government was disclosed on taking office, deprived by electors of the Parliamentary services of the Foreign Secretary, Patrick

Gordon Walker, defeated at Smethwick. This was generally seen at the time as a clear expression of popular resentment, frustrated too long by neglect, and acted as an immediate stimulus to action; the fact that it was by and large working-class Labour supporters who seemed to be involved intensified the pressures on the Government to devise some form of policy which could be put into early effect.

The initial strategy adopted fell into three parts. First, the Commonwealth Immigrants Act was renewed as an interim measure. Secondly, a mission (eventually headed by Lord Mountbatten) was to be sent to Commonwealth capitals to try to negotiate bilateral agreements. Thirdly, the new Prime Minister established his radical bona fides by a sharp attack on the new member for Smethwick, who would, he said, spend his short Parliamentary career as 'a kind of Parliamentary leper'. These initiatives taken, a search for positive policies was put in hand. In March 1965, the Prime Minister, after reviewing immigration policy and the need to 'stamp out evasion at source', announced the appointment of Maurice Foley, member for West Bromwich, as the minister responsible (in a personal capacity) 'for the co-ordination of effective executive government action with, and through, local authorities and voluntary bodies to see that much speedier action is taken on integration, in the widest sense of the word, in terms of housing, health, education, and everything that needs to be done'.[15] The Prime Minister also announced the redemption of his party's pledge to introduce legislation 'to deal with racial discrimination in public places and with the evil of incitement to racial hatred'. In drafting this legislation, the Home Secretary, Sir Frank Soskice, had the advantage of two previous detailed examinations of policy on this issue. One was his own, conducted in Opposition at the request of the National Executive Committee; the second was by a committee of the Society of Labour Lawyers, who had been given the job of revising the Bill so often moved without success by Fenner Brockway. A third memorandum had been prepared by a splinter group linking the Society of Labour Lawyers and the newly-formed Campaign Against Racial Discrimination (C.A.R.D.), calling for the use of conciliation machinery, and the setting up of a statutory agency. But neither the Home Office nor the Lord Chancellor, to whom this memorandum was submitted, were prepared to act on it.[16] Those who drafted it responded by embarking on a systematic lobbying campaign, employing a series of different avenues. The new Conservative spokesman on Home Affairs, Peter Thorneycroft, saw the potential of the conciliation principle and persuaded the Shadow Cabinet and party Home Affairs Committee, whose initial instincts had been to oppose the Bill outright, to adopt the solutions of a reasoned amendment criticizing the drafting of the Bill and calling for the introduction of the device of conciliation. After narrowly obtaining a Second Reading for the Bill, the Home Secretary withdrew the contentious sections, substituting conciliation for criminal penalties and establishing a national agency, the Race Relations Board, to supervise the conciliation process through local committees. The scope of the Bill remained restricted to public places, and the incitement provisions were untouched; in this form, the Bill survived committee stage and passed into law. It seemed, as a student of the subject has commented, a 'a haphazard, secret and inefficient process';[17] but at least it had provided the initial basis for future measures in this field by establishing an administrative agency, in the shape of the Race Relations Board.

Having evolved a solution of sorts to one policy problem, the Government now had to deal with the two main prongs of the March announcement – the integration programme and a new policy for immigration. By June, the failure of the Mountbatten mission had become evident. With the final collapse of bilateralism, any chance that the Government might have had of completing its *volte face* on the issue under cover of the symbols of Commonwealth (and, at one remove, monarchy) disappeared. The Government had to evolve its own solution, in the knowledge that a Conservative party group, sitting under the chairmanship of Selwyn Lloyd, were likely to propose extremely drastic solutions – perhaps 'one in, one out', possibly a check on dependants. This situation gave rise to complaints that the parties were engaged in a species of Dutch auction. The Government's bid was contained in the White Paper on Immigration Policy which was published on 2nd August from the Prime Minister's Office.

This White Paper, together with the Race Relations Bill that preceded it, represents the distillation of official thinking on race relations in the period immediately after Labour obtained office. As we have seen, it covers both policy on immigration and measures designed to promote integration (which we discuss, elsewhere). In essence, the immigration policy in the White Paper, as accepted in substance by both parties, was a 'Little England' policy, based unilaterally on the social and economic needs of this country as the Government defined them at that stage. This approach could reasonably be represented as selfish – for example, in its emphasis on the entry of skilled and professional migrants from under-developed countries, but its defenders represented the measures being taken as essential to the introduction of a systematic programme of integration. 'Without integration, limitation is inexcusable; without limitation, integration is impossible,' ran the syllogism put forward by Roy Hattersley, who had been among the earliest of the new generation of Labour Members to repudiate his past position on immigration control.

By this point, the Home Office had won the inter-departmental battle lost by the Commonwealth departments and its victory was shortly to be symbolized in the transfer of the junior minister responsible for integration to that department, there to combine the roles of supervisor of immigration procedure with his previous responsibility. In this victory the changing official perception of what was at stake is neatly summarized. From being an aspect of this country's relationship with the world outside, this issue had become a wholly internal problem, and one of regulation: control at entry and control of the situation resulting from entry, preservation of the Queen's Peace, prevention of discrimination and incitement to racial hatred, and the averting of inter-racial conflict. Given this bias, the question was whether the new combined structure would be capable of breathing life into the formula so neatly summarized by Hattersley and producing the integration it required. In the next section, the Home Secretaryship of Roy Jenkins is examined and assessed with these considerations in mind.

TOWARDS LEGISLATION AGAINST DISCRIMINATION

If the White Paper of 1965 was intended to restore confidence by conveying the impression of the firm smack of purposive government at work, it must be judged a failure. Its publication was followed by a disconcerting period of drift, during which the Government's posture became progressively less rather than more credible. Moreover, the temporary suspension of discussion of the immigration policy set out in the White Paper brought about by the concession of a committee of inquiry (the Wilson Committee) into immigration procedures, seemed to leave the Government even more uncertain of its course. The Expiring Laws Continuance Debate in November 1965 illustrates this uncertainty with painful clarity. Winding up for the Government, Ray Gunter informed the House: 'I defend my stand on the White Paper on the very standpoint of the Christian Gospel'; and that his officials marked the cards of coloured workers as such, 'from a sense of Christian charity because they know that if they send a man to work he will be humiliated, often not because the management wants to humiliate him but because the man on the workshop floor will not accept him.' On the selection of a number for the allocation of work vouchers, he could only say that this was 'an exercise of judgment'.[18]

With such uncertainty prevalent, not only on the manner of execution of official policy but on the aims of that policy, it was clear that not even Maurice Foley's capacity for soothing the troubled breasts of members of local authorities could avert trouble, especially if the general election, which seemed increasingly likely to take place early in 1966, produced the same kind of exploitation of anxieties over immigration as had its predecessor. This, in broad outline, was the position when Sir Frank Soskice's increasing ill-health drove him into retirement and the Prime Minister appointed Roy Jenkins, at the end of December 1965, to be his successor.

In discussing the period that followed, it is impossible to avoid discussion of the personality of the new Home Secretary. The public persona, Welsh miner's son turned Whig, has fascinated journalists without stimulating any profound analysis; the oblique style seems to baffle, the highly polished surface to reflect the light without revealing the depths. Perhaps more relevant for the present discussion were the new Home Secretary's past publications, especially that locus classicus for commentators on his Home Secretaryship, *The Labour Case*.[19] In this work, published for the 1959 General Election, Jenkins set out his criteria for a civilized bourgeois socialism. It was on Home Office issues, and perhaps in particular those (like the admission of aliens to Britain) which involved questions of individual liberty, that Jenkins discerned the sharpest divide between the parties. He characterized his Conservative predecessor's policy on the admission of foreigners as 'more suitable to a police state, terrified of intellectual infection from the outside world, than to a Britain which is the traditional refuge of the oppressed'.[20]

In short, the preoccupation with efficient management, balanced by a concern for the individual and his position vis-à-vis the bureaucracy, were together crucial in forming the assumptions with which the new Home Secretary turned to considering a problem which he identified from the outside as one which would define the style of his Home Secretaryship.

An immediate problem which arose as Jenkins began his term of office was the appointment of the first Chairman of the Race Relations Board. He brushed aside the deliberations of his predecessor and the claims of other candidates, and appointed Mark Bonham Carter, the publisher and former Liberal Member for Torrington. The aimlessness and negative atmosphere of the debate (or rather the succession of statements on the subject of immigration) on the Expiring Laws Continuance Bill in November 1965 had provided convincing evidence that the task of defining the ultimate goals of policy was not an intellectual exercise but an immediate, practical imperative. The need was satisfied with characteristic neatness and precision in the first major speech on race relations, in the course of which Jenkins produced his definition of integration as 'not a flattening process of assimilation but equal opportunity, accompanied by cultural diversity, in an atmosphere of mutual tolerance'.[21]

These preoccupations with efficiency and intellectual precision also emerged in the identification of the first (and as it turned out chief) major policy initiative in this field – the extension of the legislation against racial discrimination to cover the fields of housing and employment. Initially, the emphasis was very much on the side of employment. It is true that powerful vested interests were involved in any such extension – both employers and trade unions could be expected, for rather different reasons, to oppose a further Race Relations Act. Moreover, his predecessor, in persuading the House to accept the much mutilated Race Relations Act of 1965, had commented that 'it would be an ugly day in this country if we had to come back to Parliament to extend the scope of this legislation'.[22] But this could hardly be read as a binding commitment and the job of persuading the interest groups presented a technical problem in political manoeuvre which was not a deterrent to Jenkins and his chosen allies.

Moreover, the selection of the extension of legislation as the key issue offered an escape from the blind alley of immigration policy which the new Home Secretary clearly found extremely distasteful. It was implicit in any decision to advance on the legislative front that the immigration flank would need to be stabilized. Once the government's liberal critics had been bought off with an investigation of a possible appeals system, the main hazard was from the right; and an almost uninterrupted series of concessions on the numbers and composition of the immigration made the stabilization a difficult operation. Jenkins chose to revitalize the stale vocabulary of the debate and re-define its terms by placing the emphasis on a comparatively new factor in the situation – the 'second generation' of coloured children, British-born or educated shortly to leave school and compete for jobs and housing.

By filtering out the immigration elements of the situation and representing the case as one of justice denied by the simple factor of skin pigmentation, this approach revived the moral issue in a sharpened form and provided the best justification for legislation against such capricious discrimination.

The selection of legislation as a leading issue necessarily implied the relegation of other and more complex issues to a lower priority. The clearly formulated aim of extending legislation against discrimination was not balanced by practical proposals for official action in other directions to promote integration; although the Home Secretary talked bravely about the responsibility for providing an example, policy outside his department presented the same negative appearance as it had done in the White Paper. One conspicuous exception was the implementation in a Local Government Bill of the undertaking in the 1964 election manifesto to provide special help for areas affected by immigration. A complex formula was devised in the Home Office to provide a commitment extending to £15-million per year to offset expenditure by local authorities on staff whose employment was attributable to the presence of immigrants locally. But even here, the objectives of policy were blurred: the funds made available were useful as a palliative, when local authorities were prepared to apply for them, but not directly relevant to the solution of the underlying social problems.

A final characteristic of the style of Jenkins' tenure of office at the Home Office which is relevant to the field was his sensitivity to what was politically possible in terms of timing. Two things were clear by the end of 1965: first, that the general election then pending would be of crucial importance in clearing or clouding the atmosphere – and that if the storm were safely weathered, controversial legislation would have to come early in the lifetime of the parliament. The first of the major speeches on race relations that Jenkins 'placed' at various stages of his Home Office career, like so many stepping stones across a potentially treacherous marsh, was therefore not made until after the election.

In fact uncertainty over the outcome of the election lasted for only a short time, and concern about the possible role of the race issue for a little longer. The universal conclusion, based mainly on the defeat of Peter Griffiths at Smethwick, was that the immigration issue was no longer of major political significance. The conditions for a forward policy on race relations appeared to have been satisfied. But in launching this policy, there remained a number of basic conditions to fulfil. In particular, the strategy of the campaign for legislation also demanded a selection of priorities between the points at which pressure might be brought to bear.

The Home Secretary needed both to convince his cabinet colleagues and to ensure that their conviction was carried through to their various departments, whose attitudes towards legislation would be crucial in the forthcoming debate with vested interests in industry and elsewhere. The solution to these difficulties inside Whitehall and to the Home Secretary's problems of persuasion within the cabinet and outside lay in providing clear evidence of the extent of discrimination. From this, the need for legislation could be deduced. For a variety of reasons, this evidence would have to come from outside Whitehall. In the first place, the Home Office was not prepared to assemble it. Second, it was clearly desirable that the evidence on such a controversial issue should appear to emanate from an independent or quasi-independent source. And thirdly, the publication of the results of any inquiry conducted independently would provide the opportunity of enlisting public sympathy before officially committing the Government to take action. And public opinion would be particularly significant in determining the success of legislation designed to have an educative effect. In order to take this next step it would be necessary to turn to the race relations agencies.

In the period after the general election of 1964, the whole configuration of the race relations scene had changed. Existing organizations were shaken up and new ones created; by the general election of 1966, these organizations were just beginning to find their feet and establish formal and informal interconnecting links. In considering the possible extension of legislation the most important of these new agencies was obviously the Race Relations Board itself – if only because this body was likely to be the principal beneficiary. The Board had been established by virtue of the Act of 1965. The form of this legislation had left the board with limited scope (it covered only places of public resort) and an inadequate range of powers. The restriction of the scope was of course a political decision, persisted in despite heavy pressure, in the confused circumstances of the spring of 1965. Hepple, in his authoritative study of the law and discrimination in employment,[23] attributes much of the deficiency in the powers given to the board to a confusion over the introduction into the Bill at a late stage of the principle of conciliation. He quotes Lord Stonham as justifying this change to avoid 'bringing the flavour of criminality into the delicate question of race relations' but points out that the major raison d'être of conciliation in the American codes on which the revised British legislation was in part modelled, has been utilitarian – simply to provide a more efficient means of enforcement. By contrast, the procedures introduced by the Act of 1965 are 'unnecessarily complicated while, at the same time, being toothless'.[24] Conciliation should in practice involve not tempering the consequences of the discriminatory act for the discriminator but providing a speedy and informal means of satisfaction for the grievance of the victim of discrimination, without a clumsy top hamper of court proceedings. 'The lack of solicitude which the 1965 Act reveals for the complainant', he adds, 'is related to the inadequacy of the remedies provided'[25] – no civil or criminal proceedings (apart from an injunction) could be brought in respect of unlawful discrimination by any party other than the Attorney General. Finally, Section 6 of the Act amended the provisions of a Public Order Act of 1936 in relation to incitement of racial hatred, creating a new category of events leading to criminal prosecution. The inclusion of this section in a statute concerned with discrimination and providing for conciliation or civil proceedings has been a rich source of confusion and misrepresentation.

Faced with the patent inadequacy of the scope of operation of the Board and the likely difficulties of operating the Act in the areas in which it did apply, Bonham Carter made it a condition of appointment that he should be able to put the case, after a year's operation, for the extension of the scope of the Act and a revision of the Board's powers.

Initially, the clearly indicated strategy was to play from weakness – that is, while losing no time in putting effective conciliation procedures into operation, equally to lose no opportunity of exposing the inadequacy of the Board's powers and its inability to deal with the majority of complaints which came before it. In this way, the Home Secretary's need for manifest evidence for extension of the law would be met and the Board's own critics silenced. At the same time, the Board was able to extend its range of activity by developing initiatives in other directions. First, through carefully selected appointments to the local conciliation committees which fulfilled the twin function of creating instruments for negotiation and discussion of grievances on a local plane and influencing the formation of policy nationally. Second, by the establishment of contacts with various interested groups which had either been affected by the 1965 Act or were likely to be involved in its extension like the brewers, and the insurance companies. Similarly, the contacts built up in industry through local appointments proved valuable in enabling the Board to show that the views of employers towards the extension of legislation were by no means as monolithically sceptical as the C.B.I. wished it to be thought in the spring of 1967. By the time that John Lyttle joined the Board as chief conciliation officer from a senior post at Transport House, Bonham Carter as chairman and the Board as a body already held a central place in the developing situation.

But the Board, in order to function effectively as front runner, needed allies. Heineman has engagingly maintained that, in the initial stages, the nature and extent of the contacts between the various official and unofficial bodies active in this field was defined by what he calls 'family relations' – that is, by the personal contacts built up by a small group which he characterizes as the 'race professionals'.[26] The extent to which this was true, even in the initial stages, of a rapidly developing situation, is debatable; but if there was a convergence it was on the National Committee for Commonwealth Immigrants.

The National Committee was the senior agency in the field by six months; it had had a difficult birth in conjunction with the White Paper (an association that dogged it throughout its career) and a mixed ancestry. It had been the conviction of Maurice Foley that such an agency, operating outside the restrictive structure of Whitehall, could reach the public and influence local authorities more readily than a programme devised by a central department. But in practice these hopes were disappointed, through a series of events dealt with in greater detail in Chapter 7.

Initially, the doubts about the Committee that were later so freely expressed were not a significant element in the situation. For example, several members of the Campaign Against Racial Discrimination's executive agreed to serve on the National Committee or the specialist panels set up to discharge the advisory function. Martin Ennals, who as General Secretary of the National Council for Civil Liberties had helped to organize the opposition to the White Paper, resigned from that post in order to take up an appointment with the National Committee. The good impression initially created among sceptics by the willingness of the chairman of the Committee, the Archbishop of Canterbury, to give public expression to his doubts about the Government's immigration policy helped to encourage many of the doubtful to participate in the Committee's rapidly expanding activities. A number of immigrant organizations remained obdurate, but most of those active in what Heineman calls the 'race relations interest' associated themselves with the National Committee in the winter of 1965–66.

Not that these bodies necessarily determined the direction of policy within the Committee; but it was inevitable that with the extension of legislation in the air, those panel members who would be concerned with the earlier Bill should press for the extension of legislation to housing and employment. By May 1966, three of the specialist panels, housing, employment, and legal affairs, had prepared detailed proposals for such an extension which were submitted to the full Committee, and the housing panel had, in addition, drafted an extended survey of the situation in the housing field which was to be submitted to the Minister of Housing with a request for him to receive a deputation.

But, like the Home Secretary himself and the board, the National Committee found that the case for the extension of legislation needed to be carried one stage beyond the general arguments which had proved effective in 1965 and gave detailed evidence on the extent of discrimination. Immediately after the Home Secretary's first major speech, discussions began on the possibility of commissioning a study, coupled with the examination of the American evidence and its relevance to the British situation. By June, the decision to undertake a pair of studies and entrust the first to the independent research organization, Political and Economic Planning (P.E.P.) and the second to Professor Harry Street of

Manchester University had been taken. Although for obvious reasons the Home Secretary could not take any explicit part in the detailed negotiations, the initiative and the responsibility for the major policy decisions were both his.

The strategy of the Home Secretary also demanded a critical body representative, as far as possible, of immigrant opinion, which could both speak for the victims and act as informed critic of the status quo, putting forward proposals and criticisms which could be assimilated in a decent interval into the official wisdom. For the time being, and in default of more effective spokesmen, C.A.R.D. was cast in that role.

The main objectives of the C.A.R.D. executive committee at this stage were to build an organization which would bridge the gap between the majority society and the various ethnic groups and the class divisions within those groups, and also incorporate to some degree, in a loose coalition, the major immigrant organizations. Pressure for legislation was seen as much as a means to these ends as an end in itself. But by the end of 1965, members of the C.A.R.D. executive committee had seen their remarkable success in persuading the Government to cast their legislation against racial discrimination in the form of conciliation by an administrative agency, vitiated by the Prime Minister's White Paper and the manner in which it had been presented.

In its approach to the task of presenting the case for the immigrant, C.A.R.D. adopted a range of different expedients. One was the tactic of permeation of views through other organizations with established positions at various points in the community, the drawbacks of this technique were that C.A.R.D. did not obtain direct credit for the views expressed by these organizations and that some members felt that a certain amount of distortion was occurring in transmission. A second, and increasingly important role, was that of stimulating complaints under the provisions of the existing Race Relations Act. Their summer project, the model for which was the activities of the still undivided Civil Rights Movement, provided material for further complaints (fifty-two in all) for submission to the board. The most striking of these complaints were collected and published by C.A.R.D. in April 1967. Taken together with the general activities of

C.A.R.D. (in particular some of the local organizations with a rather more clear-sighted view of the deficiencies of the communal organizations with which C.A.R.D. had associated itself nationally) this performance provided good grounds for Martin Ennals' comment that, up to the end of 1966, 'C.A.R.D. has done an enormous job in shaping public opinion into a position where it accepts the facts of discrimination'.[27]

In October 1966, the Home Secretary delivered a major policy speech to the Institute of Race Relations. In it he made further reference to the progress of the Race Relations Board (which he described as having made 'a most encouraging start') and of the forthcoming P.E.P. report on the extent of discrimination. But in this speech, Jenkins went out of his way to stress, first, the improvement in the general atmosphere – 'I am glad', he said, 'that we appear to have put behind us the sterile debate about the precise level of the flow of immigration' – and, second, the necessity for advancing on the broadest possible front, combining 'individual example, community action, educational experience, industrial practice, and, of course, the example of Government, locally and nationally'. The Home Secretary wound up his speech by indicating a number of specific ways in which such an example could be set, outside the scope of legislation.[28]

This theme was echoed by the Home Office's Minister of State, Lord Stonham, in the Lords in the following month. After the reference to the P.E.P. report, which was becoming a ritual in official speeches at this point, Stonham referred to the measures in the National Committee's 'vigorous start' and to the growth in the provision of useful, basic welfare services and the general pronouncement of benevolent intentions, the policy gap yawned as wide as ever; in the crucial areas of housing and education the official line could scarcely be described as any advance on that in the White Paper. Nevertheless, Lord Stonham was able to round off his speech with a rousing peroration: 'We shall make a great success of this policy – a success which, I think, will be an example to the world'.[29] This was optimism of a kind which had not been heard from either front bench for three or four years – and in the long run, optimism that could only be justified if the ultimately intangible gain of confidence were supplemented by the tangible achievements that could in turn only be obtained by public policy initiatives.

Against this favourable background, the irregulars of C.A.R.D. launched the first stage of the public campaign for the extension of legislation by promoting a Private Members Bill to extend the Race Relations Act in the fields of housing, employment and insurance. Answering the Debate on the Bill, Maurice Foley indicated that the P.E.P. report would be of decisive significance in determining the Government's attitude: Charles Fletcher-Cooke for the Opposition was prepared to say in advance of the report that 'the scope of the conciliation procedure may well have to be extended to jobs and housing'.[30] A bi-partisan approach to legislation seemed probable and the scene was set for the crucial negotiations with the T.U.C. and C.B.I.

In the various stages of the negotiations that followed, the C.B.I. for tactical reasons preferred to leave the initiative to the T.U.C. And it was on the T.U.C. side that the fundamental anxiety was felt and where the entrenched opposition came – specifically among a number of individual members of the general council. Late in 1966 it became clear to the T.U.C., both from the public activities of the lobby* and from official approaches from the Treasury (initially in the context of a non-discrimination clause in Government contracts) that something was in the air. In certain quarters, this prospect did not cause great concern; Jack Jones, the Acting Assistant General Secretary of the Transport and General Workers' Union, told a Fabian conference in November 1966 that 'even in the trades unions, restrictions have been operated against the immigrant worker',[31] and made it clear that he saw the solution to this problem in some form of legislation.

But generally, the official attitude, especially of senior members of the general council and senior staff, was one of alarm and suspicion. After joint consultations with the C.B.I. a statement was drafted and presented to the meeting

* As the T.U.C. subsequently put it: 'It became clear (in October 1966) that certain bodies outside industry were attempting to secure support for far-reaching legislation.'

of the National Joint Advisory Committee in January 1967. In this statement, which was intended to represent the position for negotiation, the line adapted was that discrimination would only disappear 'with complete integration' and attention was drawn to past success and to the existence of voluntary machinery. Prominent officials told a *Sunday Times* investigation that there was insufficient evidence of discrimination to justify action; Lord Cooper, of the N.U.G.M.W., was 'not bothered a great deal with it, because I have never met it as a real problem'; as for legislation, Cyril Plant of the Inland Revenue Staff Association observed that 'the simple fact is that we are against it'.[32]

In short, it was clear that the problem of the hostility towards extension of legislation on the part of the main entrenched interests in the employment field would have to be faced as a fact of the situation. Their opposition, together with the tacit sympathy of the Minister of Labour, constituted an obstacle on a scale which would require more than the blandishments of American fellow unionists, flown over from the U.S. by the National Committee for Commonwealth Immigrants to confront their British colleagues at a specially convened conference, to overcome. But equally, the obstacle was not immovable. And the charge of dynamite that had been prepared to blow it away was almost ready for detonation.

In many ways the P.E.P. report on the extent of racial discrimination is the most important document yet to be produced on the subject of race relations in Britain. The contents of the report are discussed elsewhere; its chief significance for present purposes was the extent of the response to some of the material in it, particularly to the series of action tests of discrimination run by research services as part of the investigation. The response of the press to the evidence of extensive discrimination was far greater than the sponsors of the report and its advisory panel had dared to hope; the reaction in most newspapers both editorially and in the selection of emphasis for news items, was that an intolerable situation had been revealed which called for urgent remedial action. From this point onwards, opponents of the extension of legislation to the field of employment were on the defensive and the ground of opposition shifted – from the claim that discrimination was not a major problem to arguments in favour of a voluntary approach. And in the potentially far more sensitive area of housing, the general mandate from public opinion could now be assumed.

At the end of April, the T.U.C. General Council arrived at the predictable conclusion that 'neither the proceedings at a conference organized by the N.C.C.I. nor the P.E.P. report gave grounds for modifying the attitudes of the general council'.[33] However, the Council resolved to take steps to modify their previous position and to accept the C.B.I.'s proposal of further discussions on the desirability of establishing appropriate additional machinery to the voluntary machinery already existing in industry. More significantly, they conceded that 'even the most comprehensive of voluntary procedures' might leave an area where legislation might be thought necessary.[34]

Although the Home Secretary and his allies in the official agencies and outside them now had a strong hand to play, there were obvious advantages in avoiding an open dispute with both sides of industry – especially if they chose to present a united front. Although in the period after the election interest in race relations among politicians diminished sharply, a decline in the Government's general political fortunes presented an obvious opportunity for the Opposition. The indications were still that a bi-partisan front could be maintained – and the Home Secretary went out of his way to be conciliatory to his opposite number on this issue; but an open breach with the trade union wing of the Labour party was obviously unacceptable. In this situation, the skills of Maurice Foley might have been an important counterpoint within the party; unlike his successor he was well equipped by background and temperament to soothe the anxieties of the Congress House *apparat* and of trade union members of the House. But by the end of 1966, Foley had decided that the rapidly developing situation, with its progressive bureaucratization of activity, was unsuited to his particular gifts and had made his desire for an early move very clear indeed. So the risk was a real one; and such a split would provide an opportunity in which the right wing of the Conservative Party could hope to profit handsomely from the steady stock-piling of ammunition by Enoch Powell. Some sort of compromise was always likely.

In May preliminary discussions on the setting up of voluntary machinery were held between the C.B.I. and T.U.C., and by June these were in an advanced stage and commanded the general support of the Ministry of Labour. Also in May the Home Secretary delivered another major speech, this time to the London Labour Party. This speech, far more political in tone and emphasis, was clearly directed towards securing the explicitly Labour Party backing for a measure likely to be a cause of nervousness to a party whose painful memories of Smethwick had not been wholly erased by the general election of 1966. 'For a Labour Government to fall down on this', he said, 'would be a betrayal without excuse of everything for which the Labour Party has ever stood. If further legislation is necessary to deal with this issue, we should not be frightened of it.'[35] Clearly there was no doubt that a positive decision on legislation was now merely a matter of time.

On 19th June, the formal confrontation took place between ministers and the two sides of industry. The trade union representatives, according to their own account, referred to their statement of January, with the significant amendment that they now 'did not altogether rule out the possibility that legislation might ultimately play some residual part in the process'. Further negotiations were suggested but not on the basis that 'the Government were already committed to putting new reliance on legislation'. Was the Government not prepared to encourage a voluntary approach?

The Home Secretary's reply was apparently cautious but firm. Basing himself on the familiar second-generation argument, he explained that he 'was inclined to the view that the Government should declare discrimination illegal and that some form of ultimate sanction was necessary'. He made it clear that while it would be impossible in the new legislative proposals, on which no final decision had yet been taken, 'entirely to exclude the Race Relations Board . . . voluntary machinery established in industry should be the initial channel of settlement of cases'.[36]

This key concession obtained, the T.U.C. turned to

leisurely discussion of the outlined scheme for voluntary machinery put to them by the C.B.I., in which they were overtaken by the official announcement on 26th July of the Government's decision to legislate. 'Our preliminary studies are now complete,' the Home Secretary told the House. 'Good race relations must, of course, substantially depend upon voluntary effort and a favourable climate of public opinion. But our conclusion is that by themselves they are not enough. Further legislation is therefore necessary.'[37] It would cover the fields of both housing and employment.

To all appearances, the 'bodies' whose activities had been so justified as a source of apprehension to the T.U.C. had won a signal victory. But in the event, the significance of the prize was to fall short of expectations. For this failure, there could be two categories of explanation. The first lies in circumstances outside the immediate scope of the Home Secretary's departmental responsibilities, in the progressive loss of political authority by the Government to which he belonged.

Developments in the American situation also had increasing influence on the British domestic scene. The riots of Detroit broke out as Roy Jenkins was preparing to announce the Government's decision to introduce amending legislation. It has been (absurdly) suggested that the riots were a decisive factor in precipitating that decision;[38] there is no evidence whatsoever for such an assertion (as the analysis thus far presented should have made clear). But it is legitimate to point to the influence of the American situation in undermining much of the effect of the work he had put into the timing and content of his announcement. In December 1964, Martin Luther King had provided the catalyst for the formation of C.A.R.D. Malcom X's visit in February 1965 had suggested another style of protest. Bayard Rustin, at the beginning of 1967, had preached the doctrine of the eleventh hour, but Stokely Carmichael on his short visit in the summer of 1967, during which he was represented by the British press as a kind of black bogey silhouetted against the flames of the ghetto, had no such comfort to offer. None of these visits (except perhaps King's) deserved to be recorded for their direct consequences in the United Kingdom; but the competing claims that the visitors stood for had ceased to be local American concerns and had taken on a relevance to the British situation, and their visits were effective reminders of that fact.

If the momentum were to be maintained, public opinion, both black and white, needed to be convinced not only of the need for legislation but also that tangible benefits could be expected to flow from it. The obvious line of argument for the majority was that if effective legislation were introduced in time to deal with what was demonstrably a real grievance, the kind of civil disorder that was beginning to crucify American society could be averted. 'Let us not be Bourbons', pleaded Norman St. John Stevas in the Expiring Laws Continuance Debate of 1966, 'and let us learn cheaply and vicariously from the experience of others.'[39] It can be argued that insufficient steps (perhaps in the form of speeches by senior ministers other than Jenkins himself) were taken to bring home this point during the necessarily long delay which elapsed between the decision to introduce new legislation and the publication of the Bill. Certainly, in the interim, the debate was pre-empted by those who argued, like Enoch Powell, that such disorders were best averted not by dealing with the problems of discrimination, but by reverting to the frame of reference based on immigration and the possibility of stopping the flow altogether. This approach was greatly facilitated by the coincidental emergence of two problems associated with immigration policy: evasion of the controls by small numbers of Pakistanis (an estimated total of less than 100 by the end of 1967) crossing the Channel in small boats and the increasing concern felt both by the Government and its critics about the position of the unknown number of British citizens of Asian origin in East African countries to whom the control provisions of the 1962 Act did not apply. This was a problem to which several senior Opposition politicians, notably Duncan Sandys, whose knowledge of the problem was obtained at first hand when negotiating the Kenya independence settlement, paid increasing attention in the summer of 1967. As first one problem and then the other caught the attention of the press, the balance of the debate began to swing slowly back again to immigration – the 'sterile debate' in which the Government could not help but be on the defensive.

On the immigrants' side, the arguments for legislation were also becoming less convincing. As the Home Secretary presented it, the case was based on a form of social contract argument: immigrants must be assumed to have agreed to put up with poor conditions and some discrimination on the implied understanding that their children will be admitted into British society as full citizens. Jenkins states this explicitly in his first major speech on the subject. 'Most of those who have come here in the past decade and a half are accepting an unwritten, unspoken assumption. They have come expecting to do only the most menial jobs, because they are better than no jobs at home.'[40] But this equation, by which first-class citizenship for the second generation could be purchased by second-class status in the first generation could commend itself to an audience composed largely of young adults only if its implications were fully worked through and explained. The positive lead which the Home Secretary had promised in the same speech to provide through non-legislative action by central government, both as employer and in placing contracts, did not materialize.

Here the report of the committee headed by Professor Street into the effectiveness of anti-discrimination machinery in the United States and its relevance for an extension of the law in this country might have had some influence. However, it was decided to hold back publication of the full report until the autumn. Nevertheless, the report was widely circulated during the period of discussion and consultation that followed the Home Secretary's announcement of the decision in principle to extend the legislation.

The broad answer to criticisms that there had been failures of presentation and communication on the part of the Government was that the job of information and public education had been devolved on to the National Committee for Commonwealth Immigrants. If there were no consistent guide-lines for local and national policy on issues affecting the newcomers, then the National Committee had the duty to draw attention to the fact through the advisory function with which it had been invested. But by mid-1967 it was becoming clear that the National Committee in its current form was not really capable of filling this most important gap, for reasons discussed in a later chapter.

But, if the National Committee was increasingly attracting criticism from such sources as C.A.R.D., C.A.R.D. itself was feeling the strain of the divergence of views on the Executive Committee between those who identified colonialism as the key issue and those who wished to retain the emphasis in C.A.R.D.'s work on the bread-and-butter issue of discrimination in Britain. These groups had temporarily come together in coalition; the emphasis on further legislation had provided for a time the necessarily common aim. With its achievement, leaving only the far less glamorous task of ensuring that the form of legislation was satisfactory, and the failure of the federal structure to provide the link with the grass roots that had been vainly sought in the summer projects of 1966 and 1967, the coalition fell apart.

'Our place now is not in the corridors of the N.C.C.I. or at the meetings of V.L.C.'s but within the community at the grass roots which we have talked about for three years and failed to reach, let along cultivate',[41] wrote Dipak Nandy, but the time for such an alternative strategy had already passed and at the convention held at the end of November, the majority of the existing Executive were hustled out of office by what must have been, even by the standards of British race relations, one of the most curiously assorted coalitions ever to embark on a major tactical operation, all temporarily united under the all-embracing folds of the Black Power banner.

The summer and autumn of 1967 saw a gradual but progressive deterioration in race relations. In July, the appearance of the report of Lord Hunt's Committee on the Immigrants and Youth Service[42] provided useful additional material for a case for favoured treatment for the second generation and the pretext for Duncan Sandys to comment: 'Instead of tackling the problem at its source, the Government has just published a report which urges us to accept a large increase in mixed marriages as an essential element in our domestic policy of integration. The breeding of millions of half-caste children will merely produce a generation of misfits and increase social tension',[43] a remark for which attempts were made to institute a prosecution against him under Section 6 of the Race Relations Act, without success. This failure contrasted rather painfully with an increasing number of prosecutions brought against black orators in Hyde Park and ultimately against Michael de Freitas, who unexpectedly crowned his career with the legitimation of martyrdom. The impression made in the popular mind by the use of the Race Relations Act in this context was not the happiest of auguries for the forthcoming extension of the Act.

Positive proposals for the revision of the admission procedure for immigrants, both aliens and Commonwealth citizens, and the provision of a right of appeal against refusal of leave to enter were contained in the long awaited report of the Wilson Committee[44] but passed virtually unnoticed. The Labour Party National Executive Committee working party on race relations, publishing its report in late August,[45] came out strongly for a revised immigration procedure and for comprehensive legislation covering housing and employment and providing a substantial extension of the Race Relations Board's powers – the representative of the Trades Union Congress on the working party did not sign the final report.

Supporters of legislation received a rebuff at the T.U.C. Conference at Brighton in September 1967 where a resolution was referred back, after a sharp tussle, to discuss (as the General Council's representative put it) … 'The kind of support legislation that we would be prepared to accept to give force to the voluntary procedures which we are bringing into industry'.[46]

Supporters of legislation were luckier at the Labour Party Conference where a Society of Labour Lawyers' resolution was unanimously adopted, in conjunction with the N.E.C.'s report on race relations; but none of the eleven resolutions down for the Conservative Party Conference in the centenary year of the Party were concerned with legislation at all. There, the debate was directed entirely to immigration. A sizeable number of delegates clearly felt that official policy should be concerned, as Duncan Sandys put it, with a determination 'to preserve the British character of Britain',[47] an aim unlikely to be achieved, according to a new series of speeches made by Enoch Powell outside the conference, unless the position of the British citizens of Kenya Asian origin were speedily amended to provide against the possibility of their precipitate entry to avoid the effects of the developing policy of Kenyanization adopted by the Ken-yatta Government.

Powell's resumption of his campaign, and the obvious sympathy (notably warmer than in the case of his earlier analyses of the situation) with which his references to Kenya Asians were received, indicated that the impatience of the Conservative Party with the Government's policy was likely to find a sympathetic echo in sections of the Parliamentary party and make the continuation of the Front Benches' mutual conciliation increasingly difficult.

The Expiring Laws Continuance Debate in mid-Nov-ember in which Jenkins made the last of his series of major speeches on race relations, suggested that, for the moment, the Government's nerve held. As a progress report on two years' activity in office, this speech is less than satisfying; Commons rules of order, uncertainly applied by the chair-man in this instance, were too cramping. But the tone was still constructive. The Wilson Committee Report was ac-cepted, in principle; the entry of dependants effectively de-fended against the growing number of critics on the right. Elaborate compliments were exchanged with Quintin Hogg, who had opened with a studiously moderate speech, cel-ebrating the significance of a consensus on the issue. But on the U.K. citizens in Kenya, the tone was tentative – the Government was watching the situation, which did not in-volve the exploitation of a loophole; 'nothing approaching an exodus' had taken place.[48] Privately, the official line was that too much attention should not be devoted to a problem which might resolve itself in time.

By the end of the month, Jenkins had left the Home Office. In a discussion of the tactics adopted by the Home Secretary, William Deedes, a Conservative Member and himself once a junior minister at the Home Office, comments that 'as a political exercise' the 'joint operations' conducted by the Home Secretary were well executed and that they were 'timely and right'. But he adds that the evidence for a fundamental change in the law was derived from three docu-ments, none of them sponsored by the Government, and that there had been little opportunity for debate. This is essen-tially a House of Commons criticism and need not detain us here. But Deedes adds that the operations were also deficient as a public relations exercise in that insufficient effort was made to enlist public support on a controversial issue. It is difficult not to agree with Deedes that there was some 'failure of political communication'.[49]

There might well have been room for a flamboyant gesture. Harold Wilson's most significant contribution to the development of the debate on race relations in the first three years in office may have been his choice of epithet for Peter Griffiths in his first speech in office. But to ask for such a gesture from Jenkins is to ask for a different kind of politician altogether; flamboyance is not compatible with his chosen manner as a politician. Indeed, to some extent at least, the Home Secretary's cool, reasoned style had ensured that his audience would always be limited – and, on this issue, that is something of a weakness. But the role of the various agencies, once the announcement of the intention to legislate had been made, could well have been the subject of a little more attention, especially in the necessarily long interlude between the commitment to the legislation and its publication.

Finally, there is the flaw in the strategy that was actually adopted. It was always a precondition of the success of the campaign, conceived, directed, and in part executed by the Home Secretary, in the form of a drive towards legislation directed to the needs of the second generation that neither the difficulties of the first generation nor the grievances in the host community over immigration should become too pressing. For a brief period, it seemed as if these twin conditions might have been satisfied; that there might have been viable solutions in the formula that had been devised. But when the public anxiety about the position of the Kenya Asians was allowed to grow, and the renewed arguments about the rate of migration again began to be heard, the 'new faulty political arithmetic' duly came into play. The price of progress was once again calculated to be concessions to the unappeasable. It is the failure to face the fact that, in the final analysis, immigration policy must be fully worked out on a consistent basis and cannot be left to chance or a temporarily favourable political conjunction that makes one reluctant to make excessive claims for the policy devised in this period.

THE KENYA ASIAN EPISODE – AND AFTER

In the five years since 1964, for which immigration and race relations have been accepted as one of the range of policy issues occupying a permanent place in political debate, the terms on which discussion of the issue has been conducted have radically altered. 'All I know,' said Enoch Powell, ending his notorious speech of April 1968, 'is that to see, and not to speak would be the great betrayal.'[50] Since 1964, at any rate, the right to speak (though perhaps not the capacity to see) has been generally conceded to politicians and publicists. The doubts about the legitimacy of public discussion of the topic which were widely felt – mainly by Conservative politicians – before the general election of 1964 have evaporated. But, granted that such discussion is permissible – even essential – on what terms is it to be undertaken? The significance of the 1966 election campaign seemed at the time to be that genuine differences of opinion over policy on a difficult and controversial topic could be debated within certain understood and agreed limits. And, as we have seen, this *de facto* consensus was still in working order when Roy Jenkins left the Home Office at the end of 1967. The breaking down of this tacit understanding, which occurred during 1968, was not merely the reflection of increased concern about the subject. In addition, a willingness emerged to abandon restraints on the manner in which the debate was to be conducted. It was not merely that the solutions now proposed were those that had only previously been heard from street-corner orators; the style in which they were advocated was also one previously the prerogative of Sir Oswald Mosley. If the policies and practices of politicians have been one important determinant affecting the development of race relations, the immigration may in turn have left a mark on the manner in which politicians carry on their business.

But if the manner in which renewed debate on race relations in 1968 and after was conducted exhibited some striking new characteristics, the content of the debate remained much the same. The change lay chiefly in the balance of emphasis within the discussion. All the themes whose development we have traced in earlier chapters still preoccupied politicians: the place of the coloured minorities in our society and the terms on which they are to be admitted to it; the extent to which the Government is justified in intervening on their behalf and the rationale and technique of such an intervention. But the shake given to the kaleidoscope by the events of the spring of 1968 caused these pieces to fall into a different pattern. And although most of the arguments were familiar from earlier stages in the debate some of them took on a fresh significance in their new context. A specific example concerns the proposals in the Conservative election manifesto of 1966. In the context of the election campaign and the manner in which it was conducted, these proposals lent themselves to rational debate on immigration policy. After April 1968, they assumed a quite different significance, in terms of the way in which the debate was then being conducted.

The argument on policy is still working itself out at the time of writing, but these realignments make it essential to consider events over the past year in some detail. This will involve journalism rather than considered analysis, with all the fallibility of perspective that this implies. But these events are necessary evidence, taken together with the background information already presented, if we are to reach any conclusions from which a way forward can be mapped.

These further developments still lay in the future in January 1968 when the new Home Secretary, James Callaghan, delivered a lengthy anlysis of policy on race relations to an audience convened by the Institute of Race Relations. The Home Secretary's speech was in direct line of descent from those of his predecessor; as was Callaghan's relative lack of emphasis on the question of immigration as such. He also emulated his predecessor by attempting to lay down a formula for future policy, his aim would be to create a society in which 'every citizen shares an equal right to the same freedoms, the same responsibilities, the same opportunities and the same benefits'.[51] Yet only one month later the same Home Secretary, in tacit coalition with the Shadow Cabinet, introduced into Parliament on an emergency footing an illiberal and arguably irresponsible and opportunistic measure intended to remove from one identifiable minority a basic benefit of British citizenship.

The explanation of this apparent *volte face* lies in part in processes which had already been set in motion before Callaghan became Home Secretary. We have examined some of them in earlier sections of this chapter. The commitment to the extension of legislation against discrimination entered into by Roy Jenkins in the summer of 1967 had been followed by an elaborate exercise in consultation, involving both the official agencies – the Race Relations Board and the National Committee for Commonwealth Immigrants – and the voluntary agencies and immigrant organizations. The immediate effect was to transfer the debate on legislation to a different plane where progress was measured in terms of amendments to drafts and could of its nature receive little or no publicity.

At the same time, the pressure for further action on the other main front, that of immigration, was steadily increasing. And on 9th February Enoch Powell made another major speech on the subject, in Walsall. He told his audience, in a significant phrase, that 'you and I might as well be living in Central Africa for all they know about our circumstances'.[52] This image of remoteness was only one metaphorical illustration of the theme he and others were later to develop further: the notion that the legislators and the liberals were remote and uncaring in a situation arriving rapidly at crisis point.

The main motive force behind this renewed activity was the rapid growth in the number of U.K. citizens of Asian origin entering this country from Kenya as a result of the Kenyanization policy of the Kenyatta Government. Unlike other African governments, the Kenya Government had applied a time-limit of two years from independence within which aliens had to make their application for citizenship. Legislation passed by the Kenya authorities in 1967 created a situation in which those aliens who had not opted for Kenyan citizenship were permitted to work and live in Kenya only on a temporary basis. Six thousand Asians possessing U.K. citizenship, who were not subject to immigration control, had entered the U.K. in 1965 and in 1966. After the Kenya legislation this figure rose to 1,500 in the month of August 1967 alone, and to 2,661 in September, dropped to 1,334 in November, and built up again to 2,294 in January 1968. The initial reaction in the Home Office, as we have seen, was to watch the situation without commitment.

But the increase both in the numbers entering and in the attention paid to the subject by Sandys and Powell – almost certainly mutually reinforcing factors – compelled a re-assessment. Malcolm MacDonald, the Government's Special Envoy to East Africa, was sent to see President Kenyatta and ask for a slackening in the scope and tempo of Kenyanization. He returned empty handed; and although as late as 15th February, 1968, Lord Stonham was assuring the House of Lords that legislation to control the entry of the Kenyan Asians was unlikely as 'it would remove from them their right to U.K. citizenship and under the U.N. Convention of 1961 we are pledged to avoid any further statelessness,'[53] the Cabinet at two meetings on the 20th and 22nd February decided to act. They did so by spatchcocking into a Bill prepared some time previously, when Jenkins was still Home Secretary, a new clause to deal with what the Home Office considered to be anomalies arising in the operation of the Commonwealth Immigrants Act of 1962. This extended the operation of that Act to those possessing citizenship of the U.K. and Colonies without a substantial personal connection with this country – defined in terms of birth-place, of parents or grandparents.[54] The provisions of this Bill were announced to the House by the Home Secretary on 22nd February and received with general assent on the part of the Opposition, the Shadow Cabinet having met the day before and agreed that some phasing of the entry of Kenya Asians must be introduced.

The debates that followed were concentrated into three days and notable for their growing bitterness and the mounting disapproval of the Government's action. A full account of the episode has now been published, by a participant, and we need not refer to the detailed and technical aspects of the debate here.[55] But it is worth looking at the broad outline of the criticisms that were levelled at official policy. These centred round three principal objections. The first was the criticism levelled by lawyers (and subsequently endorsed by the International Commission of Jurists) that the Government would in fact – as Lord Stonham had implied – create a category of *de facto* stateless citizens by depriving the Kenya Asians of the right to enter the country of their citizenship. The second was based on widespread anxiety about what was seen as the breaking of an undertaking. Iain Macleod, who had a close knowledge of the situation through his own period at the Colonial Office, set out the position quite unequivocally: 'We did it. We meant to do it. And in any event we have no other choice.'[56] Duncan Sandys, the minister actually responsible for negotiations, denied that any clear agreement existed. But the Home Secretary, who was perhaps in the best position of all to know, admitted that a form of undertaking existed.[57] In addition, there was humanitarian concern for the Kenya Asians themselves – of all post-war immigrants the group best adapted to settlement in the U.K.

In its defence the Government and their backbench supporters resorted to three lines of argument. First, it was suggested that the Kenya Asians were merely the tip of an iceberg and that large numbers of other British passport-holders were likely to enter if further controls were not introduced.[*] The precise figure, cited initially as a million, grew to a million and a quarter and subsequently to two million during the course of a week, only to shrink again to a million and a quarter. Secondly, the suggestion was made by the Home Secretary,[58] and reinforced in official briefings, that a grave situation had developed in the country at large, which was now trembling on a knife edge from which it could only be retrieved by an act of major surgery – the amputation of the cause of infection. And finally, the Prime Minister maintained to the Archbishop of Canterbury that 'the criteria for exemption from immigration control are geographical, not racial. The fact that most of those who are exempt from control will be British is simply a consequence of the fact that most of the inhabitants of the U.K. are British.'[59] The measure passed through the Commons without inordinate difficulty, but to the accompaniment of a

---

* The real significance attached by the Government to the presence of large numbers of potential British passport-holders in the Far East – to whom spine-chilling reference was made by the Lord Chancellor in February – was revealed in November 1968 when the Government declined to review their dual citizenship on the ground that they had no intention of coming to the United Kingdom.

mounting barrage of press criticism, and the Government were only able to muster a majority of 24 at Second Reading in the Lords.

There are strong grounds for believing that the Government's handling of the Kenya Asian episode lay at the root of the deterioration in the situation that followed. To argue this is not to deny that the Government had an extremely awkward problem on its hands, and that the alternatives open to them seemed at the time far from clear. But what is plain enough is that any decision taken had to satisfy the test that it did not disturb confidence, either in Kenya or the United Kingdom. The Government's line of action failed that test.

In fact, there is now evidence to suggest that, had the British Government been prepared to guarantee the right of entry, few of the Kenya Asians – even in the atmosphere of 1967 – would have chosen to exercise it. An independent inquiry conducted by Martin Ennals, former Information Officer of the National Committee for Commonwealth Immigrants and brother of the Minister responsible for integration, indicates that most of the Kenya Asians would have preferred to return to India or Pakistan rather than enter Great Britain.[60] And in July a compromise agreement was in fact reached between the United Kingdom and Indian Governments, enabling United Kingdom citizens of Indian origin to enter India with a special passport endorsement. Those who did come here might well have come less precipitately, Peter Marris, who conducted an extended investigation in Kenya, found considerable evidence to suggest this view.[61] Moreover, there are good grounds for supposing that official sources grossly overestimated the numbers of those likely to come: indeed, the Government rather gracelessly admitted as much during the Expiring Laws Continuance debate in November 1968. This is perhaps not surprising, in view of the inadequacy of the existing arrangements for assembling information. In many ways this episode was the clearest possible illustration of some of the continuing deficiencies in the official apparatus: the absence of any form of planning machinery equipped to determine the scope of the difficulties and the action to be taken in the event of a situation arising within the Commonwealth involving the possible movement of population.

The passage of the Act also compromised the position both of the Home Secretary and David Ennals himself and hence the credibility of the Government's whole integration programme. Furthermore, it scattered the coalition which had come together during the period of Roy Jenkins' Home Secretaryship to link official and voluntary organizations with the Government. The National Committee for Commonwealth Immigrants took most of the strain, since it was in many ways the incarnation of the coalition. The Committee itself, which had at no stage been consulted by the Government despite its official consultative role, teetered on the brink of resignation after the Archbishop of Canterbury had paid two visits to ministers to protest against the terms of the legislation. Eventually, the Committee as an institution decided to remain in operation but individuals on the Committee, on the staff, and on the advisory panels resigned. Some of the latter then came together to assist a new lobbying organization, Equal Rights, which had been set up in the previous December and was chaired by three members of the N.C.C.I. housing panel and was chaired by the West Indian law don, Roy Marshall. The intention was to mobilize expertise to ensure that the forthcoming legislation against discrimination was as effective and far ranging as possible. A final and equally important element in the situation was the impetus that these events gave to the growing cynicism in immigrant organizations about the intentions of the Government. Informal dialogue had been interrupted with the collapse of C.A.R.D. at the end of the previous year; now benevolent neutrality changed successively to critical abstention and outright hostility.

But the most important immediate effect of the Kenya Asian episode was to provide the opportunity for which Enoch Powell had been waiting. In a situation disturbed by the publicity that these events had received and into which the Government had injected a further element of uncertainty and anxiety about the consequences of immigration, Powell's third major attempt to obtain wide attention for his views was a triumphant success. There was very little in this third speech which differed from the previous two, except in the sense that these were only new in the sense that Powell was using them for the first time. The key lay in the timing.

Powell's speech, delivered on 20th April 1968 in Birmingham, effectively blanketed in terms of publicity and public attention the Race Relations Bill which had been introduced on 9th April. This process illustrated in the most striking way possible the submergence of constructive initiatives by the reimposition of the immigration frame of reference. The Government, in introducing the Commonwealth Immigrants Bill, had recognized that the Race Relations Bill was at risk. When critics were not prepared to accept this interpretation, David Ennals had appealed to them not to press their opposition to the Government's action beyond the point of the passage of the Commonwealth Immigrants Act.[62] His intention in doing so was clearly to avoid compromising the legislation to follow. But even if they had been able to do so, the declaratory effects of the Race Relations Bill, on which the Home Secretary set so much store, were already compromised by the processes the Government had themselves set in motion.

The new Bill was in any case something of a disappointment to those who had been involved in the processes that had led up to its introduction. Although courageous in scope – both employment and housing were included, together with all commercial and public services – the enforcement procedures left a good deal to be desired, especially in the field of employment where provision was made for voluntary action in advance of statutory consultation. More generally, the Bill contained unsightly clauses allowing employers to operate racial quotas and permitting shipping companies to provide racially segregated accommodation and to discriminate against coloured seamen. Moreover, in view of the elaborate consultation that had taken place and the clear advice submitted in the Street Report, the Bill was surprisingly slackly drafted. On the general points of principle the Bill's critics' room for manoeuvre was severely limited by the changed atmosphere deriving from the events of February. The Government was able in most instances to reply to their criticisms by suggesting that in the current state of public opinion such concessions would be impossible to justify and that the main task was to prevent the Opposition from making inroads on the ground already gained. These political considerations led the Race Relations Board to swallow its private doubts about restrictions on the powers which were to be conferred on it and to issue a public statement in which the new legislation was warmly welcomed. And indeed it was inconceivable that any of those who had been concerned with the preparations for the legislation should now repudiate the results of two years' systematic preparation and lobbying.

The Bill was also the subject of some embarrassment for the Conservative Shadow Cabinet. There were those on both wings of the party who wished to take a clear-cut line, either outright rejection or conditional acceptance. Ultimately, the Shadow Cabinet decided to move a reasoned amendment accepting the principle of legislation but rejecting this specific Bill.

The extent of the impact of Enoch Powell's speech and of his subsequent dismissal from the Shadow Cabinet at the hands of Edward Heath were fully revealed when the Race Relations Bill received its second reading on 23rd April. This occasion was dominated by Powell, despite the fact that he did not himself speak. Quintin Hogg taxed his colleague with 'ficking ash' in 'a roomful of gunpowder' and emphasized that it was the manner rather than the content of the speech which had incurred the disapproval of the Shadow Cabinet. The Conservatives divided the House at the end of the debate but a number of radicals, led by Sir Edward Boyle, did not vote with the Opposition. The general upshot was to throw the Government once more back on the defensive and the debate on the means of relieving discrimination was jeopardized before it had been properly launched by the renewal of the sterile argument on immigration.

There is no space here to trace the details of the passage of the Bill through Parliament, which occupied the House from April to October 1968, involved thirteen sittings of the standing committee and 400 amendments. The Government's radical critics were only able to secure a meagre handful of concessions. Most of them were in the opposite direction, notably in the field of employment; Quintin Hogg argued in the intra-party debate still tormenting the Opposition that the Conservative front-benchers had gained sufficient ground in committee to justify not opposing Third Reading. But no less than forty-five Conservative backbenchers disagreed with him and divided the House with the approval of senior members of the backbench 1922 Committee, to provide an ill-tempered end to the lengthy passage of the Bill through the Commons.

In general, there is no reason to question the sincerity of the Government's intention in introducing this legislation nor to suppose that the Race Relations Board, which has made good use of its existing inadequate powers, will not be able to make further progress in dealing with discrimination in its new extended capacity. In this respect, John Rex's criticism[63] that the Bill is not only not half a loaf but is barely a crumb seems misjudged. But it is equally clear that an initiative which was intended to provide a sound basis in law and practice for a constructive programme of community action misfired. By its failure to devise and maintain a fair and consistent immigration policy the Government had forfeited confidence on every side.

One sign of this lost confidence lay in the re-emergence of a series of extremist organizations. They have little significance in themselves – their importance has related largely to the changing political environment in which they have worked. Until recently, they have been far less numerous than the pro-integration groups, and have still fewer organized local activities. None of the 'nationalist' political parties have made any significant headway. Nor is it likely that they now will: the line taken by the major parties is such as to take the wind almost entirely out of their sails. But the impact of the newer groups has been greater than their numerical strength. Their main importance has been to act as a conduit for potentially non-racial discontents, convincing the anxious moderates that immigrants are to blame for the processes of social change and their side effects, in a way which the anti-immigrant politicians, with their aura of disreputability deriving from the pre-war activities of the British Union of Fascists, can never do. Over the long term, they have also been able to bring openly racialist arguments back into circulation, in the guise of a defence of English culture. It is a guise, or otherwise the same people might be working on the right wing of the pro-integration groups. Occasionally individuals have in fact moved between the two: and an important part of the achievement of bodies like the Sparkbrook Association is that they have been able to divert anxieties about changing environment into constructive channels.

The other achievement of the anti-integration groups has been to help persuade people in positions of authority – editors, M.P.s, local party organizers, trades unionists – who do not share their views, that public opinion is moving in the direction of greater hostility towards immigrants. Some need little convincing: such a view chimes in with their preconceptions. Not many have the confidence to consign their letters to the wastepaper basket.

Ultimately, the extent to which these bodies have been able to make an impact on the situation is a reflection of the extent to which the overall climate of opinion has deteriorated. Their room for manoeuvre, and the way in which they have exercised it is a function of the performance of local and central government and, in particular, the politicians over the whole period of the migration.

The immigrant organizations, as we have seen, were severely shaken by the introduction of the Commonwealth Immigrants Act. Once it had been passed, it was easy to say that the Government had never meant business when it talked about not permitting second-class citizenship and easy to argue that there was a cyclic pattern of reaction in the Labour Movement from the compromise of 1963 to the White Paper of 1965 to the 1968 Commonwealth Immigrants Act. Labour leaders' judgment seemed in pawn to the prejudices of their followers. In this atmosphere the Race Relations Bill could hardly be expected to recapture lost confidence, particularly since its declaratory effect was already weakened. Coalition tactics had in any event largely lost their appeal with the collapse of C.A.R.D. and in the last year of C.A.R.D.'s activities several individual organizations had been developing a line strongly critical of the Government. Some of this criticism focused on certain provisions in the Race Relations Bill. Under the Bill, the National Committee for Commonwealth Immigrants was to be dissolved and replaced by a Community Relations Commission. A group of local liaison officers, led by an Anglican clergyman from the West Indies, Wilfred Wood, came together to draft a series of proposals which would have the effect of investing the main responsibility for the expenditure of official funds in local bodies, not with a national organization. This initiative, which reflected the disillusionment of many individuals with the notion of direction by a quasi-official agency, failed to convince the Government. In view of the strength of the case deployed, this failure reflected with particular clarity the absence of effective channels of protest.[64]

Nor were the doubts on all sides stilled when the Government eventually produced proposals for positive intervention from the centre in the problems of under-privileged inner city areas – the so-called 'Urban Programme'. This consisted in essence of a gathering together of various threads in existing Government policy: the educational priority areas (E.P.A.s) introduced as a result of the recommendations in the Plowden Report, the housing priority areas, designated as a matter of administrative practice by the Ministry of Housing and Local Government, and the fifty-seven local authorities receiving grant aid on the basis of the presence of immigrants under Section 11 of the 1966 Local Government Act, amounting in 1967–68 to £1.9 million. These criteria were combined into a new description of 'special social need' applied to the areas affected. In conception, the programme was heavily influenced by a series of different approaches put to the Government with increasing force throughout its period of office. All of these were based on the concept of relieving need rather than defining groups by ethnic origin or other special characteristics.

Moreover, the introduction of the programme signalled a recognition that these problems could not be 'thrown on to the desk of local authorities' – as Lord Gardiner had put it[65] – and that central government has a responsibility to support and where necessary supplement the activities of local government in an attempt to reach and eradicate the root causes of under-privilege in these areas.

In principle, the change was of the greatest significance: but in practice its initial impact was blunted. For by timing his announcement of the programme for the immediate aftermath of the debate on Powell's speech, the Prime Minister ensured that it would be seen as a straightforward programme of assistance to immigrant areas, in which the problem to be relieved derived quite simply from the presence of immigrants in those districts.[66] Local authorities, who had already used the opening provided by the Government's action over the Kenya Asians in February to suggest that Whitehall should step in and relieve them of all responsibility for services affected by or affecting immigrants, had some ground for hope in this pronouncement, and their disillusionment was correspondingly greater when the Home Secretary made his announcement about the detail of the urban programme in July 1968. After a sharp internal struggle within Whitehall, Callaghan had succeeded in retaining the responsibility for the programme at the Home Office. In announcing that the Government were prepared to commit £20–£25 million – in additional funds, not (as the Prime Minister had hinted) in grant aid diverted from other recipients – over four years to such a programme, he made it clear that they had no intention of defraying the accounts which had been industriously cobbled together by local authorities like Birmingham. New legislation would be introduced to supplement the provisions of Section 11 of the Local Government Act of 1966. But such a programme would be based on the extent of need, as defined by three criteria – the existence of strain on educational and housing facilities and the presence of immigrants. And only twenty-three local authorities proved to qualify under all three heads – less than half of those who receive grants under the 1966 Local Government Act provision. The bulk of the first consignment of these funds was to be spent on the under-fives, through the provision of additional nursery classes, nursery schools and additional places in children's homes.

The process of broadening the scope of the programme and refining its philosophy continued after the promised new legislation had been passed early in 1969. In the second stage of the programme – which was now joined by a community action programme, also under the general supervision of the Home Office – eighty-nine local authorities participated in a widely varying range of projects – play groups, neighbourhood advice centres, and other community-based enterprises.

For the first time, voluntary organizations were eligible for grants, if sponsored by the local authority. The original criteria for inclusion in the programme were dropped: instead, local authorities were required only to make out a case on the existing situation in their area, pending the introduction of objective measurements of deprivation. As the programme gathered momentum, the resemblances to the poverty programme in the United States became unmistakable. But there were distinctions: the sheer scale of the American programme compared with the British, for one; the reluctance still displayed by the Home Office in this country to become involved in the course of the urban programme in the basic problems of housing need in the areas concerned, in contrast to the model cities programme in the United States, for another. A marked reluctance also existed in Britain, to take the risk of channelling central government funds direct to neighbourhood organizations with no intervening filter, as had been attempted with varying results in the United States. The poverty programme's fall from favour just as the British urban programme finally shook free of the encumbrances attending its birth was another illustration of the delayed action effect of the American experience upon the British.[67]

Yet despite these welcome innovations, and the generally successful first year of operation of the Race Relations Act of 1968 – marred only by the serio-comic episode of the doctor who advertised for a Scottish domestic and found himself in difficulties with the law – the effectiveness of the integration programme remains in question. The continued erosion of confidence in the capacity of the Government to achieve solutions continues. Increasingly they came under direct assault from Enoch Powell, who followed a speech in Eastbourne in November 1968 advocating a Ministry of Repatriation with further fundamental attacks on existing policy, all advancing the same proposition: that numbers were now the sole determinant of the situation and that the only solution lay in their drastic reduction. In the long run, these speeches may prove to be less significant in their direct consequences than in their influence on the evolution of the policy of the Conservative Party. In two major policy speeches on race relations, Edward Heath took up a position which, if not in touching distance of Powell's, nevertheless lay uncomfortably close to it. At York in September 1968 he argued that entry to the United Kingdom for immigrants coming for employment should be conditional and related in all cases to a specific job, negotiated before departure. The unconditional right to reside would be conceded only after four years' satisfactory residence. In the initial period, permission would have to be obtained for any change of employment. U.K. citizenship, by a logical progression, would cease to be granted of right after five years (as at present) but conferred through an application procedure similar to that already existing in the case of aliens. Heads of household intending to bring over dependants would have to register their intention before departure: the implication being that this would reduce total numbers. Repatriation of those immigrants who had failed to settle down would be encouraged.[68]

In practice the position adopted in proposals, although presented as a new and tougher departure in immigration policy, was not very different from that of the Government – which had also been edging over as fast as its dignity would permit towards increased stringency. The long delayed implementation of the Wilson Committee Report on Immigration Appeals was made the occasion for the introduction of a compulsory entry certificate procedure – despite the Wilson Committee's reluctance to recommend such a step. And the proposal that official funds should be paid to voluntary organizations to set up welfare organizations in the countries of origin in order to ease the difficulties that might be created by an entry certificate procedure was turned down by the Home Secretary on the recommendation of Sir Derek Hilton, who conducted an inquiry into the subject[69] and came to the conclusion that such provision was not required.

The findings of two official inquiries – the Cullingworth Committee of the Central Housing Advisory Committee on the allocation of council housing (referred to in Chapter 6)[70] and the Report of the House of Commons Select Committee on Race Relations and Immigration on coloured school leavers (referred to in Chapters 8 and 11)[71] had less impact in this atmosphere than proceedings in 1969 at those two familiar ritual occasions, the Conservative Party conference and the Expiring Laws debate. At the former, the climate of opinion could be judged from the narrow majority by which Powellite opposition to the official policy of the Party was defeated and by the wave of sniggers that greeted a reference to a Sikh temple.[72] In the latter, Enoch Powell proved sufficiently fortified by the response to his earlier speeches to face his Parliamentary colleagues for the first time in a debate on this topic. Once again, his speech painted the familiar picture of the forthcoming racial apocalypse, based this time on information released to him by the Department of Health and Social Security about the number of births to coloured mothers in the inner London boroughs. As had become customary, his speech blanketed in terms of publicity the official statements of position by the Home Secretary and Quintin Hogg, together with an effective reply from Sir Edward Boyle.[73] Once more, the pace was being set – and terms of debate defined – by those who viewed the issues purely in terms of immigration control.

By the end of 1969 the situation presented an ironic contrast. By a process of trial and error, first repudiating and then adopting their critics' proposals, the Government had finally reached a position where the weapons for a dramatic assault on the problems associated with immigration had been forged – the Urban Programme, effective anti-discrimination legislation. This point had been reached at the moment when confidence on the part of the majority and the minorities alike was at its lowest ebb. The troops who had still been prepared to do battle under the banner of Roy Jenkins had finally scattered: the conviction of the majority – still essentially more tolerant than any politician was prepared to give them credit for – that catastrophe was imminent was confirmed by the lack of any effective reply to the over-publicized philippics of Powell. For the minorities, equality under the law could no longer be taken for granted, after the Commonwealth Immigrants Act of 1968.

Whether even the basic machinery so painfully put together will survive another election seems at times doubtful. The vagueness of the Conservative Party's proposals for positive action makes it difficult to forecast their likely attitude if they obtain office. However, the possibility of repeal of anti-discrimination legislation and of restriction of the scope of the urban programme on the lines of the constraints imposed on the poverty programme in the United States by the Nixon administration cannot be ruled out – especially if the election programme releases the propensity to exploit the immigration issue present in all the major political parties.

But this is speculation. What seems clear is that the Act of 1968 and the events that followed its passage gave the quietus to the argument that a gatekeeping policy of increasing severity could be undertaken without regard to the consequences for the integration programme. Since, as we have argued earlier, the factor of confidence is a decisive element in the formation of policy, the psychic wound will remain a permanent limitation on the Government's freedom of action in this field. Whether the infection is more general and more lasting it is too early to tell.

REFERENCES

1. R. v. Hunt and others (Times law reports, 16th September, 1958).
2. Cmnd. 2379, Immigration from the Commonwealth (London, H.M.S.O., 1965).
3. Economist, 7th August, 1965.
4. Published as W. W. Daniel, Racial Discrimination in England (Harmondsworth, Penguin Books, 1968).
5. Paul Foot, Immigration and Race in British Politics (Harmondsworth, Penguin Books, 1965).
6. See, for example, his article in the Daily Telegraph, 16th February, 1967, and, of course, his speech of 20th April, 1968 in Birmingham, reprinted in Race (Vol. X, no. 1, July 1968), pp. 94–99.
7. 277 H. L. Deb., col. 695, 3rd November, 1966.
8. 264 H. L. Deb., col.166, 10th March, 1965.
9. C. Senior and D. Manley, A Report on Jamaican Migration to Great Britain (Kingston, Government Printer, 1955).
10. This problem is dealt with at greater length in N. Deakin, 'The Politics of the Commonwealth Immigrants Bill', Political Quarterly (Vol. 39, no. 1, January–March 1968), pp. 25–45.

11. Foot, op. cit., 31.
12. 606 H. C. Deb, col. 369, 4th June, 1959.
13. See K. Kyle, in D. E. Butler and R. Rose, *The British General Election of 1959* (London, Macmillan, 1960).
14. C.I.A.C., *Report* (Cmnd. 2119), (London, H.M.S.O., 1st July, 1963).
15. 708 H. C. Deb, cols. 249–50, 9th March, 1965.
16. The events leading up to the Race Relations Bill of 1965 are described in detail in K. Hindell, 'The Genesis of the Race Relations Bill', *Political Quarterly* (Vol. 36, no. 4, October–December 1965), pp. 390–406.
17. Ibid.
18. 721 H. C. Deb, col. 461, 463, 23rd November, 1965.
19. Roy Jenkins, *The Labour Case* (Penguin Books, Harmondsworth, 1959).
20. Ibid. p. 137.
21. *Address given by the Home Secretary ... on the 23rd May, 1966 ... to a meeting of Voluntary Liaison Committees* (London, N.C.C.I., 1966).
22. 716 H. C. Deb, col. 1056, 16th July, 1965.
23. Bob Hepple, *Race, Jobs and The Law* (Allen Lane, The Penguin Press, 1968).
24. Ibid., pp. 136 et seq.
25. Ibid., p. 141.
26. B. W. Heineman, Jr, *The Politics of Race: a Study of the Campaign against Racial Discrimination* (unpublished Oxford B. Litt. thesis). We would like to acknowledge the help received in analysing this period in the evolution of race relations from Heineman's important pioneer work.
27. Heineman, op. cit., p. 221.
28. Speech to the Institute of Race Relations, 10th October, 1966, reprinted in *Race*, Vol. VIII, no. 3 (January 1967).
29. 277 H. L. Deb., col. 735, 3rd November, 1966.
30. 737 H. C. Deb., col. 942, 6th December, 1966.
31. J. Jones in, A. Lester and N. Deakin (eds.), *Policies for Racial Equality* (London, Fabian Society, 1967), p. 15.
32. *Sunday Times*, 8th January, 1967.
33. T.U.C. *Annual Report, 1967*, op. cit., p. 269.
34. Ibid.
35. A. Lester (ed.), *Essays and Speeches by Roy Jenkins* (London, Collins, 1967), p. 287.
36. T.U.C. *Annual Report, 1967*, pp. 270–72.
37. 751 H. C. Deb., col. 744, 26th July, 1967.
38. Dilip Hiro, in *New Society*, 27th June, 1968.
39. 735 H. C. Deb. col. 1252, 8th November, 1966.

40. *Address . . . to a meeting of Voluntary Liaison Committees*, op. cit.
41. Dipak Nandy, *The National Committee for Commonwealth Immigrants* (C.A.R.D., discussion paper, July 1967), pp. 12–13.
42. Youth Service Development Council Committee, *Immigrants and the Youth Service* (London, H.M.S.O., 1967).
43. *The Times*, 25th July, 1967.
44. Home Office, *Committee on Immigration Appeals, Report* (Cmnd. 3387), (London, H.M.S.O., 1967), Chairman: Sir Roy Wilson.
45. Labour Party, *Report of the National Executive Committee working party on race relations* (July 1967).
46. T.U.C. *Annual Report*, 1967, pp. 582–90.
47. Reported in *Daily Express*, 21st October, 1967.
48. 754 H. C. Deb, cols. 453–73, 15th November, 1967.
49. W. Deedes, *Race without Rancour* (London, Conservative Research Department, 1968).
50. Speech of 20th April, 1968, op. cit.
51. Speech by the Home Secretary to the Institute of Race Relations, 8th February, 1969. Reported in the Institute of Race Relations *Newsletter* (February 1968).
52. *The Times*, 10th February, 1968.
53. 289 H. L. Deb, col. 203, 15th February, 1968.
54. There are a variety of accounts of the genesis of the Bill. The most reliable is probably that given by the *Sunday Times* (3rd March, 1968).
55. David Steel, *No Entry* (Hurst, 1969). See also Vincent Cable, *Whither Kenyan Emigrants?* (Young Fabian Pamphlet 18, 1969).
56. *Spectator*, 23rd February, 1968.
57. In his statement to the House of Commons; 759 H.C. Deb, col. 662, 22nd February, 1968.
58. Both in his television appearances on 22nd February and in his announcement in the House the same day, in which he referred to the risk of 'racial disharmony and explosions' (759 H. C. Deb, col. 662).
59. Letter of 25th March, 1968.
60. M. Ennals, *U.K. Citizens of Asian Origin in Kenya: an independent survey* (London, Committee on United Kingdom Citizenship, July 1968).
61. P. Marris, 'The British Asians in Kenya', *Venture* (Vol. XX, no. 4, April 1968).
62. 759 H. C. Deb., col 1359, 29th February, 1968.
63. In *Matters of Principle: Labour's Last Chance* (Harmondsworth, Penguin Books, 1968).

64. See the analysis of this episode by Ann and Michael Dummett in (Lewis Donnelly, ed.) *Justice First* (London, Sheed & Ward, 1969).

65. In his speech in the House of Lords in 1965, op. cit.

66. Transcript of Speech by the Prime Minister, Birmingham, 5th May, 1968 (Labour Party).

67. The most thorough analysis of the American Poverty Programme to date is Sar A. Levitan, *The Great Society's Poor Law* (Baltimore: The Johns Hopkins Press, 1969).

68. The complete text of Heath's speech was published in *The Times*, 3rd September, 1968.

69. For a critical account of this unpublished document see, J. McNeal in *Race Today* (November 1969), p. iv.

70. Council Housing: *Purposes, Procedures and Priorities* (London, H.M.S.O., 1969).

71. Report from the Select Committee on Race Relations and Immigration, Session 1968–69, *The Problems of Coloured School Leavers*, House of Commons Paper 413-1 (H.M.S.O., 1969).

72. The resolution endorsing the party's official policy was carried by 1349 votes to 954 (*Evening Standard*, 10th October, 1969 and *Daily Telegraph*, 11th October, 1969).

73. 791 H. C. Deb., cols. 216–55, 299–306, 11th November, 1969.

Chapter Six

The Evolution of Housing Policy

Early in 1969, Parliament passed legislation 'to confer powers on local authorities to improve living conditions by improving the amenities of areas or of dwellings therein'.[1] The Housing Act which contained these powers – and others almost equally important – can conveniently be taken as one symbol of the ending of a period during which the role of central government in the inner city changed from that of passive spectator or, occasionally, a confused and ineffectual umpire, to that of an active participant. Another development – perhaps even more significant for the particular theme of this book – took place in 1969, in the shape of the Report of the Sub-Committee of the Central Housing Advisory Committee under the chairmanship of Professor J. B. Cullingworth.[2] This committee had been established specifically to review policy in the local authority sphere of activity – the sector responsible for housing over a quarter of the population of England and Wales and of especial significance in the context of the inner city. Among the many recommendations of this committee was one which tackled the question of the procedure by which local authority housing is allocated head on. *'We . . . recommend,'* said the committee, *'that there should be no residential qualification for admission to a housing list. Indeed, we go further and hold it to be fundamental that no one should be precluded from applying for, or being considered for, a council tenancy on any ground whatsoever.* Only if all applications are admitted is it possible to assess needs. . . . *We think that this rule should be made a statutory obligation.'*[3] Both the policy proposals outlined by this committee – and the powers conferred on local authorities by the Housing Act – were intended to rectify the stubborn problems of the central areas of major cities whose steady intensification alongside a steady improvement in the housing situation in general has provided such a poignant and baffling contrast over the last twenty years. These are not problems that exclusively affect coloured immigrants. But, as the Cullingworth Committee sharply concluded: 'Housing management, like industrial management, cannot do its job properly in Britain today without a conscious and positive approach to race relations.'[4] In 1969 that looked obvious enough. But it was not so obvious even four years earlier to the draughtsman who produced the Prime Minister's White Paper on Commonwealth Immigration of that year.[5] This White Paper, as we have already indicated, was the first systematic attempt to define official policy on the integration of minorities and devise solutions covering housing and other fields of social policy.

For reasons extrinsic to the migration as such, the White Paper fell at a point when the attempt by central government to operate the 'clumsy and indiscriminatory strings of the housing market'[6] had hardly progressed beyond the point reached in the fifties, when the Ministry of Housing had to circulate the local authorities in order to discover how many housing managers were serving with authorities in England and Wales. In this sense the proposals in the housing section of the White Paper illustrate the adage that immigration reveals existing deficiencies in the structure of Government.

'Commonwealth immigrants do not cause the housing shortage. It existed before they began to arrive in large numbers.'[7] This opening statement in the White Paper, while acquitting the newcomers of a charge still too often levelled against them, had little positive value. It failed to acknowledge the opposite side of the picture – the existence of special difficulties which affected Commonwealth immigrants as such. As time goes by, the dangers in the facile assumptions made by the draughtsmen of the White Paper become clear enough. But the precise reasons for the neglect of the problems of the core of major cities which predates the arrival of the immigrants are not. Explanations of national housing policy since the war lie outside the scope of this book:[8] but in the barest outline one can say that the attempts of the Attlee administration to tackle the major shortage of accommodation produced by the failings of pre-war policy and the very substantial damage caused by enemy action during the war pivoted on the local authorities and involved a strict system of controls. Their Conservative successors eventually switched their emphasis to the private sector and emphasized de-control in a successful attempt to deal with the absolute shortage of housing – an attempt which did not, however, succeed in mopping-up the pockets of poverty in the inner city. By the late 1950s the first in a succession of linked scandals about the homeless in London – usually working-class households with large families and low wages – began to break surface. In the grim paradox of misery and suffering for a minority in the middle of increased comfort for the majority, there was ample material for impassioned exposés.

Shifts in housing demand, changes in demographic and social structure, and internal and external migration had not been properly anticipated by either the central government or the local authority; and it was the latter whose incapacity to deal with the problems which had arisen in this way that was brutally exposed. As one London authority told the Milner Holland Committee, the inquiry launched as a result of the scandal provoked by the activities of the entrepreneur Perec Rachman, any attempts by local authorities to deal with the overcrowding and squalor of areas of transition in the inner city were 'creating a battlefield where a local authority cannot provide the ambulance service to take off the wounded'.[9]

This failure was particularly important since, despite the restrictions placed on their role by the Conservative Government, the local authorities still occupy a central position in the provision of housing. It is the crux of John Rex's analysis of the situation of the newcomers in Birmingham that, as he puts it, 'the system of housing allocation is one of the two major determinants of the structure of race relations in Birmingham'.[10] (The other is differential access to employment. The control of local authorities over the access of potential clients to adequate accommodation is the crux of their central role in the problems of the inner city inhabitants. Apart from the selection of tenants, their allocation within local authority owned housing, the operation of differential rent schemes and the general management of their property are all areas of local authority responsibility. Outside their own estates, demolition or closing orders on individual unfit buildings, and enforcement of public health provisions are also subject to only the most general central supervision. Over and above these important aspects of housing policy, all of which are relevant for newcomers, the detailed decisions on the deployment of financial resources and the structures devised to implement the local housing authority's policy are fundamentally matters of local discretion. And the Ministry's rule until the mid-1960s was basically regulatory.

Within the broad lines laid down for them by central government (by legislation, White Paper, or exhortation through circular), most big city authorities approached the problems thrown up by the growth of multi-occupation and immigration of all kinds on the basis that they are an irrelevance, and those affected 'transients'. In other words, the problems are a distraction from the task of providing adequate accommodation for those locally born or based members of the working class who have lived for too long in poor housing – back-to-backs or small by-law terraced housing (or, in the case of London, tenement blocks) – or with in-laws. This is a serious problem which has rightly preoccupied many authorities, but it is vital to distinguish it from the question of the 'twilight zone' of multi-occupied housing.

This reluctance to become involved in the problems of the twilight zone has been in part a function of the political pattern of the 1950s; most of the authorities affected were Labour controlled throughout this period, and, as Elizabeth Burney commented of them, 'most Labour councils make a habit of resolutely ignoring immigration, to the extent of, wherever possible, ignoring the presence of immigrants'.[11] Official reluctance is partly a function of an excessively local approach to public housing. Successive reports and Ministry circulars since 1955 urged on local authorities the importance of considering need before residence; but distinctions have continued to be made, both in obtaining access to the waiting list and in progress on it. This in turn is related to the kind of local politician who serves on housing committees. Margaret Stacey has commented that:

local authorities in all except new and expanding towns tend to be overweighted by councillors and aldermen of long local residence, members of a strong in-group attached more to maintaining the *status quo* than to welcoming strangers. The result is something like the old Elizabethan poor law.[12]

Equally, the willingness of local authorities to tackle complex and delicate problems like those arising from multiple-occupation may be related to the internal structure of local government. Problems thrown up by such conditions may affect three or four departments, and new solutions may involve a degree of collaboration which in some authorities (often for reasons of personality) is not feasible.

Finally, there may be a conventional wisdom, built up from experience of dealing with quite different kinds of minorities. 'Segregation' is a term that has a long history in the public housing field, and *de facto* separation by age or class is becoming increasingly a feature in housing of all kinds. If slum clearance or redevelopment does, for purely accidental reasons, involve an authority in rehousing coloured families, it often seems to draw on its previous experience with other low-status groups and acts accordingly. Thus, as Elizabeth Burney observes, 'any housing visitor can show you the "problem corner" – and there, like as not, will also be seen coloured faces'.[13]

But over and above all these ideological and structural reasons which made local government unable to deal with the problems of the twilight zones and their inhabitants comes the sheer scope of the problem. And this in turn brings one back to London, where all the processes described above are to some extent relevant, though the dimensions of the difficulty are obviously crucial.

The Milner Holland Committee isolated eight boroughs in which housing conditions displayed signs of increasing stress – Willesden, Kensington, Stoke Newington, Hackney, Hornsey, Lambeth, Islington, and Hammersmith. Only Paddington among London boroughs had a higher proportion of coloured immigrants than these eight. Lambeth is in many ways the most interesting case, since central Lambeth (or rather Brixton) served as a reception area for newcomers from the beginning of the migration. The first steps taken by the local authorities were in co-operation with the initial efforts of central government to arrange for their absorption: but the welfare phase gave place to the *laissez-faire* period, and Lambeth Borough Council were left to deal with its problem as best it could. Late in 1954, the mayor and the local member, Marcus Lipton, led a deputation to the Colonial Office. But the deputation was told that central intervention was not justified; it would interfere with the Ministry of Labour's efforts to disperse the coloured population through allocation of employment vacancies.

Rebuffed in turn by the Minister of Housing, Duncan Sandys (member for next-door Streatham), the council relapsed into near-total inaction – a policy described by its advocates as 'we are all Lambethans now', and by its opponents as the 'Nelson's eye policy'. Almost the only positive measure taken in the 1950s was the purchasing of two roads in the heart of the Brixton settlement area, Geneva and Somerleyton Roads, from the Beauchamp Estate. The fact that the leases were due to expire in 1966, and that with them the responsibility for the inhabitants (then thought to be overwhelmingly coloured) would fall to the council acted as a time bomb, ticking through the years of *laissez-faire*. A year before the leases were due to fall in the council executed an abrupt about-face. There were a number of explanations for this change in attitude: trouble on one of the large new council estates in the area over the re-housing of a West Indian family, the re-organization and enlarging of the borough under the provisions of the London Government Act, the advent of a new and energetic housing manager and chief public health inspector, the stimulus of a full-dress discussion with the Ministers responsible for London housing, and immigration. One symptom of the change in attitudes was the undertaking of a study to measure the precise extent of the problem, previously written off as marginal.[14] The findings of the study are chiefly valuable for the light they cast on the solution devised by West Indians for their housing problems, in a situation of some difficulty in which the local authority had declined to intervene directly.

First, and predictably, the study showed few West Indians in local authority accommodation – 5% in all, compared with 20% of the local white inhabitants. As the census results suggest, one solution that was being extensively adopted was house purchase. But the majority (two-thirds, in fact) were still renting accommodation. Here the coloured tenant was getting bad value for money. About half of them were paying over £4 per week in rent; whereas over three-quarters of the equivalent white sample were paying less than £4. A third of coloured tenants had no rent book. Although the average household size was 3–6 persons in coloured households and 2–7 in white, multi-occupancy was not a function of family size alone, independent of colour: of all households with children, only 17% of white families were in multi-occupation compared with 76% of coloured families. Nor were higher rents the consequence of late arrival in the district or the areas in which coloured newcomers settled. Although their socio-economic profile was very similar to the general population in the core area of settlement, the immigrants were worse off for amenities than the bulk of the population in that part of the borough: 23% of the coloured families had none of them, compared with only 3% of whites.

But despite the fact that they were getting poor value for money, the West Indians struck roots in Lambeth. Thirty-nine per cent of the coloured sample had lived in the borough for over five years, and such movement as had taken place tended to be within the area. Only 20% of those who had considered moving intended to leave the borough. Most of the families had passed through the various stages of expansion through migration; only 14% now expected to be joined by further children from overseas.

In sum, the Lambeth sample conformed very closely with the people of a migrant group in a big city, performing essential services but failing to obtain accommodation on an equitable basis or, until lately, any intervention on their behalf by the local authority. But despite the handicaps which the evidence clearly reveals the solutions reached have their own viability.

This same element of turning forced solutions to positive advantage is true of the substantial number of newcomers, from all ethnic groups, who have found the solution to their housing difficulties through house purchase. Elizabeth Burney comments that immigrant owner-occupation is 'a very positive source of physical and social improvement in many areas now written off as decayed'.[15] But the intending house purchaser has a series of difficulties to contend with which may have a substantial impact on his future position as an owner. There is the problem of the unsympathetic estate agent to be surmounted – too often they have tended to interpret their role as providing them with authority to direct coloured newcomers into areas which they conceive to be suitable for them. And although co-operative methods of financing may make the raising of a deposit less difficult than it would be for white house purchasers at equivalent social and economic level the question of loan finance is also difficult. Many building societies are reluctant to help immigrant house purchasers, either through anxiety about their reliability, or because of the nature of the property which is available to them, or from a combination of the two. Occasionally, estate agents are able to act as go-betweens, either with the more respectable companies, or with the less scrupulous loan and investment companies which have flourished at the immigrants' expense. Borrowing from these companies may involve the house purchaser in a cycle of difficulties stemming from the necessity to keep up excessive payments which may well land him in serious difficulties with the local authority. In this situation the local authority itself can make a significant contribution by making funds available for borrowing by potential house purchasers and, with a few conspicuous exceptions, local authorities have in the past generally risen to the situation.

However, the heyday of council mortgage schemes now lies in the past – in fact it only lasted two years, 1963–65, by coincidence following close on the peak period of Commonwealth immigration. The decline began in 1965, when the Government restricted councils to the amounts they had lent in the previous year. In 1966, they were given a little more scope, but told to keep to various 'needy' categories – interpreted in various ways. In 1967, the money was cut back still further. And although the Government have introduced an option mortgage scheme to cater for those who find difficulty in obtaining mortgages in the open market it was not until late in 1969 that some relaxation of the squeeze on funds made available to local authorities for mortgage purposes finally took place.

In the solutions reached by the new Lambethans after ten years of nightwatchman rule by their borough council there were many substantial drawbacks: some of these are vividly illustrated in the flood of cases reaching South London rent tribunals throughout the 1950s and early 1960s. But there are also virtues – as Elizabeth Burney puts it:

There is a good deal that is warm, sociable and attractive about central Brixton as its West Indian inhabitants have made it; a great potential for planners to build on if they only knew how.[16]

A verdict that many who know the area would gladly endorse. But the point is that the solutions are makeshift: the danger has been underscored by Ruth Glass, who refers to the 'quasi-solution' of allowing immigrants to remain in reception areas. The most notorious of these is North Kensington, where no solution of any kind had yet been produced, despite a decade of unremitting voluntary effort and two major social surveys. The latest of these, the Notting Hill housing survey of 1967,[17] revealed a very high incidence of over-crowding, the overwhelming bulk of which was to be found in the private rented sector. Over and above this, households with heads born overseas – in particular West Indians – have a much higher rate of over-crowding than households with heads born in the United Kingdom. The authors of the report comment: 'It is clear that we have here a high concentration of human misery in the midst of what is both a very congested and on the whole very affluent part of metropolitan London. The overall congestion of Kensington means that there is no elbow room for local street development schemes. The popularity of the better residential areas adjoining and the high purchasing power of so many people living in the borough both mean that the people we have surveyd have no chance of competing successfully in the housing market for accommodation of a reasonable standard.'[18]

In North Kensington, the problems of the newcomer – not

merely the black newcomer – are seen at their starkest: even the modest degree of security achieved by the West Indian in Brixton has no parallel; the repeatedly expressed anxiety for the value of the property which is a recurrent feature of all situations in which immigrants have begun to break through to home ownership is absent. By contrast, this anxiety – which has little or no foundation in fact – is one of the crucial elements in determining the development of the Birmingham situation, in which the potentiality for inter-racial conflict has probably reached its highest level to date.

The initial pattern of settlement in the West Midlands – and, in particular, Birmingham – followed broadly the same pattern as in London. Even by 1961, the immigrant popu-lation was not as concentrated as the popular image sug-gested, but the same marked tendency that was present in London, for the newcomers to cluster in an inner belt around the city centre partly composed of larger Victorian housing, was emerging with clarity. Behind this developing pattern lie a series of interlocking causes, which are sum-marized by Rex and Moore in *Race, Community and Conflict*, their study of Birmingham and one of its twilight areas, Sparkbrook.

Throughout most of the period between the initial settle-ment and the White Paper of 1965, Birmingham City Coun-cil was Labour-controlled; and for a large part of that period one or two powerful individuals dominated policy-making. Initially, anxious to devise acceptable means of cut-ting down the numbers of coloured newcomers to the city, these leaders had accepted with extreme reluctance the official Labour line on immigration, which they linked di-rectly with the problems of the inner belt round the city's core which was then undergoing a drastic facelift intended to drive home the image of a dynamic and successful com-mercial centre – and civic leaders.

By 1960 it had become clear that the solutions devised in the 1950s by Conservative ministers were not going to be adequate for the problems of the twilight zones and local authorities made their discontent very plain. Their pressure was a key element in the passing of the Housing Act of 1961, which, together with its successor of 1964, armed them with a series of new powers. Local authorities were empowered to make orders applying management regulations to houses in multiple occupation in an unsatisfactory state; to issue orders requiring certain work to be undertaken; to carry out the work in default and charge for it; and to fix a limit on the number of individuals who should live in a house. Equipped with these new powers, Birmingham corporation began an assault upon conditions in the twilight zone.

The effects of this assault fell almost exclusively upon immigrant landlords, for reasons which have been dealt with by Rex and Moore in their examination of Sparkbrook. Briefly, their view is that as a result of certain imperatives in the social organization of the city, a system of housing classes has been erected: a property-owning bourgeoisie which has tended to escape from the city to suburban security; the bulk of the working class, who have created 'a new public suburbia' in council estates; well-established tenants of self-contained housing; and lodging house landlords, and the tenants of furnished accommodation and lodging houses, who 'need no qualification at all apart from their willingness to pay a high rent in relation to housing space offered during an insecure tenancy'. For various reasons, the newcomer to the city is generally excluded from all but the last two categories. Some migrants can overcome the consequences of this struggle, if they are adequately motivated, but the coloured newcomer suffers from particular handicaps in relation to his skin colour. He is not the author of the city's housing problem, but he is only too likely to be made the scapegoat for it.[19]

The process of scapegoating is particularly prone to occur in the case of the immigrant – usually, in Birmingham, an Indian or Pakistani – who adopts the solution of becoming a landlord. From the ideological position taken up by both major parties the immigrant by this act puts himself beyond the pale. The fact that he might have been driven to adopt the role of landlord through necessity rather than desire, and that the methods he employed to buy the house might mean that he found himself painfully squeezed financially and that he might have binding family obligations to discharge, cut no ice. The full weight of the council's drive against overcrowding and poor conditions fell squarely upon the Indian and Pakistani landlords.

When the powers conferred by the 1961 Act proved to be inadequate for this purpose, even as amended in the Housing Act of 1964, Birmingham corporation promoted its own private Bill in 1965, with all-party support, to provide for the registration of housing in multiple occupation and the refusal of registration in cases where either the applicant or the area or house was considered unsuitable by the authority. This action attracted considerable criticism, less for the powers it conferred on the local authority than for the generally negative approach towards the problem that it revealed, and its dubious effectiveness. Seen in this light it becomes yet another ground for criticism of the White Paper that virtually the only innovation that it commended in the housing field was the introduction of legislation along similar lines by other local authorities.

Within the framework of this policy, it is fair to add, some changes have been taking place. In a long report issued in mid-1968 the Council, now under Conservative control, was able to point to an increased number of coloured people going into council accommodation – 250 per year, with 16% of the waiting list now composed of immigrants.

But the general impression from this progress report is that the basic determinants of policy did not seem to have changed – 'slum clearance', the report adds, 'will automatically engulf the poor properties unworthy of being improved, but there are relatively few immigrants in unfit houses'.[20] In other words, the increasing trend towards concentration is likely to persist, unbroken either by direct intervention by the local authority or voluntary dispersal. Only a determined application of improvement procedures, now contained in Part IV of the 1969 Act, in the inner ring is likely to bring about a long-term improvement in the situation.

An additional complication has been the resentment felt, especially in the suburban ring round the West Midlands conurbation, about the possibility of incursion by coloured immigrants. The rationale may not be very coherent – the chairman of one Midland Ratepayers Association told Elizabeth Burney that: 'You may say what's the difference except skin but I tell you they *are* different in ways we don't understand' – but the feeling is strong, and for this reason the 'suburban noose' is drawn tighter than it is anywhere else in England. The few attempts by ambitious Indians and West Indians to obtain housing in the privately developed estates of lower priced housing characteristic of the area have almost invariably provoked outbursts of intense hostility.

These outbursts have been particularly prone to occur on the fringe of the Black Country, in Wolverhampton – where, as Elizabeth Burney suggests, status differentials in housing being particularly difficult to maintain are particularly ferociously defended. The restriction of options open to immigrants, once again trapped between slum-clearance centre grants, and the suburb, is therefore even more marked than in Birmingham. The local authority has gone some way towards meeting their needs, at the time that Miss Burney made her study, by making local authority housing available. Immigrants, once they had surmounted the difficulty of qualifying in a selection scheme which emphasizes a differential qualification period for the non-English born, were getting rehoused. But far more coloured people – proportionately nearly twice as many – were finding themselves on the pre-war estates, where known troublemakers are to be found and where disturbances involving coloured tenants took place in 1965. In part, this was a function of the selection scheme. Applicants for vacancies were graded from A1 to C3 and the preconceptions of the housing visitor were likely to ensure that the immigrant did not obtain the B2 or higher mark that was required to qualify him for post-war accommodation. If this did not take place, the dispersal policy of the local authority, which overrides the selection system, would bring about the same result.[21] Wolverhampton, a city which currently has far less difficulties than many London boroughs, has rather unfairly become the epitome of a local authority with 'immigrant problems'. To the extent that this is true, the cause is not material difficulty but local attitudes. The inflexible paternalism of the local authority is effective, within its limits; but the failure of imagination, symbolized in the reluctance to employ the mortgage weapon to open the escape route for the immigrants who wish to put into practice the process of dispersal to which the council itself is pledged, shows up these limits clearly.

Other local authorities did not face the same imperatives as Birmingham and the Black Country authorities: their minds were not wonderfully concentrated. In some cases, a combination of the local housing circumstances and the attitude of the newcomers towards housing made a defensive posture tenable, in a style that makes Lambeth's *laissez-faire* approach look like a dynamic assault on the problem. Such an authority was Bradford.

Butterworth has described, with a tinge of irony, how each successive cohort of ministerial visitors has complimented Bradford on the way in which it has approached the problems involved in playing host to the largest concentration of Pakistani immigrants in the country.[22] He suggests that a good deal of this apparent success can be put down to local circumstances, and picks out the housing field as one in which the city has been particularly fortunate. Bradford, with a declining population linked to a declining industry (wool textiles) has a large stock of mid-nineteenth-century housing. The worst of this was the back-to-back cottages – now partly eliminated by the slum-clearance drive of the mid-1950s. The growing residential segregation by class, characteristic of other major cities, has meant that the larger houses of the same vintage, built in inner wards, have been deserted by their original middle-class occupants. It is in these inner wards that the Pakistani migrants, arriving to make good the labour shortage in the textile industry, first settled: by 1966, the two wards of Listerhills and Exchange had probably the highest proportions of immigrants of any local electoral area in the country, and 1,275 out of 1,417 lodging houses known to the council were owned and occupied by Indians and Pakistanis. But the crucial difference lay in the fact that there was scope for movement into adjoining areas: movement that became extremely important as family reunions made conditions in the lodging houses, acceptable to single men, undesirable for families with women to protect. By July 1965, just before the White Paper, the health department estimated that there were 1,400 families in the city.

But the local authority did not employ any of the means of intervention open to it. And by the time the slum clearance programme neared its end many of the local white inhabitants were themselves not taking advantage of the opportunity to be rehoused by the authority. The low price of housing – both rented and for purchase – meant that the authority was competing directly with the private sector; anxiety that it would not be possible to let off the housing that the local authority operated had, by the mid-1960s, reduced the qualifying period on the waiting list to nil. But immigrants, with easy access to house purchase, were on the whole slow to take advantage of this opportunity – unlike Asian immigrants in some other West Riding towns – and the local authority has preferred not to encourage them. Possibly the authority's experience with the failure of a hostel it operated may have coloured their attitude towards immigrant tenants. At any rate, by 1966, only forty-four council houses were occupied by immigrant families, and Butterworth comments that 'the majority of immigrants appear to be marginal to the immigrant community'.

Other means of positive intervention were also neglected: no mortgage scheme was thought necessary, and no steps were taken to ensure that improvement grants were used. With the pressure of multi-occupation at an acceptable level and a gradual process of dispersal taking place, the local authority could afford to let matters take their course; the absence of any substantial degree of organized pressure from public opinion or the press made the option all the easier to take.[23] But the spectacle of the levers of the housing market standing unused in favourable conditions presents an unhappy contrast with those areas where endless manipulation could achieve no result.

A more positive attitude was taken by the local authority in Bristol, where a special study has been made of the re-housing of West Indians on the city's estates.[24] A one-year qualification period operated at the time of the study, and the average time taken by West Indians in the sample to obtain housing was two and three-quarter years. The main obstacle in the way of the West Indian applicant lay not so much in the process of selection – indeed, the West Indians who had larger families and lived in poorer conditions were rehoused, on average, earlier than an equivalent white sample – as in finding out about the procedure. Given this fact, it is hardly surprising that over one-third of the successful applicants had English wives who could be presumed to know the ropes. Once arrived on the estate, the relative lack of competition for housing worked in the newcomers' favour; the processes by which they were selected were accepted as fair. And in many ways the West Indian sample approximated very closely to the normal pattern for successful applicants for council housing – in terms of skills, family size, and aspirations. But this does not necessarily imply an immediate 'fit': 'estate life', Lyon comments, 'is so finely organized around differences in status that whatever status attribute newcomers possess is likely to be critical for their prospects and their integration' – the danger in this instance being that the low esteem in which the St. Paul's area (from which the immigrants come) is held might be an alternative (and perhaps even stronger) reason for their rejection than skin colour. In practice, this process of rejection did not appear to be taking place. The West Indians, who 'wanted very much to be judged on their individual merits and not to be stereotyped as coloured people', appeared to be achieving their objective and adapting successfully to the rather tepid social life of the estate, with its emphasis on family and shrinking away from excessive contact with strangers. In many ways these particular newcomers were better equipped for success in this environment than less stable West Indian families would be; but even granted that they were to some extent a self-selected sample, the ease of their acceptance and adjustment is impressive, and suggests that the anxieties of some local authorities about accepting responsibility for rehousing coloured immigrants on ordinary estates are exaggerated.

The West Indians on the Bristol estates, however, remain a very small minority – although the P.E.P. investigation in 1967 suggested that more West Indians were prepared to consider the possibility of council accommodation (41%, in fact) than was commonly supposed.[25] A more frequent route to local authority housing lies through clearance schemes; and this leads more often to the patched or compulsorily purchased house in council hands, for reasons which are endemic in the selection process. Immigrants may, as we have seen, also be subjected to a process of 'scattering' in poorer class housing. The P.E.P. investigators' dry comment on one alibi for this process is, that while one of the 'justifications for this was that it made life easier for the immigrants by preventing unpleasantness, it was also true that it made life easier for the authority'.[26] But even these fortunates constituted a small minority (possibly even as little as 1%), as the P.E.P. investigation of the extent of discrimination was shortly to show. The majority were evolving their own solution, as we have seen, and this solution almost invariably involved both multi-occupation and house purchase. Although these solutions carried with them a built-in source of friction, the reaction of the members of the host community remained throughout this period remarkably calm and balanced (see Chapter 12).

Some local authorities had the capacity to tackle the problems of multiple occupation constructively and were not deterred when this involved them in accepting responsibility for the coloured inhabitants of the area. It is no reflection on their virtue to say that these were often also the authorities under least pressure. But not always. Leeds was one, and Lambeth was eventually to become another. But the majority of those authorities were content to hold the line either noisily (like Birmingham) or silently (like Bradford), or else to shelter behind the convenient proposition advanced by successive governments, and reaching its apotheosis in the White Paper. This was that no special measures were necessary to deal with the problem of the twilight areas over and above those taken in 1961 and reinforced in 1964. This position represents the low water mark of policy on this issue just as the narrowly-drawn Race Relations Bill of 1965 indicated the extreme reluctance and caution with which the Government had moved to take specific remedial action to deal with discrimination itself. And although a White Paper appeared in November 1965 on *The Housing Programme 1965-1970*,[27] the crucial uncertainty about the nature of the problem persisted and partly vitiated the analysis. 'First priority will be given,' said this White Paper (paragraph 39), 'to relieving the acute shortage of houses to rent in the conurbations – especially in areas which attract newcomers including immigrants from the Commonwealth – and to clearing the great concentrations of slums' (a juxtaposition which perpetuated the confusion that has fogged the issue from the outset).

But clearly the situation was not going to rest there. The stimulus of the Milner Holland Report was succeeded by that of the Denington Report on older housing.[28] Continued evidence of pressing need in the major conurbations accelerated a convergence of views on the proposal, originally advanced by the Milner Holland Committee, to designate inner areas as 'areas of special control'.

Some of these themes were gathered together and specifically related to the problems of coloured immigrants in two reports written by the National Committee for Commonwealth Immigrants' Housing Panel.[29] These reports were presented to successive Ministers of Housing and received with some sympathy. But official policy continued to stress the importance of treating the subject within the overall context of housing policy and, when pressed, ministers fell back, as Lord Stonham did in November 1966, on platitudes. 'There is', he said, 'no immediate solution to this extremely difficult housing problem; only enough low rented houses will provide the cure.'[30]

The lever which made a breach in this wall was in fact not specifically devised to deal with housing difficulties – the Plowden recommendations for educational priority areas, with their emphasis on urban renewal through community renewal, provided the necessary impetus for change. The Department of Education and Science acted rapidly to introduce positive discrimination in these areas, and the next White Paper from the Ministry of Housing, Old Houses into New Homes,[31] contained welcome recognition of the need to consider the problems of areas of multi-occupation as a whole – 'the keynote of the proposals is that the local authorities are positively concerning themselves with the conditions of the unsatisfactory private housing in their area'. And the legislation promised in the White Paper, when introduced, did indeed arm the local authority with far-reaching powers to declare 'general improvement areas' which enabled them to treat the problems of deprived districts as a whole. The intention behind the legislation is to enlist the goodwill of owners (cemented with more generous provision of grants) in order to improve rather than clear these areas: though in the overcrowded conditions in those inner city, areas which are the likeliest candidates for improvement, it seems inevitable that there will be some displacement of population – which may be particularly hard on those in the private rented sector in areas like Kensington. Here, the proportion likely to be dislodged has been tentatively estimated at 30% of the population as a whole.

This legislation also marks a further step in the development of the importance of housing associations as agents for change in the inner city. These had already been the subject of earlier legislation, the Housing Subsidies Act of 1967. This involved a change in the situation of non-profit making housing associations in relation to subsidies which improved their viability. A number of pioneer associations have been active in the field since the mid-1950s and at the height of the *laissez-faire* period, these associations, like the Aggrey Association in Leeds and the Coloured People's Housing Association in Nottingham, made a useful contribution in meeting urgent need. But by the early 1960s these associations were no longer meeting the demands of immigrants, who could afford to pay more for housing and were increasingly inclined to turn to house ownership as the preferred solution. In London, the Metropolitan Coloured People's Housing Association performed the same role, but survived to change its name and identity when a new wave of associations arose in the 1960s. These were based partly on the public indignation aroused by exposures of the worst effects of abuses in the private rented system: 'Shelter', a fund-raising and publicity organization, has helped to focus this indignation and harness it to providing resources for associations. In their report, *Notice to Quit*, Shelter drew attention to the continued deterioration in the situation of tenants in twilight areas and the relative ineffectiveness of the 1965 Rent Act, which was introduced in an attempt to stabilize the position by conferring security of tenure in the private sector. The intentions of the Act, whose provisions are not by any means as well known as they should be,[32] despite extensive advertising, have also been undermined to a considerable extent by the rapid shift of tenancies into the furnished sector – where the protection available to tenants is far less effective. Given the high proportion of immigrants to be found in furnished tenancies, this has particularly grave implications for them. In these circumstances, associations working in collaboration with local authorities can make an important contribution, as a safety net for cases which the local authority are unable for a variety of reasons to help. But, as those who work with them would recognize, their role is at present a palliative one and long-term solutions to major problems of immigrant housing are not likely to be found in this direction. Over and above this, there is the danger, recognized by Shelter itself, that local authorities may opt out altogether from the thankless job of catering for hard cases in the twilight zone. The gain for 2,330 families rehoused through Shelter in its first three years of activities may be outweighed by the consequences for the far larger group of families still awaiting rehousing, without hope of rescue from the local authorities. For them, the Cullingworth Committee's recommendations, if implemented, offer a hope of escape through the existing machinery in the public sector.

We have traced the evolution of policy on housing in some detail, because housing is in so many ways the crucial determining factor for the coloured newcomer. The familiar illustration is of the triangle of forces: housing for the adult, at the apex, determines education for the child, which determines employment for the adolescent. The failure in Government policy in this crucial field was initially, to a large extent, the result of a general misunderstanding of the processes at work in the major conurbations. Not until the 1965 White Paper, when the causes of demographic change were better understood, the bulk of the Rowntree research projects available, and the Milner Holland Report published, was the evidence on which to base a revised policy to hand. Meanwhile, local authorities were left to struggle with inadequate resources.

The evidence for failure can be seen only too clearly in the results of two investigations: the report of the 1966 sample census and the P.E.P. study of the extent of discrimination.[33] The sample survey (as we have seen) shows that in almost any significant dimension of housing circumstances the immigrant is at a substantial disadvantage. The P.E.P. report laid bare with exemplary clarity the pathology of the discrimination which has been a major factor in creating those disparities. The widespread belief among immigrants that landlords and estate agents discriminated against them proved in the course of the investigation to be only too well justified. In a series of test applications for accommodation a West Indian received less favourable treatment on 45 out of 60 occasions when approaching landlords, on 20 out of 30 occasions when approaching estate agents and on 14 out of 18 occasions when approaching an accommodation bureau. As we have seen, such discrimination is now unlawful as a result of the passage of the Race Relations Act of 1968 – the findings of the P.E.P. study were crucial in determining that such legislation should be passed. But the damage in terms of the steady entrenchment of patterns of segregation, both voluntary and forced, had already been done. The implications of this failure extend beyond the field of housing: they were also crucial in shaping the developing pattern of race relations, not only in other local authority services but also in other spheres of social contact where concentration and poor living conditions determine the reception that the newcomer receives.

REFERENCES

1. The Housing Act, 1969, cap 33.
2. *Council Housing: Purposes, Procedures and Priorities* (London, H.M.S.O., 1969).
3. Ibid, p. 54.
4. Ibid, p. 116.
5. Cmnd. 2379, op. cit.
6. Elizabeth Burney: *Housing on Trial* (Oxford University Press, for Institute of Race Relations, 1968).
7. Cmnd. 2379.
8. For some, see D. V. Donnison, *The Government of Housing* (Harmondsworth, Penguin Books, 1968), J. B. Cullingworth, *Housing and Local Government* (London, Allen & Unwin, 1966), S. Alderson, *Britain in the Sixties: Housing* (Harmondsworth, Penguin Books, 1962).
9. Milner Holland Report, op. cit., p. 96.
10. J. Rex and R. S. Moore, *Race, Community and Conflict* (London, Oxford University Press for Institute of Race Relations, 1967), p. 35.

11. Burney, op. cit, p. 188.
12. M. Stacey, 'A Fair Deal for Migrant Housing', Institute of Race Relations *Newsletter* (June 1966), p. 15.
13. Burney, op. cit., p. 76.
14. Discussed in Burney, op. cit., Chapter V. The study was carried out by Research Services Ltd.
15. Burney, op. cit., p. 56.
16. Burney, op. cit., p. 145.
17. *Initial Housing Survey*, Notting Hill Summer Project, 1967 (Notting Hill Housing Service, 1969).
18. Ibid, p. ix.
19. See the discussion in Rex and Moore, op. cit, Chapters 1 and 2.
20. Birmingham Corporation conference report, op. cit., p. 63.
21. For a full discussion, see Burney, op. cit, Chapters VII and VIII.
22. Butterworth, op. cit.
23. See, for example, for the role of the local press, Eric Butterworth, 'The 1962 Smallpox Outbreak and the British Press', *Race* (Vol. VII, no. 4, April 1966).
24. A. H. Richmond and M. Lyon, 'Immigrants in Bristol' (for the Institute's 'Survey of Race Relations in Britain').
25. W. W. Daniel, *Racial Discrimination in England* (Harmondsworth, Penguin Books, 1968), p. 195.
26. Ibid, p. 190.
27. *The Housing Programme 1965–1970* (Cmnd. 2838), (London, H.M.S.O., 1965).
28. Central Housing Advisory Committee, *Our Older Homes: a call for action* ('The Denington Report'), (London, H.M.S.O., 1966).
29. *The Housing of Commonwealth Immigrants* (London, N.C.C.I, 1967), and *Areas of Special Housing Need* (London, N.C.C.I., 1967).
30. 277 H. L. Deb, col. 733, 3rd November, 1966.
31. *Old Houses into New Homes* (Cmnd. 3602), (London, H.M.S.O., 1968).
32. See, for example, Michael Zander, 'The Unused Rent Act', *New Society* (12th September, 1968).
33. *Racial Discrimination in Britain*, op. cit.

Chapter Seven

Education

The arrival and the education of the children of Commonwealth immigrants in British schools began to be seen as a problem in the early 1960s. During the 1950s, although there was a small but regular inflow of children from the West Indies coming to join parents in Britain, the vast majority were left behind in the first stage of the migration process. Nevertheless, the remarkably high proportion of women among the Caribbean migrants indicated that there was a strong possibility that once a home could be made and the fare money raised, the children would follow. As far back as 1958, one or two schools in a very few places began to notice an increase in the numbers of non-English speaking Indian pupils, but, as shown in Chapter Three, migration from India and Pakistan only reached significant levels in 1961. Although some Indian wives and children did arrive during the 'beat the ban' rush, the family character of the Indian and Pakistani migration did not become clear until after the Commonwealth Immigrants Act statistics were published on the numbers of dependants entering the country.

Some schools already had a cosmopolitan range of nationalities among their pupils, having absorbed and educated children of the earlier post-war European immigrants. In the 1960s, however, rapid rates of increase in the number of children arriving, and their entry into schools at all ages and throughout the school year, many from non-English speaking homes, were problems for which the education system was quite unprepared. This chapter describes the policies which were developed in response to this situation.

The power to formulate policies and to put them into

practice lay with a number of different institutions, national and local: the Department of Education and Science; the institutes and colleges of education, responsible for teacher training; local education authorities, in particular their directors of education and their own local inspectorate (if any); and the individual head-teachers and teachers in the schools. Thus, there was a highly dispersed pattern of power and responsibility. The linking institution was H.M. Inspectorate. 'No other department', wrote Professor Griffith, 'supervises and assists the work of the local authorities to the same extent as does the Department of Education and Science through the medium of the H.M.I.s.'[1] However, over the education of immigrants, although individual H.M.I.s gave help and tried to stimulate interest, it was eventually left to the Schools Council, set up in 1964, to draw the threads together by commissioning a national report on the developing problems and policies of local authorities and teachers.[2]

The difficulties which the schools experienced were to a great extent due to certain basic deficiencies and inequalities in the education system, which were documented in a series of massive and detailed reports which appeared between 1959 and 1967 (1960, Crowther; 1963, Newsom and Robbins; 1967, Plowden).[3] These deficiencies hindered the schools in meeting the educational needs of the children from overseas, and affected the way in which the children were initially received. The inequalities narrowed the opportunities of children of immigrants just as they narrowed those of children of English parents. The local chief education officers, and the head teachers in the schools, on whose shoulders fell most of the responsibility for dealing with the arrival of immigrant children, had to accept most of these things as part of the facts of educational life.

THE DISPERSAL POLICY

Departmental thinking can be traced through four documents:

English for Immigrants,[4] a pamphlet published in 1963 mainly concerned, as the title suggests, with methods of teaching English; the Second Report of the Commonwealth Immigrants Advisory Council in 1964[5]; Circular 7/65 issued in June 1965;[6] and finally, the White Paper of August 1965 which, with slight changes, incorporated the Circular.[7]

The most important of these documents in the development of policy making in relation to education was the Second Report of the Commonwealth Immigrants Advisory Council, completed in December 1963 and published early in 1964. The C.I.A.C., had been set up by the Conservative Government to advise the Home Secretary on matters relating to the welfare and integration of immigrants. While the Second Report, dealing with immigrant pupils, referred to certain general problems in the education system – such as the shortage and maldistribution of teachers (which affected the reception of immigrant children in the schools) – it did not deal directly with them, and indeed found itself not competent to do so. Its main concern was with the role which the schools might play in achieving integration through the cultural assimilation of children of immigrants. The council argued:

A national system of education must aim at producing citizens who can take their place in society properly equipped to exercise rights and perform duties the same as those of other citizens. If their parents were brought up in another culture and another tradition, children should be encouraged to respect it, but a national system cannot be expected to perpetuate the different values of immigrant groups.

Integration was perceived by the C.I.A.C. very much in terms of social contact within the school between immigrant and native children. To achieve this, and to prevent any interference with the 'normal' routine of a class, the Council assumed that it was essential for the proportion of immigrants in a school or class to be small.

The presence of a high proportion of immigrant children in one class slows down the general routine of working and hampers the progress of the whole class, especially where the immigrants do not speak or write English fluently.

The evidence we have received strongly suggests that if a school has more than a certain percentage of immigrant children among its pupils the whole character and ethos of the school is altered. Immigrant pupils in such a school will not get as good an introduction to British life as they would get in a normal school and we think that their education in the widest sense must suffer as a result.

The report concluded that the location and catchment areas of schools should be planned so that they remained mixed, and that dispersal of children would be preferable, as a last resort, to *de facto* segregation.

The drafting of the C.I.A.C. report coincided with the first political crisis about immigrant children in the schools. This was a protest organized by white parents of children attending two primary schools in Southall, against the presence of immigrant children (mainly Indian). About 60% of the children in one of the schools were children of immigrants. Southall was, in fact, one of two un-named areas referred to in the C.I.A.C. Report where the build-up of immigrant children had very much disturbed the council.

Sir Edward Boyle, then Minister of Education, attended a meeting of the parents at the school. He refused to countenance any suggestions that the immigrant children be educated separately, or that children then attending the school should be moved. However, it was subsequently agreed that Southall would in the case of future admissions of immigrant children into schools 'disperse' them and try to maintain a limit of about 30% in any one school. Sir Edward explained to the House of Commons in November that year:

> If possible, it is desirable on education grounds that no one school should have more than about 30 per cent of immigrants. It was, [he said] both politically and legally more or less impossible to compel native parents to send their children to school in an immigrant area if there are places for them in other schools. Sir Edward went on: I must regretfully tell the House that one school must be regarded now as irretrievably an immigrant school. The important thing to do is to prevent this happening elsewhere.[8]

This was the origin of the official dispersal policy, which subsequently became the main plank in the programmes which the Government recommend to local education authorities.

The idea of dispersal may be interpreted first of all as a rejection of any policy of separate education for immigrants, i.e. of a 'separate but equal' philosophy. But it also implied a belief by the Department of Education and Science (D.E.S.) that the schools could correct, through their placement policies, the effects of residential concentration and the transfer of white children to other schools by their parents. The only italicized paragraph in Circular 7/65 occurred in the section headed, 'Spreading the Children':

It will be helpful if the parents of non-immigrant children can see that practical measures have been taken to deal with the problems in the schools, and that the progress of their own children is not being restricted by the undue preoccupation of the teaching staff with the linguistic and other difficulties of immigrant children.

By the time the official dispersal policy came to be set out in the White Paper in August 1965, it was presented not only as an aid to integrating immigrant children, and a way to prevent any fall in the standards of the schools, but also as a help to the organization of special English classes for immigrant children.

But this multi-purpose policy had, in 1965, no statistical basis. How many children of immigrants were there in the schools, how many of them had inadequate English, how many schools contained more than 30%; these questions could not be answered. The D.E.S. began to collect statistics in 1966. No definition of the term 'immigrant pupil' had been given. The definition of 'immigrant pupil' eventually adopted for statistical purposes included, first, children of immigrant parents born overseas, who had come to Britain, and secondly, children born in Britain to immigrant parents who had arrived within the previous ten years (the date being moved up each year).

Problems were related solely to the overall numbers of 'immigrant pupils' in a school, and no distinctions about the various age-groups were made. The problem of language was in one sense exaggerated; when the statistics were collected it was found that half the total number of immigrant pupils had no language problem. On the basis of the D.E.S.s own criteria for judging language ability, only a quarter of the immigrant pupils were found to require special teaching.[9] In another sense the language problem was under estimated for the White Paper was complacent about the need for more specialized materials, and for more in-service training courses, in English as a Second Language (E2L). 'Increasing interest is being taken,' says the White Paper (para. 47) and 'many people feel the need for further research and for the development of new materials and teaching aids'.

The problems of each school depended a good deal on the previous experience of the teachers. Sometimes a school with a high proportion of immigrant pupils experienced less 'strain' than one with fewer, because the former was used to dealing with children with linguistic and cultural difficulties.

There is little doubt that the official dispersal proposals, in Circular 7/65 and in the White Paper, tended to reinforce popular views about the danger of English children being held back. It was believed by a number of teachers that the standards of their non-immigrant pupils were falling. This was put in perspective two years later when the I.L.E.A. published the report of a study of fifty-two primary schools, where immigrant pupils formed more than one-third of the pupils. Two-thirds of the head teachers questioned felt that there had been some fall in the intelligence of their non-immigrant pupils, i.e. these children were less able than the ones of previous years. This change was due to the fact that the ablest families had been moving out of the area.* About one-third felt that there had also been some under-achievement by non-immigrant pupils, i.e. that they were not doing as well as they could. This might in theory, said the report, be due to the existence of increased class rolls, to higher pupil-teacher ratios, to a concentration of the teachers' attention on the immigrant pupils, or to a lack of mutual stimulus from other non-immigrant pupils. But the report

---

* This movement out of certain areas of the large towns was not new. Its cause was the increased housing opportunities for people after the war, to which public housing contributed as much as private. Slum clearance schemes also altered the balance of the population in the inner city area.

found that in fact the average class rolls, and the average pupil-teacher ratio in these schools, although high, were slightly lower than the average for the whole I.L.E.A. The non-immigrant pupils in the schools, who were transferring to secondary schools in September 1966, achieved scores in English, verbal reasoning, and mathematics which were the same as the average for all transfer pupils in all the authority's primary schools.[10]

The official dispersal policy also had a cool reception from local authorities. Ealing and Bradford had already adopted their own dispersal schemes and Huddersfield was to follow with its variant, and by 1968–9 about a quarter of all L.E.A.s had some form of dispersal of immigrant pupils. But those who had *not* included L.E.A.s with both the largest numbers and the highest proportions of immigrant pupils: I.L.E.A., Birmingham, Brent and Haringey. A number of arguments were advanced against dispersal, of which the main ones were attachment to the 'neighbourhood' school principle (particularly after the publication of the Plowden Report); dislike of singing out of children on the basis of national origin or, as it often appeared, race; objection to moving 5–7-year-old pupils long distances; the fact that dispersal itself could not achieve social integration, and that immigrant pupils could arrive in a group and spend the day in a special class, to return in their bus after mixing possibly even less with English pupils than if they had remained in their high density local school.[11] There was also the most important administrative problem of operating a quota policy, which excluded the movement of English children. The local education officer had to find receiving schools with spare places. Not all potential receiving schools would necessarily be anxious to accept immigrant pupils from outside their area, and there is some evidence to suggest that even in areas without dispersal, some schools are deliberately restricting their intake of immigrants even when they live in the catchment area. The department itself had by 1969 cooled from its initial enthusiasm for dispersal, and was treating it as a local option rather than a national policy. In evidence to the House of Commons Select Committee on Race Relations a D.E.S. spokesman said the department would not now be so dogmatic in recommending dispersal.

There was no evidence that dispersal had helped with language teaching in the boroughs where it had been adopted. In written evidence, the department said 'In the department's view dispersal is not in all cases appropriate but it can ease the situation in certain circumstances which local authorities are well placed to judge. A rigid policy applied from the centre would not only be a derogation of authorities' freedom but would be educationally unsound.'[12]

Local Education Authorities

While the D.E.S. might recommend, it fell to the L.E.A.s to take what action they thought necessary. Some rejected the idea of any special measures at all. For most of those who felt that they had to take some action, the problem was regarded primarily as one of resources. The main task which these L.E.A.s shouldered was the organization of special language classes for non-English speaking immigrant pupils. *English for Immigrants*, published by the D.E.S. (then the Ministry of Education) in 1963, contained an excellent early statement of the necessity for *teaching* English to pupils whose command of the language was inadequate, and suggestions about how this could be administered. The writer stressed the need for 'a carefully planned, intensive course making full use of modern methods of language-teaching'. This applied to both junior and secondary school children. 'Such special classes', the writer went on, 'should be staffed by teachers with some knowledge of modern methods of teaching English as a second language.' At this time, however, there were almost no such teachers in Britain, there were no in-service courses for teachers, graduates of university courses in E2L were going abroad to teach, and little or no thought was being given to attracting them back to teach non-English speaking immigrant children, or to helping those who came back seeking work of this kind. There were no books or classroom materials designed for teaching English to children of immigrants in Britain.

Many L.E.A.s found it hard to find and hold their ordinary teachers, quite apart from getting teachers specialized in E2L. This situation led some authorities to employ immigrant teachers specifically to teach immigrant children, not always to the benefit of the children or the longer term professional prospects of the teachers themselves.

The teacher shortage was relieved to some extent after 1965 when L.E.A.s with many immigrant pupils were allowed to employ teachers above their normal quota. This extra staffing allowance undoubtedly helped some exceptional schools which were trying new ways of organizing the teaching of immigrant pupils – for example, through a language centre in the school. But it could not increase the numbers of those trained in teaching English as a second language, and more generally, in some areas which found it hard to attract their full quota under normal circumstances, the extra allocation made little difference initially. However, by 1968/9 some 2,000 teachers were employed above quota by 51 L.E.A.s.[13]

Financial contribution from the centre came in 1967, when the Home Office began to provide a 50% rate support grant under section 11 of the Local Government Act (1966) towards staffing services affected by the presence of immigrants. Of a total estimated expenditure by local authorities in 1967/8 of just over £3,100,000 under section 11, nearly £1,900,000 was claimed for education staff (teachers and non-teaching aides). Thus the Government contributed just under £1m. to local education authorities in 1967/8.[14] Under the urban programme, which is intended to supplement services in areas of social need, not just immigrant areas, and is not restricted to staffing costs, the central Government share increased to 75%. Phase one was directed to nursery schooling. But under phase two, among a great range of different claims, some local authorities applied for support for schemes dealing with the education of immigrant pupils. For example, three quarters of the cost of 'bussing' immigrant pupils in Ealing, about £20,000, is being borne by the Home Office.[15]

The different administrative arrangements made by L.E.A.s to provide special language teaching have been examined in a number of publications,[16] mostly dating from about 1965/6, but although schemes have been expanded or modified in some areas, the basic forms of organization have not altered. The main difficulty which administrators and teachers have expressed is how to combine sufficient expert tuition, with maximum participation in the normal life of the school. There is little doubt that the most satisfactory way to combine these goals is by having a language centre within an ordinary school. This can either take new arrivals full-time initially, as at Spring Grove, Huddersfield; or take small groups withdrawn from normal classes in numbers or at times which are arranged by the language teacher and class teachers, as was the case at Gillespie in Islington (I.L.E.A.). The Gillespie language centre was notable because it always from the start catered for the language needs of West Indian as well as non-English speaking pupils. The problem of this solution was that it required an expert language teacher on the permanent staff of the school, and a room (or rooms) which could be allocated full-time to language. It is less common than other arrangements which can be briefly described as follows: full-time reception centres for newly arrived Asian pupils, set up mainly after the predictable increase in teenage arrivals after the 1965 White Paper; part-time language centres, separate from schools, to which pupils could be withdrawn for special tuition; reception classes within schools; and finally, withdrawal groups, taken either by ordinary teachers, or by a specialist on the staff, or by a peripatetic language teacher. Any one of these arrangements might differ in the length of time of the language tuition, the degree of expertise of the teacher, and the manageability of the group of children taught, e.g. whether they were of different ages, different stages, a stable or a rapidly changing group. In order to provide sufficient expertise and to take the pressure off the ordinary teachers, some L.E.A.s, of which Birmingham was the pioneer and remains the chief example, built up peripatetic language staff, who as well as taking withdrawal classes in schools, teach at the full-time centres, and do a certain amount of short in-service or pre-service training. In Birmingham, they work from a language centre which also houses *foreign* language teachers, so that here the development of techniques of teaching English as a second language is not cut off from the development of language teaching generally. Other authorities, of which I.L.E.A. and Haringey are examples have tried to build up the numbers of language teachers on school staffs. Whatever the schemes are, it is important at this stage to try to foresee the future development of language teaching need. Schemes which were devised to cater for large numbers of new arrivals of Indian and Pakistani teenagers, may have to adapt considerably to a situation of fewer new arrivals, but increasing numbers of infants from non-English speaking homes, and the more mixed language background of U.K.-born pupils in multi-national communities and schools. A report for the Schools Council by Mrs. Diana Stoker made it clear that in 1967 almost no language teaching of immigrant pupils was being done in infant schools.[17] Since then teachers have begun to take increasing interest in work with this age-group. It seems clear that the expansion of effort should in the next phase be directed to school-based teaching, with special attention to infants.

A.T.E.P.O.s, the N.C.C.I. and the Leeds Project

One of the great difficulties facing teachers of immigrant children, whether in ordinary classes or special language classes, was the absence of suitable written and other teaching material, and of information on the background of the children which could help them to understand the children's difficulties. The initiative in providing such material was to come not from the top but from the base.

The first voluntary Association of Teachers of English to Pupils from Overseas was established in the West Midlands as early as 1962. It had from the start close links with the Birmingham L.E.A. R. D. Chapman, its founder, headed Birmingham's special language department. Covering a very wide area, it had a circulation list of about 100 and an active membership of thirty or forty, including both teachers in primary schools, and university lecturers. In March 1965, the London A.T.E.P.O. was formed. During the following three years, branches were formed in the West Riding, Coventry, Bedford, Slough, and Derby, and the A.T.E.P.O.s have now been federated. Their main function has been to provide 'emergency do-it-yourself' work to help teachers deal with everyday teaching. This has meant organizing conferences and work-shop sessions, circulating duplicated bibliographies and teaching notes, and setting up study groups on special subjects. The A.T.E.P.O.s have also functioned as ginger groups to obtain more resources and help from L.E.A.s through developing fruitful links with local H.M.I.s and administrators. Getting more adequate training facilities has been one of the main objectives, and the A.TE.P.O.s have also tried to build up contacts with colleges of education.

Another voluntary organization, whose impact upon the situation was less immediate but covered more ground, was the Education Panel of the National Committee for Commonwealth Immigrants. The panel brought together for monthly meetings a number of educationalists of high calibre, and operated as a stimulant to action on the part of established bodies, in particular the institutes and colleges of education. In 1967, the teacher training sub-committee held two major conferences on the subject, organized with the co-operation of H.M. Inspectorate. Two pamphlets, one on the educational background of West Indian children, the other giving practical advice to teachers of E2L, were published.

The work of the N.C.C.I. panel has been continued through its successor, the Education Advisory Commission.

It was largely as a result of A.T.E.P.O. and N.C.C.I. pressure that some progress was made in teacher training. In September 1965, Ann Blatch, now Ann Fraser, formerly a teacher in Huddersfield, started the first one-term in-service training course in E2L at the Institute of Education, London, attended by fifteen teachers. In 1967, her course was taken over by the I.L.E.A. in July 1968, the N.C.C.I. was able to list only two colleges of education which provided similar in-service training.

At the beginning of 1967, few teacher training institutions were showing interest in language teaching or race relations. Two years later there had been a considerable improvement. A survey of colleges conducted by Ken Millins, principal of Edgehill College at Ormskirk, late in 1968, obtained a 63% response. Two thirds of respondents were providing or intending to provide courses in teaching of immigrant pupils (i.e. primarily language teaching) and just over 30% were offering courses in Education in a Multi-Cultural Society. Many of these courses were optional. Of the compulsory ones, just under half occupied at most 10 hours.[18]

Thus, most of the burden of teacher training has been placed on the L.E.A.s and the teachers' own voluntary groups. Some L.E.A.s have provided a range of in-service training. (The I.L.E.A. holds, in addition to its one-term course, one-week full-time courses for its new recruits from training colleges, part of an existing training provision for teachers going to schools with special difficulties.) But not all L.E.A.s were interested, and it was not impossible in 1967 for a probationary teacher to find herself, without warning or preparation, placed in charge of a reception class for forty infant children of immigrants.

Meanwhile, the most important attempt to meet the needs of teachers on a sufficiently large scale arose from the in-itiative, late in 1964, of June Derrick, University of Leeds. She drew up a proposal for the establishment of a national centre to pro-vide practical help to schools admitting large numbers of immigrant pupils. The proposal was submitted to the newly established Schools Council, whose reaction was to sponsor a feasibility study, undertaken by June Derrick, to find out the extent to which local education authorities were aware of the factors involved, the size of the immigrant in-take into local authority schools, and the nature of the pedagogical problem. The results, which have never been published in full, formed the first comprehensive study of local authority practice, and, in fact, of teaching practice in the individual schools. It seemed likely to the council that the survey would show the need for development work in the preparation of new materials suitable to the classroom situation and the real life experience of the immigrant children. On the basis of June Derrick's report, a three-year development project ('the Leeds Project') was set up at the Institute of Education of the University of Leeds in September 1966, with an initial budget of £50,000 later raised to £77,000.

The objectives of the Leeds Project were to provide teach-ing materials for pupils with inadequate English, of Asian and Southern European parentage. Its first aim was the pro-duction of an introductory two-term course for children aged from 8 to 13. Approximately 150 teachers in thirty-eight L.E.A.s were involved in trying out the new materials during the project, so that, in effect, it also functioned as a training for teachers. The introductory course was published in January 1969.[19] But in addition, it was planned to produce a more advanced course for the same age group, a course for the newly-arrived teenagers, and to conduct research into the situation of 5-to 7-year-olds. The Leeds Project was therefore oriented in an extremely practical way, and began to affect the school situation from the start, through the teachers involved in the trial of the new materials and by becoming, inevitably, an information source for many others. In the autumn term of 1968 the small project staff were committed to running two complete short courses in different colleges of education. The Leeds Project may be said to represent the first attempt by any of the central institutions of the educational system to tackle the problem of resources. June Derrick's feasibility study, together with the report on infant schools subsequently conducted for the Leeds Project by Diana Stoker, remain the only comprehensive and detailed studies of schools where there are immigrant pupils with inadequate English.

West Indian Children

All these activities were devised to meet the needs of the non-English-speaking child, and in the provision of special classes, the production of materials, and the analysis of the classroom situation, attention was in practice focused on children of Asian or Southern European parents. Only in a few exceptional schools and authorities was there evidence of a serious attempt to meet the education needs of children of parents from the Caribbean countries, or to help class teachers to overcome the difficulties which they felt in tackling the problems.

Both June Derrick and others were aware of the need for analysis and for the production of materials to help teachers of West Indian children, and in 1967, a project with aims similar to those of the Leeds Project began at Birmingham University, under Professors Sinclair and Taylor. The Schools Council contributed the budget of £20,000. The lack of an objective study has meant not only that teacher training and teacher-aid programmes have been held back, but also that almost all comment tends to be about 'problem' children. Moreover, the problems are often defined exclusively from the point of view of the teacher, who may not be free from bias.

The problems faced by very many pupils who have come from the Caribbean, or whose parents did, seem to spring from several different sources. There is, first of all, for a minority of these children an unexpected linguistic barrier when they first enter school; they cannot follow the teacher, nor make themselves understood. Unlike children from non-English speaking homes, they are unlikely to have been warned about this. A rather larger proportion may be able to follow and make themselves understood, yet their command of English may be inadequate for educational purposes. In a return which Birmingham L.E.A. made to June Derrick's Schools Council inquiry in 1965, of 8,242 immigrant pupils so designated, over half were children of West Indian parents. Nineteen per cent of the West Indian pupils in the I.L.E.A. sample were said to need further intensive language-teaching. The D.E.S.s criteria for assessing language ability are likely, as John Power has argued, to conceal rather than to illuminate the linguistic needs of West Indian children.

Secondly, many of the problems the children face derive from economic circumstances. A high proportion of Caribbean families in Britain are living in one-room homes; a high proportion of Caribbean mothers go out to work. These factors alone mean that it is common for the children to have led unusually confined pre-school lives, and to have had only limited opportunities for proper exercise and stimulating play and talk. These problems are shared with many non-Caribbean families.

Thirdly, some teachers take the view that West Indian parents are exceptionally demanding of their children, that they expect them to do well at school, and at the same time to contribute to domestic chores and share family responsibilities at home. This may create difficulties, especially for children who have arrived in Britain after long separation from their mother or father, who may have been strongly attached to their substitute parents in the West Indies, and are now having to live in a totally new family.

Finally, there are problems which derive from prejudice and low expectations of teachers, and the effect on the pupils' motivation and relationships in school of racial prejudice and discrimination outside school.

The vast majority of Caribbean children have simply entered ordinary classes in their local schools, and have been dependent upon the interest and energy of head and class teachers. On the whole they have not been included in the available specialized language classes. At the secondary level, many have been placed in 'lower' streams or remedial classes. Some teachers are clearly worried about this situation, and this concern was expressed very clearly in discussion groups of London teachers at a conference on English for English-Speaking Immigrants in January 1969.[20]

We should remain especially alert to the possibility that immigrants are failing to reach their potential attainment simply because of their difficulties with language ... an apparently undue proportion of immigrants remain in our 'lower streams' and ... in some schools immigrants are put into remedial classes, without any special encouragement to move out to courses with stronger academic ambitions as soon as they have mastered their language difficulties. They may then tend to respond only at a remedial or backward level.

The group was worried by 'remedial' class expectation which was unusually low, over-specialized and led to under-achieving. This is particularly worrying when the ease with which West Indian pupils make their way into 'remedial' classes is considered.

Another worrying problem, which affects smaller numbers of children, but which may represent a significant injustice, is the disproportionate placement of West Indian pupils in schools for the 'educationally sub-normal'. The I.L.E.A. Report[21] suggested that many West Indian pupils in E.S.N. schools should not be there, and other boroughs have published figures which raise considerable doubts about the referral system, particularly when there seems as yet to be no 'culture free' or 'culture fair' test of children's ability. In an interesting article published in October 1969, a community relations worker from the London borough of Ealing contrasted the attention devoted to Asian pupils (11%

of all pupils) by the L.E.A with the lack of attention to West Indian pupils (6% of all pupils). At the same time, the proportion of these groups in special schools was, respectively, 3% and 19%. The article concludes: 'there is the possibility of a whole racial group being labelled as less capable in the area of school attainment, with all the dangers of this becoming a self-fulfilling prophecy'.[22]

Achievement

The problems of Caribbean children in schools overlap with those of Asian and South European and other non-English speaking groups, and also with those of some English children. What prospects have all the immigrant pupils of achieving educational equality with English children of English parents, i.e. of achieving a similar spread of attainment? Two studies[23] suggest that those who have had all their schooling in the U.K. are doing at least as well as their English peers, but the number of such children surveyed is only just over 100, and there is some evidence to suggest that within this group, children of parents of some nationalities may do worse than others. It would be rash to generalize about the achievements of the 'second generation' on the basis of research so far conducted. Reports from teachers of immigrant children in infant schools give ground for concern that a lack of knowledge of English, or lack of mastery of other basic skills, may hamper immigrant pupils at each subsequent stage in their school career. There are, of course, counter-examples, children who start in a backward primary group, and finish in a grammar school sixth form. But enough is known generally about the cumulative effect of 'failure' in the early stages of learning, for this to be regarded as a major handicap for immigrant pupils.

As for the children who are themselves immigrants, it is fairly certain that as a group they will find themselves in the 'below average' categories of attainment, and that their academic attainment will be less than their spread of intelligence would have permitted.

CONCLUSIONS

There is no doubt that the most important single decision during the entire evolution of policy was that taken by the

Schools Council in 1965 to commission June Derrick's study of L.E.A. and classroom practices. It led, of course, to the productive and immediately useful work of the Leeds Project. More significant, however, was the perspective of the project, which provided a more realistic and a more reputable basis for the development of policies in the future. This perspective was radically different from that of the Commonwealth Immigrants Advisory Council in its Second Report, of the Department of Education and Science in its Circular 7/65, and of the Government in the White Paper.

The main policy issue defined in the earlier period, 1963–65, was the problem created by the numbers of immigrants entering the schools. The policy-makers' main concern was to minimize disturbance to the normal (i.e. the previous) routine of the class or school. They expressed fear lest the class teachers would devote too much time to immigrant at the expense of non-immigrant pupils. The school's role in the process of integration was seen as a social one: it would train immigrants to be British, and provide a location where they could mix with English children.

The Leeds Project was set up to equip teachers for a specific education job – the teaching of English as a second language. It was concerned to do this whether the teacher had 2% or 100% of immigrant pupils in his class. The proportion of children with inadequate English would affect the organization of language classes, but teachers with low proportions needed help as much as those with high proportions. The evidence from June Derrick's and Diana Stoker's reports suggested that some of the most effective teaching of non-English speaking children was taking place in schools which had had high intakes of immigrant pupils over a number of years. The greatest danger, stressed in both reports, was not that immigrant pupils received too much attention, but that the attention they received was too limited and too inexpert and that they became mere passengers, instead of participants, in the educational process. This danger was greater where they formed very low proportions in class. The reports found that the simple presence of immigrant and native-born pupils in a class, still less in a school, did not amount to integration in any real sense. Without more attention to their particular educational needs, the children were unlikely to be able either to join in the life of the school, or to compete on equal terms after leaving school.

The main instrument of official policy, devised on the basis of the pre-1965 perspective, was dispersal: L.E.A.s were advised by the D.E.S. to intervene to prevent the proportion of immigrant pupils rising above a third in any school. But the main policy imperatives revealed by June Derrick's and Diana Stoker's reports were the need to provide language materials, books, and in-service training for serving teachers; the need to alter initial training courses so that language-teaching for immigrants was included; and the need to provide nursery schools in areas of immigrant settlement.

The dispersal proposals were not linked with any real attempt by the D.E.S. to tackle the lack of resources, particularly the shortage of appropriately trained teachers, and of equipment to help them. As a result, they appear as an attempt to dodge the issue of resources, by making the problem 'disappear' by sleight of hand. When there were only a few children of immigrants in a class, they often hardly impinged at all on the teacher's consciousness. The dispersal policy also fitted some teachers' definition of their problem in terms of discipline: they wanted to reduce the numbers of immigrants in order to reduce their disruptive potential.

Some, but not all. As we have seen, there was a powerful feeling among many teachers, especially those in primary schools, that the schools should serve the neighbourhoods in which they were sited. These teachers were prepared to adapt their techniques, and to give their time. They received no leadership from the D.E.S., practical or political, in a situation in which there was a need for in-service training, for liaison between teachers, and for teachers' centres. Above all, there was a need for an interpretation of events which would attract teachers into schools with immigrant pupils, rather than repel them from the situation. This was not provided.

Why was it that the central response to the presence of immigrant pupils was so negative and so slow? It is impossible on the basis only of published material to give a full answer. The D.E.S, the most 'interventionist' in style of all the social service departments, was at its weakest when it came to planning for new developments in the system. Theoretically, H.M.I.s could have foreseen the increases in the number of children of immigrants, and could have made plans to provide the necessary information and to examine in advance the various arrangements which would be necessary to receive and to teach the children. This was not done. As John Power has pointed out:

The structure and traditions of the department would have tended to inhibit its inspectors from doing more than-arranging (or stimulating others to arrange) various conferences and courses, while hoping that interested groups and individuals among teachers and others might emerge to take more positive action.[24]

Generally, the reduced emphasis on the dispersal policy is to be welcomed, since it allows the real issues to come to the fore. In particular it should now be possible to distinguish between a policy aimed at keeping schools *racially* mixed, and one aimed at creating mixed-*class* schools, or breaking up schools with very high proportions of deprived or disadvantaged children. The former goal would apply to fewer schools, since the majority of schools where there are coloured pupils have been mixed schools. Figures for January 1967 showed that about 3,700 schools had 2% to 20% of immigrant pupils (D.E.S. definition); about 500 had 20% to $33\frac{1}{3}$%, and 345 had over $33\frac{1}{3}$%.[25] London figures for January 1968 showed that half the immigrant pupils in primary schools formed less than 30% of their schools, another 28% formed less than 50% and 6.5% were in schools where they formed over 60%.[26] Analysis of immigrant households in 1966 suggests that the numbers of schools with high proportions of children of coloured immigrant parents will increase at least up to 1971 as the under-fours become of school age.[27] On the other hand the numbers of new arrivals are falling. Whether the high concentrations continue into the late 1970s will depend upon housing policies, particularly as these affect the second generation of West Indians in Britain. It is possible that the numbers of schools with over two-thirds of their enrolment black could nonetheless be kept multi-racial, if this were the goal, through careful administration of catchment areas – in some cases re-drawing them, in others insisting that schools paid attention to them and did not reject immigrant pupils. If on the other hand, the second aim, that of achieving mixed-class schools, were the goal, this would be a more complex policy to work, and would, of course, involve dispersing white English as well as children of immigrants.

At the present time, however, there are a whole set of problems faced by the predominantly black school, the de-prived white school, and the typical multi-racial school. These are problems both of academic results, and of social relationships within the school, between pupils, and between teacher and pupil. They involve deprivation, and in the multi-racial schools problems of cultural and linguistic difference, and problems of race relations. A partial solution may be seen in the full implementation of the Plowden rec-ommendations on E.P.A. areas; in particular its recommen-dations on pre-school provision. Another partial solution lies in revising teacher training curricula, and the teaching prac-tice experience of student teachers. But even a major re-allocation of resources of this kind would be insufficient, because the schools, perhaps particularly the secondary schools, are directly affected by race relations in the outside world. For the multi-racial schools to succeed, a stronger political commitment to a multi-racial society is required.

REFERENCES

1. J. A. G. Griffith, *Central Departments and Local Authorities* (London, Allen & Unwin, 1966), p. 523.
2. For a description of the report, carried out by June Derrick, see *English for the Children of Immigrants*, Schools Council, Working Paper No. 13 (London, H.M.S.O., 1967).
3. *15 to 18* (The Crowther Report) (London, H.M.S.O., 1960). Terms of reference: to consider in relation to the changing social needs of our society, and the needs of its individual citizens, the education of boys and girls between 15 and 18, and in particular to consider the balance at various levels of general and specialized studies and to examine the inter-relationship of the various stages of education. *Half our Future* (The Newsom Report) (London, H.M.S.O., 1963).

Terms of reference: to consider the education between the ages of 13 and 16 of pupils of average or less than average ability who are, or will be, attending full-time courses either at school or in establishments of further education. *Higher Education* (The Robbins Report) (London, H.M.S.O., 1963). Terms of reference: to review the pattern of full-time higher education in Great Britain, and in the light of national resources to advise H.M. Government on which principles its long-term development should be based. In particular, to advise whether there should be any changes in that pattern, whether any new types of institution are desirable, and whether any modifications should be made in the present arrangements for planning and coordinating the various types of institution. *Children and Their Primary Schools* (The Plowden Report) (London, H.M.S.O., 1967). Terms of reference: to consider primary education in all its aspects and the transition to secondary education.

An excellent summary of all these reports and the Albemarle Report on the Youth Service has been written by Anne Corbett for the Council for Educational Advance: 'Much to do about Education – a critical survey of the fate of the major education reports',

4. *English for Immigrants*, Ministry of Education pamphlet No. 43 (London, H.M.S.O., 1963).
5. Second Report by the Commonwealth Immigrants Advisory Council (Cmnd. 2266) (London, H.M.S.O., February 1964).
6. *The Education of Immigrants*, Department of Education and Science Circular 7/65 (June 1965) to local education authorities and certain other bodies.
7. *Immigration from the Commonwealth* (Cmnd. 2739) (London, H.M.S.O., August 1965).
8. Hansard, Vol. 685, cols. 433–44, 27th November, 1963.
9. D.E.S, *Statistics of Education*, Vol. 1 (London, H.M.S.O., 1966). There were 131,043 'immigrant pupils', making 1.8% of all pupils: 44% came from the West Indies, 19% from India, 10% from Cyprus, and 6% from Pakistan. Forty-nine per cent had no problem with English; 26% had reasonably good spoken English but weak written English; 19% had some English but needed further training; 6% had no English. The quarter needing further intensive language teaching made up 0.45% of the total school population. For a critical analysis of the department's criteria of assessing language ability, see John Power, *Immigrants in School: a survey of administrative policies* (London, Councils and Education Press, 1967).

10. Inner London Education Authority, *The Education of Immigrant Pupils in Primary Schools: report of a working party of the inspectorate and the school psychological service* (London, I.L.E.A., 1967), para. 44, and Appendix 3, Table F.

11. Ealing International Friendship Council, Education Committee, *The Education of the Immigrant Child in the London Borough of Ealing* (London, E.I.F.C., 1968).

12. Evidence given by the Department of Education and Science to the Select Committee on Race Relations and Immigration on Coloured School Leavers (13th February, 1969).

13. Evidence given by the Department of Education and Science to the Select Committee on Race Relations and Immigration on Coloured School Leavers (13th February, 1969).

14. Estimates submitted to the Home Office by local authorities under Section 11, Local Government Act, 1966.

15. Home Office press release on 'Urban Programme – Second Phase' (30th June, 1969).

16. See, for example, N. Hawkes, *Immigrant Children in British Schools* (London, Pall Mall Press, for Institute of Race Relations, 1966); Schools Council, Working Paper No. 13, op. cit; June Derrick, *Teaching English to Immigrants* (London, Longmans, 1966).

17. Schools Council, unpublished.

18. Evan Reid, education correspondent, 'Rationalising Teacher Training', *Race Today* (December 1969).

19. 'Scope': an introductory English course for immigrant children: Stage 1 London, Books for Schools Ltd, for the Schools Council, 1969.

20. 'English for English Speaking Immigrants', Report of a conference held at Stoke d'Abernon. I.L.E.A. (duplicated) 1969.

21. Inner London Education Authority, 1967, op. cit.

22. Ealing: 'Education and Race', *Race Today* (October 1969).

23. See Inner London Education Authority (1967) op. cit. Appendix III table A–E, also Alan Little *et. al.*, the Education of Immigrant Pupils in Inner London Primary Schools, *Race* (Vol. IX, no. 4, April 1968), and Sylvane Wiles, 'Children from Overseas', Institute of Race Relations *Newsletter* (February and June 1968).

24. John Power's book review in *Education* (Vol. 131, no. 23, June 1968), p. 766.

25. D.E.S. *Statistics of Education*, 1967 (London, H.M.S.O., 1968).

26. Unpublished figures supplied by the I.L.E.A. research department.
27. David Eversley & Fred Sukdeo, *The Dependants of the Coloured Commonwealth Population of England and Wales* (London, I.R.R. 1969).

Chapter Eight

Employment

Earlier when we discussed the migration to Britain in Chapter Three, we concluded that it was the search for jobs that was the prime moving force. It was the jobs that the migrants thought that they could get that drew them to Britain and it is the jobs that they actually obtained which determine their place in British society. The position of any group in society is determined as much by the jobs that its members hold as by any other factor. From our discussion of 1966 census data, it became clear that the coloured immigrant communities have not, as yet, achieved anything like a comparable position to that of the indigenous population in the field of employment. Census data suggest that in part this was due to the reluctance of employers to employ immigrant labour, for reasons above and beyond those of skill. In this chapter, we will pursue this topic and examine it in the whole context of industrial relations. While attention will be paid to the skills of the coloured worker, our primary focus will be on the host society's reaction to the presence of the coloured worker in the labour force. Specifically, this means the examination of the attitudes and behaviour of employers and employees, the policy and the practice of management and unions, and the intervention or non-intervention of the Government and other public bodies.

THE PATTERN OF DISCRIMINATION

The level of jobs that coloured workers have achieved has been considerably lower than that of the rest of the population. In part this has been due to the level of skills of coloured workers (a topic we shall discuss later in this chapter) but we shall take as our starting point the direct evidence concerning discrimination in British industry.

The most important evidence is contained in the P.E.P. report, which was based on research carried out in six selected areas in 1967.[1] Using a threefold approach – interviewing immigrants, interviewing persons in a position to discriminate, that is, employers, and situation testing – the investigators concluded that there was substantial discrimination, largely based on colour, against coloured applicants applying for jobs. In interviews with employment exchanges and employment bureaux it was reported that a large percentage of the users of these facilities discriminated against coloured labour. On another level, a recent study by Bob Hepple cites seventy-five selected examples of discrimination, reported in the press, covering engagement procedures, training, promotion, terms and conditions of work, dismissal procedures, and trade union practices.[2] In studies, such as those by Sheila Patterson in South London[3] and Peter Wright in the Midlands and the North,[4] evidence of discrimination against coloured workers is presented. Recent reports have suggested that coloured graduates are paid less than their white counterparts and that racial discrimination can even operate against the best qualified of scientists.[5]

The pattern of discrimination against coloured workers in British industry disclosed in these and many other studies appears to be so widespread and pervasive that an innocent stranger (or a frustrated black job applicant) could well believe that it is the result of a centralized directive, enthusiastically implemented, that the employment of coloured labour be restricted to those jobs that white men do not want. This would be a mistake: none of the central triumvirate of the Government, the C.B.I. (for employers), or the T.U.C. (for workers) has ever laid down a deliberate policy of discriminating against the coloured worker. What statements there have been from these bodies have almost always stated a belief in equal opportunity, and expressed confidence in the inherent sense of fair play of the British public – and in particular, of employers, workers, and customers – to see that discrimination on the grounds of race does not occur. But despite these pronouncements, the P.E.P. report showed that many firms had no coloured employees and most of the remainder placed severe limitations on the types of jobs that coloured workers could do. The

Keighley Junior Chamber of Commerce reported in 1966 that they could not find a single white-collar job for coloured school leavers in the town and had found amongst employers in the town every attitude from 'wooden indifference to frank hypocrisy'.[6] This discrepancy between public pronouncement and general practice is a theme that repeats itself throughout the whole employment field.

The coloured worker in Britain has been attempting to enter an industrial system resistant to change, in which decisions are often taken not at national or even regional level but at plant level. In this situation, the employer faced with a coloured job applicant was far more likely to be influenced by local and personal factors than the remote declarations of racial equality by the Government, the T.U.C., and the C.B.I.* In some cases, probably a small minority, the employer would refuse to employ a coloured man because of his own prejudices. More frequently, especially in the earlier days of coloured immigration, the coloured man was an unknown quantity, and the employer's attitude to his employment potential may have been influenced by uninformed views derived from the British colonial experience. Employers were doubtful of the possible contributions that a coloured man was capable of making and feared the reaction of the other workers or customers. For their part, workers were suspicious of coloured labour and of the use that employers might make of it. It was feared that coloured workers might be used as strike-breakers and that unscrupulous employers would pay coloured workers lower than standard wages. Both workers and employers were ignorant and suspicious of the standards prevailing in the countries from which the immigrants had come and were unwilling to believe that the West Indian or the African could be a skilled man.

Most employers therefore approached the question of whether to employ coloured immigrants with some trepidation. The easiest answer was to do nothing. In a conservative milieu where anything new and strange could disturb the delicate equilibrium of industrial relations, the best policy seemed to be to stay with the known, tested

* The C.B.I. made no specific statements on racial equality prior to 1967. See below, Employers' Associations, in this chapter.

labour supply. A few employers and workers were willing to give the newcomers a fair chance to prove themselves. But the foundation of a pattern of discrimination against the coloured worker was laid down by the mass of employers, unwilling to look at this new source of labour unless they had no other choice. However, the continuous labour shortages of the 1950s and early 1960s created a situation in which some employers seemed to have no alternative but to employ coloured labour. Thus the majority of firms only started employing coloured labour when no other sources of labour were readily available.[7]

In a situation in which only certain employers were willing to employ coloured workers and then only for limited types of jobs, concentrations built up. Demands for quotas were made by white workers and the resultant quotas – usually informally agreed – reduced to an even greater extent job opportunities. Once it was known by labour exchanges and the coloured community that a particular firm would employ them, the number of applicants they received increased and often demands for quota restrictions from white workers would also increase. Some employers, less scrupulous than others, took advantage of the employment difficulties of coloured workers and confirmed the worst fears of English workers by using coloured labour as cheap labour, often to work in intolerable conditions. These were exceptions, but rare though they may have been, they exacerbated suspicions between white and coloured labour.

Bars on the promotion of coloured labour to supervisory positions became fairly general throughout industry. Instances of upgrading to supervisory positions with some authority over white workers have been almost non-existent. The P.E.P. report stated 'at manual worker level coloured people had positions of authority only over other coloured people'.[8] The reason has been a fear of the resistance of white workers to taking orders from coloured supervisors. This bar on promotion has also had some effect on recruitment in jobs where a worker might reach a supervisory position over a number of years.

In this way, despite repeated Government statements and exhortations and T.U.C. resolutions on equality, a pattern of discrimination has been established in employment. This discrimination has manifested itself in recruitment, the type of job available, quotas, ethnic work units, and opportunity for promotion. It was caused by the mass of employers and workers acting in what they perceived to be their own best interests. Employers, unwilling to experiment and fearful of disturbing the industrial peace, and workers, suspicious of both the coloured man and their employers, combined to exclude the stranger.

Government

Throughout the 1950s and the early 1960s, the official policy of the Government was occasional exhortation, not usually backed up by any action. In periods of recession and at the time of Notting Hill, Government exhortations became more frequent. The general policy however was one of *laissez-faire*: it was assumed that such problems as arose in the field of employment would work themselves out over time. By 1961, the only action the Ministry of Labour had taken was unofficial counts of coloured unemployed which continued on a new basis after the Commonwealth Immigrants Act of 1962.

However, the Government was involved, from the very start of the migration, with the coloured worker's search for work. Sheila Patterson reports the manager of a South London employment exchange as saying: 'Even without reading the papers I can always tell when a new shipload's arrived. Next morning there'll be seventy or more round at the exchange bright and early. You can't say they're not keen to work.'[9] Employment exchanges were run on the general *credo* of public service with no discrimination on grounds of race and they came into direct collision with employers' preferences. Until 1954, any vacancy notified which put 'unreasonable restrictions' on the kind of worker wanted was to be refused. From 1954 until 1964, exchanges were to attempt to persuade an employer to change his mind, but if this was not possible they were to accept 'no coloured', or 'whites only' requests. This policy left the employment exchanges in an ambiguous position, in which they could be accused of pandering to an employer's prejudice. They answered that they were protecting the coloured job appli-cant from unnecessary humiliation.

In July 1964, the Minister of Labour told the House of Commons that exchanges had to note restrictions laid down by employers, otherwise they would send men for jobs they had no chance of obtaining and would be unable to continue the process of persuasion to have these restrictions withdrawn. Later in his speech, after critical questions, the Minister said, 'to the extent that where it is shown that continued resistance is due to prejudice, eventually and after due consideration we are prepared to withdraw the facilities of the unemployment exchanges'.[10] The final sanction of withdrawing facilities has almost never been used and the procedure by which this is done is extremely cumbersome.[11] The policy was further strengthened towards the end of 1966, but the ministry would accept quotas where a 'reasonable proportion' of coloured workers are employed. The 1968 Race Relations Act has legitimized quotas in its racial balance clause. It is not completely clear what the Department of Employment and Productivity will do in the case of discrimination coming to the notice of its labour exchanges. In evidence to the Select Committee on Race Relations in 1969 the D.E.P. showed itself reluctant to contemplate withdrawing facilities and possibly reporting an employer to the Race Relations Board.[12] The D.E.P. wished to influence employers by persuasion and also would seem not to want to endanger the voluntary and co-operative relationships which exist between officials and employers.

The Youth Employment Service has faced similar problems to those of the labour exchanges and in a report in 1968 suggested that apart from the question of discrimination immigrant school-leavers presented other problems. These were educational inadequacies and over-ambitiousness among some of the less able.[13] David Beetham, in his study on school-leavers in Birmingham, identified what he described as 'unrealistic aspirations' among immigrant children (most of whom were newly-arrived). Considerable debate has ensued on this subject; the Y.E.S. in evidence to the Select Committee accepted uncritically the thesis that unrealistic aspirations are the main problem for coloured school leavers and discrimination is not a very serious problem.[14] (See also Chapter 11.)

Government policy has generally reflected their reluctance to be actively involved in this field and attempts to introduce legislation dealing with racial discrimination in employment came to nothing before 1965. In 1966 Roy Jenkins as Home Secretary undertook to start consultations on the possible amendment of the Fair Wages Resolution, which all government contractors have to agree to comply with, to include a non-discriminatory clause. In October 1969, after a succession of reports endorsing this policy, Roy Jenkins, as Chancellor of the Exchequer, finally stated that Government departments would be prepared to withhold contracts from firms practising racial discrimination in employment.

Another indication of Government's unwillingness to become involved has been its attitude to the collection of statistics distinguishing by colour or ethnic origin. Until recently no need for such statistics was seen; it was argued that to collect them was discrimination in itself. Without any reliable statistics the real dimensions of the problems that were developing could be ignored and when they finally forced their way to the attention of policy-makers the basis for informed action was absent. In the last two years official views have changed and in a number of statements in 1969 Government has agreed to keep records and to encourage other bodies to keep them.[15]

Government has been intimately concerned as an employer with the problems of race relations in employment from the very start. Either directly in the civil service or indirectly through nationalized industries or the social services such as the National Health Service, Government is by far the largest employer in the country. There have been considerable variations in the policies adopted and it has been suggested by some critics that the official record does not always reach the exemplary standards which are desirable. In their report, the Select Committee commented that Government should give a lead: while welcoming the extent of recruitment of coloured people to responsible positions in the civil service, they thought that more might be done in recruiting coloured candidates.[16] The Select Committee was more critical of the record of local government as major employers:

... they could and should set a good example locally ... In most of the places we visited, however, few coloured people ... seemed to be employed by the authorities at the town hall in positions of responsibility.[17]

They therefore recommended that local government should, like the civil service, take positive steps to recruit coloured workers.

Because of the reluctance to keep or to admit to keeping statistics, it is difficult to assess the relative performance of different sectors of public employment. According to the Civil Service Department in 1969 a recent estimate of the number of coloured civil servants was that there were approximately 17,500 of whom 850 were executive officers and above (including professionals), and 3,300 clerical officers.[18] Very detailed statistics have been supplied by the army on the number, rank, length of service and corps of coloured male soldiers. In 1969 just under 46% of coloured male soldiers were N.C.O.'s compared to just over 41% in 1968. This compared with 52% of all soldiers who are N.C.O.'s and this small discrepancy is probably mainly accountable in terms of length of service. Thus over half of all coloured soldiers with nine or more years' service hold the rank of sergeant or above.[19] The information on the army is exceptionally interesting in its detail and the way it shows change over time. The civil service and army evidence is also of interest in view of the marked reluctance of private industry to promote coloured workers to positions of authority over white workers. The figures for the army also show that a very high proportion of coloured soldiers are tradesmen (60%), and in the civil service there are a high proportion in white-collar jobs. These figures provide an oblique comment on private industry's assessment of coloured workers' skills and potential.

Through the National Health Service, Government employs a very large number of coloured workers ranging from highly qualified medical staff to ward orderlies and catering staff. As we saw in earlier chapters a very high proportion of some immigrant groups were working in medical and dental services and new migrant doctors receive the majority of all B vouchers. In 1967 approximately half the

junior doctors working in N.H.S. hospitals were born outside the U.K. and Eire; but only about one-sixth of those in
the grade of senior registrar were born outside the U.K. and
Eire. Generally, overseas doctors work in the non-teaching
hospitals and they tend to be concentrated in the least
'fashionable' specialities such as geriatrics. Similarly there is
evidence that coloured nurses are less likely to be in teaching
hospitals than their white colleagues, and that promotion is
more difficult for them.[20] Despite the very large numbers of
skilled staff employed in the health services and their essential role in these services, they do not seem to have achieved
as yet full equality of opportunity.

Some of the very biggest employers of coloured labour
have been the nationalized industries and in theory they
have operated policies of non-discrimination, although practice has varied between industries and within industries. Two
of the most important employers of coloured labour have
been British Rail and London Transport. Both have recruited labour directly outside the U.K., in Barbados, and
both have employed coloured workers from the very earliest
period of coloured migration. It is easier to describe London
Transport's policy and practice than that of British Rail, as
the former has a very highly centralized recruitment and
promotion system, while that of the latter is far more diverse. Recruitment by London Transport for bus and train
staff has operated on a basis that would seem to be free of
discrimination. Records are kept for the number of coloured
staff in certain jobs and in 1969 there were 4,700 bus drivers
and conductors and some 2,200 railway operating staff.
However, the reluctance and the length of time which it took
for the first coloured bus inspector to be appointed in the
latter half of 1968 provoked considerable adverse comment.[21] There has been some promotion on the railways,
where seniority is of great importance, and the L.T.B. themselves have stated that it is on the railways side that most
promotions have occurred.[22] It is possible that the greater
difficulties experienced by the L.T.B. over promotion on the
buses is due to the peculiarly exposed and isolated position
of a bus inspector compared with most supervisory jobs,
including those on the railways.

In general, the L.T.B. has followed a policy of dispersing

coloured workers, where possible, without restricting itself to any quotas. This has helped the absorption of coloured workers and has given the L.T.B. more flexibility in its recruitment policies.[28] The picture on British Rail is more confused and in general it is fair to say that there have been more obstacles to promotion on British Rail than in London Transport. In certain areas, no coloured staff have been recruited, while in others, there have been bars on coloured workers except in the lowest grades. Often, wide variations in recruiting policy have been seen in adjacent areas falling under different jurisdictions. Thus, in 1966, a West Indian working as a guard at Marylebone applied for a transfer to Euston and was officially informed that it was a policy at Euston not to employ coloured guards. Following disclosures in the press, the policy at Euston – stated to have been agreed between management and men – was rescinded and the transfer effected.

Finally, in reviewing official policy, it is worth mentioning some other sectors of public employment. Many municipal bus companies and also bus companies which are subsidiaries of the Transport Holding Company (a public corporation) have operated, and some still continue to operate, bars on the recruitment of coloured staff. Directors of transport companies have stated that coloured conductors and drivers are unable to do the work or are unacceptable to the general public – despite the contrary experiences of those bus companies elsewhere who do employ coloured labour. One explanation for the absence of coloured staff has been that white labour is available – an ingenuous explanation that implies coloured labour will only be considered if white labour does not want particular occupations. Some local bus companies have also become embroiled in bitter disputes over the right of Sikh employees to wear turbans. The diehard fanaticism of the resistance of some local transport departments has contrasted strangely to the placid acceptance of the turban by other bus companies.

To summarize local government employment practice is more difficult than for any other sector of public employment. In local government, diversity of policy as well as practice is to be found. Different departments of local authorities are often almost separate enterprises, and it has been not unknown for one department of an authority to recruit coloured labour and another department of the same authority to operate a colour bar. Most major local authorities do employ coloured staff and some local authorities have been among the best in offering full opportunities for coloured staff. Nonetheless, as a generalization the Select Committee were probably correct in suggesting that there was considerable scope for local authorities to re-examine their employment practices towards coloured workers.

Discrimination undoubtedly exists in many forms in employment in the public sector, but certain aspects differentiate it sharply from that in the private sector. Due to its nature, public employment recognizes standards of pay, unions, and so on, and the extreme exploitation of coloured workers, such as occurs – if only occasionally – in private employment, is rare or non-existent. The use of ethnic work units which is fairly common in some sectors of private industry and which produces a situation of go-betweens, straw-bosses, and is an open invitation to corruption and bribery, is very rare in public employment. Finally, discrimination in much of the public sector is restrained by the *credo* of non-discrimination. In the last resort, discriminatory practices in central government employment and the nationalized industries are the responsibility of a minister of the Crown who is forced to act if the discrimination is too blatant and the publicity too great. Throughout the field of public employment those who make policy at all levels and those who implement policy are publicly accountable. This public accountability is not of such a searching quality as to eradicate discrimination, but it does limit its scope and inhibits to a degree those who would practice a policy of discrimination. Hence, while discrimination exists in the field of public employment, the coloured worker is likely to find that his employment opportunities are a great deal better than normally obtain in private employment.

Trade Unions

At its annual conference in 1955, the policy of the Trade Union Congress was stated clearly and explicitly:

This Congress condemns all manifestations of racial discrimination or colour prejudice whether by Government, employers or workers. It urges the General Council to lose no opportunity to make trade union attitudes on this issue perfectly clear.

Since then resolutions have been passed at annual conferences of the T.U.C. declaring the trade union movement's opposition to all forms of racial discrimination. The trade union movement, as a whole, stands firmly on a policy of equality and non-discrimination. But a closer examination of the situation shows that policy and practice are not always in step.

At the centre, the policy is clear, but as one moves nearer the shop floor, the picture becomes blurred. Little advice seem to have filtered from national offices of unions to regional, district, and branch officials. Beryl Radin, writing in 1966, revealed that the T.U.C. had not communicated with local trades councils on the subject of co-operation with the local voluntary liaison committees set up to promote integration.[24] Trade union policy also suffers from the confusion that to make any special provision for the special needs of coloured workers would be to act in a discriminatory manner which would create or accentuate problems. An illustration of this attitude was Lord Collinson's answer on behalf of the T.U.C. to a question from the Select Committee about special training facilities.

This is the fundamental position of the T.U.C. We believe that if you start creating special machinery for coloured people then you are underlining the differences – the thing we should be seeking to avoid. Coming to this question of special training facilities, I think the answer is contained in this: if we had separate schools, primary schools and so on, for coloured people and white people. ... we would say 'This is apartheid and all wrong', so this is an extension of this into industry.[25]

The confusion in this statement between special provisions for certain specific needs, which can often be met by flexible adaptations of existing facilities, with 'separate development' is blatantly obvious. Nonetheless, there have been some unions and union officials who have attempted to meet the needs of immigrants by providing literature in different languages, explaining more carefully the role of unions and British industrial procedures, and generally taking time and care to integrate immigrants fully into union activities. But the more common attitude however has been that there is no need to make any special effort at all.

Most of the evidence available on trade union membership suggests that West Indians are as willing to join as English workers when approached. A study carried out in Nottingham found that rates of union membership of West Indians and English were very similar.[26] In some instances, unions have been introduced into factories that were previously non-union by coloured workers, especially Indians. The evidence on the membership rates of Indians and Pakistanis is more confusing and many union officials report difficulty in dealing with these groups.

A study of the interaction of unions and coloured workers is currently being carried out in Bradford by a team under the direction of Mrs. Sheila Allen, and some of their preliminary findings are worth noting.[27] The most frequent response of trade union officials to questions on recruitment was that no special difficulties were encountered in the recruitment of immigrants. Where difficulties were cited they included language problems, and disillusionment with and lack of trust of unions by coloured workers. Nearly all the officials thought that the unions were doing everything possible to involve immigrants in union affairs. Despite this, immigrants were less unionized than indigenous labour in Bradford and this was due only in part to the type of industries in which they worked. One explanation offered was that in the trades in which immigrants were most concentrated, unions were often weak and did not pursue active membership policies. It was suggested that any ignorance and suspicion which the immigrants may have shown was reciprocated by many of the officials.

On the other side of the picture immigrant workers' views of trade unions were also studied.* Just over half the Pakistanis interviewed thought that trade unions could be of help to immigrants, but many of these replies were qualified and conditional on trade unions changing certain of their

---

* Only Pakistani responses have as yet been analysed.

practices with immigrant workers. Often Pakistani respondents felt that unions had not helped or responded to their needs, and were only helpful for English workers. Immigrant views could be summed up as a series of demands for direct representation in the union structure, especially where a majority of workers were immigrants.

The Bradford study concluded that unions had failed to take action, 'not only on the level of disputes and compensation – but also on the general level of discrimination'. It is suggested that the problems raised by immigrants are only part and parcel of the problems of organization and participation faced by unions today. Better communications, which the unions often regard as the solution, is not seen as anything like the whole answer.

Many immigrant organizations encourage their members to join trade unions and actively participate in their affairs. Beryl Radin found that a number of unions had coloured shop stewards and also a few coloured branch chairmen, treasurers and other officials, sometimes in predominantly white branches.[28] A number of other studies have also indicated the presence of coloured shop stewards. Participation of coloured members in education courses and week-end schools run by unions has also been noted. Nevertheless, it would appear that few, if any, coloured trade union members have reached the higher decision-making positions in trade unions or are paid full-time officials of unions.

In a number of cases, lack of consultation by union officials acting on behalf of coloured workers has led to bitter disputes. In a strike at Preston, the workers, mainly Indians, did not accept an agreement which raised their work load for a small wage rise and went on strike. Their fellow white workers did not support them and the union stigmatized the strike as 'racial' and gave it no support. After a bitter three-week strike, the strikers returned to work.[29] However, at a later date the white workers were forced to accept the same conditions which were originally imposed on only the coloured workers.[30]

Another strike which ended in total disarray was in Southall where district officials of the union gave support to the strikers (mainly Indian). The union had been introduced into the firm (which was extremely anti-union) by Indian workers. After a long history of disputes, the sacking of an Indian led to a full-scale strike. While officials of the union on the industrial side supported the strikers, the administrative wing of the union refused to make the essential declaration that the strike was official. After a six-week strike the workers returned to work beaten and disorganized. Peter Marsh in his study of the strike,[31] showed that the indecisive attitude of the union was the result of structural factors: the union officials responsible for organizing workers and negotiating on their behalf. Added to this there were complications in communication and inflexibility of interpretation by certain union officials, all of which led to the Indians involved believing that the union had totally failed them. (See also Chapter 11.)

It would be unfair to leave the impression that the unions have done nothing for their coloured membership or have acted in a consistently hostile fashion. The trade union movement is made up of hundreds of unions and millions of members and a body of this size not unnaturally displays a vast diversity of behaviour. Additionally, an assessment of union practice is complicated by two interrelated factors; first, the autonomy of many branches and, secondly, the difficulty of carrying white workers in support of union policy. Thus, the actions of many local branches – openly expressed opposition to the employment of coloured workers or hostility towards the wearing of turbans and beards by Sikhs – are in part due to local officials giving expression to the feelings of their white members. Similarly, the refusal of local officials to support coloured workers' complaints can be due to a fear that they would not be able to carry their members with them. There have been occasions when unions have supported coloured members' claims but have not carried white workers with them and thus the claim has failed.[32] These incidents are a reflection on the inability of the unions to educate their members in the basic principles of trade unionism – unity and brotherhood. The inability of unions to educate their members is not so surprising when the attitudes of some leading trade unionists are examined. The belief that coloured workers contribute little and take greatly is not entirely absent among the upper echelon of trade unionists. Coupled with these stereotypes, the approach of leading trade unionists does not inspire confidence in the whole-hearted way in which they approach the problems faced by coloured workers. The Select Committee stated:

What was disappointing was what appeared to be the somewhat negative reaction of some of the T.U.C. witnesses to the parallel call for positive action to help young immigrants overcome some of their particular problems in employment, including colour discrimination.[33]

The T.U.C. evidence to the Select Committee was hardly a clarion call to equality but rather a fearful look over the shoulder at the prejudice of the general population.[34]

The reactions of the trade unions to coloured workers have been varied. Their policy has been welcoming in theory, but in practice they have often alienated the coloured worker. The sins of the unions have been like those of Government – ones of omission rather than commission. They have failed, with a few notable exceptions, to organize and involve the coloured worker, or to make allowances for the differing cultural and industrial backgrounds from which coloured workers have come. Moreover, they have displayed a rigidity and lack of understanding in their dealings with coloured workers which could have grave repercussions. Finally, and most crucially, the unions, again with a few notable exceptions, have failed to educate their members to face the challenges presented by the presence of the coloured worker in British industry.

Employers' Associations

The role of employers' associations in the field of industrial relations is, in general, more limited than that of unions. Their role in bargaining is usually confined to industry-wide agreements on wages and hours of work, while negotiations on bonus rates, piece rates, and conditions of work are usually the product of bargaining at local level. Questions such as quotas and promotion, would not normally involve an employers' association. And only in the event of disputes would an employers' association be involved. Despite this,

T–H

employers' associations can be influential in advising their members on policy and representing their members' views to the Government and the general public.

The silence of the Confederation of British Industry, on questions of race relations in 1967, ended when the discussions on the extension of Race Relations legislation to cover employment had already made some progress. Among the different strands of the C.B.I. position that have emerged, the first has been that the problem is minimal. At a conference on racial equality in February 1967, a C.B.I. spokesman stated: 'our (C.B.I.) experience is that up to now no serious problems have arisen'.[35] The Director of the Engineering Employers' Federation (the largest industry association in the country) stated: 'We have in our industry to our knowledge little evidence of a serious state of discrimination.'[36] Since the publication of the P.E.P. report in April 1967, the playing down of discrimination as an important factor has been more muted. Secondly, it has been stated that discrimination is more a question of employee and customer resistance rather than the prejudice of the employer. Finally, it has been claimed that the established voluntary machinery in use in industry was more suitable for dealing with complaints of racial discrimination than any intervention by an outside body.

As we saw in Chapter 5, the C.B.I. and the T.U.C. issued a joint statement in January 1967 opposing legislation and expressing confidence in voluntary procedures. Following this the C.B.I. recommended that employers' associations should begin discussing with the appropriate unions to consider setting up voluntary machinery. The Engineering Employers' Federation and the Confederation of Shipbuilding and Engineering Unions set up voluntary machinery in July 1967[37] but after the Act came into force the unions withdrew taking the view that there was no longer any need for the machinery. The opposition of the C.B.I. and the T.U.C. to the 1968 Race Relations Act did have the effect of shaping the very complicated procedures for dealing with employment cases. The Act which allows for industrial machinery to be set up to deal with complaints is a prime example of the tenacity of voluntary procedures in industry and of the shaping of new administrative instruments to the old existent pattern.

The policy of the C.B.I. and other employers' organizations to the presence of the coloured worker in British industry is basically similar to that of Government and unions. Until 1967 the presence of coloured workers was ignored. Since then, stimulated by the threat of legislation and intervention in their preserve, the C.B.I. has been active and helped to set up machinery that seemed to have two purposes: first, the reduction of discrimination by enunciating a general policy of non-discrimination and encouraging the creation of *ad hoc* machinery to deal with complaints and, secondly the avoidance of outside intervention. Recent C.B.I. statements since the passing of the Act have been like those of the T.U.C., full of doubts about the extent to which leadership could be expected from them.[38]

The Coloured Worker

Employers often cite the lack of adequate skills as the reason why they do not employ coloured workers either throughout their organization or in particular posts within the organization. Complaints are made of coloured workers' qualifications and abilities, their slowness, the quality of their workmanship, their inability to communicate in English, their attitude towards work and supervision, their frequent job changing, and the length of time it takes to train them. These and similar complaints are also heard at times from fellow-workers and union officials. In his study, Peter Wright found that the majority of employers thought that the skill levels of coloured workers were lower than those of British workers. Just over half Wright's respondents said that coloured workers were less flexible and needed more supervision than British workers. Finally, the majority of firms said that the labour turn-over of coloured workers was lower than for British workers. One of the most interesting facets of Wright's study was his description of the different ways in which different employers assessed the situation. Not only did different employers assess coloured workers differently but often they contradicted each other's assessments. Furthermore, while some employers thought that West Indians were good workers and other groups bad, other employers gave reverse assessments. In one firm it was claimed that Pakistanis were more educated than Indians, and in an adjacent firm that Indians were more educated than Pakistanis. Both firms preferred to employ the group believed to be less educated.[3,9]

In a study in the wool industry in the West Riding in 1967, twelve out of fourteen employers found Pakistani workers generally comparable in all respects to local labour.[40] Some employers thought that Pakistani labour was superior to other labour that could be recruited for these particular jobs. However, two employers thought that Pakistani labour was inferior with regard to both the quality and quantity of work. Possibly, the most significant point made by many of the respondents satisfied with the standard of Pakistani labour was the need for careful selection. A similar emphasis on careful selection, this time of West Indian workers, was made by employers to Sheila Patterson in her studies in the late 1950s in South London. Quite a few employers indicated that there had been initial problems with standards of work until they learnt to select good West Indian workers.

A study of employment opportunities in office jobs, undertaken by Julia Gaitskell in 1966-67, showed that the belief that coloured workers were not suitably qualified for white-collar work was widely held and self-reinforcing.[41] While the average standard of coloured applicants was probably lower than that of white applicants, many of those with suitable qualifications were rejected. Sometimes the justifications produced to prove that the coloured applicant was not suitable in terms of skill were highly improbable. The manager of one company explained why he had rejected an applicant for a secretarial post - 'Asian . . . a charming woman, 40-ish, capable, been here a long time. Her English was good although not her first language. But we both felt (he and the personnel officer) that if she got excited her English would fall down.' Later in the interview he expressed the opinion 'they (coloured people) do get wildly excited'.

In the very different environment of the East End of London, McPherson found that opinions as to the skills of coloured workers varied as much as elsewhere.[42] In some cases, coloured workers were considered the most valued workers in firms whilst, in others, they were thought to be lazy and poor workmen. In one case, a clothing manufacturer stated that he would not employ immigrants as they could never became tailors or cutters – they were not born to it. This was a surprising statement as the clothing industry had the highest percentage of immigrant workers of any industry in the area and immigrant workers were generally reported to be highly valued by their employers. Another widespread belief about coloured workers is that they frequently change jobs, especially if they think they can earn more money. A study carried out in Nottingham in 1963 found that 63% of West Indian workers had been three years or more in their longest job.[43] The P.E.P. inquiry found that nearly half of all immigrants had been in their present job for three years or more.[44] There is also evidence that the Barbadians, directly recruited by London Transport, have a much lower wastage rate than all other London Transport staff.[45]

Many employers state that coloured workers make extravagant claims about their skills and past experience. Most investigators would agree that some coloured workers, especially those unfamiliar with British working conditions, do overstate their abilities. However, the blanket disbelief that some employers and trade union officials have shown over claims to skills, whether acquired in Britain or abroad, is undoubtedly unjustified. For example, private employment bureaux reported that well over a third of coloured applicants for clerical work did in fact reach an adequate standard.[46]

The most striking thing about reports on coloured workers' abilities is the apparent conflict of evidence. Sometimes a person will contradict himself, as did one union official when he said that immigrants were 'pretty good workmen' and 'take pains', but he later said that the 'danger' was that they are 'not concerned with quality', and finally, that their attitude paralleled any newcomer to the mill.[47] However, one major difference does emerge and this is that most employers who report favourably on coloured workers either mention the importance of good selection or differentiate between good and bad coloured workers whom they have employed.

The success of coloured workers in a whole variety of occupations, ranging from doctors to textile workers, from administrative class civil servants to London Transport staff, shows that within the coloured population all grades of skill and industry are present. A substantial number of coloured workers accordingly stand to suffer from the generally held stereotype of the unskilled immigrant. It seems possible that the assessments of coloured workers' abilities given by some employers and trade union officials owe as much to their own personal attitudes and racial stereotypes as they do to the qualities of the workers concerned. The irony is that the employer with 'bad' immigrant employees will probably fulfil his own worst fears and confirm his own stereotypes.

Finally, the claim by British industry that it is not discriminatory practice but lack of skills that has held back the coloured worker spotlights the failure in training. It can be argued that to use labour for limited purposes and not to adequately train that labour is an abdication of responsibility as serious as overt discrimination. Industrial training has been weak in this country for a very long time and the coloured worker, because of his special needs as a newcomer, has possibly suffered more severely than most. British industry's failure to capitalize on the ability and aspirations of the coloured immigrant with imaginative and flexible training schemes has been almost total. The use of the 1966 Industrial Training Act to teach English to non-English speakers has been minimal.[48] Generally industrial training boards have been extremely slow to use or encourage the use of powers under the Act for vocational training suitable for immigrants. The attitude which sees no necessity for special provisions has operated with exceptional strength in this area, where British industry is traditionally weak. Courses to teach additional industrial and commercial skills designed for the needs of coloured workers have been limited or non-existent. Two related areas where problems have also emerged are the induction of new workers and safety training. Both have suffered extreme neglect by many employers, and coloured workers because of their particular vulnerability have often suffered disproportionately. In all these instances the 'problems' of coloured workers are more often the problems of the industrial system they have entered.

SOME ECONOMIC PERSPECTIVES

At this stage in our discussion, it will be useful to discuss the role of immigrant labour in British industry and some of the economic effects of immigration. In doing this we will draw heavily on the contribution of Professor Maurice Peston in *Colour and Citizenship* on this subject. We will not examine the economic causes of the migration, which were touched on earlier in Chapter 3, but will confine ourselves only to the economic consequences for the receiving society. It must be stated at the outset that we do not believe it is possible at present to quantify these economic consequences and to arrive at a final balance sheet. We must also stress that whatever the overall effect of immigration economically for the community, there will always be some groups that will lose and others that will gain.

There are certain hypotheses which are inter-related that have been put forward concerning the economic consequences of immigration. These are:

(i) immigration causes unemployment;
(ii) immigration reduces the rate of economic growth;
(iii) immigration reduces the rate of technical progress;
(iv) immigration leads to a deterioration in the balance of payments; and
(v) immigration causes inflation.

For convenience we have separated out each of the above statements and will attempt to examine these in very general terms.

Starting with the question of unemployment we saw in Chapter 4 that immigrant unemployment followed a similar cycle to that of the total population and that immigrants form an increasing share of the unemployed in the downswing. Two reasons which may contribute to this are that immigrants as the latest arrivals are more likely to be laid off first and also that immigrants are most concentrated in those occupations most likely to experience the greatest amount of unemployment.

The fact that immigrants may experience more unemployment than the home population is not the same as saying that unemployment among the home population will rise as a result of immigration or even that unemployment among the total population will rise. This may be seen in a variety of ways. First, for the economy to work effectively in the short run, it must have a degree of slack, made up partly of physical capacity and partly of human capacity. To the extent that this slack is made up of immigrants, it will not be made up of the home population. As a result the effect of immigration is not to increase unemployment but merely to take over the burden of unemployment from the home population. Secondly, if immigration is responsive to labour demand the pool of unemployment in the domestic market is minimized. This was the case in West Germany and also to some extent here in the 1950s.[49] Thirdly, economic efficiency requires mobility which is geographical as well as occupational and industrial. The greater mobility of immigrants allows the domestic population to be less mobile and offsets inter-regional migration. Finally, if some unemployment results from Government's attempt to deal with inflation then if immigration is anti-inflationary this may reduce unemployment. To sum up, the view that immigration necessarily leads to increased unemployment need not be correct, in fact what evidence there is suggests the contrary.

Turning to the question of economic growth Professor Peston concluded that there was no reason why immigration should reduce the rate of economic growth. In view of a number of considerations, especially the effects of shortage of labour on growth, the effect of immigrant labour on technical progress and the greater propensity of immigrants to save, it seemed that on balance immigration had probably been beneficial to growth.

As far as technical progress is concerned, it is sometimes argued that this is increased in conditions of labour shortage, thus making it imperative to develop and employ new labour-saving techniques. There are two arguments to be set against this. One is that technical progress means change, and an immigrant labour force may be less well entrenched and more willing to change than the domestic population. Secondly, technically advanced equipment may be situated in unattractive places or may need to be worked continuously through the day and on every day of the year, and an immigrant labour force, especially if it has fewer family ties, may be more willing to work in this way.

A number of studies have shown that there is a considerable concentration of immigrant workers on night shifts or changing shifts. In a study of the wool textile industry it was found that:

The degree to which new capital investment and the employment of immigrants go together is surprising, and it would be fair to conclude that the employment of immigrants has facilitated new capital investment in the sample of firms under study. This is because new machinery is too expensive to be worked only forty or forty-eight hours a week and it must be employed as intensively as possible thus necessitating shift work. This is a trend not confined to the wool industry and may well, in the future, make headway into more white-collar occupations. It is well recognized that there is a general disinclination to work nights or changing shifts, and higher rates of pay are the general rule. The immigrant (Pakistani) workers are usually more willing to take this work than local labour....[50]

In a number of other industries which have been studied it has been found that the introduction of new machinery and processes requiring multi-shift operation have resulted in a sharp increase in the number of coloured immigrants employed.[51] In general, therefore, the hypothesis that immigration has adversely affected technical progress seems unlikely and the reverse is probably more likely.

As far as the effect of immigration on the balance of payments is concerned, this turns mainly on whether immigration has an inflationary effect on the economy. The greater the degree to which immigration relieves excess pressure of demand in the labour market, the more inflationary pressure is relieved. To quote the obvious example, the ability of West Germany to grow at an extremely fast rate with little or no unemployment and minimal price inflation is attributable in large part to the availability of immigrant labour. It has been argued that the demands made by immigrants, especially on social capital, outweighs the value of their labour.[52] This, if correct, would mean that immigration of the type Britain has received in the last 15 years has had an inflationary effect. This argument may be criticized partly in terms of its assumptions. It is not necessarily the case that all immigrants place a greater burden on the social services than they pay in taxes, even in the short run. Secondly, even if this aspect of immigration were inflationary, it would have to be set against other aspects which may be non-inflationary. Thirdly, the point is often made that many of the social services in the United Kingdom are staffed to a considerable extent by immigrants. If those immigrants were barred from the United Kingdom, the cost of the social services would be higher, and that is certainly inflationary. A crucial piece of evidence in all of this was presented by Mrs. K. Jones in 'Immigrants and the Social Services'.[53] It seems to follow from her investigation that, presumably partly as a result of the different demographic structure of immigrants and their higher participation rates, the pressure of expenditure on the social services is less than that of the domestic population. It should also be noted that the immigrant's demands for social capital are often met from old, under-utilized and/or obsolete stock rather than from new capital.[54]

It is by no means unlikely, therefore, that the efficiency of some or all of the economy may rise as a result of immigration, and it is possible that inflationary pressures will be reduced. It follows that it cannot be argued with certainty that immigration will lead to a deterioration in the balance of payments. It may well lead to an improvement in the balance of payments, and in the case of West Germany most certainly has. There is, however, one special aspect of immigration which might be presumed to have a deleterious effect on the balance of payments. That is, that it is not unreasonable to argue that immigrants coming from foreign lands may have a high propensity to import compared with home-born citizens with the same incomes, and, in particular, they may have a high propensity to remit sums to their original homeland, either to raise the income levels of their poor dependants left behind or to help them meet the cost of becoming immigrants themselves. There is no doubt that West Indians, Indians, and Pakistanis remit significant sums home, although it is worth noting that these financial flows are to the sterling area. Even here, however, the matter is not quite as simple as all that, because in these days of foreign aid it is not inconceivable that now or in the future these remittances may take the place in part of aid that would have been given by the richer country to the poorer. In other words, although there is every presumption that from this point of view the effect of immigration would be to worsen the balance of payments, the net effect may be less than the sum remitted.

To summarize: immigration has on balance proved beneficial to the economy. While the effects are closely matched it would seem that the great mobility and flexibility of the immigrant population coupled with the lower burden of demand placed on the social services are decisive. It is reasonable to infer that it has led to a rise in the general standard of living of the domestic population and an upgrading of the domestic population in the occupational hierarchy. Two final points are that firstly not everyone in the domestic population has benefited and secondly, that the scale of the benefits and costs of immigration when balanced against the size of the national economy is probably very small.

Before leaving this topic it seems worth exploring briefly some of the possible alternatives to the movement of Commonwealth immigrants. As we have already seen, it was demand for labour that was the main dynamic for the migration and before large-scale migration from the Commonwealth there was heavy migration from Europe to meet the labour shortages of British industry.

It has been alleged that British industry has been wasteful and uneconomic in its employment of labour and the responsibility for this lies with management and unions. It can be argued that a flow of migrant labour has delayed the much-needed structural changes by supplying a pool of cheap, available labour. While structural reorganization may well be an ideal long-term solution of Britain's recurring labour shortage, most employers would certainly have used a series of short-term measures that seemed to offer a quicker and more certain solution. It is possible that greater capital investment may have reduced the demand for immigrant labour but, as we have already seen, new investment often increased the need for the type of labour that only immigrants would supply. More efficient organization of the labour force or greater investment might have been the ideal answer to many of the problems of labour shortage. However, given the conditions existent in British industry in the 1950s or even in the present day, these methods of dealing with shortages of labour supply were never the most probable. If the coloured immigrant had not come to Britain the major employers would probably have attempted to widen their area of recruitment to other parts of the U.K., Eire and Europe. Thus the alternatives to Commonwealth immigrants would have been immigrants from elsewhere.

CONCLUSIONS

For any new and easily identifiable minority group entering a society, one of the main, if not the main, determinants of achievement in the field of employment is the reaction of the host society. This was, and is still, especially the case with the inflow of coloured workers to the British industrial system. For workers with little or no capital, the possibility of establishing themselves outside the existing framework is severely limited, and they must therefore enter the tightly organized industrial system controlled by British employers and workers and not by members of their own minority groups.

Our analysis of the British reaction to the presence of coloured workers has of necessity been general in nature. In part, this is due to the extreme diversity of the employment scene where employers range in size from the Government and nationalized industries, employing hundreds of thousands, to small private employers. But among private employers the range also varies from the industrial giants with a hundred thousand or more employees throughout the country, with thousands of employees in a single plant, to the small shop, workshop, or garage with one or two employees. The diversity of employers is mirrored by that of the degree of organization of workers, which varies within industries and between industries, and is often dependent on the nature of the work and the size of the firm. The inter-dependence of the job for which a coloured worker is being recruited and the jobs of other workers varies from one place of work to another and again makes it more difficult to generalize. The picture is therefore one painted with a heavy brush; but, despite the very real and important differences between employers, industries, regions, unions and each particular and peculiar local situation, certain general patterns have been the rule. Employers willing to accept coloured workers for reasons other than labour shortages, workers willing to accept coloured workers as fully equal, especially in regard to promotion, have been exceptions and not the rule.

The one fact that stands out above all others is that throughout the field of employment, discrimination is widespread and pervasive. It manifests itself in recruitment, training, promotion, and a host of other ways. This discrimination is not a result of any centrally inspired policy of Government, unions, or employers' organizations, but is determined by decisions at local level. As long as the criteria by which management are expected to make their decisions are short-term and limited, then the situation of the coloured worker can be expected – without active intervention from outside – to remain on the margins of the industrial relations system. The role in which British industry has cast the coloured worker is that of spare man or reserve – to be used only when necessary.

The immediate costs of such policies are not borne by the discriminators but by the wider society. The decisions, freely taken at the periphery, become a practice with long-term implications so damaging that a decision must finally be taken at the centre to intervene, however reluctantly. In fact, the problem of the coloured worker is only one of many examples which have arisen through the individual decisions of a host of employers.

In effect, the question of the coloured worker raises the whole question of whether private industry has a social as well as a business role. Decisions taken by private industry can, and often do, have vast social consequences, and while these may seem irrelevant, as far as the business efficiency of any single firm is concerned, the state sometimes feel justified in placing obligations upon individual firms. Examples of this are recent legislations such as the Contracts of Employment Act 1963, laying down minimum periods of notice, and the Redundancy Payments Act 1965, giving an employee an entitlement to redundancy pay from the employer. Some private companies, usually the very largest, consider that their social role is important and contribute money, materials and manpower to local educational and community facilities. The degree to which this is part and parcel of public relations is debatable, but undoubtedly many companies go much further in these and other activities than would be justified by balance-sheet consideration.[55]

The conflict between the short-term, limited considerations of employers and the wider, long-term needs of society has meant that the Government has a crucial role to play in the satisfactory absorption of the coloured worker in industry. In such a situation, a hands-off non-intervention policy of doing nothing for fear of discriminating in favour of the coloured worker is a policy of acquiescing in widespread discrimination. With the growth of the coloured population and discriminatory practice, a whole host of new fears and practices grew up. Much of the responsibility for this has lain with the Government – first, for allowing the situation to deteriorate, and then, when finally it decided to take action (in 1968), for permitting the action to be half-hearted and lacking in conviction.

Part of the paradox of the British resistance to the entry of the coloured worker is that often this resistance has gone much of the way to reinforcing the worst fears of the resistors. Each particular group of British workers, each individual employer, and each union branch, acting on what it perceived as its self-interest and excluding coloured workers, has created situations which seem to confirm their worst fears. Unions, inactive in recruiting, have seen the exploitation of coloured workers with its inevitable side-effects on their own members. Factories or departments, protecting themselves against coloured workers, have seen factories or departments near by with majorities of coloured workers.

As in so many other spheres, the coloured worker in the British industrial relations system is less of a problem and a challenge in himself than an indicator of much that is inefficient, poorly organized, and socially unacceptable in the whole system. The coloured worker is also a prime example of the inability of the system to adapt to the pace of change which is the single most important factor in our social and economic life. As the Royal Commission on Trade Unions and Employers' Associations 1965–68 (Donovan Commission) indicated, informal structures have grown up alongside formal ones, and the attempt to fit the informal structure to the formal has inevitably led to severe frictions. But the Commission, while attempting to catch up with changes that have been taking place over the last fifty years, failed totally to look at a more recent development – the coloured worker and discrimination. The most careful search of Donovan will reveal only a passing comment on race or colour.

'Will it need more dockers marching – and another Royal Commission – to convince those who are called on to implement the Donovan reforms that "racial disputes" are not on the periphery of our industrial situation, but symptomatic of its central conflicts?'[56]

REFERENCES

1. Political and Economic Planning Report, *Racial Discrimination in Britain* (London, P.E.P., 1967), and W. W. Daniel, *Racial Discrimination in England* (Harmondsworth, Penguin Books, 1968).

2. Bob Hepple, *Race, Jobs and the Law in Britain* (London, Allen Lane, The Penguin Press, 1968), Appendix 1.

3. Sheila Patterson, *Dark Stranger* (London, Tavistock Publications, 1963 and Penguin Books, 1965). Also *Immigrants in Industry* (London, Oxford University Press, for the Institute of Race Relations, 1968).

4. P. Wright, *The Coloured Worker in British Industry* (London, Oxford University Press, for the Institute of Race Relations, 1968).

5. See Chris Selby Smith, 'Racial Discrimination in Salaries' (*Personnel*, February 1969) and Brian J. Ford, 'Coloured Scientists Search for Employment' (*Race Today* August 1969).

6. Keighley Junior Chamber of Commerce, Immigrant Project, published 1967.

7. Wright, op. cit., pp. 44–46.

8. Daniel, op. cit., p. 108.

9. Patterson, *Dark Strangers* (Penguin). op. cit., p. 126.

10. H. C. Deb., Vol. 699, col. 16, 20th July, 1964.

11. Hepple (op. cit., p. 71) states that up to November 1967 the sanction of withdrawing employment exchange facilities has occurred only once.

12. Select Committee on Race Relations and Immigration, Minutes of Evidence 30th Jan., 1969 and 15th May, 1969.

13. 'The Work of the Youth Employment Service 1965–8', a

report by the National Youth Employment Council (London, H.M.S.O., 1968), pp. 4–6.

14. David Beetham, *Immigrant School Leavers and the Youth Employment Service in Birmingham* (London, Institute of Race Relations Special Series 1968). For a discussion of unrealistic aspirations, articles by Dipak Nandy, David Beetham and Sheila Allen in *Race Today* May 1969, Oct. 1969, Nov. 1969 and Dec. 1969. For the Youth Employment Service opinion see evidence to the Select Committee especially Minutes of Evidence 6th February, 1969.

15. See especially Home Office memorandum to Select Committee on this subject, Minutes of Evidence 21st May, 1969.

16. Report of the Select Committee on Race Relations and Immigration, Vol. 1, p. 34.

17. Ibid, Vol. 1, p. 34.

18. Ibid, Vol. 4, Appendix 12.

19. 1968 figures are given in *Colour and Citizenship*, p. 306, 1969 figures were supplied in a letter from the Ministry of Defence (Army) 14th October, 1969. The interpretation of the information supplied is that of the authors and not the Ministry of Defence.

20. Oscar Gish and Andrew Robertson, 'Where Immigrant Doctors Go and Why', *New Statesman* 14th March, 1969 and Oscar Gish, 'Training and Advancement of non-British Nurses', *IRR Newsletter* (Nov.–Dec. 1968).

21. See *The Unsquare Dead* (London, West Indian Standing Conference, July 1967), and also *Guardian* 3rd, 5th, and 11th April, 1968.

22. Report of the Select Committee, Vol. 4, Appendix 29.

23. We wish to acknowledge the help given by Mr. Dennis Brooks. He has been carrying out a study of coloured immigrants in London Transport, commissioned by the Institute's 'Survey of Race Relations in Britain'. All interpretation of the information supplied by Mr. Brooks is that of the authors of this report.

24. Beryl Radin, 'Coloured Workers and British Trade Unions', *Race* (Vol. VIII, no. 2, October 1966), pp. 157–73.

25. Select Committee Minutes of Evidence, 30th April, 1969.

26. F. J. Bayliss and J. B. Coates, 'West Indians at work in Nottingham', *Race* (Vol. VII, no. 2, October 1965)

27. Unpublished research conducted by Mrs. Sheila Allen on the work situation of Pakistanis in Bradford, supported by the Institute's 'Survey of Race Relations in Britain'.

28. Radin, op. cit.

29. P. Foot, 'The strike at Courtaulds, Preston', Institute of

Race Relations *Newsletter* (July 1965, Supplement).

30. Radin, op. cit.

31. P. Marsh, *The Anatomy of a Strike: Unions, Employers, and Punjabi Workers in a Southall Factory* (London, Institute of Race Relations Special Series, 1967).

32. See, for example, Peter Marsh, 'Asians and Jews – Some Similarities' (*Race Today*, Dec. 1969).

33. Report of the Select Committee, Vol. 1, p. 37.

34. Minutes of Evidence, 30th April, 1969. See especially answers on coloured meter readers by Sir Frederick Hayday (Q 3470) and also T.U.C. role in positive policies (Q 3477).

35. N.C.C.I., *Racial Equality in Employment* (Report of Conference held in London, February 1967).

36. Ibid, p. 88.

37. Report of Select Committee, Vol. VI, Appendix 34.

38. Ibid, Vol. 1, p. 36 and Minutes of Evidence 30th April, 1969.

39. Peter Wright, op. cit.

40. B. Cohen and P. Jenner. 'The Employment of Immigrants: a case study within the wool industry', *Race* (Vol. IX, no. 1, July 1968).

41. Klim McPherson, Julia Gaitskell, *Immigrants and Employment: Two Case Studies in East London and in Croydon* (London, IRR Special Series 1969).

42. Ibid.

43. Bayliss and Coates. op. cit.

44. P.E.P. Report, op. cit.

45. Brooks, op. cit.

46. Gaitskell, op. cit., and P.E.P. Report, op. cit.

47. Sheila Allen, op. cit.

48. See Report of Select Committee, Vol. 1, p. 46. Also for a fuller discussion of some aspect of training see articles in *Race Today*, July 1969, by Len Squire and Roy Williams.

49. G. C. K. Peach, *West Indian Migration to Britain* (London, Oxford University Press for Institute of Race Relations, 1968); also Peach, 'West Indian Migration to Britain: the Economic Factors,' *Race* (Vol. VII, no. 1, July 1965).

50. Cohen and Jenner, op. cit.

51. Current research being carried out by The Industrial Society and the Joint Unit For Minority and Policy Research.

52. E. J. Mishan and L. Needleman, 'Immigration, Excess Aggregate Demand and the Balance of Payments', *Economica* (May 1966).

53. K. Jones, 'Immigrants and the Social Services', *National Institute Economic Review* (No. 41, August 1967).

54. See *Colour and Citizenship*, p. 648.

55. The social role of private industry is a topic being increasingly discussed in the U.S.A. See *Report of the National Advisory Commission on Civil Disorders* (Kerner Report) (New York, Bantam Books, March 1968), especially Appendix H.

56. Bob Hepple, 'The Donovan Report and Race Relations', Institute of Race Relations *Newsletter* (October 1968).

Chapter Nine

Health, Welfare and Police

THE HEALTH AND WELFARE SERVICES

The health and welfare of the immigrants have become problems for British society in very much the same way as other aspects of their lives. The extreme stereotype of the coloured immigrant, which was circulated widely, was of someone who brought disease into the country, and who, once here, created a risk of epidemics because of his origin and living conditions. On the welfare side, the immigrant was seen as a sponger, living on benefits, or as part of a group which, collectively, caused shortages of essential services: housing, educational facilities, maternity beds in hospitals. Taking the social services as a whole, as Mrs. K. Jones has shown, the immigrants are an asset, not a burden:

The adult working population supports the old in the community. An inflow of young adult immigrants therefore – so far as current expenditure on the social services is concerned – provides a once and for all gain for thirty years in which they add to contributors but not to dependants. This more than outweighs the additional social service costs which may be incurred because of the immigrants' special health or educational requirements.[1]

The high rate of economic activity of the immigrants and their age structure has given them an overall 'positive balance'. At the same time, immigrants are in contact with services dealing with the health and welfare of families, and the people operating those services face problems of language, cultural conflict, and cross-cultural communication. Poor housing conditions mean that certain services are likely to be under extra pressure; and in general the economic situation of the immigrants and their various cultures are likely to involve some deployment of extra resources, or new approaches in some existing services.

The Health of Immigrants

The illnesses affecting immigrants are likely to differ in some ways from those affecting the host population for two reasons. First, the immigrants (like all travellers) may import infections which are endemic in the areas from which they come; secondly, they may, for immunological or environmental reasons, be at special risk to diseases occurring in the U.K. In this section, we will briefly consider some of the diseases whose incidence is known to be higher among immigrants than among the rest of the population. A survey, in Paddington in 1965 found that the rate of illness among the parents of one-year-olds was approximately the same for West Indians as the rest of the population, but most of the West Indian mothers thought their health had deteriorated since their arrival in this country.[2]

Of all the specific diseases to which immigrants were thought to be susceptible, tuberculosis attracted the greatest attention. Rates of TB infection among Paskistanis have been found to be substantially higher than the average. In Bradford, in 1961, the incidence of tuberculosis was 23.94 per thousand in Asians, compared with 0.64 per thousand in the whole population. In the early 1960s, although the Pakistanis in Bradford formed only about 2% of the total immigrant population in Britain, they contributed nearly 10% of all tuberculosis notifications. A similar situation has been reported in Birmingham and Nottingham. It is thought that perhaps half the cases are imported, and then spread to compatriots; according to Dr. D. K. Stevenson, a Bradford expert, there is no evidence of cross-infection between the local and Asian populations.[3] The high incidence of TB among Pakistanis in Bradford reflects not only their place of origin but their conditions of life and work: Eric Butterworth discusses the effect of the Bradford environment on the incidence of the disease: overcrowded lodgings and employment in the wool industry, where occupations involve the carding and combing of wool, have always been associated with a high incidence of tuberculosis.[4] Fortunately, preventive techniques for identifying tuberculosis and limiting the spread of the disease are well-established. An extensive programme of prevention was begun in Bradford in 1956, including the use of mobile radiography units and the examination of immigrant schoolchildren and new arrivals. Since 1964 new notifications have again started to fall, and there was a 24% fall in cases of pulmonary tuberculosis in 1964–65. Despite the incidence of TB among immigrants the number of new cases attending chest clinics has been lower in every year since 1965 than it was in 1959, and by 1968 was almost 27% less than the 1959 figure.[5]

How far could the importation of TB and other diseases have been prevented? The 1965 Report of the British Medical Association estimated that about half the cases of tuberculosis in Pakistanis, identified in the first year after arrival, would have been identified by an X-ray at the port of entry or in the country of origin, and the B.M.A. recommended that all immigrants should be medically examined before entry to Britain, preferably in the country of origin.[6] This view was supported by the 1965 White Paper and the National Committee for Commonwealth Immigrants. However, a scheme of this sort would have been extremely difficult to operate given the general suspicion with which immigration officers regard all documentary evidence presented by prospective immigrants, and health controls have therefore been operated at the port of entry. X-ray apparatus was installed at London Airport at the beginning of 1965. Under the 1962 Commonwealth Immigrants Act, all Commonwealth citizens, except dependants entitled to enter and returning residents, became subject to medical examination at the ports of entry, and could be refused permission to land on grounds of health. The 1968 Commonwealth Immigrants Act extended medical examinations to entitled dependants and returning residents. Although they cannot be refused permission to land, they are admitted subject to the condition that they report to a medical officer of health in the area where they are going to live. Failure to do so is an offence punishable by imprisonment and a possible recommendation for deportation. The number of those refused entry on health grounds has been very small. In 1966, of 15,340 Commonwealth immigrants examined, only 50 were refused entry; in 1968, of 53,327 examined, 59 were refused entry. The proportion of refusals has been consistently higher for aliens.[7]

In contrast to tuberculosis, the overall number of reported cases of venereal disease in the total population has been rising since 1957. The number of patients seen at venereal disease clinics for the first time was 68% higher in 1968 than in 1959.[8] This rise has been a world-wide phenomenon and is not confined to countries with significant immigration. Immigrants do not introduce venereal disease into this country, but contract it in disproportionate numbers after they arrive here.[9] The B.M.A. Report stated that gonorrhoea was a greater problem than syphilis, and that 'it is the experience of venereologists in charge of clinics that gonorrhoea and syphilis amongst male immigrants are most frequently contracted after arrival and often through the agency of white prostitutes.' Hinds gives a vivid account of the way in which a white prostitute may exploit the colour factor,[10] and Dahya describes the systematic exploitation of immigrants by pimps using white prostitutes.[11] Caribbean patients formed 28% of male patients in 1962, but a much lower percentage of female patients. Since then the number of Caribbean patients and their proportion in the total has substantially fallen, and in 1966 they formed 18% of the total.[12] The steady fall in the number of cases of venereal disease in immigrants since then can be taken to be the result of the formation of families or stable unions.

Some cases have been found in this country of imported helminth, or worm, which is endemic in parts of Asia and of yaws and sickle-cell anaemia.[13]

Immigrants may be at special risk to infections associated with the British climate. A survey of 3,250 children in London found that a high proportion of West Indian children (48%) suffered from respiratory infections compared with 32% of Irish children and 23% of English children.[14] The frequency of rubella (German measles) among Jamaican women has been related to the low incidence of the disease in the areas from which they come.

There are no overall figures on the mental health of immigrants. Christopher Bagley[15] and Dr. Farrukh Hashmi[16] have drawn attention to stress factors in Britain which may cause mental illness among some immigrant groups. In a study of three London mental hospitals, only eighteen out of some 18,000 patients were West Indian, which seemed to indicate that the rates for severe psychiatric illness were not high for this group. However a six-month study of a general practice in the same area suggested that there was a high rate of less severe psychiatric illness among West Indians [17] and studies of immigrant mothers have shown a relatively high incidence of depression among West Indian mothers. [18]

The Health of Immigrant Children

The range of health and welfare problems which have been found to arise particularly among immigrant mothers and babies present a more serious and intransigent problem than any of the infectious diseases mentioned above, for their prevention and solution is a complex matter. Some children of immigrant parents have been found to present symptoms which were common to poor working-class children before the war – deficiencies in diet have resulted in anaemia and in the appearance of rickets in some children. [19] A study of young children found a withdrawal, non-communication syndrome occurring specifically in children of West Indian parents – this has sometimes been misdiagnosed as deafness. [20] The case histories of the children in this last study frequently shared the following characteristics: maternal depression, economic pressures on the parents, mothers too exhausted to give time to or enjoy their children, inadequate housing, inadequate care of children, and multiple fostering (i.e., child minding). There have been deaths from fire, often caused by oil-heaters which may be the only available form of heating in some buildings. [21]

A study of 101 West Indian one-year-olds in Paddington in 1965 showed that they were subject to more frequent minor illnesses than the non-West Indian group (42% compared with 15%) mainly due to minor respiratory or gastro-intestinal episodes, and were also more often hospitalized (15% versus 2%). There was no evidence of physical neglect, disease, or deformity, and developmentally the majority came within normal limits. The standards of physical care were high (although some diets were excessively high in milk and carbohydrates) and the mothers had taken advantage of the local authority's facilities for immunization. The relative ill-health of the West Indian children was due to bad housing and grossly inadequate conditions of child-minding. Half the West Indian mothers were working (compared with 18% of the control) and were often unable to follow the health visitor's advice either because their homes were so overcrowded or because they had little control over the child-minder. Although the motor development of the children was well-advanced, they were often deprived of stimulus and space to play in, and their environment might have an adverse effect on their later development. The one-room home, found to be the typical West Indian dwelling, might for the one-year-old be a cosy and secure environment, apart from its oil-heater, 'but a little later when the one-year-old becomes an active toddler, it must be confining, frustrating and hazardous.'[22] Dr. Eric Stroud summed up a review of the health of immigrants as follows:

Nearly all the medical problems of immigrant communities are related to environmental factors. There are many diseases and injuries to which the children of immigrant people are particularly liable, and it is essential that doctors working in immigrant areas should be aware not only of these conditions but also of their aetiologies, for one factor these diseases and injuries have in common is their preventability.[23]

To an increasing extent, the health of immigrants will cease to reflect their place of origin or recent arrival, and will be determined by the conditions in which they live in this country. Eric Butterworth illustrates this point by using the statistics showing infant mortality rates among immigrants and children of unskilled and semi-skilled workers: in 1965 the rate of infant mortality in Bradford was 10 per thousand in professional-class homes and 30 per thousand in homes of unskilled and semi-skilled workers. Among immigrants, the rate was 50 per thousand in 1965, but this dropped to 35 per thousand by the end of 1966. He sums up his study of health and the Bradford local authority by concluding that 'the pattern of health is more likely in future to approximate to social class rather than ethnic characteristics'.[24]

The Hospital Services

Apart from the problem of maternity beds, immigrant groups make less demands upon the hospital services than the native-born. Given the age structure of the immigrant population we can say that they provide few geriatric patients, and are unlikely in the near future to place much demand on local authority homes for the aged because of the strong cultural traditions in which grandparents remain within the family and are cared for by their grown-up children. Nor, as we have seen, do they occupy a high percentage of psychiatric beds. However, immigrants do require a high proportion of maternity beds relative to their numbers. This arises from the age-structure of the immigrant groups – the higher proportion of women of child-bearing age results in a higher number of live births per thousand of population [25] – and from housing conditions which are unsuitable for home confinements. Many immigrant families have settled in areas from which the native-born families have been moving for some years in search of improved housing, and so in some areas of poor housing a very high proportion of young families are immigrant families. Richmond's Bristol survey showed that the Caribbean-born population of St. Paul's contained a higher proportion of 'normal' households than the other national groups. For these reasons a high proportion of maternity beds in some hospitals are occupied by immigrants. In West Bromwich, for example, the percentage of hospital births in 1964 was approximately 58% (953 births) for 'white' mothers, and 94% (217 births) for 'immigrant' mothers, while at the time there were only 8,000 immigrants out of a total population of 97,000.[26] Dr. Galloway, former Medical Officer of Health in Wolverhampton, has said that 'social grounds were responsible for two-thirds of the admissions of immigrant mothers in Wolverhampton, and for only a fifth of the other mothers who had their babies in hospital'.[27] The need for maternity beds – which is assessed by domiciliary midwives – can only be met by resorting to early discharge after confinement. This situation can lead to additional problems because the burden of providing domiciliary midwives to look after the mothers after their discharge from hospital falls directly upon a local authority service – no extra grant for midwifery is payable under Section 11 of the 1966 Local Government Act.

As we have seen, immigrants are apparently under-represented among patients, but immigrants from many Commonwealth countries contribute heavily to staff. Since 1966 the number of overseas doctors coming to work in Britain has increased from 2,000 to 3,000 a year. Most of these doctors are from the Commonwealth, and in 1968 71% of all category B (i.e. skilled) work vouchers went to doctors, the majority from India. 14,000 overseas doctors in Britain represent 22% of all doctors, and 25% of all N.H.S. medical staff. However, they are not evenly distributed throughout the hospital service, and are concentrated in the junior and middle grades, and in non-teaching hospitals, particularly those in the provinces. In 1967, 51% of registrars and 63% of senior house officers were born outside the United Kingdom and Irish Republic, compared with only 12% of consultants. Non-teaching hospitals contain well over nine-tenths of the hospital beds in the country, and no less than 85% of registrars and 88% of senior house officers at these hospitals are of non-U.K. birth.[28] Nor were the foreign-born doctors evenly distributed between the specialities: between 80% and 90% of registrars and S.H.O.s working in geriatrics (the least glamorous speciality) were born outside the British Isles. Not all these doctors remain permanently in Britain, but there is an estimated net inflow of 500–600 per annum, and the maintenance of the existing hospital services clearly depends on the continued immigration of doctors to compensate for the 'brain-drain' to the United States and Australia.

In nursing, the percentages of overseas-born are smaller, but still significant. The proportion of overseas-born nurses and midwives in Britain is estimated at between 25% and 35%. At the end of 1966, 25% of the nurses and midwives training in hospitals were born outside the U.K., and three-quarters of this group were Commonwealth-born. But like the medical staff, they were unevenly distributed: only 4% of the Commonwealth student nurses were training in teaching hospitals compared with 24% born in the U.K. and Eire. A study of overseas-born midwives showed that 71% of those who had completed their training in the four years prior to January 1968 had remained in Britain, and this group were twice as likely to be actively engaged in midwifery practice after their training than the British-born.[29] These proportions are likely to rise in view of the preference for nursing training shown by coloured school-leavers, as this is one profession where colour is not a barrier to entry.

Immigrants and the Social Services

The 1965 White Paper declared that the immigrants' needs were 'different in degree rather than kind', and that the general objective must be 'to treat them in the same way as other citizens' (para. 53). The underlying principle of official policy has been that immigrants should be instructed how to use the existing social services, and local community relations councils are not intended to provide a separate service for them. The effectiveness of these voluntary bodies will be discussed in the following chapter; we are concerned here with the extent to which immigrants have special requirements in the broad area of social welfare, some of the difficulties which have been experienced by professional workers in this field, how far the immigrants have taken advantage of existing facilities, and how far the central government and local authorities are meeting their needs. The major areas of housing and education have already been considered. Although we will here be assessing the special needs of immigrant groups, we do so with the proviso that their problems can only be understood and (hopefully) solved within the context of the wider problems of the inner city.

In the early stages, there was only one aspect of the problem for which special policies were thought necessary: the risk of the importation of infectious diseases. But there were from the outset certain obvious needs, including a programme of education explaining the working of the National Health Service and the social services. The White Paper laid considerable stress on the subject of communication, and various attempts at health education have been made through the provision of written information in appropriate languages at the port of entry. In the absence of centralized organization, the provision of information has varied according to the assiduity of individual local authorities or voluntary bodies.

Some of the services available do not necessarily require extensive advertisement; for example, the existence of the National Health Service seems to be widely known among immigrants and there is some evidence to show that it is adequately used. To take one case, an indication of the use of the maternity and child welfare services by immigrant mothers was obtained from the study of West Indian one-year-olds in Paddington referred to above. The survey included the compilation of a 'use of services' score, which showed that the use made of G.P.'s and the maternity and child welfare services by West Indian mothers was high (the mean percentage score was 72%) and similar to that of other mothers in the neighbourhood. A higher percentage of West Indian mothers regularly attended infant welfare clinics (82% compared with 69% of the control group) including the majority of the mothers who were out at work all day. The proportion of children immunized was also higher (81% compared with 77% of the control). When the G.P.s testing the sample were questioned about the use of their services by their patients, 67% thought that their West Indian patients used their services proportionately more than others on their list, but only seven out of the 31 felt this was a problem, and the majority advanced sympathetic explanations, such as the need for reassurance or for a father figure.[30]

The Department of Health and Social Security is currently compiling statistics showing the use of all social services by immigrants in the Greater London area, but at the time of writing these were unpublished. However, it is likely that the use of services by the immigrants will reflect the extent to which various borough authorities are offering an efficient service, making provision for immigrants' requirements, and attempting to publicize the services available. Some examples drawn from other areas illustrate the close relationship between communication and the provision of services. Elizabeth Burney found that almost no coloured families had been housed on Nottingham's council estates and suggested that one reason for this was the 'extraordinary ignorance' among immigrants of Nottingham's council house system.[31] The Cullingworth Committee has called for better publicity, better public relations and a housing advice service to help overcome the immigrants' ignorance.[32] Bradford, in attempting to provide hostel accommodation for Pakistani male immigrants, failed to take account of the existing household structure among this group: many households were composed of close-knit kinship groups, sharing a communal kitchen and sitting-room. When the local authority provided a hostel without communal rooms, and with cooking facilities in self-contained bedrooms, it failed through lack of tenants, partly because of high rents, partly because it had failed to take account of cultural differences.[33]

Cultural misunderstanding has also been suggested as a reason for the excessive use of a service by an immigrant group. Katrin Fitzherbert suggested that the numbers of West Indian children received into care 'give an exaggerated picture of the size of the problem of deprivation among West Indian children, and reflect the reluctance of the children's department to treat West Indians as a separate cultural group, with distinct family patterns and attitudes to child-rearing.'[34] She argues that far from being unable to make effective use of the services, many West Indian parents see the child care service as a convenience, rather than a last resort service. Mary Dines argues that, on the contrary, pressure of circumstances – in particular the need for both parents to work and the lack of day nursery care – create realistic grounds for families requiring help from local authorities, particularly if the mother has to go into hospital or becomes otherwise unable to look after her children.[35] 'It is important,' Mrs. Dines adds, 'not to confuse situations that arise through force of circumstances with any natural inclination to lead a particular way of life.' The possession of differential characteristics by a minority may also lead to the assumption that this characteristic is unique to an immigrant group; on investigation, this may be found to occur in native-born people as well. Dr. Simpson, a Bristol G.P., notes that 'Having decided to keep a record of patients that are co-habiting because it is part of the Caribbean way of life, I find that it is not uncommon among the English' among all age groups.[36]

These examples illustrate some of the problems arising from cultural diversity. This is a subject of considerable importance, since the range of social workers (in the broadest sense) meeting the immigrants as patients, 'clients', 'cases', 'problems' and offenders is extensive. It includes case-workers in child care and family service units, health visitors, housing visitors, public health inspectors, TB visitors, doctors, nurses, teachers, officers in the youth service, the staff of the local Ministry of Social Security and Employment Exchange, the youth employment service, and the police. This list is not exhaustive, and in dealing with immigrants all the professional workers involved will face difficulties arising from linguistic and cultural diversities. Bessie Kent has shown the inadequacy of some basic principles of social work when the case-worker encounters someone from a different cultural background:

> British social work is based on the belief that man can alter his own destiny; confronted with a client whose culture has taught him that man is a pawn of destiny and can do nothing except to meet with dignity whatever fate has in store for him, the British social worker will not only have an opposing perception as to the fundamental purpose of existence, but may well be infuriated by the client's 'refusal' to do anything about his problem.[37]

In some situations, when the traditions and beliefs of im-migrants conflict with those of the social worker and of the host community, the social worker will have to choose be-tween two sets of values. Peter Hutchinson illustrates this difficulty in cases involving the status of women in Indian and Pakistani communities. If the social worker supports a girl who desires to avoid an arranged marriage, or a badly-treated wife who wants to leave her husband, the worker will have to choose between the wishes of the client and those of her family. If she is advised to reject the family plan she will be isolated, and will require long-term support and help if she is to make an independent life.[38] In other cases, the problem of language may be the main difficulty. Dr. Simpson has given some vivid examples of language difficulties, and adopted various solutions to overcome them. These include the use of language cards, giving various medical phrases in different languages with the English translation. He also made a noteof the medical terms used by his Jamaican patients, which often differed considerably from the normal English ones.[39] The

West Indian mothers in the Paddington survey saw their doctors whenever they or their children had caught a 'cold'; when this was discussed, however, it was discovered that in the West Indies a cold commonly heralded the onset of a severe illness and therefore it was still felt to be cause for concern.[40]

The difficulties for social workers resemble those they encounter in communicating across the class barrier, but are in many ways more acute:

> Especially in the services which depend on effective communication, groups which do not share the cultural norms of the majority ... are at a distinct disadvantage. ... The providers of these services ... must be wary of the types of bias which can operate in professional people working with members of ethnic minorities or groups on a different social class level from their own – biases which may make more difficult, even block, the attainment of the desired professional goal.[41]

Many officers in the health and welfare services have discretionary powers which, if they are influenced by hostile stereotypes, can lead in certain circumstances to *de facto* discrimination against minorities. John Lambert's investigation of this problem in relation to the police is discussed in the second part of this chapter. But Lambert has recently pointed out that other local officials also have discretionary powers and may display 'stereotypes, prejudice and well-intentioned but offensive attitudes'.[42] Elizabeth Burney also drew attention to the danger of bias in any system of housing allocation which accords housing visitors too great a degree of discretion.[43] At present, they receive a scanty training which does not equip them for the complex process of assessing the needs of individuals from differing cultural backgrounds. The Cullingworth Committee was extremely critical of the capacity of the housing departments to make assessments in difficult cases. The Committee found a moralistic attitude in some housing departments, whose 'underlying philosophy seemed to be that council vacancies were to be given only to those who deserved them. Thus unmarried mothers, cohabitees, dirty families and transients tended to be grouped as "undesirable".' The Committee concluded that 'coloured immigrants, like any group from cultural back-grounds which are "strange" to housing visitors, may also tend to be unfavourably treated. This stems from the prac-tice of assessing applicants according to their housekeeping: a practice of which we are severely critical.' The report recom-mended that cases which presented difficulty should be assessed by the health and welfare departments.[44]

Problems of this type have important implications for social work training and methods of health education. But above all, they demand a revaluation of priorities by local authorities and the central government.

As far as training is concerned, change may be inhibited by the existing diffuse structure, with many kinds of training institutions covering many disciplines. There is no doubt however that the experience of social workers coming into contact with immigrant families has contributed to a general re-thinking of methods. The National Committee for Com-monwealth Immigrants and the Association of Social Work Teachers (which spans several disciplines and institutions) produced a pamphlet suggesting possible changes in the syl-labus. Through the London Boroughs Training Committee four two-day courses for senior social workers were organ-ized, and a pilot project of a series of weekly seminars for residential staff. There have been a number of other efforts on these lines, but courses or seminars cannot, of course, amount to training in themselves. The purpose has been to provide some orientation for professional groups who are bound in the course of their work to come into contact with immigrants. They are seen as a stimulant to more widespread and systematic changes in training within the profession.

The normal health and welfare of immigrants and their families, as for everyone else, are the responsibility of local authority health and welfare services, and the general prac-titioners. Local authorities are required by law to provide a number of services, including health centres, maternity care, midwives, health visitors, home nursing, and vaccination and immunization. Local authority child care services come under the Children's Department of the Home Office, and a local authority may employ a family case-worker and subsidize an intensive case-work agency such as a family service unit, and an advisory service such as a citizens advice bureau. The provision of services by the local authorities varies widely. One vital area where they have failed to meet the needs of immigrants is in the provision of healthy and safe day-care for pre-school age children whose mothers are at work. There is no need to labour the point which has been most recently and forcefully made in the Plowden Report and the Seebohm Report and echoed by all organizations concerned with children's welfare. Nursery places benefit all families where the mothers work, and among immigrants this means particularly the West Indian families. Indian and Pakistani women go out to work less, but, even then, mixed nursery schools would enable non-English speaking children to learn some English before going to school.

Since 1949, the number of day nursery places provided by local authorities has steadily declined, in accordance with the ministry's policy that places be provided only for those in special need. Even after the arrival of immigrant families in the cities, the number of nurseries has continued to fall. In December 1956, there were 547 local authority day nurseries, in December 1964, 455. Meanwhile, the number of registered private child-minders rose from 881 to 2,994,[45] and that of the unofficial childminders, catering for a public largely composed of immigrant parents (as far as can be seen), even more rapidly. Associated with this growth was an increase in health hazards which caused anxiety to local authorities and voluntary organizations and eventually led to legislation being introduced to control minding. It was expected that nursery education would be provided to an increasing extent in schools by the local education authorities. But until recently this did not happen. The result has been that local voluntary agencies have struggled to provide pre-school play groups and to put pressure upon local authorities to provide them. Ultimately, provision for assistance was belatedly included in the second stage of the urban programme.

The Hunt Report, *Immigrants and the Youth Service*,[46] sharply criticized the youth services for failing to make provision for immigrants, while acknowledging that the service is understaffed and reluctant to take on an additional burden. Birmingham and Bristol have appointed youth leaders for multi-racial activities, but specific funds and training are necessary if the numbers of young immigrants attending youth clubs is to be increased, and if the possibility of young people thereby continuing to participate in multi-racial contacts after leaving school is to be enhanced.

In general, the inadequacies in the provision of health and welfare services stem from structural weakness in the system of local government, which has been analysed in the Seebohm Report. The success of any health and welfare measures has, as the report notes, to be judged within an existing framework of housing circumstances and income which may be the source of the problems. Until 1966, local authorities were presumed to be able to handle any special provision for immigrants with their own resources. A step forward was taken in section 11 of the Local Government Act of 1966, referred to in earlier chapters. However, it was left to each local authority to make expenditure claims according to its own priorities and policies and there was consequently considerable variation between different authorities as to what they spent Section 11 funds on. In the first year of operation, 1967–68, the largest estimate in all major authorities, except Manchester, were for education. Manchester's largest estimate was for public health inspectors (£44,016) with education next (£36,260). Estimated expenditure on day nurseries varied considerably: Birmingham, £16,219; Wolverhampton, £1,173; Bristol, £11,600; Brent, £21,680; Ealing, £3,515; and Haringey, £1,540. Ealing's estimate for health visitors was £18,253: Haringey's which, like Ealing, has a large non-English speaking population, is only £2,820.[47]

These variations do not only reflect the varying populations and proportion of immigrants in the local authorities, but also differences in policies towards immigrants, and, in particular, differences in health and welfare policies between authorities, which characterize the administration of social welfare in Britain generally. What they illustrate in the present context is that although the Government decided to make a substantial contribution to the costs of certain services through Section 11 of the 1966 Local Government Act, no overall guidance accompanied this provision.

However, official recognition finally emerged that the process of migration and the functioning of control machinery might themselves generate welfare needs. The

Wilson Committee on appeals procedure, set up owing to the dispute over the new proposals for immigration control in the 1965 White Paper, recommended the creation of an independent body to provide an advisory and welfare service.[48] (An independent, unofficial body, backed by over 100 immigrant organizations, the Joint Council for the Welfare of Immigrants, had already been set up in December 1967.) The *Immigrant Appeals Act 1969* – using evidence from the Wilson Committee and of an *ad hoc* working party set up by the Home Office which in July 1968 submitted proposals for the establishment of an independent Port Advisory and Welfare Service – provides for a Government grant 'to any voluntary organization which provides advice or assistance for, or other services for the welfare of, persons who have rights of appeal'.

By 1968 there had also been a definite change in the whole approach of the central government. The Plowden Report established the principle of compensatory provision for deprived areas,[49] and, as we have seen in Chapter 6 a parallel concept of housing priority areas evolved from a variety of sources. This process culminated in the announcement of the Urban Programme, which will be discussed in Chapter 13. But we should note here that in the first year, projects were mainly in the field of nursery education, general education and child-care.[50]

In general, as we argued earlier, the placing of problems of immigrant areas within an overall problem of urban deprivation is a hopeful step. Whether compensatory provision will be made on a large enough scale to make a significant difference is another question. The selection of initiative for projects undertaken in the course of the urban programme will not now be left entirely to the local authorities, but will be planned in accordance with some overall perception of priorities.[51] The Seebohm Report's recommendation of a single local authority department for personal social services should also encourage a planned distribution of resources by providing an instrument by which efficient allocation can be undertaken. The assumption of a degree of central direction after a decade of drift comes opportunely, but it remains to be seen whether these developments in themselves are sufficient to justify optimism.

THE POLICE AND LAW ENFORCEMENT

The survey among police officers carried out for the Royal Commission on the Police (1962) revealed that many police felt 'that coloured people had grown more resentful of them recently'.[52] In 1967, the late Sir Joseph Simpson (then Commissioner of Police for the Metropolis) wrote:

> Complaints of police 'brutality', of West Indians afraid to complain at police stations for fear of being 'beaten-up' and protest marches and deputations in support of these allegations, have all been part of the deteriorating background to the pattern of police and immigrant relations during the last six months.[53]

The West Indian Standing Conference, in a study entitled *Nigger Hunting in London?*, claimed that 'threads of objectionable prejudice seem to be inter-woven into the fabric of police and immigrant relationship. It must be maintained that many instances have proved that the police are malicious and sometimes exceptionally hostile.'[54]

But although the claim that relationships between police and immigrants have been deteriorating is one that has frequently been made, culminating in a full-scale confrontation in the B.B.C. television production *Cause for Concern* in August 1968, substantive evidence on the state of the relationship is not easy to come by. There is no shortage of assertions – all organizations connected with civil liberties or race relations have files full of complaints about police practice. The absence of validated material is a by-product of the machinery which exists to examine these complaints; and the way in which this machinery functions is at least partly responsible for the penumbra of suspicion that surrounds this topic. What is indisputable, at least in certain areas, is that an attitude of suspicion and mistrust has grown up between the police and the immigrant community[55] – this, ironically, at a time when the police are trying to bring about a better understanding between themselves and immigrant groups, and when more police officers are devoting their attention to the problem than ever before. How then has this situation come about and how is it likely to develop? In order to begin to answer these questions, we will need to consider the place of the police in the structure of society, the function of social control which they perform and the specific tasks which they are called upon to undertake in order to discharge this function, and the effects on all these of changes in society as a whole.

The Life and Labour of the Police[56]

The general objective of the police force laid down by the first Metropolitan Commissioner of Police still stands. This makes 'the principal object to be attained ... (the) prevention of crime ... Security of the person, the preservation of public tranquillity and all the other objects of a police establishment, will thus be better effected, than by the detection and punishment of the offender, after he has succeeded in committing the crime.' To this end a great deal of importance is attached to relations between police and public. Hence the sentiment expressed in the Report of the Chief Inspector of Constabulary in 1965, that the 'police service as a whole is deeply conscious of the need to have the goodwill and support of the public at all times',[57] is echoed in most official police reports and by most Home Secretaries, and is emphasized in police training.

The police must both prevent and detect crime: but in practice these two roles conflict. In the prevention of crime the policeman needs the help and co-operation of the public and in its detection the policeman 'by profession must be inquisitive and interfering'.[58] The police simultaneously desire both the unquestioning respect of the public in the execution of their duty and their understanding and help.

The police are hampered in performing the crime prevention role because they are an identifiable minority and are to some extent shunned by the non-police public.[59] This isolation, together with the hierarchical structure of the organization under which the police are constrained to work, may generate values opposed to those associated with good community relations.

In the decaying areas of cities where crime ratios are high the local community are unlikely to see the police as helpful allies. The police in turn are likely to 'close ranks' against the hostility they experience and have little feeling of identity with the inhabitants of these areas. In recent years an over-riding concern for the crime wave and clear-up rate indicates an emphasis on the 'thief catching' as opposed to the prevention or social role. Furthermore new legislation has increased police duties and increased the number of people who come in contact with the police for infringement of the law. One obvious example of this are motoring offences which constitute such a high proportion of all offences.

An essential feature of the operation of the police force is the use of discretion. It is essential 'on the beat' where the individual policeman must determine the most appropriate action in dealing with specific situations, and at higher levels where the decision on how best to deal with reported or prospective incidents must be taken. Although it is a crucial element in police procedure, misuse of discretion occurs. This is witnessed by the number of complaints against the police which may frequently turn on a disputed use of discretion. Discretion inevitably leads to a discretionary style of policing; it can give rise to a feeling by an individual or group of being singled out for special attention.[60] For example, prosecutions for male importuning in Manchester increased dramatically with a change of chief constable in 1959.[61]

Public attitudes to the police are likely to vary from area to area and to depend to some extent on social class, but one obvious index of public regard for the police is the rate of complaints about police misbehaviour. Though changes in the procedure for recording complaints in 1964 may have caused administrative increases, two interesting examples indicate how complaints are a barometer of the public's attitude, though perhaps not so accurate as a measure of police misbehaviour. After the shooting of three policemen at Shepherds Bush in 1966, there was a 'distinct drop' in the rate of complaint.[62] The adverse publicity of the Sheffield inquiry contributed to the increase in the number of complaints in 1965. Table 16 indicates the rising trend of complaints over the last few years. But the proportion of substantiated complaints, notably in the Metropolitan area, has not risen.

The system of investigating complaints against the police through an internal quasi-judicial procedure has been the subject of much discussion. In support of the present

Table 16. COMPLAINTS AND SUBSTANTIATED COMPLAINTS AGAINST THE POLICE, 1964–68 [63]

| | Metropolitan area | | All other areas | |
	Complaints received	Complaints substantiated	Complaints received	Complaints substantiated
1964	1,870	197	3,363	408
1965	2,460	237	6,736	756
1966	2,412	235	5,771	699
1967	2,639	220	5,885	756
1968	2,924	202	6,357	956

procedure it has been argued in a recent report of the Chief Inspector of Constabulary that 'the principles to be considered in any system for dealing with complaints is that justice must be seen to be done … and that police morale should not be undermined in order to secure this objective', and, he added 'the present procedure seems to justify these principles.'[64] It is also argued by Sir John Waldron, the present Metropolitan Commissioner, that the police are the only people with the ability to investigate complaints thoroughly.[65]

The N.C.C.L., in a recent pamphlet,[66] present two main arguments against the present system: first, that there is evidence to show that not all complaints are dealt with satisfactorily and in such a way that justice is seen to be done; secondly, that the police are not disinterested judges of their own cause, 'in each of the (fortunately few) major police scandals of recent years … senior police officers persistently denied that anything was wrong until a public outcry arose. And in each of these cases numerous policemen … knew what had happened and kept quiet.'[67]

There is some doubt about whether the serving policeman accepts that the present system is satisfactory, Whitaker found that the majority of the policemen interviewed thought that serious complaints should be independently investigated,[68] but in the five years that have intervened since his inquiry, police opinion may have hardened against any system of external review. An independent body would not solve all the difficulties connected with the present procedure.

In many cases court proceedings will be pending; either the complaint must be investigated and dealt with while the case is *sub judice* which is unsatisfactory or else complaint proceedings must take place against a background of a conviction or acquittal by a court. In the latter case there is the obvious danger that the court proceedings will determine the outcome of the case. However, for other cases, the veil of secrecy which covers the investigation of complaints will be lifted and the reasons for decisions on complaints may at least be made public.

As we have pointed out, the role of the police inevitably involves conflict and as an identifiable group, to some extent isolated from the community, they are a target for prejudice and resentment. The grievances and the resentment of the public are expressed through the complaints machinery which is not seen to be impartial and may thus tend to reinforce resentment and prejudice. This is as true whether the complaints are substantiated or not. Complaints adjudged frivolous, trivial, or deriving from a misunderstanding may be just as damaging to public confidence as a massive scandal. Many unsubstantiated complaints indicate a decline in police-public relations and, particularly where racial or class attitudes are involved, the need in a complaint procedure should be less to prove or justify behaviour as to reassure an offended person. The procedure is thus vital to the background against which police-immigrant relations need to be considered.

Police–Immigrant Relations

Initially, the police were regarded by the authorities in Whitehall simply as the means of ensuring that law and order in areas of immigrant settlement was efficiently preserved. In other words, they should simply continue to execute the traditional function of keeping the peace. Thus, the Home Secretary was able in 1958 to pay tribute to the way in which the Metropolitan Police had prevented the disturbances in Notting Hill from getting out of control, and it was generally agreed that the disturbances in Dudley two years later had been handled with considerable skill by the local police. In addition to this function of preventing the emergence of open conflict between immigrant minorities and the white majority, the police were employed in an intelligence role – they were the medium through which most of the scanty information about the minorities reached Whitehall. At this stage, the idea that the police might perform a mediating role between the coloured and white communities had not yet been put forward: as we have seen, the general objective of official policy towards minorities in the late 1950s and early 1960s precluded any direct involvement of this kind. This confining of the police to a purely regulatory role may well have had something to do with the deterioration of relationships, which began to be noticeable in the early 1960s and which found expression in the increasing numbers of protests raised by organizations like C.A.R.D. and the West Indian Standing Conference. These complaints stemmed almost exclusively from the experience of West Indians. By the mid-1960s the rate of complaints (*per capita*) by coloured immigrants in the Metropolitan Police area exceeded those made by whites by three to two. C.I.D. and senior police officers were virtually unanimous in the view that the relationship between the police and the coloured minorities had never been worse.

In this atmosphere, complaints about police misbehaviour have received a good deal of publicity. But it is difficult to establish how much this reflects on actual police performance. To extend an earlier quotation: 'it is understandable that a police officer by profession must be inquisitive and interfering, will at times himself become the object of suspicion, particularly by those who themselves feel insecure or perhaps harassed'.[69] In addition where there are immigrant organizations which are capable of gathering and transmitting complaints effectively, it is possible that the rate will increase. Finally, changes in the situation of the immigrants and increased expectations may well create increased sensitivity and produce more complaints.

Though senior police officers are often liberal in their views towards coloured immigrants and have become more understanding in their dealings with immigrant groups, it is not established whether their attitudes have influenced the police on the beat. Complaints (which do not of course customarily involve senior officers) are certainly becoming more frequent; but the fact that the rate of substantiated complaints is lower for coloured immigrants, at least in the Metropolitan area, than it is for white complainants (2.5% as opposed to 8.8%[70]) has been put forward as evidence that immigrants are particularly prone to make frivolous complaints arising out of their own insecurity (the 'chip on the shoulder'). However, it is of the essence of complaints that they arise from intensive or prejudiced remarks or behaviour by the police that they are difficult to substantiate and usually depend on the unsupported assertions of the complainant.

It is readily conceded by senior police officers and federation officials that the police share the prejudices of the indigenous population.[71] Some add, however, that these do not influence police behaviour in carrying out their duties. But, granted the degree of flexibility deriving from the discretion exercised at all levels, it is difficult to be entirely confident on this score. Michael Banton's remark that 'to explain what a policeman actually does it is necessary to see his activities as being governed more by popular morality than by the letter of the law'[72] can readily be extended to behaviour of officers towards immigrants.

Many coloured immigrants, of course, live in the decaying areas near the centre of cities. As these areas often coincide with areas of high incidence of crime, it will often happen that the inhabitants will have their reputation determined by their association with the area. For coloured immigrants, this reputation will be reinforced by their visibility. This must inevitably affect police attitudes, for it is in just these areas where police work is greatest that detection and apprehension take precedence over prevention.

If there were in fact a high recorded incidence of crime among immigrants in these central areas, there might be a realistic basis for differential treatment of immigrants on the part of the police. But this does not seem to be the case. The main sources of information are an article by Bottoms,[73] Lambert's work, and in the evidence to the Select Committee on Race Relations. Bottoms found, on the little evidence available, that crime among immigrants tended to be low except for violent crimes, where domestic disputes predominated. The rate of violent crime needs to be treated carefully as it probably involves people at greater risk by age and environment factors than for the population at large.

Coloured immigrants have also been over-represented in drugs charges, mainly possession of cannabis, as compared with the white population. Lambert confirms these findings: 'fewer than 5% of arrests made in the significantly coloured neighbourhood are in fact coloured people. . . . Only in offences related to drug trafficking are coloured immigrants over-represented.'[74] The Select Committee found that in the 15–20 age group, the incident of delinquency was lower than for the equivalent white age group.[75] This evidence, apart from contradicting a widely-held stereotype (to which even the judiciary have been known to subscribe), also suggests that prosecution is not used by police as an instrument of discrimination – although it must be borne in mind that prosecution is the ultimate police sanction and there are lesser sanctions at their disposal.

There are certain bright spots around the country which should be noted. In Warley, in the West Midlands, and Birmingham, when immigrant school children were asked about policemen they spoke in terms of the help, advice, and friendliness they received. This can be contrasted with the experience of a London police officer talking to a class of mainly West Indian girls, who met with the unanimous assumption that everybody who went inside a police station was beaten up.[76] For adult immigrants in West Bromwich, Detective Sergeant Till had 'helped them to organize peace and contentment' for which they presented him with a silver plate.[77]

The Police and Integration

As the pendulum has swung away from the concept that the police role should be confined to the prevention of disturbances or open conflict and as the provision of special facilities designed to promote integration has become acceptable in terms of general policy aims, the Home Office have begun to consider measures for the promotion of better relations between police and immigrants. When he first came to the Home Office, Roy Jenkins made this one of the areas on which he placed particular emphasis. As the Chief Inspector of Constabulary put it in his first report to the new Home Secretary:

In 1966, you became responsible for co-ordination of measures to promote integration of coloured immigrants into the community and caused inquiries to be made about action that was already being taken by Chief Officers in areas in which it was known that large communities of coloured immigrants were resident. As the year advanced ... the Police Service took a more intense interest in the problem.[78]

Two areas in which this intense interest was shown were in the field of liaison between police and immigrants through the appointment of liaison officers and in the recruitment of coloured policemen. In particular, the Metropolitan Police were concerned with the deterioration of the atmosphere and made increasing efforts to devise a structure which would enable this trend to be reversed.

Though police liaison officers existed before Roy Jenkins issued a circular on the subject of police authority in July 1967, this central initiative gave added impetus to the idea. In the Metropolitan Police and elsewhere the liaison officers are virtually self-appointed, in that officers with special interest in the field of race relations are asked to put themselves forward. Their function, in the Metropolitan area at least, is 'to establish and maintain a dialogue with the local immigrant community and particularly its leaders; to arrange talks and discussion by police officers with immigrant audiences, as well as vice versa; to conduct 'Surgeries'' or make similar arrangements for assisting immigrants with their problems, and to eliminate in any way possible, mistrust and differences which may exist.'[79] Section I of the A7 Branch at Scotland Yard has been set up to coordinate the activities of the liaison officers, to carry on a dialogue with the leaders of the immigrant community, and to carry out a general education function. This department organized a two-day conference for police officers in the Metropolitan area which has been mentioned previously. It has also organized lectures for police officers on race relations and is now producing a leaflet explaining the police role to newcomers.

Liaison officers are on two levels; the divisional officers who inform A7 Branch of the local situation and maintain formal contact at a local level, and the station liaison officers who maintain a non-intimate contact with the local community.

Little training is given to liaison officers; a two-day course of lectures at Scotland Yard was all the London ones had, and more training may well be necessary if they are to operate effectively. However, courses in Urdu and Hindi have been organized and officers of the A7 Branch have attended university courses and visited America, India and Pakistan to increase their knowledge of immigrant communities and race relations. In one case a station liaison officer visited the West Indies.[80]

Altogether, according to an analysis of the results of a questionnaire issued by the National Committee for Commonwealth Immigrants (now the Community Relations Commission), thirty-seven local liaison committees have at least one police representative, generally of inspector rank or above; and ten have more than one. So far the Metropolitan Police have about 100 liaison officers, twenty-five of whom sit on the voluntary liaison committees established under the auspices of the Commission. The basic rationale for the participation of police officers in their activities has been presented by a serving police officer as the promotion of improved communication and understanding and 'to lend stress to the principle that the administration of criminal justice in all its ramifications is totally a community responsibility'.[81]

It is within this general framework of education and social action that the work of police liaison officers has so far been. Great scope has been given to individual police officers of the uniformed branch in creating their own variations on the theme of liaising throughout London with the various committees set up under the auspices of the Community Relations Commission. One divisional liaison officer will make a personal liaison with one or more committees, sometimes as a mere observer, and at other times will fully participate in the work of the committee and its subsidiaries. Together with this activity, some officers have devised their own approach to the community at large – for example, by publicizing their availability at specified times at their police stations.

In the rest of the country, the liaison officer system is growing, with some variations on the Metropolitan system. Bradford for example, has appointed a Pakistani and an Indian civilian liaison officer as well as a uniformed liaison officer. In all, over thirty police forces outside the Metropolitan area have appointed about 100 liaison officers.

In provincial forces, the role of the liaison officer is often not defined. Inspector J. P. Steer, the liaison officer for Warwickshire, when asked about his work, replied that: 'We are not setting out to be social workers. We have no terms of reference at all. . . . What we are trying to do is find out what they expect from the police and tell them where they stand and what exactly we can do to help them.'[82]

The immigrant community is to some extent suspicious of the liaison officers scheme. The West Indian Standing Conference (London branch) is reported to have 'believed that police did not intend to treat black people fairly and impartially and that liaison on the part of the police was "simply to whitewash and hoodwink the community and especially the black community into believing that the police are the fairest in the world"'.[83] However, these public denunciations are not necessarily paralleled in private practice. Since 1964, the Standing Conference has maintained contact with the special officers appointed at Scotland Yard and although public criticism is frequently voiced, these contacts have been maintained. Indeed Mr. Jeff Crawford, the Secretary of the Standing Conference, has commented that 'the Metropolitan police are the most progressive section of the white community'.[84]

It is too soon to say whether the liaison system will produce results. We have argued that some degree of conflict between the police and the immigrant community is inevitable. The liaison system will not eliminate this but can bring about a better understanding of the particular causes of conflict. To tackle the problem successfully, the liaison officers should be full-time appointments and they should be full participating members of local committees. This will present the police with a difficult manning problem and, in a situation where there is a great manpower shortage, may not be possible. However, if the scheme operates successfully and some dialogue is established between the police and the community, this may compensate for the loss of a man on the beat. The liaison officer, in any case, need not be strictly off the beat but a free-ranging agent acquiring an intimate knowledge, if he does not already have this, of the problems within his particular division. In the future there should be scope for this officer to develop into a community liaison officer without particular reference to immigrants.

It is essential that liaison officers are not seen in the context of a public relations exercise, an activity of which many police forces are becoming increasingly enamoured. This would be a negation of the concept of liaison between two equally concerned parties.

The second prong of the police effort to salvage the deteriorating situation is in the recruitment of coloured policemen. Unfortunately, the police have dragged their feet over this issue. There is little doubt that some chief constables, who were in principle favourably disposed towards recruiting of coloured policemen, allowed themselves to be dissuaded by fears of the reaction of serving policemen. There was widespread anxiety in the police about the capacity of coloured officers to exact from the public the degree of respect and compliance which the police would ideally like to receive; this found expression in an anxious correspondence in the Guardian.[85] Other critics, from a more positive position, were concerned that coloured police might be recruited merely in order to police areas of immigrant settlement. Until Roy Jenkins became Home Secretary, no real attempts were made to recruit coloured policemen, but, as a result of the stimulus administered by Jenkins, the policy of most forces changed from defensive assertions that no sufficiently qualified applicants had presented themselves to a positive attempt at recruitment. The Association of Chief Police Officers stated through their secretary in October 1966 that they 'would welcome more coloured applicants'.[86] Yet a survey among policemen in the Metropolitan area revealed that 62% of those questioned 'did not want coloured policemen recruited in areas where there were large numbers of coloured immigrants'.[87] At the time of writing there is still only one black policeman serving in the Metropolitan area.

One should add that there have been practical difficulties over the recruitment of coloured policemen. Part of the general shortage is due to the high standard, especially of physique, required and the conditions of work. Language is frequently cited as a barrier. Though the total number of coloured applicants to date is not known, the Metropolitan Police, for example, considered only one applicant in thirty suitable before 1964.[88]

The impact that the recruitment of coloured policemen could have had has to a great extent been lost. Belated attempts to improve the situation only serve to underline the previous reluctance of chief constables and the Metropolitan Commissioner. It cannot be that suitable applicants have only been coming forward since 1964. An appointment of a coloured policeman much earlier would have had a much greater impact on public and immigrant attitudes than it does now.

Finally, there are the police efforts to improve the training of new recruits and to educate serving policemen in social problems with particular reference to the immigrant community.

Police training for recruits consists of a twelve-week full-time course at a police district training centre, followed by a two-year probationary period on the beat, during which time the constable attends classes and lectures under the guidance of a force-training officer. In a document for the N.C.C.I., the Metropolitan Police state that in the initial training:

> The purpose is to train an officer to be a policeman first, and although consideration has been given to guiding the trainee towards an appreciation of what is required in community relations, race relations is only a small part of the formal training.[89]

Ninety-six lectures will have been delivered at the various recruit training establishments during the course of 1968. To quote further: 'The widely held opinion amongst senior officers that the practical experience of the policeman has more importance in this field has a great deal to commend it.'[90]

Training thus lays stress on the legal aspects of policing with a smattering of information on community relations. It is presumed that knowledge about the community will be achieved mainly through practical experience. In practice the attitudes policemen acquire during their two years' practical experience are to a great extent derived from older police-men. In addition, prejudices are likely to be reinforced if the only practical experience of immigrants is gained on the beat, in areas where the general population is most hostile to the police, and where the older officers have little time for further training. The new recruit will neither be exposed to informed or balanced attitudes, nor will he have time to relate his experience to what he has previously learned about community relations.

Apart from this initial training course, there are special courses for particular types of police work – for example, the C.I.D. – which need not be discussed here. In addition, there is a special course for constables at the Police College at Bramshill House intended for those who show promise, and serving as an avenue for accelerated promotion. It is broader in content than most other police training, and includes economics, politics, and social studies.

For higher ranks, the official further training courses for those singled out for eventual promotion to the highest levels are mainly (though not exclusively) concerned with police administration. No doubt this should be the main emphasis. But it can be argued that as policemen rise through the hierarchy they should gain a greater understanding of the complexity of life in an urban society and not just of one institution in that society.

However, the most important part of all police training is that given to police constables, because, as one policeman has put it, 'it is not the chief inspector the immigrant is worried about – it is the policeman walking down the Harrow Road, now'.[91] It is, in fact, unlikely that one part of the training can be changed without some reshaping of the training at all levels. The course for probationary policemen has changed little over the last twelve years and, apart from the new situation presented by immigration, it is time that courses took account of the new environment and the changing expectations both of the police and the community. The legal aspects of policing should be less emphasized and less reliance should be put on the part played by experience on the beat in the local setting and the influence of older colleagues. A greater importance could be attached to social studies in the form of elementary psychology and sociology. In this way, the road to improved police–community relations may be made a little easier.

CONCLUSIONS

The response of the police to the decline in their relations with the immigrant community has in some ways been encouraging, but it still leaves much to be desired. It would be unrealistic to hope for too dramatic a change, but already existing machinery can be adapted without too great a strain on police goodwill.

Certainly there is no doubt that the organization of the police is such that discrimination against any group in the community can be dealt with effectively. The way the police work is supervised and organized can drastically curtail the opportunities for discrimination. But against this must be set the question of police discretion which militates against the detailed supervision of the police task. However, the curtailment of discrimination does not so much require direct interference in detail as the adoption of disapproving attitudes and the disciplining of actions which are suspected as being discriminatory. This is why the Home Secretary's failure to persist in his earlier decision to introduce an amendment to the police disciplinary code, making it an offence to display prejudice or act in a discriminatory fashion, is regrettable. Although it has been strongly challenged by the Police Federation, it would stand as an official recognition that certain standards must be observed.

Finally, it is clear that, as Michael Banton indicates in his study of the police, change in our society will modify both the role of the police and the expectations and attitudes of the general public. These changes will place a considerable strain on the police and test their adaptability to the limit. As so often, one of the functions performed by the immigrants has been to display in its sharpest form a dilemma already arising as a result of processes at work in our society as a whole.

REFERENCES

1. K. Jones, 'Immigrants and the Social Services', *National Institute Economic Review* (No. 41, August 1967), pp. 28–40.
2. T. E. Oppé et al., *Children of West Indian Immigrants: A Study of One-Year-Olds in Paddington* (London, Institute of Race Relations, Special Series, 1970).
3. *The Times* (5th December, 1969).
4. Ibid.
5. *Digest of Health Statistics 1969* (London, Department of Health and Social Security, H.M.S.O., 1969).
6. British Medical Association, *Medical Examination of Immigrants: report of the working party* (London, B.M.A., 1965).
7. *Digest of Health Statistics 1969*, op. cit.
8. Ibid.
9. Ministry of Health Memorandum (November 1968).
10. D. Hinds, *Journey to an Illusion: The West Indian in Britain* (London, Heinemann, 1966).
11. B. Dahya, 'Pakistanis in Birmingham and Bradford' (for the Institute's Survey of Race Relations in Britain).
12. Statistics on the incidence of venereal disease are from the studies of the British Co-operative Clinical Group, 'The Gonorrhoea Study, 1965', *British Journal of Venereal Diseases* (Vol. 43, no. 1, 1967; R. R. Willcox, 'Immigration and Venereal Diseases in Great Britain', *British Journal of Venereal Diseases* (Vol. 42, no. 4, December 1966), pp. 225–37; B.M.A. Report, op. cit.
13. On the health of immigrants, see for example *Postgraduate Medical Journal* (October 1965).
14. T. E. Oppé, 'The Health of West Indian Children', in *Proceedings of the Royal Society of Medicine* (Vol. 57, no. 3, April 1964).
15. C. Bagley, paper presented to the Anglo-French Conference, Brighton, 9th–13th September, 1968, and 'Schizophrenia in Immigrant Groups', *Race Today* (October 1969).
16. F. Hashmi, paper presented to the Anglo-French Conference, Brighton, 9th–13th September, 1968.
17. A. Kiev, 'Psychiatric Illness among West Indians in London', *Race* (Vol. 5, no. 3, January 1964), pp. 48–54.
18. C. Eric Stroud and V. Moody, 'One Hundred Mothers: a survey of West Indians in Britain', *Maternal and Child Care* (Vol. III, no. 26, June 1967).

19. B. Gans, 'Health Problems and the Immigrant Child', in Ciba Foundation, *Immigration, Medical and Social Aspects* (London, Churchill, 1966).

20. B. Gans, op. cit., and see also W. H. Israel, *Colour and Community: a study of coloured immigrants and race relations in an industrial town* (Slough, Council of Social Service, 1964).

21. G. Stewart Prince, 'Mental health problems in pre-school West Indian children', *Maternal and Child Care* (Vol. III, no. 26, June 1967).

22. Oppé *et al.*, op. cit.

23. Professor C. Eric Stroud, 'The New Environment', *Postgraduate Medical Journal* (October 1965).

24. Eric Butterworth, op. cit.

25. K. Jones, op. cit.

26. H. M. Bulla, 'Immigration – past, present and future: attitudes and official policies of local officials in West Bromwich to coloured Commonwealth immigrants' (Dissertation for B.A. degree, University of Bradford, 1966).

27. J. Galloway, 'Some Aspects of Immigration', *The Medical Officer* (Vol. 118, no. 5, 4th August, 1967), pp. 69–70.

28. Oscar Gish and Andrew Robertson, 'Where Immigrant Doctors Go and Why', *New Statesman* (14th March, 1969).

29. Oscar Gish, 'Training and Advancement of Non-British Nurses', I.R.R. *Newsletter* (November–December 1968).

30. Oppé *et al.*, op. cit.

31. Burney, op. cit.

32. Central Housing Advisory Committee, Housing Management Sub-Committee, *Council Housing: Purposes, Procedures and Priorities*, 1969 (Chairman: J. B. Cullingworth), Chapter 12, Summary of Conclusions and Recommendations.

33. Eric Butterworth, op. cit.

34. K. Fitzherbert, *West Indian Children in London* (London, G. Bell, 1967), sponsored by the L.C.C., Lewisham Children's Department and the London Boroughs Social Work Training Organization.

35. Mary Dines (London Council of Social Service), 'The West Indian Family', *Race* (Vol. IX. no. 4. April 1968).

36. R. E. D. Simpson, 'Morbidity survey of general practice with a large proportion of immigrants' (for the Institute's Survey of Race Relations in Britain).

37. B. Kent, 'The Social Worker's cultural pattern as it affects casework with immigrants', *Social Work* (October 1965), pp. 14–22, and in Institute of Race Relations *Newsletter* (January and July 1968).

38. Peter Hutchinson: 'The Social Worker and Culture Conflict' *CASE Conference and ASW News* (April 1969).

39. R. E. D. Simpson, op. cit.

40. Oppé *et al.*, op. cit.

41. Ibid.

42. J. Lambert, 'Local Authorities and the Police'; background notes for Race Relations Conference, 4th, Birmingham, September 1969.

43. Burney, op. cit.

44. Central Housing Advisory Committee, op. cit.

45. See, for example, National Labour Women's Advisory Committee, *Labour women's national survey into care of children's final report* (London, N.L.W.A.C. 1967), Part 4: The education of immigrant children.

46. The Seebohm Report, op. cit.

47. *Immigrants and the Youth Service* (London, Department of Education and Science, July 1967). Chairman: Lord Hunt.

48. *Report of the Committee on Immigration Appeals* (Cmnd. 3387), (London H.M.S.O, August 1967). Chairman: Sir Roy Wilson.

49. Estimates submitted to the Home Office under Section 11, Local Government Act 1966. H. of C. Written Answers, Vol. 764, 98–9, 8th May, 1968.

50. *Children and their Primary School: A Report of the Central Advisory Council for Education* (London, H.M.S.O., 1967). Chapter 5. Chairman: Lady Plowden.

51. Statement (press release) on the Urban Programme by the Home Secretary, the Rt. Hon. James Callaghan, 22nd July, 1968.

52. Ben Whitaker, *The Police* (Harmondsworth, Penguin Books, 1964), p. 14.

53. *The Job* (the newspaper for men and women of the Metropolitan Police), in the editorial 'Man to Man' (8th December, 1967).

54. Joseph A. Hunte, *Nigger Hunting in England?* (London, West Indian Standing Conference, London Branch, 1966).

55. See *Race Today*, Vol. 1, no. 2, June 1969, pp. 54–56, also Evidence of the Select Committee on Race Relations and Immigration (Proof). Questions 1704–12 and 1834–9.

56. Much of the information for the section is drawn from *Police: a social study* (London, Church Information Office for Church Assembly Board for Social Responsibility, 1967); and Ben Whitaker, op. cit. The principal source, however, was from research commissioned by the Institute's 'Survey of Race Relations in Britain' by John Lambert, who has

examined police operations in Birmingham. It will be published as *Crime, Police and Race Relations* by O.U.P. later
in 1970.

57. *Report of Her Majesty's Chief Inspector of Constabulary for
the year 1965* (H.C. 251), p. 72.

58. *Report of the Commissioner of Police of the Metropolis
1967* (Cmnd. 3659), p. 16.

59. Royal Commission on the Police: minutes of evidence 1960–2
(Chairman: Sir Henry Willink) (London, H.M.S.O., 1963).

60. For a detailed discussion see John Lambert 'The Police can
Choose', *New Society* (18th September, 1969), pp. 492–32.

61. Ben Whitaker, op. cit., p. 30. Other examples of this sort of
activity are to be found in M. Banton, *The Police and the
Community* (London, Tavistock Publications, 1964), Ch. 5.

62. Cmnd 3315, op. cit., p. 30.

63. Compiled from the Reports of the Commissioner of Police
for the Metropolis and the Reports of Her Majesty's Chief
Inspector of Constabulary for 1965, 1966, 1967 and 1968.

64. *Report of Her Majesty's Chief Inspector of Constabulary
for the year 1967* (H.C. 272), p. 85.

65. *The Times* (3rd December, 1969). A report of a broadcaster,
on B.B.C. Radio 'Woman's Hour' on 2nd December, 1969.

66. 'The Police and the Citizen', prepared by Mervyn Jones for
the N.C.C.I. (London, October 1969).

67. Ibid.

68. Ben Whitaker, op. cit.

69. Cmnd. 3659, op. cit., p. 16.

70. This analysis was obtained from New Scotland Yard A7
Branch.

71. 'I wouldn't think of suggesting to you that the police force
does not share proportionately the prejudice of the society
from which its members are drawn, and to which they belong.' (Robert Mark, Deputy Commissioner of the Metropolitan Police Force, transcript of *Cause for Concern*, B.B.C.,
August 1968).

72. Michael Banton, op. cit., p. 146.

73. A. E. Bottoms, 'Delinquency among Migrants', *Race* (Vol.
VIII, no. 4, April 1967)

74. *Sunday Times* (30th July, 1967).

75. *Report from the Select Committee on Race Relations and
Immigration*, Vol. I, p. 54, para. 250.

76. From John Lambert's material. But a small-scale study, conducted by the Metropolitan Police in North London, showed
that police stations were frequently entered by local West
Indians for a wide variety of purposes.

77. *Birmingham Post* (25th April, 1967).
78. *Report of Her Majesty's Chief Inspector of Constabulary 1966* (H.C. 544), p. 9.
79. Minutes of Evidence to Select Committee, Memorandum from Chief Superintendent D. Merricks, p. 997, para. 9.
80. Ibid, p. 998, paras. 13–20.
81. N.C.C.I. *Police Training Procedure and N.C.C.I. Role.* Chief Inspector K. L. Lee (Metropolitan Police), NC/TRG/68/5, Appendix 2, p. 5.
82. *Coventry Evening Telegraph* (18th August, 1967).
83. *Guardian* (31st July, 1968).
84. Minutes of Evidence to Select Committee, Q. 3218, p. 1012.
85. Letters to the *Guardian*, (19th and 30th November, 1964).
86. *Evening Standard* (12th October, 1966).
87. *Bolton Evening News* (8th November, 1966).
88. In the past, the failure to recruit coloured police has sometimes been put down to the low quality of applicants. In one year, for which information is available (1966), thirty-six coloured men applied to join the Metropolitan Police – five were asked to attend an interview, but four failed to turn up. The fifth was rejected as being below standard. Of the rest, over half were recent immigrants and the others were rejected for lack of education or on medical grounds. The Home Secretary regarded these results as disappointing. (Vol. 740, H. C. Deb., Written Answers, Cols. 278–9, 7th February, 1967.)
89. Chief Inspector K. L. Lee, op. cit, p. 1.
90. Ibid, p. 2.
91. Transcript of *Cause for Concern*, B.B.C., August 1968.

Chapter Ten

Co-ordinating Voluntary Effort

In this section we will consider the role of some of the agencies, statutory and voluntary, which are concerned with race relations in Britain. It is impossible to cover all the varieties of voluntary organization which were set up to help solve 'race' or 'community' problems, or which, set up for other purposes, tried to influence the situation. Attention here is focused on those bodies set up locally and nationally to promote 'good relations' between immigrants and the native population. From the beginning, as the preceding chapters have indicated, integration was regarded by White-hall as essentially a matter for local institutions – local government, and local offices of central departments – and much was expected from voluntary organizations, for the inevitable complement of *laissez-faire* at the centre was re-liance on volunteers. The passage of the Race Relations Act of 1965 did not alter the fact that local effort was seen as the key to the situation.

On a national level radical lobbying organizations have not participated in this field to anything like the extent that might have been predicted. Explicitly political organizations of the left, like the Movement for Colonial Freedom, have displayed only spasmodic interest and the National Council for Civil Liberties' involvement only dates from the period of the Mosley punch-ups in 1962. One hybrid, Racial Unity, briefly combined the style of a radical organization and the welfare approach of a religious body during the early stages of migration. The Society of Friends and the Salvation Army have spanned the religious and secular spheres of activity in a style closely related to other organizations functioning at a local level. The Community Service Volunteers is one of the few organizations that has applied in local situations a broad approach deriving from its general concerns. The role of leadership within the immigrant communities will be discussed in Chapter 11. The influence of the Campaign Against Racial Discrimination (C.A.R.D.) has been discussed in the chapters dealing with the formation of Government policy. The Institute of Race Relations (which initiated the Survey of Race Relations on which this book is based) is primarily a research organization, while the Runnymede Trust – set up in 1968 – is actively concerned with the dissemination of information.

THE CHURCHES

The Churches might have played an important part in promoting racial harmony. Few people would deny that the Churches in Britain regard racial prejudice as being anti-Christian, and there is no lack of statements and publications from the Churches bearing witness to the need for racial tolerance. The British Council of Churches (to which all the main English Churches, except the Catholics, belong) has kept a watching brief on immigration since 1956, and has published strongly-worded resolutions on race relations.

The Board of Social Responsibility of the Church of England, individual churchmen (particularly Nonconformists), the Catholic Institute for International Relations, and the Race Relations Committee of the Society of Friends have all published pamphlets and teaching material expressing liberal views, and providing information intended to lay the various myths which have grown up about coloured immigrants. Moreover, in 1968 the whole Bench of Bishops and the Nonconformist representatives in the House of Lords voted against the Government in the debate on the admission of Kenyan Asians. But from the point of view of the immigrants – who in the main, occupy the decaying central areas of cities – these public statements are less important than local action, and here there has been a lack of communication between the leadership and the parish clergy. The rapidly changing character of urban life has created a whole series of problems for which the Churches have been unprepared, and their participation in community life has been weakened by the tradition that pastoral care is mainly concerned with individual church members in distress. The

Church of England has suffered a great decline in central urban areas due to the flight of the middle-class population; the Catholic Church and the Free Churches have strong working-class congregations, but the Catholics have traditionally avoided 'political' activities, and the smaller following of the Free Churches has weakened the impact of their social commitment. There have been further variations in the role which individual churchmen assume in relation to the immigrants. Some see them as one aspect of the general problem of Christian action in a changing environment; some see the arrival of West Indians as an opportunity for Christian revival because of their strong church-going traditions; some actively seek cultural integration; others are hostile to the Pentecostal sects because of their heterodox practices, and a few see the arrival of Asians as an opportunity for missionary work in the church backyard.

The evidence on church attendance among West Indians shows considerable variations, but it is likely that, as in the case of the Irish, migration has been associated with a decline in church-going. It is often the case that one or two churches in an area will account for all the church-going immigrants because of the efforts of a local minister. Where the churches have large West Indian congregations they will often also run advisory centres, community centres and play groups. Churchmen are also often active in local organizations concerned with immigrants. The wide range of activities undertaken by some churchmen shows that the contact of the local church with the immigrant community is frequently very much greater than church attendance figures indicate.[1] However, many churchmen and immigrants feel that the Churches have failed to help them in the way they could and should; the activities of the individual minister are negligible when viewed against the overall task. As one said recently, 'You work away in your own little plot, with your nose to the grindstone, and when you have time to look up, the whole race situation seems to have become much worse.' The achievements of individual ministers mask the inactivity of the Churches as a whole.

The Churches in England, and the Church of England in particular, own some very valuable assets, many of which are not utilized fully, even for ritual and congregational activities. The assets of the Churches which are of particular interest from the local communities' point of view are the churches and church halls. Control of these buildings is often split between the diocesan commissioners and the parochial councils. If there is agreement between these two bodies on the use of their buildings for social purposes, there is a great gain by the local community. If, however, as often happens, there is disagreement, or, more likely, a lack of local or diocesan initiative, then valuable buildings remain under-used or unused. In addition, changes in use or redevelopment of church premises for housing or community centres are often prevented by the legal aspects of church ownership.

This problem can be overcome and there are various Christian housing associations who have built on church land. But this activity, however, is only touching the fringe of the problem – 'the number of Churches considering using land for housing is very few indeed, despite the present need'.[2] Direct help for the immigrant community through housing associations has also been undertaken.

Connected with this problem of mobilizing church buildings for community activities is that of the duplication of buildings between denominations. This emphasizes the need for a national policy on the part of the Churches if any real progress is to be achieved. It impinges on the whole question of the role of the Churches in the urban areas with long-standing social problems related to housing, health and welfare. It will be mainly in these areas that immigrants will live for some time to come. The local churchmen individually cannot be expected to deal with these problems unsupported, and the use of church buildings is one very vital aspect of the problem.

There is another group of assets over which the Churches, particularly the Church of England and the Catholic Church, exercise control, that of schools. In 1963, places in denominational schools both primary and secondary accounted for 21% of the total places available.[3] They can thus have a strong influence on the educational policy on racial issues throughout the country, and some steps have been taken in this direction, as was mentioned earlier.

The welfare services run by the Churches do not directly impinge on the problems that have been discussed. They reflect, however, aspects of Christian concern for the deprived members of the community, and the traditions of Christian action for the community. Consideration of these services draws attention to the Salvation Army and the Quakers who have made large contributions in the field compared with their following in the community. It also draws our attention to the sort of effort the Churches can make in areas where they feel Christian action is needed. If similar efforts could be made by all the Churches in tackling the problems in the decaying areas of cities, it would go some way to bringing some measure of social justice to those who live there.

American students of race relations frequently express surprise that there has not been in this country any commitment on the part of the Jewish community equivalent to that in the United States. There have been exceptions in the case of individuals and certain synagogues, but until lately only the brief recrudescence of fascism on the pre-war model has been sufficiently powerful a stimulus to involve the Board of Deputies in the field of race relations. However, in 1969, the Board of Deputies set up a working party to investigate the possibilities for action by the Jewish community to improve race relations and at the time of writing, a preliminary report had already been produced.

VOLUNTEERS FOR INTEGRATION

The main contribution of voluntary organizations has, as we indicate above, been made at the local level. The early voluntary liaison committees* date from the early 1950s and were intended to deal with problems created by the new arrival of immigrants: 'liaison' could mean co-operation between different social welfare and other agencies. Others were formed after the 1958 Notting Hill and Nottingham 'riots' with the purpose of promoting racial harmony. The perspective of the early voluntary organizations can be partly defined in negative terms: they did not see the problems as racial ones. Mary Grigg has characterized the voluntary liaison committees as 'the voice of conscience of the local

* The title of voluntary liaison committee was conferred on these organizations when the N.C.C.I. was set up in 1965. We use the term to describe them even before this date.

establishment. They were built up on a belief that a few newcomers needed some help and friendly guidance and that there was nothing fundamentally wrong with the local community.'[4] Some committees seem to have been overtly paternalistic, like the Bristol Committee for the Welfare of Colonial Workers, which did not survive the long winter of *laissez-faire* in the 1950s. More typical of the later pattern was the Nottingham Commonwealth Citizens Consultative Committee, formed in 1954. Its main purpose was to provide practical help for immigrants, broadening activities started by the local Council of Social Service (which was one of its sponsors) in 1951.

The 1958 'race riots' did not fundamentally alter the perspective of these organizations. The most significant change seems to have been a shift away from the idea of 'welfare for immigrants' towards the idea of 'education for the host community'. One of the first actions of the newly formed Willesden Friendship Council, for example, was to commission research to assess the amount of prejudice among local residents, and, on the basis of the findings, to recommend a major educational programme to the council.[5]

Paradoxically, one of the effects of the Notting Hill episode may have been to disguise problems of discrimination. It is true that racial violence took place; but British society, in the person of Mr. Justice Salmon, condemned it, and some at least of the culprits were severely punished. But one corollary was that 'bad' race relations were equated with violence; 'good' race relations merely with the absence of violence. The attitude of many local authorities in 1959 was 'we have no problem' or 'we are watching the situation and it is fully under control' – they viewed race relations as a problem of public order. Many local authorities were reluctant to become involved at all, and none followed the example of Birmingham and a consortium of Black Country authorities who had formed the Commonwealth Welfare Council for the West Midlands, by employing full-time welfare officers. The attitude of the local authorities was important not only because they had decision-making power but also because the voluntary committees were often dependent on them for funds. The reluctance of the local authorities to commit themselves was also reflected in the avoidance of the issue by elected representatives. Only a few individuals conceived their role as including activity on behalf of immigrant constituents.

The various local 'liaison' committees set out to promote their goal of peaceful integration by undertaking a variety of activities on a rather limited scale. Mixed social gatherings, 'international' exhibitions or events, functioned as symbolic offers of welcome to immigrants, and could provide mild propaganda for the host population if they were attended by local dignitaries. No commitment to a policy more specific than harmony and friendship was required. The function of the social occasion varied. If organized merely to 'mix' people, they could become a matter of non-representative English meeting non-representative immigrants, a dilemma familiar to many middle-class voluntary workers in other fields. Collins described such a meeting in a school at which, 'on kiddies' chairs ... [the] middle-class elite, M.P.s, reverends and idealists ... unblinkingly faced the robustness of the migrants, and with their beautiful English manners politely observed the invisible gulf which existed between themselves and their dark brothers; that bridge which could be crossed only by the new West Indian quasi-elite, who inserted himself in the middle, in a kind of social no-man's-land.'[6] But where these meetings took place to celebrate, for example, the opening of a new community centre for an immigrant group, they could be a kind of social sealing-wax, a friendship ritual closing a period of conflict about the establishment of the centre. They could simply provide entertainment or enjoyment, or occasionally they could provide an opportunity for real co-operation. Some committees exercised a kind of U.N. trouble-shooter role: Willesden Friendship Council sent a multi-racial team to try and settle disputes between landlords and tenants. Nottingham lawyers attempted to conciliate in cases of housing discrimination, but their experience showed the need for legal sanctions; effective action on this front had to await the passage of legislation against discrimination.

During the 1950s no attempt was made to co-ordinate the activities of the voluntary committees; the move towards co-ordination sprang from the development of the liaison committee concept by Miss Nadine Peppard, who from 1957 was Secretary of the Immigrants' Advisory Committee of the

London Council of Social Service. In April 1964 she was appointed secretary of a small national advisory committee set up by the Commonwealth Immigrants Advisory Council to supervise the development of local committees and co-ordinate information. These were all non-statutory bodies. With the publication of the 1965 White Paper their work was legitimized with the establishment of the National Committee for Commonwealth Immigrants, which sanctioned the concept of Government involvement through the direction and financing of voluntary effort. The work of the committee on a national level has already been touched upon in Chapter 5; we are concerned here chiefly with the local activity of its constituent committees. A small full-time secretariat was set up at the centre under Miss Peppard's direction and grants were provided towards the salary of liaison officers serving with local committees. However, co-ordination remained a loosely-conceived operation. The central body dealt, one might say, with the N.C.C.I.'s output, with conferences, pamphlets, relations with local committees; the input – analyses, ideas, policy recommendations, written work – rested almost exclusively on volunteer effort. (The specialist panels of the N.C.C.I. – whose work is discussed with the subject areas concerned – were in effect voluntary bodies.)

The functions of the National Committee was defined in its first annual report as two – advisory and community development. From the start there was tension between these two roles. The function of liaison demanded the holding of a very delicate balance at local level between the local authority and the members of the local immigrant community in order that mutually accepted policies could be evolved. But, simultaneously, the committee had to discharge the function of advice-giving in such a way as to command the Government's attention without jeopardizing its conciliatory posture in local situations. There was no necessity for these functions to prove mutually exclusive, but the strain of discharging them can be seen in the general secretary's comment in the 1967 annual report: 'A body dedicated simultaneously to "liaison", conciliation, the eradication of injustices and the propagation of a new spirit, is constantly confronted by choices which seem impossible to make.'[7] In a situation where success, as the 1967 annual report put it, 'depends on retaining the confidence of the authorities in order that one's views will be heeded when it comes to policy-making [but] no less important the confidence of the immigrants, who may often interpret co-operation with the authorities as condoning of what may be discriminatory policies',[8] there was clearly a serious risk that conflicting pressures will lead to evasion of the difficult issues.

In the estimation of its successor, the Community Relations Commission, 'the N.C.C.I.'s most notable achievement was no doubt the part it played in gathering evidence and presenting the case for more comprehensive and effective legislation against racial discrimination'.[9] The N.C.C.I. was joint sponsor with the Race Relations Board of the P.E.P. Report on discrimination and the Street Report on anti-discriminatory legislation, whose impact on the passage of the Race Relations Act of 1968 is discussed in Chapter 5. Through the work of the advisory panels there was an unspectacular but valuable penetration into the training procedures of a number of professional groups – teachers, police, social workers in particular – and the provision of some additional services on a voluntary basis. A substantial grant from the Gulbenkian Foundation in 1967 provided for an extension of welfare work. However, the housing panel's recommendations of 1967 for a radical overhaul of policy towards twilight areas were entirely neglected (only to be taken up in an emergency situation a year later). The N.C.C.I. gave evidence to a number of statutory committees, including the Wilson Committee and the Seebohm Committee, but its signal failure to influence Government policy came with the passage of the 1968 Commonwealth Immigrants Act. Despite its official advisory role, the committee was at no stage consulted by the Government, and teetered on the brink of resignation. Eventually the Committee as an institution decided to remain in operation but individuals on the committee, on the staff, and on the advisory panels resigned.

The problems of identifying a coherent role have shown no sign of decreasing since the N.C.C.I.'s replacement under Section 25 of the 1968 Race Relations Act by a statutory body, the Community Relations Commission. In fact, the contradictions have been written into the statute, under which the functions of the C.R.C. are defined as 'to encourage the establishment of harmonious community relations' and to co-ordinate on a national basis the measure adopted for that purpose by others, and to advise the Home Secretary on matters referred to the Commission by him or on matters which the Commission considers should be brought to his attention. The Commission came into operation in November 1968 under the chairmanship of Frank Cousins, formerly General Secretary of the Transport and General Workers Union. The Commission was given a grant of £200,000, from which it could in turn make grants of up to £1,500 p.a. for the appointment of a local community relations officer. In 1969–70 this was raised to £300,000 and the maximum grant to £3,500. In addition to its support for local community relations committees the Commission has powers to provide training courses, arrange conferences and establish information services to advise local authorities and community relations councils. It is significant that since 1966 neither the N.C.C.I. nor the C.R.C. have succeeded in spending their total grant. In 1966–67 the N.C.C.I. spent £77,528 from a grant of £120,000, and in 1967–68, £131,735 from a total of £170,000. At the end of its first year of operation, the C.R.C. had an unexpended balance of about £14,000, out of £200,000, although it had obtained an increased grant from the Government. At the end of its first year of operation, in November 1969, the C.R.C. was under attack from a number of directions. There had been some important resignations both among the senior staff and of experienced community relations officers, and growing scepticism among some immigrant groups and radical critics. However, in reply to a question from Sir George Sinclair, Conservative M.P. for Dorking and a member of the Select Committee on Race Relations and Immigration, the Home Secretary said: 'The Commission has been in existence for less than a year. It is operating in a difficult area, but its annual report, which has been laid before Parliament, shows that a good deal of positive work has been done.... It is a new body, and it has its teething troubles.'[10]

When the N.C.C.I. was set up there were three main kinds of local organizations in existence: immigrant organizations, including some formed and run by West Indians but with an

T–K

inter-racial membership; local 'campaign' committees established to oppose racial discrimination; and local voluntary liaison committees, established with the broader aim of promoting harmonious integration of immigrant groups. The role of liaison committees was defined in the White Paper of August 1965 in terms of involving people of influence in the community as well as immigrants. The majority of the English-formed local voluntary committees had adopted this strategy and it was these who were singled out for official recognition and support by the N.C.C.I. A major part of the work of the N.C.C.I. and its successor, the Community Relations Commission, has been the promotion of such committees. After the establishment of the N.C.C.I. there was a spectacular increase in the number of voluntary liaison committees. Thirty-two were formed in the first two years of the committees' operations – many with a full-time secretary paid for from official funds – and by May 1969 there were 78 community relations councils (the new name dates from the establishment of the Community Relations Commission).

Throughout, the effectiveness of these local committees has varied. To some extent this can be attributed to the presence or absence of a full-time worker, but as a class the local organizations suffered from a form of the malaise of their parent body. There was constant tension in their conception of their role between the desire to act on behalf of immigrants, and the anxiety to retain the confidence of the local authority. From their original inception the voluntary liaison committees tended to discourage protest, in the form of marches or demonstrations. Most were inhibited from taking a more active part in opposing discrimination by their commitment to the idea of preserving racial harmony and bringing people together. They rejected confrontation, even as a last resort, partly as a result of a conviction that getting on with the powers that be was likely to produce better results than protest, partly from scepticism about claims of discrimination, and partly from the general view that sources of conflict between groups should not be stressed. In contrast of their parent body, few voluntary liaison committees played any part in the prolonged campaign to extend the Race Relations Act of 1965. This led to radical criticism of their position, expressed by Dipak Nandy:

Voluntary liaison committees have always had a choice, one which has been masked by the imprecision of the concept of 'liaison' (for it suggests a symmetrical two-way relationship which does not obtain in real life). The choice is between interpreting the demands for equal opportunities of the minority to the dominant white society and, on the other hand, acting as spokesman of that society to the minority group. In effect, the voluntary liaison committees have uniformly chosen the second alternative.[11]

The Nottingham Commonwealth Citizens Consultative Committee, for example, succeeded in obtaining local authority support in the 1950s, and Eric Irons (later the first coloured J.P.) was appointed as an educational organizer with special reference to the needs of coloured people. A recent study has shown that Irons became a channel for all contacts between the coloured community and the local authority, while acting as a buffer between them. Political discussion was discouraged within the committee, but its secretary, Miss Dorothy Wood, has commented that 'It has been awfully difficult for us to know how far we could go in supporting immigrant demands without alienating the council'.[12]

Most of the voluntary liaison committees, and many other voluntary organizations, have attempted some form of 'welfare' work: advising individuals, helping to fight court cases, setting up housing associations or children's play-groups, and so on. Inevitably, only a handful of people could possibly benefit from these efforts. The White Paper of 1965 explicitly discouraged the voluntary liaison committees from undertaking welfare services specifically for immigrants and so the committees have come to see their role as one of encouraging the adaptation of the existing statutory agencies to meet the needs of a society with immigrant populations: basically an advisory and information-giving role. If a local committee can muster sufficient expertise, it is possible to see how this function can be useful to the various professional workers coming into contact with immigrant groups. But the amount of influence the voluntary liaison committee has depends to a great extent on the professional workers' own attitudes, the composition of the voluntary committee, the attitude of the local authorities, and the extent to which the committee's recommendations conflict with the views of the local authorities. The more vigorous voluntary committees have often crossed the line from adviser to protagonist. For example, Ealing International Friendship Committee produced a detailed criticism of the local education authority's 'dispersal scheme' and called for basic changes in the way it is organized.[13] In Oxford, the local committee, O.C.R.I. (Oxford Committee for Racial Integration) has had some success in ending discrimination by local employers by using the threat of publicity as a sanction. It was unique in its acknowledgement of the extent of racial discrimination and the lengths to which its members and officers went in order to deal with cases of friction but in order to end a discriminatory practice. O.C.R.I. members were willing, not to disturb public order, but to run the risk of being accused of doing so, in order to publicize and end discrimination. Their picket of a hairdressing salon, after months of negotiation, was, however, very much out of line with the attitudes of most of the liaison committees. Both in Manchester and Brent, the local branches of C.A.R.D. complained that the voluntary liaison committees had tried to prevent protest action against alleged police misconduct in the area.

Another committee, C.C.C.R. (Camden Committee for Community Relations) has pushed the orthodox concept to the furthest point so far achieved. It is in Camden that the most ambitious campaign of public education has been undertaken and where the attempt to reach various key groups with influence over vital aspects of the lives of immigrants, like estate agents, has been tackled most systematically. Both in the provision of play groups and the sponsoring of housing associations, Camden's contribution has been better co-ordinated than that of other comparable committees.

The concept of 'community work' now adopted by the community relations councils has been best demonstrated in action by other kinds of organizations. The Sparkbrook Association,[14] working in an area with only 15,000 residents, has shown what can be done to improve the amenities and morale of a neighbourhood on a non-political basis. The incidental success of the association has been to prevent problems of 'urban decay', turning into race relations problems. The association had no views on some of the most important issues of race relations, such as immigration control or, locally, the implications for race relations of the Birmingham Corporation Act, which increased the local authority's power to limit multi-occupation. It was not intended to deal with racial injustice. Its function was to channel grievances into practical work to improve the area.

A broadly similar range of activities was undertaken by the Notting Hill Social Council in North Kensington. A deluge of voluntary organizations of all descriptions had burst upon the area after the disturbances of 1958, but in most areas the sheer scale of the problem had been too much for their limited resources. As Burt commented in 1960, 'the necessarily limited scope of any individual welfare project in North Kensington can only be overwhelmed by the uncontrollable magnitude of the problem confronted in the area.'[15] The Social Council, based on a Methodist group ministry, survived, where other voluntary bodies were engulfed, to undertake a series of practical projects directed towards community organization to tackle grievances held in common: it was still functioning effectively when in 1967 the flamboyant descent of a new wave of volunteers on the area began the cycle of activity and frustration over again.

In a different style altogether were groups like the Islington branch of the Campaign Against Racial Discrimination. Local C.A.R.D. groups began to be formed in 1966, at first largely as a result of individual action rather than any central planning. Most of the groups followed patterns of action established by the earlier 'campaign' committees such as the Campaign for Racial Equality groups in Leicester and Bradford: individual casework, collection of evidence of discrimination, 'counter propaganda,' and protest action. One of the main activities of Islington C.A.R.D. was to organize tenants to protect or gain their rights under the various Rent Acts. This was a highly political group, formed to deal with racial injustice. Its activities were intensive and involved aggressive protests against some local landlords and sometimes the local housing authority. Its ideology was popular participation, not the provision of services. But, as in Sparkbrook, the effect was the joint organization of efforts to combat problems common to immigrants and non-immigrants.[16]

Looking back upon the whole period from 1955 to the present day, it is clear that it was too much to expect that 'integration' could be decisively promoted or effected by the local voluntary committees unless they had had more political backing. Race relations in Britain were formed by forces beyond their control, and their own attitudes were influenced by the same forces. There was bound to be an element of 'tokenism' in the voluntary efforts to provide services which would be of real use to immigrants. Nevertheless, on a limited scale, the provision of a special training course, of a day-nursery, of a legal advice service, which would not otherwise have existed was not futile activity, especially in the smaller boroughs. Michael and Ann Dummett have argued that the committees' relationship with the N.C.C.I. or C.R.C. and the local authorities has encouraged conformism, that those liaison committees which applied for a grant for a liaison officer 'delivered him bound hand and foot into the power of a frequently hostile local authority', and that the growth in the number of liaison committees since the establishment of the N.C.C.I. has merely represented 'the artificial reproduction of rigidly stereotyped bodies' who are over-anxious to avoid areas of conflict. They argue that a unique opportunity was lost when, in the Committee stage of the Race Relations Bill, no serious consideration was given to the Rev. Wilfred Wood's proposals for a National Commission for Racial Equality, a body which was to include elected representatives of immigrant communities, and 'where the immigrants' voice, rather than the British Establishment's voice, would be heard'[17] (The political background to this episode is described in Chapter 5.)

Certainly the N.C.C.I. and C.R.C. did not meet one of the expectations of the White Paper – the building up of 'a comprehensive body of doctrine which can be flexibly applied to a variety of local situations'. Once a local committee has appointed a community relations officer, the C.R.C., if it agrees to make a supporting grant, can only offer advice, which may be refused. In reaction to what was felt to be excessive flexibility under the N.C.C.I., the C.R.C. has responded by a more rigid exercise of its powers of control over appointments, and there have been cases of conflict over the choice of some committees. There have also been problems arising from lack of communication between the C.R.C. and the community workers, and in November 1969 a field officers' association was formed to by-pass the existing two-tier structure and bring the first-hand experience of the field officers to bear on training and decision-making. Ann Dummett gave a vivid picture of the difficulties of liaison work in describing her reasons for resigning as community relations officer in Oxford:

Community relations workers are ... the front-line troops charged with attacking the key positions. And alas, we sometimes look more like Fred Karno's army. Heterogeneous and ill-equipped, the members of the local community relations council, and their officers, are being asked to do the impossible.[18]

For many of the English participants in the committees, contact with immigrant representatives was their introduction to the problems of racial discrimination. Ideally, this interaction between 'people of influence' – both from the 'host' and immigrant communities – would give the immigrants a share in the decision-making process, and increase the understanding of the English. But this ideal rested on an assumption about the goodwill of the host community – particularly the decision-makers – which has been steadily eroded in the past ten years. This does not mean that the strategy of seeking to involve people of influence has become invalid, although its validity may well vary from borough to borough. It does mean, however, that the methods used to achieve this, and even more important, the actual content of the involvement, need to be re-examined. The danger facing the community relations committees is that they may become remote, both from the ordinary citizen, and from the springs of power within their area, and become window-dressing for local authorities indifferent and even hostile to equal rights for minorities.

REFERENCES

1. See, Rev. C. S. Hill, *West Indian Migrants and the London Churches*, Chapter III; and the Methodist Church Manchester and Stockport District Christian Citizenship Committee: Social Responsibility Project, Group 6 Race Relations Report, August 1966, these give some figures for other forms of contact.

2. Memorandum from Rev. W. J. Milligan to the British Churches Housing Trust, January 1968.

3. *Facts and figures about the Church of England*, No. 3 (Central Board of Finance of the Church of England, 1965), Table 83.

4. Mary Grigg, *The White Question* (London, Secker and Warburg 1967) pp. 135–36.

5. Joan Maizels, *The West Indian Comes to Willesden* (London, Willesden Borough Council, 1960).

6. W. Collins, *Jamaican Migrant* (London, Routledge & Kegan Paul, 1965).

7. Report for 1967 (London, N.C.C.I. 1968), p. 14.

8. Report for 1967 (London, N.C.C.I. 1968), p. 14.

9. Annual Report of the Community Relations Commission (London: Her Majesty's Stationery Office, 1969).

10. Hansard, 20th November, 1969.

11. Dipak Nandy, 'An Illusion of Competence', in *Policies for Racial Equality*, A. Lester and N. Deakin (eds.) (London, Fabian Society, 1967).

12. Quoted in I. Katznelson, *The Policies of Race under the Impact of Migration: the U.S.* (1900–30) and the U.K. (1948–68): Unpublished thesis submitted for Ph.D at Cambridge University 1969.

13. *The Education of the Immigrant Child in the London Borough of Ealing*, a report of the Education Committee of the Ealing International Friendship Council (April 1968).

14. For a full account of the work of the Sparkbrook Association, see J. Rex and R. Moore, op. cit., Chapter IX.

15. Robert A. Burt, *Colour Prejudices in Great Britain* (Unpublished thesis submitted for B.A. degree, Princeton University, 1960).

16. See Nigel Baseley's (unsigned) article in *Campaign*, No. 1, Newsletter of the Campaign Against Racial Discrimination.

17. Michael & Ann Dummett, *The Role of Government in Britain's Racial Crises* in Lewis Donnelly (ed.), *Justice First* (London: Sheed & Ward, 1969).
18. Ann Dummett: 'What to Do' (*Race Today*, June 1969).

Chapter Eleven

The Immigrant Response

Earlier chapters have described the societies from which the immigrants came, the kinds of people they were and some major factors which have determined their life in Britain, in particular the jobs they are in and the housing which they have been able to obtain. This chapter describes in a little more detail some of the ways in which the minorities have been developing in Britain. Several cautions are necessary: a variety of different 'responses' to British society should be expected, not only and obviously between the various national groups, but also within those groups. There is also one particularly important distinction to be drawn which cuts across all national groups, and that is the generation difference. The voice of the younger generation, and the British born generation, has so far been heard even less than that of their parents. When they are heard, this response to British institutions and their account of their role in them may differ radically from that of the original immigrants. They are already, among some groups, a very sizeable minority. For example, according to one estimate, nearly 40% of people living in Caribbean households in 1966 were under 15, and of those under 11 at that time, the overwhelming majority were born in Britain.[1] It is therefore possible that what we describe here under the heading of 'immigrant response' may soon be out of date, and there may be quite a different definition of problems under the heading of minority response.

WEST INDIANS

Of all the national groups, the Caribbean migrants were the most diverse and individualistic. They came from many islands, from many occupations, and from different colour-groups in what Professor Gordon Lewis has termed the Caribbean 'pigmentocracy'.[2] From almost casual beginnings there developed a flow from all the islands which was the result of a number of individual initiatives. At a later stage, the communities in the U.K. were reinforced as relatives came to join relatives, but the migration remained a movement of individuals whose obligations were limited to themselves and their immediate family – partner, children, and in some cases parents. There was nothing like the system of sponsorship or the elaborate network of village or kinship which had so much influence on the pattern of migration and settlement of Indians and Pakistanis. There was nothing in the West Indian family system, nor in the organization of the migration, which encouraged the concentration of the migrants in large separate settlements.

The West Indians were, initially at any rate, the most assimilationist of all the coloured immigrant groups because of their cultural identification with Britain, an identification which was the product of slavery and colonialism in the Caribbean. The West Indians took their British citizenship seriously, and many regarded themselves not as strangers, but as kinds of Englishmen. Everything taught in school and institutional life in the Caribbean until recently encouraged this belief. As one provincial spokesman put it, 'We are not immigrants in the true technical sense: after all, we are members of the realm, we are British.'[3]

There is no shortage of examples of conformity to British norms among West Indians in Britain. There is the demographic evidence that West Indian women are marrying earlier and limiting their families. The evidence of the falling West Indian birth rate in Birmingham (reviewed in Chapter 4) is supported from the records of general practitioners. In one Bristol practice with a large number of Jamaican patients, there is conclusive evidence of a sharp decline in the birth-rate over a period of five years.[4] In a study of 200 West Indian mothers (40% Barbadian, the rest mainly Jamaican) in Reading, Professor Bell found that 90% were married, and that three-quarters of those who were unmarried when they came to England had got married within two years of their arrival.[5] For most of them illegitimacy carried no stigma at home, yet in England they (half of them) felt it was important to legitimize their children. Bell also found that husbands were actively helping to rear the children; 56% of the women were working and in half these cases, husbands were caring for the children during the day. They were on nightshift. This was a very different pattern from that prevailing in the West Indies, in fact they participated more than the average English father. It would be wrong to generalize from this. Many Caribbean families in Britain are still matriarchal in form, the stable unit the mother and children born to one or several partners. Nonetheless, with job security providing the economic basis which was seen as the prerequisite of marriage in the West Indies, West Indians in Britain are increasingly following a family pattern which is typically British. In their study of Sparkbrook in Birmingham,[6] Rex and Moore found that the West Indians who came from a number of islands, followed a 'largely English culture pattern' with their community and social activities centred around sports clubs; some of the West Indian families reminded them of the Victorian middle class, and they write of the 'petit bourgeois respectability which pervades so much of West Indian life'. The Victorianism of the West Indians is a theme developed strongly by Professor Gordon Lewis: 'whereas for the English *The Forsyte Saga* is a romantic dream only, for the West Indian that story still reflects much of the Caribbean class reality.'[7] One example of this is the much discussed authoritarian attitude of West Indian parents towards their children. For example, their use of corporal punishment and suspicion of youth clubs has brought them into conflict with British social workers. Another example is the fact that West Indians are often the main support of the Churches in working class areas. Yet another example of West Indian respectability is the low crime rate among West Indians, compared with the rest of the population in the areas where most of them live. They tend to live (for reasons discussed in Chapter 4) in areas of cities with the highest crime rates and criminal residences; they also belong very largely to the age group (15–44) which is the most prone to crime; and yet the incidence of crime among this first generation appears to be far lower than for the population at large. John Lambert's study of the police division in Birmingham[8] with the highest crime rate showed that West Indians (who at the 1966 census,

though only 6.4% of the division's population, were concentrated in the criminal areas where they comprised 17% of
the population) accounted for only 3% of all indictable
offenders. As Lambert says, 'They seek success within the
general framework of their own values and rise above the
delinquent and criminal standards prevalent in the areas in
which they live.' This general law-abidingness was also a
feature of West Indian migration: there was no black market
in currency, no reported attempts to evade passport control
or immigration regulations, West Indian children invariably
arrived with entry certificates in the period when these were
recommended, but not compulsory. In the work situation,
the West Indians' acceptance of British institutions has been
demonstrated by their readiness to join trade unions and
their active participation in unions. Beryl Radin found that
many coloured shop stewards had been elected in branches
with predominantly white workers, and one West Indian was
chairman of a branch with nearly all white workers.[9] She
quotes a union official in London who reported that on two
building sites where West Indians had been elected as shop
stewards and where there were a number of Irish and other
'foreigners', the West Indians were the most 'English' of all
the men there.

But the Englishness of the West Indians was not perceived
by many in the so-called host society, particularly in the
rapidly changing areas in which many of the migrants lived.
Most of the Jamaicans interviewed in Richmond's study of
St. Paul's in Bristol in 1966 supported the view that immigrants should adopt English customs and rejected the suggestion that immigrants cling together and do not want to be
friendly with the English.[10] The vast majority of the
English in the area took the view, however, that 'the immigrants' background and way of life make them altogether
different from English people round here' – although they
failed to agree when pressed on the specific ways in which the
migrants were different. Even disregarding cultural differences, the disparities between the age and family structure of the two communities in areas like St. Paul's would
have been a barrier to communication. Most of the migrants
were young adults with young children; many of the English
living in these areas were much older, with children who had

grown up and left home. Rex and Moore observed that nostalgia for the past glories of the neighbourhood added to the resentment felt by older people in Sparkbrook against the newcomers.[11] The Bristol researchers found that the feeling that St. Paul's had lost status produced a greater antipathy towards West Indians among their neighbours than among English residents elsewhere in the city.[12]

In contrast, the small group of West Indian and mixed families on three Bristol housing estates were nowhere thought to be lowering the status of the neighbourhood. This finding was the more remarkable in view of the concern for respectability prevalent among the residents. The study of the 45 West Indian families rehoused affords an encouraging picture of successful social integration.[13] The West Indians have a similar outlook to the English on the estates and faced the same problems of making a start in finding friends. The main differences seemed to be that the West Indians were rather more sociable than the English. Very few of the West Indians had been there longer than two years. They found the English good and helpful neighbours and the estates friendlier places than the inner city areas where they had lived before. Gardening was a useful common bond. The most successful relationships seemed to be established where there were families with young children, although on the whole the West Indian children were younger than the English. Difficulties occurred with elderly, reserved neighbours, repeating the pattern of the gap between generations in the twilight areas. Most of the West Indians had formed good friendships, and there was nothing like the social isolation which was characteristic of many of the English families interviewed. It was also very striking that there was little tendency for the West Indian families on the estates to draw together, although some of them made frequent visits back to St. Paul's to see friends or to shop for West Indian food. Nor did they favour joining West Indian clubs, as they felt this might prevent their being accepted on the estates. Equally striking was the low degree of prejudice among their English neighbours on the estates, few of whom were prepared to hold stereotyped views about colour but saw the West Indian families as individuals whom they welcomed or not, on their merits.

But, of course, the council estate context was not the typical one for West Indian families in Britain. St. Paul's was typical, where the opportunities for social integration were limited both by the material struggle to obtain a reasonable living standard, and by the non-communication observed between English and immigrant populations. Paradoxically, it has been the assimilationist, Anglophile West Indians who have been most disillusioned by life in Britain and their experience here has led many to shed their former identification with this country. In the P.E.P. report's survey of immigrant opinion,[14] over half the West Indians said they had found life in Britain worse than they had expected, while only 12% said it had turned out better. The problem of finding housing and jobs were mentioned as reasons, but the greatest source of disappointment, the one which affected most people, was said to be racial and colour prejudice and unfriendliness towards foreigners. The disillusion was in part, for the most Anglophile, the shock of finding that the England they had been told about did not exist: 'The British people whom I and the rest of us met were to us paragons of everything manly, courageous, wonderful. How can I or any other West Indian live down this great lie? Is this the homeland of the great John Wesley, the birthplace of Nurse Cavell ...? It is not the material England alone that draws immigrants ...'[15]

The writer of this letter to a provincial paper in 1958 expressed what has been repeated again and again by West Indians writing about the integration of their countrymen into British life. It was also partly that in leaving the carefully graded colour-class system of the West Indies, the newcomer faced the crude 'coloured or white' categorization employed by the English. Those West Indians for whom migration had been seen as a step towards middle-class, or 'white' status were doubly frustrated; those who were fair skinned, and/or part of the middle class found themselves sharply demoted. 'There are certain unusual features of my experience,' wrote a former Minister of Labour from Trinidad, 'I was accepted as a white person in Trinidad. For all practical purposes, I am "coloured" in England.'[16] Gordon Lewis has summarized the West Indian dilemma in Britain in the following way: 'On the one hand, his image of a liberal England, fed by generations of laudatory colonial school textbooks, disables him; and this produces the literature, already voluminous, of West Indian disillusionment. On the other hand, his Victorian background equips him to understand the new, virulent forms of English social snobbishness. The Americans, observed the Chicago wit Mr. Dooley, defeat their enemies, the English disqualify them; and what the black immigrant meets is a series of English disqualification exercises, implemented with all the massive ingenuity of English hypocrisy. He meets them with tolerant, unvindictive good humour, although clearly there is a limit to his patience. He can be seen, indeed from this viewpoint as the last of the English gentleman type surviving in a society where the last of the English gentleman class is rapidly on the decline."[17]

Lewis warns against the myth that West Indian society is culturally akin to British society. It is, he argues, *sui generis*, and even the most pro-English sectors developed early on a distinct psychological separatism, which divorced them from English values. 'All that needs to be done now is to break the cord.' And the recent tendencies in West Indian life and organization in Britain in the late 1960s, he suggests, can be seen possibly as a breaking of the cord.

Tracing the policies expressed by leading West Indian organizations from 1958 to 1968, a clear shift is observable away from assimilation and multi-racialism, towards self-help and emphasis on a distinct West Indian identity. It is also possible to observe the changing reaction to the English community: from expectation of fair play, to apprehension, to certainty of foul dealing.

The earliest kind of West Indian organizations formed by post-war migrants were in fact models of separate, self-help groups – the numerous joint savings and credit schemes ('pardners'), Pentecostal churches, and social clubs formed usually on an island basis. But these had no political ideology or goals. Despite earlier pre-war examples like the West Indian led, anti-colonial, League of Coloured Peoples, no political organizations emerged until the late 1950s – discouraged alike by divisions within the West Indian population in Britain, and by the reluctance of the English to recognize that immigrants were distinct and had difficulties as groups. Of particular importance in holding back the development of strong leadership, or, to put it rather differently, the development of secure followings for West Indian spokesmen, were colour-class divisions carried over from the West Indies.

The disturbances in Nottingham and Notting Hill in 1958, led to the formation of a number of organizations concerned about integration and the position of minorities in Britain, but many of these were short lived. The most significant individual initiative was that of Claudia Jones, Trinidadian and former member of the Communist Party of the U.S.A., who had been deported from there to Britain in 1957 after her imprisonment under the Smith Act. *The West Indian Gazette*, a weekly paper founded by her in the same year, rapidly gained circulation and for a while became an effective platform for the views of West Indians on major policy issues.

Of very different political character were the initiatives taken at this time by the Migrant Services Division of the West Indian Federal High Commission. It was under its auspices that the West Indian Standing Conference was created in 1958. A London-based federal organization, it functioned at first as a discussion group on the problems of integration, in which both West Indians and white sympathizers joined. The formula fostered by the High Commission, both in Standing Conference and in provincial organizations formed or encouraged by it, was that of careful multi-racialism. Two major events in 1961 precipitated a change of policy within Standing Conference. The first was the break-up of the concept at the federation, as a result of Jamaica's rejection of the concept at the referendum of September 1961 (see Chapter 5). There is no doubt that this came as a shock to West Indian leaders in England, all of whom appear to have supported the idea of the federation, regardless of their island of origin, and to have regretted its collapse. With the Federal Government went its High Commission in the U.K. and the Migrant Services Division. At the same moment (indeed, the two events were connected, as we have seen in Chapter 5) the British Government decided to introduce control of Commonwealth immigration. Thus, the presumption of British fair play, which was nurtured by the High Commission and to some extent justified by British reactions to Notting Hill, was exposed as unreliable and the strategy based upon it was discredited. From this point onwards, Standing Conference began to move slowly away from the original formula of a multi-racial discussion group, and to develop a policy based on the proposition that a separate strategy for West Indians in Britain, dependent neither on acceptance by the hosts nor on support by the High Commissions, would have to be devised.

The election campaign of 1964, when Peter Griffiths won at Smethwick on an anti-immigration platform, and the drastic curbs on immigration of the White Paper of August 1965, could only deepen the disillusionment of the West Indian organizations. In Neville Maxwell's *The Power of Negro Action*,[18] Standing Conference produced in 1965 a reasoned statement of policy which started from the rejection of the concept of assimilation as a goal for West Indians in British society. Maxwell concedes that 'by and large the West Indian until recently has been concerned less with the self-identification, West Indianism, negritude or call-it-what-you-will, than with the unconscious drive to establish a minimal level of communication with the native community'. But now he has no alternative, white leadership and white perceptions of the Negro's place in British society are equally damaging to his future prospects in Britain. The solution lies in capitalizing on weakness; the geographical concentration in the incipient ghetto provides a framework within which to organize and the preoccupation of most immigrants with 'bread and butter issues' became a conscious policy of economic development (the parallel made is with the Jews). In proper Samuel Smiles style, what is required is an Operation Boot Strap. In the meantime, anything which helps to provide a degree of unity and stimulate interest, even cricket, must be encouraged, and class divisions based on middle-class values minimized.

In 1968, after the Kenyan Asian episode, and the start of Enoch Powell's series of anti-immigrant speeches, Standing Conference's public line became even more defiantly separatist: 'We are not British' the Legal Panel argued in a long statement issued after Powell's first speech, 'we are citizens of the Commonwealth, not of the British Commonwealth which does not exist. . . . The fiction of the "Mother Country" is to be blamed for the failure of both the British Government and the High Commissioners to respond to their respective duties to black people in Britain at the height of the racialist violence and threats.' Something like this same development of attitudes seems to have occurred in most of the provincial West Indian communities. In an article on three West Indian organizations in Wolverhampton in 1969, Jennifer Williams reported that irrespective of their degree of militancy, all had changed from their original social club function, and were now concerned with self help, more conscious of having political and economic aims, and showing increasing disenchantment with the official multi-racial structure.[19] Gordon Lewis, after travelling widely in Britain in 1968–69, found that 'most West Indian organizations oscillate between rejection, root and branch, of the "host society", and a search 'to make the best of its better radical tradition'.[20]

All this, however, remained at the time of writing more a matter of opinion than of actual organizational change, of wishes rather than success. There were local examples of valiant self-help work by West Indian groups, particularly for instance in organizing youth clubs, and of campaigns on individual issues which had some effect. But West Indian organizations remained on the whole small and fragmented. Their spokesmen were hardly ever sought out by the mass media, whose representatives, in 1968, still turned first of all to figures like Lord (Learie) Constantine. As Gordon Lewis remarks however, 'this essentially unformed, even inchoate, character of the immigrant organization scene is understandable of course, once it is remembered that it is the product of a tiny time-period in the history of British race relations'.[21]

PAKISTANIS[22]

Of all the migrations from the Commonwealth, the Pakistani presents the greatest contrast to the West Indian. If to many West Indians Britain was the mother country, to Pakistanis it was a foreign land whose language, customs, religion, and way of life were totally alien to them. Their loyalties were to their own new nation, to their region, to their village, and above all to their kin. They came to England asking nothing of their hosts except to settle for a while, work, and earn for their families at home, to whom they meant to return.

What distinguishes this migration from all others, and not simply from the West Indian, is its demographic imbalance. For cultural as well as economic reasons, it has remained predominantly male, selecting male children to join male relatives in this country. The imbalance between the sexes is far greater among Pakistanis than among West Pakistanis, who have recently begun to bring their wives over[23] – even then, those who do so are generally men who came during the 1950s, and the number of families in which a mother is present is still fairly small. When the Pakistani Government began to restrict the issues of passports, travel agents emerged to fulfil the new and profitable role of supplying forged documents and of sending 'religious' travellers to Britain via the Middle East. The organization of this traffic depended to a large extent on there being sponsors in England who could provide shelter and an introduction to a job, and in many cases, the money for the fare. The effect of the 1962 Commonwealth Immigrants Act was to perpetuate the selective process of migration, as kinsmen and fellow-villagers stood an even better chance of being sponsored under the voucher system than those who had no kinship links with Britain.

A very close reciprocal relationship is set up between sponsor and client. Some form of sponsorship by friends and relations in Britain on the basis of village-kin ties is a necessary insurance for the immigrant against possible hardship during his early days in Britain. This, as much as a desire to be with kinsmen and friends, explains the emergence of village-kin groups in Britain, which has become the pattern of settlement, not only among Pakistanis but among the Gujaratis as well.[24] The sponsor has an equal interest in the relationship. He looks first for kin to help him to achieve his economic goals, whether in running a business or in managing houses. If close kinsmen do not exist, he sponsors distant kinsmen, friends, and fellow-villagers. It is not necessary for a prospective migrant to know his sponsor personally, provided there is a mutual friend known to both parties.

A Pakistani sponsor in Britain becomes a patron to all those whom he has sponsored, no matter how widely dispersed they might be in Britain.

In Pakistan, men and adolescent boys spend their leisure hours in the company of male members of the *baradari* (or brotherhood, which comprises a number of extended families within a clan) at the *baithak* (a kind of club or resting place). Here, a family's male guests will often sleep with their host or with another male member of the family. Among Pakistani immigrants in Britain, the sponsor and his 'family', or the house-group, are the substitutes for the traditional functions of social control exercised at home by the *baithak* and the *baradari*. Within the all-male dormitory houses, the Pakistani is reminded of his primary obligation, which is to discharge his debt to his sponsor or to his family (who have probably mortgaged their land to pay for his passport and passage) and then to remit sufficient funds to Pakistan to sponsor other kin and to improve his family's fortunes.

The Pakistani sacrifices material comfort to pursue his economic objectives, and the dormitory house, with its low rent of 15s a week, is an important means to this end. Food is bought on a co-operative basis at bulk rates and he can live on as little as £2 10s 0d a week, other expenses consisting of 2s. for flour, 7s. for milk, 16s. for groceries, and 10s. for bus fares. In his first few years every penny is saved to discharge obligations: many Pakistanis remit as much as half their earnings. It was estimated that in 1963 remittances amounted to as much as £26 million, or more than the inland revenue of East Pakistan.[25] The dormitory house also serves as a kind of insurance policy or provident society, for rent is excused to a kinsman who falls out of employment. It is, therefore, not surprising that a plan by the Bradford City Council to provide hostels for single Pakistanis, with separate cooking facilities in each room, at a rental of 30s. a week failed to evoke any response. Their goals are more likely to be reached through mutual support and austere living than through dispersal into the wider community.

Joint living in these dormitory houses with their group activities and total lack of privacy ensures that the immigrant conforms to the norms of his community in respect of diet, thrift, recreation, language, avoidance of contacts outside the sub-group, and modest hospitality to visiting kinsmen. Apart from visiting friends, leisure hours are spent in the house or in watching Indian and Pakistani films. This self-sealing process is carried over into working hours, especially if the immigrant is recruited into an ethnic gang, sometimes on the night shift, where contact with his employers is maintained through an English-speaking foreman.

These closely knit and self-segregated communities are served by their own shops and other services provided by fellow-countrymen: the growth of these services and the emergence of the Pakistani entrepreneur in the last few years is a measure of the growth of separate communities. In Bradford in 1967, there were fifty-one Pakistani grocers and butchers, compared with only two in 1959. The number of cafes increased from three to sixteen, of barbers sixfold. The city now has five Pakistani banks. In 1967 an article in *Asia Weekly* compared Bradford's Lumb Lane to a bazaar in some prosperous city of Pakistan. The same kind of development has taken place around other Pakistani communities. For example, in Balsall Heath, whereas ten years earlier there were five Pakistani shops or cafes, in 1967 there were sixty. Glasgow's population of 7,000 Pakistanis is served by one hundred retail grocers and twenty-five wholesale stores.[26]

This picture of a community organized along village-kin groupings has emerged only in the last few years and is the result of massive reinforcement from Pakistan since 1961. In the earlier years, Pakistanis settled together irrespective of origin, but as the rate of immigration accelerated, subgroups, based at first on regional identity, soon fragmented into village and kinship units. The community was further divided by religious sects, namely, the Sunnis, Shias, and Ahmeddiyas. Thus, the growth of the Pakistanis in Britain has developed from a fusion of the migrant community to fission and segmentation. Personal relationships between immigrants from outside their area of origin are kept to a minimum. East Pakistanis live exclusively apart from West Pakistanis, even in London where the acute housing shortage might have brought them together. In Bradford there is no sharing between West Pakistanis from different regions – Pathan tribesmen live on their own, and there is a similar division between Punjabis and non-Punjabis. Houses are apt to be grouped according to area of origin.[27]

This effect of fission through reinforcement is familiar from the pattern of settlement of immigrants in other countries,[28] but whether it will persist among the Pakistanis depends on the rate at which families are reunited in this country. If a wife comes to join a husband, the family moves to a house away from the areas of dormitory settlement. At first, such families were few and isolated, on the margin of the settlement, but already there is a perceptible clustering of family houses in certain streets cutting across regional and kin boundaries. In its third stage families are thrown out to the margin, leading in the next stage to a clustering of family houses with a return to fusion, and finally to the stage where the dormitory house may itself become marginal. There are still Pakistani settlements which have been formed fairly recently, in places like Luton, Bedford, and Watford, which have not got much beyond the stage of fusion; earlier settlements in Bradford and Birmingham exhibit the second stage fully and the beginnings of the fourth stage of family clusters.

Before the 1965 White Paper virtually closed the door to adult male immigrants, it was possible for brother to replace brother in the emigration, and when Rex and Moore were working in Sparkbrook in 1964, they found that many Pakistanis expected to follow this pattern. The effect of the White Paper was to substitute adolescent schoolboys for their uncles in the emigration; after a short period in English schools, they too would become worker-bees sending honey back to the hive. Thus, the Government restrictions did not change the pattern of the settlements, except to lower the age of entry. But they did force the immigrant to face the fact that he would probably not return to his country, except on a visit. This may have led a certain number to decide to bring over their wives who would not have otherwise done so; subsequent restrictions imposed by the British Government accelerated the process. The effect of the 1968 Commonwealth Immigrants Act, which closed the door to dependent children unless both father and mother were in Britain, remains to be seen. It may result in many more wives coming over to join husbands, but cultural inhibitions may still prove too strong.

The male settlers exhibit many of the characteristics of the transient. They ask little of this country except to be allowed to earn and prosper materially. If this is conceded, they are not very much concerned with their social or political rights. The Race Relations Board has received very few complaints from Pakistanis. The P.E.P. report showed that they are not particularly aware or resentful of discrimination because they avoid situations which would bring them into conflict with outsiders, with whom they seek only a *modus vivendi*.[29]

Once a Pakistani decides to bring his wife and children to this country he is breaking out of the web of connections that has tied him so closely to home, kept him sheltered from the outside world, and prevented him from psychologically putting down roots in Britain. Bringing over a wife and children is in many ways a most decisive step. But it does not mean that there will be any loosening of the bonds of his own culture: in fact, they may well become stronger.

The arrival of wives in Britain serves to reinforce Muslim culture in other ways. They are kept in strict purdah and effectively isolated from the world around them. A Muslim woman who visited several Pakistani families in Bradford reported on the extreme loneliness of the wives and their dependence on their husbands.[30] Removed from the companionship of other women in the joint family, they cannot leave their house without their husbands, who still spend their leisure with other men outside the home. The traditions and taboos of the joint family are carried over even into the small nuclear household: husband, wife, and children eat their meals separately and the wife must eat unseen by her husband. Even if there were not the barrier of purdah, they would be isolated by their total lack of English. As more are reunited, this social isolation will no doubt be broken down, but it seems certain that the first generation will be zealous guardians of their culture and will see that it is transmitted to their children.

Pakistanis in Britain regard themselves as a people apart. They classify themselves as *Kâlé* (black or coloured), and Europeans as *Gôrélok* (literally 'white people'). Negroes are referred to as *Sîdîs*, irrespective of their origin, and are not part of the *Kâlé* category. The distinction between *Kâlé* and *Gôré*, the insiders and the rest, is primarily a social distinction, based on culture and religion which transcends class distinction and the connotation of colour is often forgotten.

This classification of the world into 'us' and 'them' has a close parallel to the practice of Jews, and may tell us a good deal about the way this community will seek to maintain a separate cultural existence in Britain.

There is no sanction in Islam against inter-marriage with people of another faith, and Pakistani seamen who arrived in the early 1950s frequently married English wives.[31] But in spite of the very great preponderance of single men in the emigration, there appears to have been comparatively little inter-marriage with the *Góré lok*, although correspondence in the two Urdu papers shows that 'marriage out' is sufficiently widespread to be regarded as a deviant pattern of behaviour and a threat to the culture of the community.

Meanwhile, the majority of Pakistanis in this country remain single, and they appear to be achieving their econ-omic objectives. The great mass of workers are still engaged in labouring jobs in textiles, heavy engineering, and in trans-port. It may be deplorable that they tend to be concentrated in industries which are declining and, for the long run, there is a danger that Pakistanis will be associated with this kind of occupation, unless a much wider variety of jobs and job op-portunities is made available to them. But at this stage of the immigration there is, as we have seen, little feeling of dis-crimination, and, in many cases, there may be none because they are not looking for other types of work which might pay less: those who take white-collar work sacrifice material pro-sperity for status. Among Gujaratis, according to Desai, oc-cupations which entail wearing a uniform are not highly regarded, as they lower the prestige of immigrants belonging to high castes.[32] This is not the case with Pakistanis; with whom to be a bus conductor or driver has a high status, because it requires a good knowledge of English and the uniform bestows authority on the wearer. However, from both Glasgow and Bradford, it is reported that Pakistanis are unwilling to accept promotion to inspector as they would earn less and they are afraid of incurring resentment if they had to criticize and check white employees.[33] This is con-sistent with their general avoidance of situations which might bring them into conflict or competition with British workers.

Alongside the mass of manual workers, there is a class of

entrepreneur who is prospering through providing services to his fellow-countrymen and has a vested interest in the immigrant community remaining separate. There are other successful Pakistanis whose savings go into investment in the home country. A distinction must be made between the entrepreneurs, who live in or near the immigrant colonies, and the educated elite of Pakistani professionals resident in Britain, who are doctors, teachers, lawyers, journalists, and officials of the High Commission. The hierarchical nature of Pakistani society is carried over into the emigration, not in the settlement areas, but in the attitudes of the High Commission and of many of the elite who find the immigrants' way of life in Britain an embarrassment. The mass of the immigrants, in turn, feels that the High Commission is out of touch and does not look to it for leadership.

In spite of cleavages, particularly between East and West Pakistanis, and regional differences in village and kin loyalties, community feeling is strong among Pakistanis in Britain. It is founded mainly on pride in Pakistan and on a sense of belonging to a new nation. This patriotism operates in times of crisis, like the 1965 war with India, when large sums of money were raised for defence, and it expresses itself not only in loyalty to the home country but in the value attached to maintaining the culture and traditions and transmitting them to the children. The immigration is far too recent for there to be many signs of a process of adaptation to the norms of British culture; but it remains to be seen what effect the British educational system is having on the children. Even among the first generation of adults, there are already some indications of change. The Asian film club in Bradford now finds that American and British films are more popular than Indian or Pakistani productions – this would have been unthinkable ten years or even five years ago.

Although it may still be psychologically important to the single male Pakistanis to think of themselves as 'birds of passage' and though they may express their intention to return to Pakistan, they know that they are unlikely to do so. Compared with what they can earn in Pakistan, where the average income is £30 a year, Britain is indeed an El Dorado, and their brick-built houses, even though they have poor amenities, are *pukka*. So much is expected from them at home that even if there were no other motive for staying, they are more or less compelled to remain as worker bees outside the hive. Very few will return. For many the migration offers an escape from the hereditary bonds of caste, as caste distinctions can no longer be maintained in an urban society. Some men who have prospered have even been able to arrange marriages with women of a higher caste belonging to locally influential families, thus acquiring a new status – these marriages would never have been possible in Pakistan. There is an obvious contrast with the West Indian who finds his hopes of escape from the handicap of colour frustrated in the emigration.

The fact that the Pakistani immigrants were able to some extent to satisfy the limited goals of the migration, and that these were, for the majority, very closely linked to their family in Pakistan, meant that organizations concerned with their position as migrants in Britain were very slow to emerge. Such organizations as did evolve – burial societies, mosque committees, and, occasionally, informal welfare organizations – were concerned 'with Pakistanis as a national group and not as immigrants in a foreign country'. Even these were split between East and West Pakistanis. The High Commission had made a number of gestures towards administrative streamlining; England was divided, in a kind of Cromwellian system, into a number of areas for which officers (in most instances majors) on the High Commission staff were to be responsible. But Rex and Moore comment that the staff 'knew little of, and sympathized less with the interests of the ordinary migrant. It is an organization of diplomats in a situation where sensitive community leadership and the skills of social work are needed.'[34]

A misleading appearance of involvement in host community activities was given by the candidature of individual Pakistanis in local elections in 1963 and in one case in the general election of the following year. These were prestige candidatures; the audience was the immigrant community and the electoral processes were being manipulated to demonstrate the numerical support possessed by the individuals.

It is against this background that the attempt to form a National Federation of Pakistani Associations in 1963 must be seen. Five years after its founding the federation was savagely attacked in an editorial in *Asia Weekly* which called for unity and deplored factionalism among Pakistanis and the failure of the so-called leaders to tackle the problem of the immigrants. 'We openly declare that the National Federation is a useless and meaningless organization which is tantamount to saying that its title is a misnomer.'[35] The paper stated flatly that there was no association in any British city which could be said to be a representative organization of Pakistani immigrants. If the Federation has never been very effective, this is largely because of its strong bias towards East Pakistan. But any organization, whatever its regional bias, would have to contend with the pre-occupation of individual Pakistanis with their economic problems which has exceeded even that of the West Indians, and the fact that individuals who have assumed the leadership role have been even more isolated and atypical.

SIKHS

Of the three main groups of coloured immigrants from the Commonwealth, the Indians are the most homogeneous, the most cohesive and the best organized.[36]

Like the Pakistanis, they demanded at first little of Britain, except to be allowed to earn a living and remit their savings to their families, and the emigration was at first confined to men. But, unlike the Pakistanis, the Sikhs brought over their families when immigration control seemed to be imminent. This process continued, and the balance between the sexes approaches the West Indian pattern, except that whereas there are many West Indian women living alone in Britain, all Sikh women are living with their husbands. When a family is reunited, it has been usual for all the children to come with their mother, instead of arriving one by one.[37]

As well as the migrants from the villages – mostly small farmers, with some landless labourers – there was a movement of professional and white-collar workers from the towns in the Punjab who accepted labouring jobs in Britain in which they could earn more than as teachers, clerks, or non-commissioned officers in the army or the police in India.[38] These migrants settled and worked alongside the peasants, again distinguishing the Sikh from the Pakistani settlements, among whom there has been very little mixing of the educated elite with the peasantry. This is perhaps one reason why the Sikhs in Britain have thrown up so many leaders, and have been able to organize community services on a much larger scale than the mutual aid to village kin which has characterized the Pakistanis. There is certainly a greater sense of identity between the illiterate and the educated among the Sikhs than either among Pakistanis or West Indians in Britain.

Their pattern of settlement, and employment, depended very much on a good knowledge of English. This knowledge enabled a man to take employment alongside English workers, for example, in transport, where there was a strong union organization. It enabled him to find his own housing. But the majority did not know English, and many were also illiterate, and had to rely on English-speaking compatriots to act as go-betweens with employers. In the factories, they were isolated by language from the English workers, and in many cases, by working on night shift. The earliest Sikh settlers in Southall came along a chain which led from the Punjab to Woolf's rubber factory, whose personnel officer had met members of a Sikh regiment in the Middle East during the war and was prepared to take Sikh labour. By 1965 90% of the unskilled labour at Woolf's were Sikhs.[39] Woolf's example was followed by four or five other firms, none of them, initially, unionized. It was often necessary to bribe a foreman to get employment and, later to be given overtime; indeed, this appeared to the ordinary migrant as a British norm. At a later stage the Sikhs began to organize themselves into unions.

Few English people were prepared to take in the Punjabis as lodgers, and housing had therefore to be provided by compatriots. The early days of severe overcrowding, renting of beds rather than rooms, and squalid conditions, brought the Sikhs – like all immigrants – into a disrepute which still lingers. When families were reunited a different type of overcrowding occurred as heads of families felt obliged to house their kin in the small single family houses which they were able to buy. But the arrival of women brought great changes. In the period of the rush to 'beat the ban' every room in Indian-owned houses was used for sleeping, but three years later in many family houses the front rooms were reserved as sitting-rooms and furnished with three-piece suites. This improvement in standards and move towards a 'Western' style of living became accepted signs of economic success, and they led to a reduction in overcrowding as younger kinsmen left to form their own households. But the concentration of Sikhs in certain districts grew with numbers of arrivals, partly because estate agents directed Indian clients to those areas. (Although, as we have seen in Chapter 4, with the exception of one Southall ward, Indians are more dispersed than the West Indians.)

A number of influences have operated to enhance the sense of identity and cultural distinctness of the Sikhs in Britain. One of the most publicized issues has been that of turban-wearing. Most of the younger Sikhs cut their hair, shaved their beards and discarded the turban even before they left the Punjab; they were prepared to abandon these outward marks of religious allegiance as they might be a handicap in getting work in England.[40] It has been generally the older Sikhs from the villages, and the younger urban Sikhs who have managed to get white-collar jobs who wear turbans in Britain. On the other hand, attempts by British organizations (typically, municipal transport undertakings) to forbid the wearing of turbans have led to increasingly strong public reaction from the Sikhs, and some of the most substantial protests by any immigrant group. This solidarity in defence of their social rights marks off the Sikhs from the other immigrant communities.

The *gurdwara* (Sikh temple) plays a very important part in maintaining the cohesion of Sikh communities, and acts as both a religious and a social centre. The *gurdwaras* were strengthened by the arrival of wives, for, like the Muslim wives, the women are more inclined than their husbands to observe the rules of their religion, keep the fasts and maintain religious observance in the home. At the same time one major break with custom which many Sikh wives have made is in going out to work. In the Punjab, although they might mean a loss of prestige. Patnaik found that many working work in the fields, for a Jat woman to work for hire, would wives had concealed this fact from their relatives in the

Punjab. Moreover, this change has carried on to their daughters, many of whom are allowed to work on leaving school – probably the single greatest result of an English education, and one which inspires many conflicting emotions in Sikh parents.

Religious ties have been preserved and strengthened by visits to and from India, and by the growth, in recent years, of missionary activity from the Punjab. One group, the Shiromani Khalsa Dal, has raised demands for Punjabi to be taught in schools and for religious instruction to be provided by the local education authorities.[41] This has been one response to a situation in which the London gurdwara at Shepherd's Bush had been running a monthly service in English for some years 'because the number of young Sikhs was growing who were less conversant with Punjabi than with English.'[42] Political ties with the Sikhs in India have been equally important.

Since 1964 the Sikh religious party – the Akali Dal – has been a major party in the Punjab. This change has been reflected among Sikh organizations in Britain. Sant Fateh Singh, the President of the Akali Dal, visited England in 1966 and created an Akali group.[43] The establishment of a Punjabi-speaking state in India, and the conflict over the position of the capital, Chandigarh, are live issues to Sikhs in Britain – to some, more vital than British political issues.

At the same time, there has been growing interest in Sikh rights in Britain – it was the Akalis who organized the mass demonstration in Wolverhampton in 1968 against the ban on turbans by the town's transport services. The demonstration drew support from all over the country; eventually the campaign was successful.

Ties with home were maintained by the ordinary immigrant also through letters, new arrivals, and visits. Many have returned to see their parents, their wives, to attend marriages, or to be married themselves. The majority of immigrants have their marriages arranged in the Punjab, and even when a marriage occurs between two people in England, it is often arranged through the home villages – the link between Coventry and Newcastle is in Jullundur.

Marriage is an institution in which caste distinctions survive the process of migration. For the Sikh men, leaving the village meant leaving caste. Aurora gives a ranking order of nine qualities thought desirable among the Sikh migrants at one of the main areas of settlement in Britain: at the head of the list is a good knowledge of English, followed by influence with employers, leadership of the Indian Workers Association (the main secular organization of the Sikhs in Britain) and so on, down to the ability of an ordinary un-skilled worker to earn and save good money, followed last of all by membership of a high caste. Thus the traditional cri-teria of social status are almost turned on their head in the diaspora. However, in some areas there have persisted two gurdwaras – the Jat, which is the larger and more pros-perous, and the Rangarhia whose members are drawn from the carpenter and blacksmith castes and are regarded as belonging to a somewhat lower caste.

The effect of migration has also been to weaken the caste system generally among the small Hindu community living in Britain. However, they, even more than the Sikhs, insist on strict observance of caste distinctions in marriage. This is a more educated community, more urban, than the Sikhs, but also more closed to English influences. The joint family and village kin group have much the same importance for them as for the Pakistanis. Larger social organizations like the gurdwaras or the I.W.A.s are lacking.[44]

The Sikh religious organizations have forged a link be-tween the preservation of cultural and religious values, and the broader struggle for the rights of minorities in Britain. But their activism has been fairly recent. At least two other kinds of initiative to improve the position of the migrants had been made earlier on by the secular organization of the Punjabis – the Indian Workers Associations.[45] These in-itiatives were unionization, and intervention in English party politics.

The I.W.A.s were first set up in the early 1950s – a revival of a pre-war working class migrant organization. By the mid 1960s most of the areas where Sikhs had settled in Britain had at least one I.W.A. – in some areas two rival groups reflected ideological or factional divisions. The I.W.A.s have been remarkable in that many have involved nearly all the Punjabi men in their areas. In this they present a striking contrast to both West Indian and Pakistani groups. Their original day-to-day functions were to provide a welfare service, recreation facilities (including reading rooms and, notably, film shows) and to help in finding jobs and dealing with British officials on behalf of migrants. The strength of the I.W.A.s was founded firmly on the homogeneous character of the Punjabi migration, and strong kinship and village ties which helped to draw individuals in to participate. But almost equally important in the development of the I.W.A.s was the role of members of the Communist Party of India. This was to be expected among migrants from the Punjab where C.P.I. activity is strong, and their Communism was of purely Indian relevance. As DeWitt John puts it 'Punjabis have grown up in a political atmosphere where non-Communist and even conservative religious leaders co-operate with the Communist Party.' It is expected of a Party member that he will be politically more zealous and less prone to corrupt practices than non-Communists. The prestige that has gone with observation of this practice has permitted the Communists to function in I.W.A.'s politics without the apparatus of contacts and kinship employed by the non-Communists. At the national level, however, the prominence of the Communists may have acted as a hindrance to united action, as splits between the activists in Britain exactly paralleled the splits which occurred in the C.P.I. For example, the Chinese invasion of India in 1962 not only damaged the prestige of the Communists in the I.W.A.s, but caused a fundamental split between the 'left' or 'Maoist' faction (who dominated Birmingham I.W.A.) and the 'right' or 'revisionist' faction, whose chief protagonists came from Southall, the largest of all the associations. As a result Southall left the national federation, which thereafter for some time functioned largely as an appendage of the Birmingham group. These differences over Indian or international issues frequently accompanied differences over the strategy to be employed in British race relations, with the pro-Moscow faction taking a rather more integrationist approach than the Maoists.

The I.W.A.s provide one example of immigrants as a group making approaches to British trade unions. Individual I.W.A. leaders have taken an active part in union affairs and, in Southall, the I.W.A. introduced unions (or made strong attempts to do so) in some companies in which they had hitherto not existed. In one well documented and notorious case, the strike at Woolf's rubber factory, the Punjabi[46] workers failed in collective action largely because of lack of support from the Transport and General Workers Union. After four years of activity the Indian workers at Woolf's had succeeded in organizing a union. Once the union was recognized, the workers came out on strike over the suspension of a man and remained on strike for six weeks. On the grounds that most of them had lost their union membership through non-payment of dues, the T. & G.W.U. refused to grant any strike benefits even to workers who were fully paid up. The Indian community gave some financial support, but the strikers could not continue without union backing and were taken back on the company's terms; their local branch was broken.

Another initiative taken by the I.W.A.s both in the West Midlands and Southall was their approach to the Labour Party. Prior to the 1964 general election, negotiations were conducted with the local parties by the serving officials, on the basis that the communities' vote could be delivered to Labour in return for measures that would lift some of the pressure on the migrants.

In at least two cases pacts were in fact made, and Labour can be shown to have benefited at the election in consequence. In the local elections in Southall in 1968, a Sikh Labour councillor was elected, and a Sikh Conservative (the Party's narrowly defeated candidate) appointed alderman.

Southall I.W.A. was also the largest and the most representative of the immigrant organizations to participate in C.A.R.D. (the Campaign Against Racial Discrimination) between 1965 and 1967 – the first major attempt at concerted action by all the main Commonwealth immigrant communities. It was part of the basic strategy of C.A.R.D. that the immigrant organizations were the key to the situation. They were assumed to understand the situation at local level and to participate in it. Their claims to representativeness were taken at face value, especially in the case of Asian groups. The assumption was that a genuine representative nature could be achieved by building coalitions. Heinemann argues that in practice, this was a mistaken view, and amounted to little more than multiplying powerlessness, like zeros.[47] After the White Paper of August 1965, C.A.R.D. saw its position to be on the left flank of a radical coalition, working both for liberalization of the immigration laws, and for the introduction of laws against discrimination. Both involved contact with immigrants, and documentation of cases, achieved where possible through immigrant organizations, or through local inter-racial organizations, or through C.A.R.D.'s own local groups. But most of the activists were individuals working outside immigrant organizations, or if they did hold office in them, separately from their roles as immigrant leaders.

After the collapse of C.A.R.D. in December 1967, another national organization has been built up on the basis, primarily, of the support of immigrant organizations, plus a wider range of inter-racial groups. This is the Joint Council for the Welfare of Immigrants. Founded in 1967 with the support of C.A.R.D., its purpose has been to provide a full-time advocacy service at Heathrow airport on behalf of immigrants whose credentials are challenged by immigration officers. It has also provided information and pressed generally for the rights of immigrants. These are issues on which the maximum degree of unity could be expected from immigrants in the U.K., particularly Indians and Pakistanis many of whom, if families are to be reunited in Britain, still have wives and children to bring over.

SECOND GENERATION

Almost all the research and reports about immigrant communities have concerned themselves primarily with the first generation. Even when they have been concerned with children and young people, they have typically seen the problems associated with this group in terms of cultural adaptation of foreigners to British society. The most obvious example here has been the concentration of the education authorities on language teaching. This was indeed an urgent problem for the schools and the non-English speaking children. Yet, as Ann Dummett has asked, 'when one looks at the children themselves, the schools they are in, the day today life they experience and the kind of jobs they look for, can we be certain that the attainment on their part of perfect standards of English is the answer to the main problem they face?' And she goes on to argue that the roots of this problem lie in the attitude of their school staff, of their white contemporaries, of other children's parents and of course of the whole society around them: 'the attitude that regards them as different and inferior.'[48] Rather more graphically, a West African sixth form girl described this problem in a B.B.C. discussion programme in September 1968: 'Well let me put it this way. They think we are sub-human. They don't think us equal to them. So we have no right to own a house, have chairs, eat with a knife and fork, or drink from a glass, or dance to music or us young girls wear mini-skirts. They don't think we are equal to that.'

Earlier chapters have described the economic position of immigrant groups in Britain, and the complex of handicaps which may be grouped under the heading: Poor housing – low income. They have also described the special hazard of baby-minding, which appears to apply in particular to West Indian and West African children. The confined pre-school life which children who are 'minded' suffer (or children living in one room), could retard them throughout their subsequent school careers. This is a hazard faced by the U.K. born, as distinct from the immigrant parent. There are other distinctions which may tentatively be drawn between the parent and second generation. In the case of most of the parents – or at least, the fathers – they have chosen, albeit under various pressures, to come to Britain. In the case of the children this was not so, and those born in the U.K. will, in contrast to their parents, be brought up in a society which has in many ways treated them during their formative years as a problem-creating minority. Membership of a group which has been generally regarded as inferior by the dominant society can in itself pose difficult problems of identity for the second generation of Commonwealth immigrants in Britain, quite apart from value conflicts which may arise between the generations. Recent research among 5- to 8-year-olds in Bristol suggests that the seeds of such difficulties have already been sown, and that they are likely to be particularly acute for children of West Indian parents.[49] The experiment used brown and white dolls and pictures, and the children were asked various questions about these: e.g.

which doll looks most like you? Which do you like best? Which is the bad doll? etc. 25% of the West Indian children in one low density area (60% in a high density area) claimed that the white doll 'looked more like them'. In the low density area 65% of the West Indians and 50% of the Asians consistently chose white dolls to play with, sit next to, etc. Over 50% of the West Indian children said the brown doll was 'the bad doll' when shown dolls identical except in race and given no other clues. When asked why, the following replies were received: 'Because he kills people', 'Because he do rude things' – and, from a white boy aged 5: 'Because he should have learnt the language before he came over here.'

That the immigrants are commonly seen as posing problems, rather than facing them, was noted by the Select Committee on Race Relations and Immigration, in its investigation into coloured school leavers.[50] 'Our aim has been to examine the problems of coloured school leavers. It was surprising how often this was not properly understood. It was a standard opening to most witnesses to ask a question on the line of "what do you see as the main problems facing coloured school leavers?" A number replied, in effect, that they themselves had no problems or that there was no problem of race relations within their experience. In other words they did not see the coloured school-leavers as posing a problem for them, but equally they failed to look at the situation from the coloured school-leavers' point of view. This is unfortunate ...'. The investigation produced perhaps more information about the assumptions and the practices of agencies dealing with coloured school-leavers, than about the leavers themselves, about whom the evidence given tended (not surprisingly) to be contradictory.

The evidence given by the Youth Employment Service (some of it echoed by the Departments of Employment and of Education and Science) defined the problems very much from the limited viewpoint of the agency itself, and also tended to stress solutions which relied on cultural adaptation.[51] Great emphasis was placed on the over-ambition of immigrant leavers compared with English peers – the problem of 'unrealistic aspirations' – which was regarded as one of the main problems facing Y.E.O.'s. The thesis of 'unrealistic aspirations' was developed by David Beetham in a study carried out in Birmingham in 1965–66.[52] He suggested that many immigrant boys were seeking jobs for which they were not qualified on leaving, and would not succeed in qualifying for through further education courses; and that they were seeking jobs among a narrow range of occupations which were in short supply: typically, mechanical or electrical engineering jobs. The cause he attributed to assessments based on the job market in the country of origin (at least in the case of West Indians) and the lack of knowledge of the British labour market. The solution he saw in terms of counselling or general 'socializing' which would lower immigrant aspirations or change them. Beetham's study has subsequently been criticized, but nevertheless it remains widely accepted.[53]

In the opinion of Y.E.O.'s, school leavers have usually obtained jobs commensurate with their abilities. Beetham also thought that those in his sample did as well as white school leavers. There is little evidence about apprenticeships, and jobs with training. Those studies which have been completed relate to 1965 and 1966, and are based on very small samples. A study in Birmingham found that 20% (8) of the West Indians and 14% (5) of the Asians obtained apprenticeships compared with 23% of the English.[54] On the other hand the head of a secondary school in the city with large numbers of immigrant pupils has said in 1969 that 'Whereas non-academic white pupils could secure well-paid jobs, the same was not true for non-academic West Indians.'[55] Figueroa in his study of West Indian school leavers in North London, in which as far as possible the abilities of West Indian and English groups were matched, found that four out of twenty-one West Indian boys got apprenticeships, compared with eight out of twenty-one English boys. Of all those who secured jobs with some form of training, far more of the jobs of West Indians involved training 'on the job' rather than through apprenticeships or further technical training in classes.[56]

There is general agreement that coloured leavers' opportunities are limited by discrimination in the white-collar and retail sectors, especially outside London, and that Y.E.O.'s have to spend more time in securing placements for them.

Once they are in work, there is consistent evidence of dis-satisfaction, especially among West Indians.

Outside work there appears to be little social contact between coloured and white teenagers. It has been observed, both in primary and secondary schools, that children of different nationalities tend to choose their friends from within their own group, whether they are English or immigrant children. On leaving school, teenagers are made even more aware of the distance which separates the coloured and white groups. The Hunt Report,[57] although it pressed generally for insistence on multi-racial clubs, found that the efforts of youth clubs to bring about social contact were good only by exception. The Select Committee found that 'the success of a multi-racial club as such may be short lived. They tend all too soon, to become all coloured or all white, although this, in its turn, may change again.' The committee found it 'pointless to dogmatize about what type of club is best'. Since the Hunt Report, there has been an increase in the demand for their own clubs, particularly from West Indian groups. But one of the problems which immigrant teenagers are likely to face if they want to join clubs is resistance from parents. This may apply both to West Indian and to Asian girls, although rather more to the latter. Indian girls are sheltered in adolescence and expected to stay at home after school. But as they increasingly enter the labour market, it is probable that their economic independence will lead to more social freedom. Sanctions against inter-marriage are likely to remain strong, however, and if the Indian pattern of early marriage is continued many girls will be betrothed before they leave school and married by eighteen. The Muslim parents exercise even closer supervision over their daughters. Many immigrant parents are torn between ambition for their children's future and anxiety that they may lose them to an alien culture – both of which feelings may well produce tensions within the home. For the teenager particularly, the conflict between the values of parents, school, and peer groups is likely to be felt more acutely than it will be by the average white teenager.

Some of the difficulties of the second generation may perhaps be gauged from a report on teenagers in Cardiff and Liverpool, cities which have had a coloured population for at least forty years. A working party of the Liverpool Youth Organizations Committee found in October 1968 that the position of coloured youth in Liverpool was dismal. They were convinced of the existence of discrimination, and when they moved outside the coloured quarter of the town, they felt very insecure. The inquiry left the working party with a 'deep sense of unease'. It also feared the danger of conflict unless an active policy of integration was urgently adopted.[58]

Len Bloom's study of Bute Town in Cardiff draws an almost equally depressing picture. We see a second and third generation which lives in a quasi-ghetto, is denied the opportunities available to white English-speaking immigrants, is less ambitious, and achieves less than they do. They have a fair amount of social contact with whites, but they fear they will meet colour prejudice outside Bute Town. They choose to stay in the coloured quarter because it is safer to trust their own people.[59]

REFERENCES

1. David Eversley and Fred Sukdeo, *The Dependants of the Coloured Commonwealth Population of England and Wales* (London, I.R.R. Special Series, 1969), Table 27.

2. Gordon Lewis, 'Race Relations in Britain – a view from the Caribbean', *Race Today* (July 1969).

3. A West Indian spokesman from Derby. In an interview conducted as part of a survey for United National Institute for Training and Research by the Institute of Race Relations (unpublished).

4. Dr. R. E. D. Simpson, 'Study of a General Practice with a large proportion of Immigrants', research commissioned by the Institute's Survey of Race Relations in Britain.

5. Prof. Robert R. Bell, of Temple University, Pennsylvania, 'The Lower Class Negro Family in the United States and Great Britain', *Race* (October 1969).

6. J. Rex and R. Moore, *Race, Community and Conflict* (London, O.U.P. for I.R.R., 1966).

7. Gordon Lewis, op. cit.

8. John Lambert, 'Study of Immigrant Crime and Relations of the Police and Immigrants in a Division of Birmingham', research carried out for the Institute's Survey of Race Relations in Britain.

9. Beryl Radin, 'Coloured Workers and British Trade Unions', *Race* (Vol. VIII, no. 2, October 1966). See also, F. J. Bayliss and J. B. Coates, 'West Indians at work in Nottingham', *Race* (Vol. VII, no. 2, October 1965); Bayliss and Coates found that 66% of West Indian men were in trade unions, compared with 78% of white Englishmen in their sample.

10. A. Richmond and M. Lyon, 'Study of the St. Paul's area and of three housing estates in Bristol', research commissioned by the Institute's 'Survey of Race Relations in Britain'.

11. J. Rex and R. Moore, op. cit.

12. A. Richmond and M. Lyon, op. cit.

13. A. Richmond and M. Lyon, op. cit.

14. Political and Economic Planning and Research Services Ltd., *Racial Discrimination* (London, P.E.P., April 1967).

15. Letter to the *Oldham Evening Chronicle*, 14th October, 1958, in C. E. Fiscian, 'Minority Group Prejudice: a study of some sociological and psychological correlates of anti-English prejudice among West Indian immigrants to London' (Ph.D. thesis, 1960).

16. Albert Maria Gomes, 'I am an immigrant', *Listener* (Vol. 80, No. 2062, 3rd October, 1968) (Third Programme talk).

17. Gordon Lewis, op. cit.

18. Neville A. Maxwell, *The Power of Negro Action* (London, the author, 1965), p. 22.

19. Jennifer Williams, *Race Today* (November, 1969).

20. Gordon Lewis, op. cit.

21. Gordon Lewis, 'Protest Among the Immigrants – the Dilemma of Minority Culture', *Political Quarterly* (October–December, 1969).

22. For this section we have drawn heavily on unpublished research conducted by B. Dahya in Birmingham and Bradford for the Institute's Survey of Race Relations in Britain, and also on unpublished research in Bradford commissioned by the Survey from Eric Butterworth.

23. Dahya reports that there were approximately ten East Pakistani wives in the whole of Bradford by 1967 and 142 East Pakistani dormitory houses. Similarly, in Balsall Heath there were ninety-two East Pakistani dormitory houses and only four family houses. The figure for West Pakistanis in Balsall Heath were 229 dormitories and seventy-nine family houses.

24. See R. Desai, *Indian Immigrants in Britain* (London, Oxford

University Press, for the Institute of Race Relations, 1963).

25. *Why a Federation?* (Organizing Committee, National Federation of Pakistani Associations, London, 1964); and a report in *Oldham Evening Chronicle and Standard*, 18th January, 1964.

26. Karam Elahi, 'Some Aspects of Social Adaptation of Pakistani Immigrants in Glasgow' (M.A. thesis, Edinburgh University, 1967).

27. Dahya lists 983 Pakistani houses in Bradford in 1964, broken down as follows: 142 East Pakistani, 190 Chacci (Campbellpuri), 24 Pathan, 3 Gujarati Muslim, 135 Punjabi, 489 Mirpuri.

28. Price shows that the Greeks of Central Sydney, who had come from a number of islands and the mainland, were fusing together as a national group and assimilating themselves to Australian society; but thirty years later, after the second world war, there was so much reinforcement from different islands that the Greek community broke up into a federation of Greek district groups and the process of assimilation was much retarded. In one case, the Kytheran Greeks, inter-marriage came down from 42% to 10%. C. A. Price, *The Cultural Integration of Immigrants*; W. D. Borrie (ed.) (Paris, U.N.E.S.C.O., 1959), p. 281. Also C. A. Price, *Southern Europeans in Australia* (Melbourne, Oxford University Press, 1963), p. 260.

29. Over 70% of Indians and Pakistanis had never applied to a white landlord for lodgings. W. W. Daniel, *Racial Discrimination in England*, Penguin Special based on P.E.P. Report (Harmondsworth, Penguin Books, 1968), p. 41.

30. Z. Dahya, 'Pakistani Wives in Britain', *Race* (Vol. VI, No. 3, January 1965), pp. 311–21.

31. Sidney Collins, *Coloured Minorities in Britain* (London, Lutterworth Press, 1957), pp. 160–73.

32. R. Desai, op. cit., p. 70.

33. Karam Elahi, op. cit.

34. J. Rex and R. Moore, op. cit. p.171.

35. *Asia Weekly* (10th February, 1968).

36. For this section we have drawn on unpublished research commissioned by the Institute's Survey of Race Relations in Britain and conducted by Narindar Uberoi and Anjali Patnaik (both in Southall), by Ian Thomson in Gravesend. We have also drawn on DeWitt John, *Indian Workers' Associations in Britain* (O.U.P., for I.R.R., 1969).

37. Narindar Uberoi, 'Sikh Women in Southall', *Race* (Vol. VI, No. 1, July 1964), pp. 34–40.

38. G. S. Aurora, *The Frontiersmen* (Bombay, Popular Prakashan, 1967), pp. 18 and 30.

39. Ibid, p. 77.

40. Aurora, op. cit., p. 94. Narindar Uberoi found that 75% of the Sikhs in Southall in 1965 were clean shaven.

41. *Middlesex County Times*, 26th August, 1966.

42. Preetam Singh, a London barrister, introduced the service on 29th September, 1963.

43. Autar Dhesi, 'Anatomy of Sikh Politics', *Race Today*, October 1969.

44. R. Desai, *Indian Immigrants in Britain* (London, Oxford University Press, for I.R.R., 1963).

45. For the description of the I.W.A.'s we have drawn mainly on DeWitt John, *Indian Workers' Associations in Britain* (O.U.P., for I.R.R., 1969).

46. Peter Marsh, *The Anatomy of a Strike* (London, Institute of Race Relations Special Series, 1967), p. 16.

47. Quoted in B. W. Heineman Jr., 'The Politics of Race: a Study of the Campaign Against Racial Discrimination' (unpublished B.Litt. thesis, Oxford, 1967), p. 103.

48. Ann Dummett, 'What to Do', *Race Today* (July 1969).

49. D. Milner, 'The Effects of Prejudice', *Race Today* (August 1969).

50. Report from House of Commons the Select Committee on Race Relations and Immigration: 'The Problems of Coloured School Leavers' (London, H.M.S.O., 1969).

51. Minutes of Evidence to Select Committee, 6th February, 1969.

52. David Beetham, *Immigrant School Leavers and the Youth Employment Service in Birmingham* (London, Institute of Race Relations Special Series, 1967), p. 22.

53. See, for example, Dipak Nandy, *Race Today* (May 1969); and Sheila Allen, *Race Today* (December 1969).

54. F. Milson, *Operation Integration Two: The Coloured Teenager in Birmingham* (Birmingham Westhill College of Education, September 1966).

55. Mr. George Meredith, headmaster, William Murdoch School, Birmingham. Cited in a report of a conference, 'English for English-Speaking Immigrants', held at Stoke d'Abernon, January 1969, I.L.E.A.

56. Peter Figueroa, 'Study of West Indian School Leavers in North London', research carried out for the Institute's Survey of Race Relations in Britain.

57. *Immigrants and the Youth Service*, Report of a Committee

of the Youth Service Development Council (Hunt Report) (London, H.M.S.O., 1967) p. 3.

58. Liverpool Youth Organization Committee, *Special but not Separate: a Report on the Situation of Young Coloured People in Liverpool* (Liverpool, Liverpool Youth Organizations Committee, 1968).

59. Leonard Bloom, 'Study of Bute Town, Cardiff', research carried out for the Institute's Survey of Race Relations in Britain.

Chapter Twelve

The Incidence and Form of Racial Prejudice in Britain

To measure the extent of racial prejudice is one of the most difficult tasks to ask of social science. Prejudice is a relative concept.* In societies which have institutionalized a racial hierarchy, 'prejudice' – as a dynamic element – is often lost against a background of conformity with the cultural and social norms of ethnic stratification. In a society completely free of ethnic stratification, racial hostility might be regarded as a personal aberration and not a social force worthy of sociological investigation. Britain lies between these extremes: the climate is in a state of flux, which places limitations upon the degree of accuracy in the measurement of prejudice.

Nevertheless, some promising lines of investigation have been gradually evolved through past research – largely conducted outside Britain. Others can be derived from ideas generally prevalent in Britain about the consequences of immigration and its effects on attitudes. Some of these notions were brought together at the beginning of the investigation of attitudes conducted by Dr. Mark Abrams for the Survey of Race Relations and provided the starting point for this study. There was, for example, speculation about the effect that contact between majority and minority had on attitudes. Were these effects simply the consequence of proximity? Or were the circumstances of the contact the main determinant? What significance should be attached to personality factors in the individual member of the majority or to his social

* 'Prejudice is a negative, unfavourable attitude towards a group or its individual members; it is characterized by stereotyped beliefs; the attitude results from processes within the bearer of the attitude rather than from reality testing of the attributes of the group in question.' – a definition of prejudice by Marie Jahoda, in J. Gould & W. L. Kolb: *A Dictionary of the Social Sciences*, Tavistock Publications, London, 1964.

situation? What implications did changes in that situation (in the individual's own lifespan or between generations) have in shaping attitudes?

With these considerations in mind, it was decided to open the inquiry with an attempt to compare a representative sample of the whole white population with a more limited group who were more likely to have experienced day-to-day contact with coloured people. Over a series of key questions (some reported later in this chapter) no significant difference was found between the views of the two groups.

Having established that simple proximity to coloured minorities (as opposed to face-to-face contacts) is not in itself a major element in shaping attitudes, it was decided to proceed to an intensive study conducted in areas of high immigrant settlement. In such a study detailed examination of responses to situations of contact between black and white would be possible, together with an analysis of the significance of personality factors and elements in the social situation. As a device for establishing the extent of prejudice four key issues were selected from a schedule of fifty questions, as being crucial measures of racial hostility. At different points in a long interview, people were asked:

(1) Whether they would avoid having coloured neighbours even if they were professional people.

(2) Whether they regarded coloured people as their inferiors solely on the basis of skin colour.

(3) Whether the authorities should refuse housing to coloured tenants even if they had been on the waiting list the required time.

(4) Whether a private landlord should refuse accommodation to coloured tenants even if he knew that they would care for his property.

(These are, of course, summaries of questions asked in a multi-stage pattern.)

People who gave no hostile replies to these questions can be regarded as exhibiting tolerant attitudes – or perhaps more accurately as showing no overt prejudice; those offering one hostile response as mildly prejudiced; those with two hostile responses as prejudiced; and those with three or even four hostile replies seemed to be wholly rejecting in their attitudes towards coloured people and may be regarded as 'intensely prejudiced'.

In 1967 the entire 50-item questionnaire, covering various aspects of the subject's personality, family and social characteristics, was administered to 500 people, selected at random, in each of five boroughs: Lambeth, Ealing, Wolverhampton, Nottingham and Bradford; each of these boroughs contains substantial concentrations of coloured people. The four key questions divided the total sample of 2,500 like this:

Table 17: INCIDENCE OF UNFAVOURABLE ATTITUDES

	%
No hostile answers	35
One hostile answer	38
Two hostile answers	17
Three or four hostile answers	10

Thus, in those areas having relatively high proportions of coloured residents, over one-third of the white population showed no prejudice, and a further two-fifths made only an isolated prejudiced response. A further one-sixth may be regarded as prejudiced but, following a common British trend, they were prepared to make exceptions. This leaves one tenth whose antipathy to coloured people seems unconditional. It must be emphasized at once that this is not an absolute scale, but a relative judgment made by the social scientists concerned, in the light of their analysis. One cannot be dogmatic about the degree to which these categories correspond with reality because 'reality' in this context is ultimately dependent upon the value system of our society.[1]

Rather more interesting than the absolute scores are the differences in the distribution of scores when, on the basis of the information in the remainder of the questionnaire, the sample is divided in demographic and social terms like sex, age, class and politics. These differences were never startling, ranging in this order:

30–40%:	No hostile answers
34–42%:	One hostile answer
12–20%:	Two hostile answers
6–14%:	Three or four hostile answers

However, within those ranges there were some significant differences and these variations provide some clues to the concomitants, if not the causes, of high and low prejudice. First, women were slightly less inclined to display prejudice than men.

Table 18: ATTITUDE SCORES BY SEX

	Male	Female
	%	%
No hostile answers	30	39
One hostile answer	41	35
Two hostile answers	18	17
Three or four hostile answers	11	9
	___	___
	100	100
N (sample) =	1,136	1,358

Second, the incidence of expression of intense prejudice was highest among people aged 45-54 and fell away on both sides with the lowest levels of intense prejudice among those under 35 and over 65.

Table 19: ATTITUDE SCORES BY AGE

Age	21-34	35-44	45-54	55-64	65+
	%	%	%	%	%
No hostile answers	37	37	31	31	38
One hostile answer	38	35	31	40	37
Two hostile answers	17	17	40	19	16
Three or four hostile answers	8	11	12	10	9
N =	573	425	551	477	467

Women showed consistently less prejudice than men throughout the age-range, especially among those who had become adults in the last ten years.

Third, when the sample was divided by socio-economic grades, the lower middle class and skilled manual workers emerged with the highest incidence of extreme prejudice while the professional, managerial and the unskilled and semi-skilled workers had much lower levels.

Table 20: ATTITUDE SCORES BY CLASS

	Professional/ Managerial	Lower Middle Class	Skilled Working Class	Other Working Class
	%	%	%	%
No hostile answers	33	32	31	40
One hostile answer	45	38	37	36
Two hostile answers	14	19	19	16
Three or four hostile answers	8	11	13	8
N =	344	528	778	844

These variations are, of course, simply trends and it must be remembered that one-third of the two middle groups showed no prejudice while one in twelve of the two less prejudiced classes expressed intense prejudice. People who were educated beyond the age of fifteen expressed less prejudice than others: this is particularly true of people (only 4% of the population) who received full-time education after the age of nineteen. A disproportionately high ratio of those with education beyond fifteen are still in the under thirty-five age-group who show a lower level of prejudice. Taking the sixteen + education group sub-dividing into those aged thirty-four or less and thirty-five and over, only 3% of the younger group showed intense prejudice while over 9% of their elders (with the same educational background) fell into this category. It seems that education does reduce prejudice; but its effect is difficult to distinguish from that of age.

Moving from the purely personal attributes of respondents, it was found that variations in prejudice were also associated with other characteristics. People who at the time of the survey would have voted Conservative expressed more prejudice than Labour supporters and still more than Liberals.

It is sometimes argued that middle-class Labour voters are much less prejudiced than their working-class allies; this view gains no support from the survey which found no differences between the two groups. Nor did any such difference emerge among Conservatives. The survey also separated out those who were members of the Labour Party (4%) and the Conservative Party (5%) and compared their responses to the first key question ('superiority' or 'inferiority' of coloured people) with the responses of their respective electoral supporters. It was found that while members of the Conservative Party were again more hostile than Labour Party members, members of both parties were less egalitarian than those who supported them, but were not members. Labour Party members had scores almost identical with those of Conservative voters. This apparent anomaly seems due to the over-representation of skilled working-class men

Table 21: ATTITUDE SCORES BY VOTING INTENTION

	Conser-vative %	Labour %	Liberal %	Others %
No hostile answers	30	37	36	39
One hostile answer	40	37	44	34
Two hostile answers	18	17	16	17
Three or four hostile answers	12	9	4	10
N =	904	1,056	145	389

among Labour members – this group has already been shown to be more prone than average to give hostile responses.

The incidence of rejection was highest among tenants of private landlords and lowest among owner-occupiers; the scores of council tenants fell in between. The differences between the two groups were, however, small.

The survey found no support for the view that travel abroad reduces prejudice. In fact, those who had travelled to Asia and Africa (mainly ex-servicemen) were less likely to be found in the categories expressing low prejudice. Nor did the ethos of brotherhood and solidarity implied by trade union membership seem to have any effect upon scores. The sample contained almost a thousand working-class people in employment, 38% of whom belonged to a trade union; their scores were almost identical with those who were not trade unionists.

People who, compared with their parents, had experienced upward social mobility were a little more likely to express prejudice than those who had fallen in the social scale. But again it was found that nearly all the upwardly mobile group were also lower-middle class and skilled working class and these groups, again, tended to score higher on prejudice irrespective of whether they had experienced upward mobility or not.

From the evidence examined so far, it seems that personal attributes like age, sex, class and education do have some effect upon the expression of prejudice but that social variables like political affiliation, social mobility, travel and housing tenure, have only a marginal effect. The next stage of the inquiry was to isolate groups of respondents according to six personality factors and their perception of their social situation. Two of these factors shed no light on the identification of prejudice.

People who felt that their neighbours all shared exactly the same kind of interests and problems as themselves displayed almost exactly the same views as those who felt that they had nothing whatever in common with their neighbours. Similarly, people who said that they would miss most of their neighbours if they moved were only slightly less inclined to express prejudice than the rather larger group of people who said that there was no one they would miss.

The next two factors followed on from the information on social mobility discussed earlier. People were asked whether they felt they had achieved more or less than their parents: 75% thought they had improved upon their parents' earlier position while only 7% considered themselves worse off. Again contrary to a popular notion, those who felt that they had fallen in the social scale did not express greater prejudice than those who felt they had improved their situation. Indeed, as in the results for respondents objectively mobile in the social scale, the trend was in the opposite direction. On the other hand, when people were asked to speculate about their future prospects, the 60% who felt that things would get better for them over the next 5-10 years expressed slightly less prejudice than the 11% who were pes-simistic about their future.

Two other factors in this section differentiated those who expressed prejudice from those who did not. First, 15% of the sample showed a high 'social potency', in that they de-clared that they would give active support to a local move-ment which concerned itself with problems of community action, and felt that the authorities would heed such action. This group showed considerably less prejudice than a further 10% who would offer no active support and felt that such action would, in any case, be ignored by the authorities.

Table 22: ATTITUDE SCORES BY SOCIO-POLITICAL POTENCY

	High Potency	Low Potency
	%	%
No hostile answer	36	33
One hostile answer	40	34
Two hostile answers	18	22
Three or four hostile answers	6	11
N =	380	241

Second, people were asked to express approval or disap-proval of six statements unconnected with colour but of a kind often used in personality tests to determine each re-spondent's degree of 'authoritarianism'. Briefly, an 'author-itarian personality' (Adorno et al, *The Authoritarian Personality*, 1950) is someone who – among other things – regards social problems as the handiwork of malicious indi-viduals whose activities should be curbed by greater exercise of authority; a 'non-authoritarian' person resists such stereo-typed thinking. The 21% of the sample who were con-sistently authoritarian displayed much more prejudice than the 11% who were consistently non-authoritarian.

These two factors are almost certainly related. It seems logical to suppose that the authoritarians are also likely to be those with a low social potency – because they will be prone to believe that all power should reside in the authorities to suppress social deviants. Conversely the non-authoritarians are likely to have faith in community action and to believe in the reality of government by consent.

Table 23: ATTITUDE SCORES BY AUTHORITARIANISM

	High Authoritarian %	Low Authoritarian %
No hostile answer	30	39
One hostile answer	34	41
Two hostile answers	21	13
Three or four hostile answers	15	7
N =	527	282

In what form is the prejudice revealed in this study expressed? Concentrating once more upon the five-borough data, the following table details the way in which people rated the British in comparison with the peoples of other Continents.

Table 24: ATTITUDES TOWARDS THE BRITISH COMPARED WITH PEOPLE IN OTHER PARTS OF THE WORLD

British people are	Africa %	Asia %	Europe %	America %
Definitely superior	33	27	8	5
Superior to some extent	32	34	28	18
Same	18	20	52	58
Inferior	4	3	4	11
Don't know	13	16	8	8
	100	100	100	100

While a majority conceded equality and some even superiority to Americans and Europeans, a greater majority regarded Africans and Asians as inferiors. Later in the interview when the issue was put in a much more personal manner, 53% expressed the view that coloured immigrants were their inferiors, 11% were unable to decide and 31% rated them as equals. Those who declared themselves superior to coloured immigrants were asked to state why they reached that conclusion, and their reasons are summarized in Table 25.

Table 25: REASONS FOR REGARDING COLOURED PEOPLE AS INFERIOR

	All %	Men %	Women %	Middle Class %	Working Class %
Skin colour	5	3	6	4	5
Lack of education	44	53	35	51	40
General cultural differences	38	37	41	35	41
Specific differences: cleanliness	10	7	13	8	11
Specific differences: other	10	9	10	10	9
Lack intelligence	7	8	5	6	7
Not civilized	3	3	3	3	3
Other reasons	9	9	10	9	9

Only 5% of this 53% justified their views on grounds of skin colour. In the current climate of opinion, prejudice on grounds of colour alone is not generally socially acceptable. Many of the other replies appear to reflect covert prejudice; some may be realistic appraisals of the different characteristics of coloured people in Britain. Among the 53% of the sample who declared that coloured immigrants are inferior, this pattern of acceptance of alleged inferiority (for which incidentally there exists no supporting evidence) was extended to people's appraisal of the differences in the 'way of life' in the migrants' countries of origin. Nearly a third of the sample said they knew too little about Cyprus or Greece to make such a judgment, but only 10% felt similarly handicapped in relation to India, Pakistan, and the West Indies – the great majority concluded that there is a large gulf between these countries and Britain. In a similar fashion, over 90% of the sample assigned 'the majority of coloured people in Britain' to the unskilled, or at best, semi-skilled working class – a picture that does not altogether correspond with reality.

An issue which usually comes to the fore in public concern about immigration and race relations is the fear that the country is in danger of being 'swamped' with immigrants. As

Table 26 demonstrates, the survey showed that grossly exaggerated estimates of the coloured population have gained considerable currency among the public.

Table 26: ESTIMATES OF THE SIZE OF THE COLOURED POPULATION

	%
One million or less	27
2–5 million	23
More than 5 million	24
Don't know	26
	100

Even when given the correct total population of Britain as a guide, (about 50 millions) three-quarters of the sample gave estimates of the coloured population at least double the true figure.

People were also asked to consider whether each group of immigrants took more out of the country than they contributed. At least 60% of the sample thought that all three groups did just this; in Wolverhampton 75% thought so. While about three-quarters of the sample felt that, in general, all immigrants benefited disproportionately from the social services, a majority acquitted white immigrants from this charge. This last point is important because it divides those who specifically believe that coloured immigrants exploit the social services from the remainder who may have based their judgment of the immigrants' lack of contribution upon their recent arrival.

Similar erroneous – and often derogatory – stereotypes emerged at various stages of the interview; for example, many people justified their support for more stringent controls upon coloured immigration by reference to 'disease', 'dirt', 'strain on schools', and 'overcrowding'. Altogether, the survey found a great deal of widely diffused anxiety, confusion and misunderstanding about migration to Britain, its composition and the migrants' backgrounds – all leading to a predisposition towards rejection. In such a climate, hostile stereotypes, used to justify overt rejection, are bound to flourish.

Against this background, it would appear reasonable to predict that contact between British people and coloured immigrants on a personal level is likely to be characterized predominantly by symptoms of rejection or avoidance. In fact, the evidence tends to lead to rather more varied conclusions. In total, 9% of the five-borough sample claimed to have coloured people living next door to them, 47% within five minutes' walk and 12% within half an hour's walk and these three groups were all questioned about their contacts with their coloured co-residents. Contact was not extensive – 25% of those having coloured neighbours had never spoken to them, and neither had 59% of those living five minutes' walk away. On the other hand, what contact has occurred seems to have been mostly of an agreeable nature; only 8% claimed *not* to have got on well with West Indians, 9% with Indians and 18% with Pakistanis. Those who said that they have become more favourably disposed towards coloured people tended also to be those who had spoken to and got on well with them. The main scenes of contact were these:

Table 27: LOCATION OF CONTACT WITH COLOURED PEOPLE

	%
At work	37
Living in the same house or next door	20
In the street or shopping	17
Through friends	11
Through children	5
Elsewhere	10

While most of the encounters occurred at work, only 44% of the sample had actually had an immigrant colleague and this figure varied from over half in Ealing to a third in Nottingham. Two thirds of the youngest age-group claimed to have an immigrant colleague and, rather surprisingly, so did 45% of the middle-class group. In all, 13% reported friction with West Indians at work, 16% with Indians and 23% with Pakistanis. The children of many respondents shared a school with immigrant children, ranging from 49% in Nottingham to 89% in Lambeth. These parents were asked to judge how their children got along with their coloured schoolmates and 13% reported difficulties with Pakistani children, 11% with Indians and 8% with West Indians. For many of the adults as one would expect, these direct contacts were supplemented by a good deal of informal and occasional contact on buses, in pubs and so on.

The last major stage of the interview was to place people in four imaginary situations, two related to employment and two to housing, within which they were invited to make a choice involving a 'colour' element.*

1. Suppose there were two workers, one white and one coloured, who do exactly the same work. If one, and only one, had to be made redundant should it be the white or the coloured worker?

Fifty-six per cent declined to discriminate on grounds of colour and said that the decision should be based on considerations of merit and service; 2% thought the white worker should go, and 42% would dismiss the coloured worker, usually on grounds of a universal white preference. In the national sample described at the beginning of the chapter the pattern of response was precisely duplicated. Relating this result to the other data in the five-borough sample, it was found that those less ready to dismiss the coloured worker out of hand were younger people, those higher up the social scale, those who had received extra full-time education, trade unionists (but only marginally), but most of all *people who had actually worked with or had experience of direct personal contact with coloured people.* These groups can by now be recognized as those with lower prejudice scores on the scale described at the outset. There were other interesting variations on this issue, for example: in Wolverhampton, considerably more Labour than Conservative supporters would dismiss the coloured worker but in Lambeth these positions were reversed.

2. Suppose there were two workers, one coloured and one white, who do exactly the same work. If one, and only one, had to be promoted, should it be the coloured or the white worker?

Again, the two samples (national and five boroughs) gave identical scores with a clear majority refusing to discriminate merely on the basis of colour and over one-third

* These questions were asked, of course, prior to the 1968 Race Relations Act which made much discrimination of this kind unlawful.

awarding promotion to the white worker. Among the boroughs a pattern of response emerged closely resembling that to the first question. Those less likely to support promotion of the white worker were the young, those in higher social class categories, the educated and, to a certain extent, the Labour voters and trade unionists. And again, the crucial factor was work-place and personal contact – people with these experiences were least likely to decide the question of promotion simply on grounds of colour.

The two housing questions (3 and 4) were two of the key prejudice questions (above) and so the distribution of hostile response will by now be obvious. Overall, 49% raised no objections to the letting of council dwellings to immigrants. Of those who refused, more than half dropped their objections where the immigrant family had been on the waiting list for the full qualifying period, which left 20% whose opposition was unconditional. Among this 20%, hostility was usually justified on the grounds that council housing was a reward for fully paid up membership of the Welfare State and as such ought to remain the exclusive right of British people. This kind of opposition was greatest in Lambeth and Ealing and least in Bradford, with Wolverhampton and Nottingham in between. The wide difference between Bradford's acceptance and Lambeth's rejection of coloured municipal tenants may be due to the predominant type of tenure in each borough; while each borough has 25% council tenants, in Bradford the majority of the remainder are owner-occupiers and in Lambeth exactly the same majority are in privately rented accommodation (most of these will have their names on housing lists) and only 20% own their own houses.

The pattern of response on the question about private letting was similar with 60% rejecting discrimination. Half of those who initially objected reversed their position on the qualification that the immigrants concerned were known to care for the property, leaving an intractable 10%. Again, the shortage of accommodation in London was reflected in marginally greater hostility (12-13% against 7% in Bradford); a negative reply tended to be couched in terms of a landlord's freedom of choice.

Altogether, the data from these four questions indicate

that two major factors may modify attitudes: (a) the extent of realistic competition for scarce resources like housing, and (b) personal contact in the workshop or office, especially among young people. While these conclusions tally well with people's own reports of agreeable exchanges, discussed earlier, the question of contact with particular immigrant groups creates a more complicated picture. One of the reasons for the choice of boroughs was the differential distribution of each immigrant group within each borough: Ealing's immigrants are predominantly Indians (3% of the total population), Lambeth's and Nottingham's are mostly West Indians (5.2% and 1.6% of the total respectively), Wolverhampton has an even balance of West Indians and Indians while Bradford has a predominantly Pakistani immigrant community. In each borough, the ethnic group not represented locally was the most popular one and this held true when people were asked to select members of one of the immigrant groups as new neighbours. This point might have important implications for all the survey's findings because it suggests that at least some of the acceptance that has occurred in the white community has emerged in a form more symbolic than actual.

Some of the questionnaire's supplementary items did throw some light on the profile of current opinion and possible clues for change. For example, of the 30% of the sample who felt less sympathy for disadvantaged coloured immigrants than they did for white people in similar trouble, more than half abandoned this view if all the coloured family had been born in Britain – only 10% of the whole sample carried their hostility to a position of rejection regardless of place of birth or upbringing. A request for suggestions about how coloured people might improve their own situation produced a motley collection of ideas, not all of them helpful or complimentary. Eleven per cent offered no ideas, 3% thought no solution possible, 7% bluffly recommended coloured people to 'return home'. Most people thought 'adopting a more English way of life' an appropriate course and recommended many acts of conformity, avenues for educational and economic improvement, and made special references to their alleged need for higher moral standards. It is interesting to interpose here some detail from another Research Services survey* which indicated that many immigrants, especially Asians, regard British workers as unclean, lazy, overfond of gambling and swearing and – most especially among the young – morally lax; this being a source of serious concern to Asian parents. So it would seem that conformity does not guarantee acceptance, especially if it is misconstrued on both sides. On a more optimistic note, one of the most significant findings of the survey is summarized in Table 28.

Table 28: IMPORTANCE ATTACHED TO PRESENCE OF COLOURED PEOPLE AS IT AFFECTS RESPONDENTS PERSONALLY

	Five boroughs	National Sample
	%	%
Very important	14	9
Quite important	18	16
Not important	38	37
Not at all important	30	37
Don't know	–	1
	100	100

Here the importance to whites of 'the colour problem' is placed in perspective. Over two-thirds of a sample regarded the issue with varying degrees of emphasis as 'unimportant'; only 14% regarded it as 'very important'. Of the 32% who were worried, 31% feared a deterioration of their area, 'because of immigrants', 25% feared intermarriage and 22% feared that immigrants would become a local majority. On the other hand 60% of both samples felt that the issue generally would either remain or become important in the future.

CONCLUSIONS

The conclusion that emerges most clearly from this attitude survey is that, however one divides up the sample – by age, sex, class, politics, the housing people live in and so on – each group will contain some people who are intensely prejudiced. Despite all variations discussed so far, it seems that intense racial prejudice is not strongly associated with

* Published in the *Daily Express* (9.7.69).

any demographic or social factor. The representation of intense prejudice in some measure in all groups indicates that these manifestations of social hostility are rooted in the personality of the intensely prejudiced individual. This indication is to some extent confirmed by the finding that the two factors which did discriminate sharply between the intensely prejudiced and the unprejudiced ('social potency' and 'authoritarianism') were both psychologically-based measures of personality. The authoritarian personality's exaggerated need to submit to authority and his acute hostility towards people physically, culturally or socially unlike himself and his own (the 'out-groups') is said by Adorno to 'spring from underlying hostility towards in-group authorities, originally the parents. The individual strives to keep his hostility in check by over-doing in the direction of respect, obedience, gratitude towards the in-group authorities and by displacing the underlying hostility towards these authorities on to "out-groups"'.

The essential features of this theory have been validated in many Western countries and have some important policy implications.

Ten per cent is not an insignificant minority and the intensely prejudiced cannot be ignored. But their views should be recognized for what they are – irrational 'solutions' to the inadequacies of undermined personalities which will persist in the face of any proof or policy. Our first concern must be with the 55% of the population whose doubts and uncertainties contain numerous exceptions. A programme of public education, carried out by community leaders, can offer immediate aid to those whose anxieties spring from misapprehensions like the notion that 'There are over 5 million immigrants.' In other instances, criticism is generated by realistic competition for decent houses, education and medical attention. A carefully managed reduction in this competition – which can be degrading in itself – may well lead to more favourable predispositions towards coloured immigrants than those which have been described here.

REFERENCES

1. See the correspondence between John Rowan, Danny Lawrence and Mark Abrams in *New Society*, 14th, 21st September and 4th, 11th October, 1969, Abrams' article in *The Listener*, 6th November and Lawrence's article in *Race Today*, October 1969.

Chapter Thirteen

Towards a Consistent Policy

In this chapter we shall begin the process of pulling together the threads of the discussion so far. In order to do so, it is essential first to establish the basis upon which the evidence is to be considered and evaluated, and for this we need a frame of reference within which to examine it and on which the recommendations for action could be securely based.

Oscar Handlin, the American social historian, has suggested three overlapping ways in which the evidence of the effects of the process of migration on a substantial scale can be examined. The first is the demographic. That is, one can consider the consequences of population change and the situation of the newcomer in purely statistical terms. The evidence presented earlier in this report on the situation of the coloured man in Britain in 1968 reveals a substantial degree of inequality over quite a wide range of areas – housing, jobs, and, to some extent, educational facilities. Moreover, it is clear from the investigation of immigrant attitudes carried out as part of the P.E.P. report that this inequality is perceived and resented by the majority of coloured people in this country – although there is evidence of sharply differentiated responses between one immigrant group and another. In this realistic experience of deprivation, and the perception of deprivation that results from it, lies one basis for action, and a precise one, too, in that it suggests where remedial action can immediately be applied. But this evidence by itself, valuable though it is, cannot be regarded as sufficient. Such an assessment provides items for only one side of a balance sheet. Remedial action directed to the material needs of the minority, although indispensable to satisfy their grievances does not cater (except indirectly) for those of the majority. It could even be that such action may base an additional strain on the majority – either because they resent the process of satisfaction or because it affects them directly and materially. One of the first coherent statements linking the two sets of grievances and attempting to reconcile them was that of Philip Mason's, and the field in which he argued that a concession to majority feeling is necessary was that of immigration. He suggested, at the beginning of 1965, that the aim of official policy should be defined as follows:

We are determined to treat those immigrants who are here as kindly as we treat our older citizens; we are determined to cut down sharply the number of fresh entries until this mouthful has been digested.[1]

It is a prescription which has since become the political orthodoxy. Whether this separation is satisfactory in concept or practical in execution is another matter; but the notion that stringency in control could be justified by reference to a constructive policy in domestic race relations has had an enormous influence on the evolution of policy generally.

But with immigration policy, another set of considerations comes into play, including the second criterion for the determination of policy suggested by Handlin – the economic. It is possible to evaluate the entry of newcomers into our society purely in terms of economic costs and benefits and this process has been attempted by Professor Peston. He concludes that immigration has been economically beneficial and that excessive restraints upon it might have adverse effects on the economy at large.

Clearly these findings have important policy implications for the numbers and composition of immigration alike. Yet, as Professor Peston himself is the first to accept, these considerations cannot in themselves be decisive for the formation of immigration policy. Other calculations must enter the picture – in particular, the capacity of the social structure, as distinct from the economic system, to absorb newcomers. This introduces the third of the categories devised by Handlin, the socio-cultural, and it is this perspective with which we will now be chiefly concerned.

However, in this dimension, unlike the economic, precise

calculation is not feasible. It is true that in the rationalizations for the restriction upon numbers and rate of entry advanced by politicians, the restrictions are conceived of and justified directly in terms of material stress upon social services. Strain, that is, placed either on existing resources – housing stock, educational facilities, provision of health services – or on the capacity of the natives to accept the arrival and settlement of the newcomers. This argument from stress was the chief plank on which the case deployed in the Labour Government's White Paper of August 1965 rested. It is implied in the formula subsequently devised by Roy Jenkins: that 'immigration should not be so high as to create a widespread resistance to effective integration policies (nor) so unreasonably low as to create an embittered sense of grievance in the immigrant community itself'.[2] But it is significant that neither at the time nor subsequently has any attempt been made to explain the basis on which the detailed calculation of the numerical quota was made. As we have seen, Ray Gunter (as Minister of Labour responsible for the employment voucher system, which serves as regulator) declined to do so. Nor is it possible to devise a formula in relation to the outflow of emigrants from the British Isles since the composition and basis of the emigration is necessarily quite different from that of the immigration, which it substantially exceeds.

The difficulties of devising objective measurements of stress multiply when subjective criteria come to be considered. The levels of effectiveness of local services are to some extent quantifiable. But once the concepts of cultural assimilation or psychological stress enter the picture, precision is inevitably lost. And even in such areas as the changes in use which frequently take place with property in areas of immigrant settlement and the effects on amenity of the differing life styles of the newcomers, objective assessment is effectively impossible.

Furthermore, anxiety about the extent of immigration and its consequences is based very largely on irrational – and consequently unquantifiable – factors. Moreover, the focus derives from an element which is objectively irrelevant – the colour of the newcomers' skin. That the roots of the attitudes which make up the main element in the public reaction are irrational is indicated by the findings of the survey of attitudes reported in Chapter Twelve.

The fact that anxiety is often irrational does not mean that it can be ignored. But it poses a problem of evaluation and the implications for policy are not clear. Edward Heath has stated – and there is truth in his assertion – that current public anxiety derives largely from the ordinary voter's fear that the Government has lost control over a phenomenon that affects him personally. The moral that Heath draws is that he himself must immediately be seen to be advocating the most stringent possible control of immigration; but the conclusion that this is the only way to recover confidence is a *non sequitur*. One cannot base policy indefinitely on conciliating opinion as such, regardless of the justice of the demands that are made. Most politicians realize this, and their repeated demands for stringency of control are a platform device in which the importance lies in the gesture struck and not the practical consequences. But such gestures have the effect of reinforcing the anxiety, not of relieving it – and hence intensifying the demands which must in turn be satisfied with further gestures, *ad infinitum*.

While all the factors we have discussed must be taken into account when policy decisions are taken, they are not necessarily the decisive ones – important though they are in many ways in their implications for the quality of life in this country. There are other perspectives in which the issue can be viewed.

At the outset, it was generally considered, as we have seen, that the external factors deriving from Britain's relationship with the outside world decisively overrode all domestic considerations. Julius Isaac wrote of Commonwealth immigrants in 1955:

Their presence must be welcomed from an international point of view. They are a challenge to those who regard racial prejudice, discrimination and the colour bar as unjustified, immoral and incompatible with the ideal of mutual aid and the common destiny of mankind. By fighting symptoms of deep-rooted racial prejudice, such people help to create a climate conducive to friendly international relationships. They have a powerful and less emotional argument to support them: the importance of this immigration for the cohesion and survival in its present form of the British Commonwealth.[3]

This kind of statement derives from assumptions about the relative significance of international and national policy objectives and has gradually lost significance as the one has diminished in importance and the other increased. We have described the process by which a Labour administration came to adopt first what we have called a 'Little England' policy on race relations and then, in the throes of rejecting a last post-imperial responsibility, lapsed during the Kenya Asians episode into a 'White Britain' posture. From the assumption that any form of control would infringe inalienable rights to an equal status, there had been a rapid decline to the complete dismissal of the notion that the Commonwealth connection imposes obligations that should remain binding.

But whether the British Government chose to concern itself with these considerations or not, British policy has implications both for the Commonwealth countries and internationally. The perspective exists, even if it is not employed. Robert Gardiner, reviewing the problems of international race relations in the 1965 Reith lectures, concluded that:

It seems to me that problems of migration and the treatment of settlers, which are now within the exclusive jurisdictions of individual countries, will eventually have to be examined collectively in a world organization.[4]

Such a voluntary surrender of an admittedly important aspect of national sovereignty would certainly have important implications and might well be impractical in practice: that it is not totally a fantasy has been shown by the success of the E.E.C. countries in abolishing all restrictions on the movement of immigrant workers and their families within the European Community. But it is not, in the present climate of domestic opinion, practical politics. Nor, in present circumstances, are arguments (like those of Dr. Isaac) deriving from a discarded view of the significance of the Commonwealth connection. To the extent that they still persist among politicians, these attitudes can no longer be regarded as relevant for policy.

In any discussion conducted upon the terms so far outlined the individual is largely excluded. Arguments on broad grounds of principle employing purely symbolic terms are justly suspect when applied to social problem issues in which questions of human suffering are involved. They may also embody assumptions which have never been put to the test of free consent.

Policy-makers in the past have proceeded from the assumption that the act of migration implies a willingness to accept not only the material conditions obtaining in the new surroundings but to take on the values and customs prevalent in that society. Migration has, since the nineteenth century, implied the entry of future citizens. And, although the increasing recognition given to cultural diversity has modified this assumption in the case of the migrant himself and restored a degree of identity to individuals who were once regarded purely as objects on a totem pole, it has been transferred, often in an intensified form, to their children – the second man on the pole. There is a feeling, to which one cannot help applying religious metaphors, that the 'Black British' will redeem our sinful society: that by making them first-class citizens we will wipe out the sin of the second-class status of their fathers. In short, what one could call a new social contract. In one version, they will become the simulacrum of Englishmen – their skin colour a constant reminder of our virtue in their equality, in another, the less patronizing, there will be a new mixed youth culture, with multi-racial and multi-cultural characteristics. Norman Bentwich has written of the generation of German Jewish refugees who came to this country at the end of the 1930s, that their children 'may yet produce the best fruit from the meetings of the two cultures . . . the return which the new citizens have already made is a rich reward for the virtues of tolerance and the asylum that Britain signally offered'.[5]

This notion of cultural amalgamation is clearly a stage beyond the crude assumption of Anglo-conformity with which their parents were confronted and with which coloured newcomers are still confronted by the host population generally. But it is still based on the presumption that a contract which for one party has not been offered on a footing of free choice has already been entered into. In most of the policy decisions taken in the past on race relations the consent of the minority has been assumed. The possibility that it can no longer be taken for granted has not been subjected to any serious scrutiny.

American Negroes, it is often suggested, have ceased to be prepared to accept the overdue concession of justice if it is offered as an act of charity. The same might come to be true of the equal citizenship offered to the coloured Briton by British politicians. For instance, it may be that some of the inducements offered to him may not be as attractive as the white majority have assumed them to be. To be a visible example of British tolerance may not be a very satisfying role to perform. To take an obvious example, for a white house-owner, the arrival of a black neighbour, according to the unshakeable folk-lore, will diminish the material and hence the psychological value of his property. A contrary assumption is no less tenaciously subscribed to; that for a coloured man, white neighbours confer vastly increased social status. But, like some black Americans, a coloured Englishman might decide that rather than face the personal stresses of entering an all-white neighbourhood, remaining in an area of coloured concentration would provide not only increased security but ultimately a basis for political power.

Faced with a challenge to the cultural imperialism which has been unthinkingly accepted for so long, what degree of pluralism can our society, its homogeneity already under assault from other directions, tolerate? The separatism of the Indian and Pakistani communities has been the subject of both criticism and defence: criticism, on the grounds that it constitutes an impermissible degree of communalism, and defence on the grounds that the phenomena involved are of a temporary nature and have a certain exotic value in terms of style of life. In neither case has the problem of the evolution of separate institutions and the extent to which they can be conceded parity of esteem been considered. The idea has rarely been entertained that British society might move, like American society in the model devised by the American sociologist Milton Gordon, towards a chess-board pattern in which class and ethnic differences divide society horizontally and vertically. And the problem of keeping the way open for those who decide to leave one system for another has therefore not been examined, although the experience of previous migration suggests that this transition is far more painful and difficult than the process of migration itself.

One difficulty about charting a secure passage through these rocks is that the debate on cultural diversity has so far taken place on such a superficial level. Because discussion has concentrated on a limited number of manifestations of different life styles, there has been a general tendency to mistake temporary fringe phenomena for the more significant differences that they reflect. Many justifications of the migration have been mounted on the rickety platform of these transitory, lower order differences. One can classify these briefly in terms of the senses which register them. The visual variety, such as the differences in skin pigmentation, dress, and styles of decoration, makes up the image of cosmopolitanism which many people consider appropriate to large cities; as does diversity of cuisine, which is perhaps where the notion of cultural amalgamation has been closest to realization; and, in the case of the young, musical tastes which reflect all kinds of diverse influences – American Negro, West Indian, Indian. Furthermore, distinctions in use of the English language, dialect, slang, and, on a more serious level, the special contributions of African and Caribbean novelists, all have a significance – though one that can be exaggerated.

In all these directions, and in others, there has been an assumption that the behaviour and style of the newcomer will make a special contribution to modifying the Englishman's own style of life. Thus, he will exemplify the virtues of relaxation, persuade the Englishman of the value of living in the present, and communicate the notion that the enjoyment of sex is a legitimate and important part of life. It may well be that this kind of interpretation of the position of the immigrant in our society contains as much cultural patronage as the earlier assumption that all migrants were instant Englishmen. But a more serious criticism of this attitude is that it overlooks the intense puritanism of most migrants, who would reject the life style with which they are associated in this theory with far more vehemence than the white middle class. Although amalgamation in a multi-cultural and inter-racial setting is possible, this is not the kind of footing on which it can be launched, except by footloose young. If we are to evaluate the prospects for pluralism satisfactorily, it will have to be done on a more systematic basis than this.

Not merely should discussion extend beyond the purely exotic aspects of the migration: it must transcend the limitations implicit in the politicians' definition of the issue as 'the immigration problem' – a concept implying equally restricted views of causation and the aims of future policy. For, in practice, the issue has not been an isolated feature in the political landscape. By throwing light on a series of major social issues, culminating in the whole debate about the relief of poverty and maldistribution of resources, the immigrants illuminate the strengths and weaknesses of our social system and indicate the surgery which it requires. For the effects of the deprivation of rights cannot be viewed in isolation: the perspective in which it must be placed is ultimately that of the debate about these concepts in the wider society. Equally, the implications of pluralism relate to the basic structure of that society and the basis on which certain facilities are provided within it. In short, our society is in important respects an unjust society organized in such a way as to perpetuate these injustices. Immigration, by stimulating a concern for social justice, may also provide the solvent for the inflexibility which helped to produce the symptoms now ascribed to the presence of immigrants.

This perspective has provided the focus for the diagnosis made by a number of eminent social diagnosticians. Professor Peter Townsend, in his discussion of the social policy of the Labour Party in office, wrote:

There has been a marked shift of emphasis away from social equality as a national objective. The White Paper on Immigration from the Commonwealth in 1965 (together with the later failure to promote integration) can now be perceived as representing a major retreat from universalistic values, which inevitably sapped the moral authority of the Government in other social spheres and affected the whole delicate structure of community services ... The interdependence of institutions and values (ensures) that changes in one part of the social structure are bound to affect other parts of that structure. The restrictive social policies reflected by the White Paper and by measures like the Kenya Asians Act (sic) were bound to make racial equality harder to achieve. But they make social equality harder to achieve too.... After the White Paper of 1965 the term 'equality' could no longer be used unselfconsciously by members of the Labour Party. Much more important, the concept could no longer lend coherence and simplicity to the Government's long-term objectives.[6]

This perspective is also crucial at a time when the whole functioning of the Welfare State and the provision made for those who fall below the minimum subsistence level have come under close and critical scrutiny. Douglas Houghton has pointed out that the entire structure of the Welfare State has come into existence in one lifetime: 'Everyone now over pensionable age was born at a time when the only institutional care provided by the State was the Workhouse and the Lunatic Asylum.'[7] Yet the institutions are already displaying the signs of stress and wear and tear appropriate to a far older structure. The governing assumption of the 1950s had been that the minimum living standard envisaged by Beveridge had been achieved; a safety net was presumed to exist which symbolized society's commitment to ensuring that individuals would not find themselves living in poverty.

Yet the evidence for the wholesale abolition of poverty in our society was never satisfactory and on closer examination it became clear that the increased prosperity of a large section of the working class had left behind it substantial pockets of poverty, made more visible and painful to those who endured it by the relative success of the majority. Galbraith's famous use of the classical tag about private affluence and public squalor underlines the important element in this residual poverty – the poor quality of the services which were available to a substantial section of the population in the inner areas of great cities. The 'cheerful' school could point with justice to the enormous changes in life style and access to amenities enjoyed by a large section of the population. We have quoted one such analysis, that of Dr. Abrams, in Chapter 1. Professor Titmuss has put the other side of the picture:

In Britain, in 1951, there were few who would have thought that in the years ahead the proportion of children and old people considered to be living in poverty would increase; that incomes would become more unequal; that the distribution of personal wealth would be found to be more highly concentrated in the top 5 per cent of the population; that there would be no narrowing of the differentials between working class and middle class children in the higher reaches of the educational system.[8]

The rediscovery of poverty, that endless cyclic process through which every generation passes, had this much in common with earlier revelations: the quite unexpected extent of the suffering revealed had an electric effect on the social conscience of the nation. But there is a distinction which sets this process of discovery apart from previous ones – the complicating and illuminating presence of an element of coloured immigration.

There was another distinction besides, which may in the long run prove to be more important. The poor, in the mid-twentieth century, are not conceived of as constituting a physically or socially separate section of the community. They are not separated from the body of society, as the nineteenth-century pauper was, by formal deprivation of social rights. Nor are the areas of poverty remoter, as C. F. G. Masterman portrayed the Edwardian slums, than China or Peru. The mass media see to that. As Professor Townsend has put it: 'The extent of poverty and the current methods of treating the poor are inescapably linked to the prosperity and expectations of other sections of society.'[9] And the responsibility for remedial measures has been by and large accepted, once the diagnosis was admitted to be sound. Nevertheless, a deprivation of social rights is suffered by those whose income or family size confines them to the rented accommodation in the inner areas of large cities and forces them to accept unskilled work for themselves and poor educational facilities for their children. Professor Townsend goes on to comment: 'It is not surprising that they (the poor) *feel* stigmatized. To a large extent they *are* stigmatized.'[10] Or, at best, the processes of exercising those rights are clogged by the complexities and inefficiency of the machinery devised to satisfy them. And the coloured poor, suffering in common with their neighbours this deprivation, have additional disadvantages deriving both from discrimination and from the neglect deriving from the *laissez-faire* integration policy of the 1950s which embodied a failure to recognize the need for separate facilities to cater for their needs.

Professor Titmuss has suggested that there are three ways of classifying the benefits or uses of social security and social service provision. It can be regarded as a form of investment on the party of society or the individual or it can be seen as a method of distributing income or command over resources; or, finally, it can be seen as a form of compensation for deprivation – for example, inadequate access to existing services or welfare provisions. The means to achieving these ends, he argues, lies in the provision of a range of benefits on a universal basis. He concludes that 'there can be no answer in Britain to the problems of poverty, ethnic integration and social and educational inequalities without an infra-structure of universalist services'.[11] This is, of course, a view that has been strongly criticized by those who feel that if need can be accurately identified it can be satisfied in a less wasteful way than by the provision of benefits on a universal basis.

It is not part of our purpose here to suggest that universal benefits, at least as provided at present, are necessarily always the most efficient way of dealing with all the needs of the minority with which we are particularly concerned. In the case of a minority differing in age structure and family size from the population at large, there may be objective arguments for a degree of variation in the provision of services. The time scale of need may also be different; there are additional – but temporary – needs arising from the migration process which have to be satisfied in the short term but whose satisfaction should not be built into any long-term solutions. The deprivation for which compensation is necessary may also need to be satisfied in different ways. And some services provided for the population at large may at present not be relevant for the needs of this minority: for example, there is very little use made of the geriatric services by immigrants, both for cultural reasons and as a result of their age structure. But none of these propositions is inconsistent with the general case for the provision of the kind of re-inforcement of the universal infra-structure for which Professor Titmuss is arguing.

A programme which involves, even in a partial way, distinguishing a particular group and giving them access to benefits not provided for the population at large presents formidable political and practical difficulties. As Professor Titmuss comments, the problem of redistribution presents such a formidable challenge precisely because 'it is inextricably mixed up with the change of social rights as well as civil rights for coloured citizens'.[12] This is in many ways the crux of the whole issue. One strategy already proposed would go a long way towards surmounting this obstacle. It is one which will already be familiar from discussion of policy and its evolution – the application of the principle of territorial welfare justice. That is, the identification for action of the geographical areas in which the burdens of under-privilege bear particularly hard on inhabitants of all colours. This is the policy adopted in defining the Plowden educational priority areas (E.P.A.s) and the other devices for promoting 'positive discrimination' since introduced. The rationale for this approach is that the handicaps of poverty are cumulative: a disproportionate amount of the social cost of change is concentrated on certain social groups occupying certain geographical areas and the burden of unemployment deriving from technological change will fall particularly heavily on these groups. It is also these groups that will feel the impact of urban renewal and have to put up with poor quality services and a poor quality environment in the inner urban areas. Ultimately, effective community services, preventive in outlook and of a high quality (both in terms of facilities and personnel), should provide the main answer, but in the interim there must be a redistribution of resources to compensate for what Titmuss calls the 'diswelfare' imposed by the factors detailed above. Such a programme would represent something of a revolution in social priorities. And even if such a revolution left certain specific needs of coloured minorities unsatisfied it would still represent, for them as for their white neighbours, an enormous advance on the present position. Furthermore, it could provide the context within which any additional special measures could be set in perspective.

In any programme involving positive discrimination, whether it is in favour of a group defined by area of residence or one distinguished by ethnic origin, the major justification for action must be past negative discrimination. Such discrimination must be recognized as existing, and accepted for what it is. As the evidence from the attitude survey suggests, the average Englishman recognizes no responsibility for the immigrants who have entered his society. Like Lord Carron, he feels that they have not made sufficient contribution to justify permitting them to obtain benefits on a scale equivalent to that to which the population at large is entitled, let alone to benefits over and above these. However, a degree of responsibility is admitted in the case of those born here. Action on their behalf could take the form of corrective legislation to restore the social rights which they are unlikely to be permitted to enjoy in present circumstances or administrative action to enable them to exercise them. It is important to emphasize that these rights are available to them as citizens: there should be no implication of a special contract entered into between them and the State which differs from the reciprocal rights and obligations which apply in the case of all British citizens. Providing access to services and amenities of right should not involve the narrowing of their area of choice and personal behaviour – the friends they choose, the places they live in, their tastes in food and clothing. They must not be expected to be more British than the British.

The broad principles for special programmes are hard enough to devise, even in the case of the Black Britons: in practice, their application presents even more formidable difficulties. Such programmes are hedged round with the psychological problems of identifying need without ascribing responsibility for its existence.

The suggestion that the presence of immigrants has an absolute rather than a relative significance has been a major source of difficulty in this area. Poor housing conditions and inadequate educational facilities are adequate indices of social deprivation; the presence of immigrants can mean any number of things, depending on local circumstances and one's perspective, but there is no one-to-one relationship between the fact of an immigrant residing in the area and the existence of a material problem – indeed, the individual migrant may find himself deprived even within an area in which there is overall prosperity. By encouraging the view that immigrants were in themselves one form of natural disaster, the initial ministerial explanation of the urban programme nourished the illusion that the problems of areas of settlement would disappear if the immigrants departed – either voluntarily, through dispersal, or compulsorily, through repatriation – and impeded the formulation of realistic objectives for central and local government.

We have already suggested that part of the difficulties involved lie in the structure of central Government. The proposals in the Seebohm Report for the co-ordination of personal social services at local authority level may point the way to a solution to some of these structural difficulties, but it is imperative that the task of defining the scope of the special needs of coloured citizens and the most effective means of relieving them is entrusted to a department capable of making a realistic appreciation and well equipped to devise remedial measures. The deployment of personnel and resources, the organization of the services, and the access to information has in the past been wholly inadequate to those needs.

Finally, Professor Townsend has commented that poverty should not be regarded as an absolute but as a relative condition and 'for it to be alleviated there has to be a complex reconstruction of the systems of rewards in society, as between those at work and those who are not at work, those with and without dependants, and those who live in depressed and prosperous regions'.[13] We cannot urge that the significance of race relations is such that the entire reconstruction must be undertaken with a view to resolving this issue alone. Nor, even in the broader context of meeting the needs of the underprivileged as a whole, can the necessity for such a reconstruction be completely decisive for the evolution of policy. It is attractive to see the focus of government action purely in terms of 'social growth', but at this point other factors come into play and involve us in issues beyond the scope of this book. The touchstone by which our proposals must be measured is the extent to which they contribute to a situation in which a redistribution of resources can be undertaken on a socially just basis, between citizens with full and secure access to social, civil and political rights, employing means which permit the exercise of the maximum degree of choice compatible with these overriding aims.

REFERENCES

1. P. Mason, *Guardian* (23rd January, 1965).
2. In a speech to the National Committee for Commonwealth Immigrants, 23rd May, 1966.
3. Julius Isaac in *The Positive Contribution by Immigrants* (Paris, U.N.E.S.C.O., 1955), p. 62.
4. *A World of Peoples* (London, B.B.C. Publications, 1966), p. 23.
5. Quoted by Isaac, op. cit, p. 65.
6. Peter Townsend in *Social Services for All?*, Part One, Fabian Tract 382 (London Fabian Society, 1968), p. 2.
7. Douglas Houghton, *Paying for the Social Services* (London, Institute of Economic Affairs, 1967), p. 7.
8. R. H. Titmuss, *Commitment to Welfare* (London, George Allen & Unwin, 1968), p. 161.
9. P. Townsend in *Social Services for All?*, Part Four, Fabian Tract 385 (London, Fabian Society, 1968), p. 110.
10. Ibid, pp. 110-11.
11. Titmuss, op. cit, p. 123.
12. Ibid. p. 114.
13. Townsend, Fabian Tract 382, op. cit, p. 6.

Chapter Fourteen

What is to be done?

Colour and Citizenship originally ended with 78 recommendations addressed chiefly to central government, covering all the main subject areas treated in the main report. In a debate on the report in the House of Lords, on 16th December, 1969 Lord Shepherd, speaking on behalf of the Government, indicated that there had been an official review of these recommendations and that the Government's overall conclusion was that 'on the two main issues of employment and housing . . . there is no difference between the Government and the authors of the Report on the objective to be achieved'.[1] Together with his ministerial colleague, Baroness Serota, Lord Shepherd went on to review these recommendations in some detail. On some of them, it appeared, the Government felt sympathetic but entertained doubts about the practicability of what was proposed. On some, action was in the process of being taken – or had been taken – since the publication of the report. For example, there were the new provisions in the Housing Act of 1969 and the implementation of the much delayed proposal to introduce a nondiscrimination clause into Government contracts (October 1969).

On other recommendations still the Government could not accept the proposals that had been made. For example, there was the proposal that Section 6 in the Race Relations Act of 1965, dealing with incitement to racial hatred, should be either repealed or transferred to the Public Order legislation. Answering a letter from the Board of Deputies, the Home Secretary said 'The provisions of the section had a salutary effect, particularly in the distribution of literature which is racially offensive. I think the section continues to be useful . . .'[2] Similarly, the Government did not, perhaps hardly surprisingly, agree with the views expressed in the original text on the question of the co-ordination of official action. As Baroness Serota put it: 'The need to co-ordinate the policies of individual Departments and relate them to a common theme was recognized very early on in the life of this Government: first in the condition that one Department, the Home Office, should undertake the responsibility and, secondly, that special Government machinery was needed to co-ordinate policies and action. I think that evidence of the effectiveness of the machinery which the Government established in this sphere is the success of the urban aid programme'3 (which was not established until the summer of 1968).

In addition to this official consideration of issues raised in the course of the concluding sections of *Colour and Citizenship*, two further reports containing recommendations addressed to the Government have appeared since the publication of that volume. These are the Report of the House of Commons Select Committee on Race Relations and Immigration, on school leavers, and the Report of the Sub-Committee of the Central Housing Advisory Committee on policy in relation to council housing. Since these two reports share the status of official enquiries, they possess – with their other virtues – the additional advantage that their recommendations can be acted upon by government without the danger of damage to official dignity implied by admitting that outsiders have a substantial contribution to make on issues of policy. A White Paper giving the Government's detailed response to the Select Committee's recommendations is to be issued in the near future.4

All these further developments make it impractical simply to restate the programme outlined in *Colour and Citizenship*. The situation is in a state of very rapid change; and the essence of any effective programme in this field is that it should be sufficiently flexible to accommodate itself to such changes. Most – though not all – of the changes in policy that have been made recently are in our view likely to have constructive effects. Indeed, in the original report, the authors went out of their way to stress that some of the innovations that date from the period after mid-1968 – the introduction of the Urban Programme and the second Race

Relations Act – were extremely encouraging.[5] Nevertheless, we still cannot wholly endorse Lord Shepherd's complacency about the record of Government in this field. 'The Government,' he claimed, 'have been taking, and will continue to take, a positive attitude to problems of race relations in this country, and ... in dealing with them we are striking a reasonable balance between seeking solutions within the development of our general social policies and paying due attention to the special difficulties created by differences of language and culture, and by racial prejudice'.[6] The distance that has had to be travelled between this sort of statement, with its unexceptional balancing of priorities, and the pronouncements made by the same Government in their White Paper of 1965 is a far sharper indictment of past negligence in official policy than any contained in the original text of *Colour and Citizenship* – which Lord Shepherd dismissed as 'essentially political judgments (which) cannot claim ... scientific objectivity'.[7]

But if straightforward repetition of a programme already partially overtaken by events would not be of any great value it may nonetheless be useful to restate some of the basic guide lines laid down for policy in *Colour and Citizenship*, on which a strategy for reform can, in our view, be based. It is, of course, fair comment to say that in viewing the issue as one of devising strategies for reform the authors are making a judgment about the nature of the task that faces our society. Some critics have made the point that tinkering with a system that has so far conspicuously failed to deliver the goods to minorities may be worse than useless and that the dependence on political personalities involved in such an approach has already been demonstrated to be ultimately unsatisfactory. We disagree with this view: in our opinion non-violent change is still possible within the existing system and a just society that provides an equitable distribution of rewards and opportunities can still, we believe, be achieved by peaceful methods. We share some of the anxieties of our critics, based on the past performance of politicians of all parties: but we see the scope for manoeuvre within the existing system, under any circumstances that we can at present foresee, as still wide enough to justify putting forward the proposals that follow.

INSTRUMENTS FOR REFORM

One of the allegations most frequently made about the evolution of policy on race relations is that those responsible for making policy (by which is meant both Parliament and Whitehall) lost control of the race relations situation through a failure to undertake any systematic forward planning. As our analysis would suggest, we would agree that there has been such a failure, although there are now encouraging signs that some of the difficulties and inhibitions have been overcome. In our view, this failure has stemmed partly from the placing of the responsibility for race relations within the structure of government and partly from the attitudes of those in authority about the legitimate aims of policy.

In our view the way to reform lies initially in distinguishing policy on race relations from policy on immigration. Each demands a different approach; each the deployment of a different range of services. The two problems cannot be considered in isolation from one another, but the suggestion that they must be indissolubly linked for administration purposes is untenable.

In the previous chapter we argued that in the long run efficiency and social justice both demanded that solutions to the main problems associated with immigration should be sought within a broad strategy directed towards the problems of the city and based on need and not race. As we have just shown, the Government now accepts this proposition. But we would go further than Lord Shepherd did in the statement we have quoted: we would argue that recognition that the needs of minorities must be considered in the context of general social policy strongly suggests that policy affecting them should be made in a department whose responsibilities lie in the mainstream of policy-making. In the original report, we went on to argue from this that the logical point from which strategy could be directed would be from the office of the Secretary of State for Social Affairs. We went on to argue that responsibility for integration should be transferred to the Department of Health and Social Security – the embryo from which such a ministry might be expected in due course to develop.* As we stated in the original text (page 684) it may well be that this is not the right time at which to transfer such an important responsibility. Events since the original volume was published have reinforced this impression and we would not now wish to suggest that such a transfer should take place immediately. There are also grounds for arguing that the experiences gained over the past two years by the Home Office should not be dissipated by a transfer. Nevertheless, we do not accept that the arguments put forward by Government spokesmen elsewhere in the House of Lords debate – that the Home Office remains the most logical place for this responsibility – are conclusive and we would like to see this whole matter reconsidered, as part of the series of inquiries conducted by the House of Commons Select Committee on Race Relations and Immigration.

Should a transfer of functions eventually be decided upon, there are a number of related activities – for example, the grant-giving function in Section 11 of the Local Government Act of 1966, the responsibility (barely exercised to date) for undertaking research, and (far more important) the supervision and co-ordination of the Urban Programme – which should also be transferred.

Finally, reform of the structure of the integration machinery would be only half the battle. The style in which the machine is operated is almost of equal importance in a situation where confidence is so vital. Any new structure must be open to outsiders; access as a matter of course to all levels should be routine. Full advantage should be taken of the recommendation of the Fulton Report on the Civil Service about the exercise of responsibility by officials.

PRIORITIES FOR POLICY

There are a number of subjects which are central to all recommendations on this subject, and which occur as a common theme throughout the discussion of policy. The most important of these is the causes and consequences of concentration and the extent to which the policy of dispersal

---

* Although we should have made it clear that the Secretary of State exercises two distinct functions—one co-ordinating and one departmental. It is the first that we had in mind when making the recommendation.

is desirable. There are, as yet, few if any coloured ghettoes in this country; but many cities have coloured quarters in which coloured people may come to be in a majority. These concentrations have an immediate practical importance in that they are reflected in the changing composition of school populations in the areas concerned. The Secretary of State for Education (Mr. Edward Short) has gone on record as saying that the emergence of all-black schools which is likely if the concept of the neighbourhood school is retained, would be undesirable. But while such a development may indeed have its negative implications, the matter may well be beyond the control of a local education authority to regulate; it may be a by-product of the same authority's housing policy. And in determining this housing policy there is still, in many cases, an option open to local authorities: the question 'to disperse or not to disperse', will increasingly come to confront the planners as the coloured quarters of our cities come to be cleared and be developed.

In the past the assumption shared by all concerned in making policy has been that the aim is the dispersal of minorities. However, we agree with the Cullingworth Committee[6] in concluding that dispersal is not in practice always the right policy to follow. This is not to say that there is any virtue in the continued concentration of coloured people in overcrowded housing in quarters of our cities with poor educational facilities and a deteriorating environment. On the contrary, these problems pose great dangers which are particularly threatening in the case of West Indians. There is a danger of perpetuating disadvantage and of a cycle of disability from which escape eventually becomes impossible.

But despite these dangers, we would not feel justified in recommending drastic measures which would be necessary to promote wholesale dispersal. This is chiefly because there is no prescription which can be universally applied. As we have shown in our earlier chapters, the differences that separate the different coloured communities from one another generate entirely different needs which will achieve satisfaction in different ways. For the Indian immigrant there are many virtues in the communal settlement which provides security in the early stages of the settlement. In our view, there is no case for a policy of active dispersal in the case of

Indian settlements, although it is desirable that the Indians should not be involuntarily confined to particular areas of any town. The situation of the Pakistanis is likely to be similar to that of the Indians, but its development will be slower because of the demographic imbalance in the immigration.

The situation of the West Indians is different and more complex. In some places there are communities which have established themselves and despite poor housing prefer the neighbourhood in which they are established because it is near to work and provides a number of familiar facilities. Yet in many ways, the West Indians are the archetype of the council house tenant – the skilled artisans whose wives are prepared to go out to work to add to the family resources. If present obstacles were to be removed it seems to us likely that they would follow the Irish into acceptance in the public sector. Others would willingly buy homes if credit were available; the home ownership rate among West Indians is already far higher than among their white neighbours. Such people need to be helped to get out of the areas in which they are often involuntarily segregated.

The key to the situation is to allow individuals from all different backgrounds the maximum degree of choice. For those West Indians who do not wish to leave concentrations in the inner city – either through fear of the unknown or because they feel threatened or rejected by the majority – and for the established communities who do not wish to be moved, the alternative should ultimately be rehousing within the area for those who are displaced through development schemes or assisting property owners to rehabilitate their homes.

But if these alternatives prove to be justified, two essential preliminaries need to be satisfied. First, free exit from areas of settlement must be safeguarded and, secondly, the link between colour and squalor which is firmly cemented in the public mind by conditions in the twilight areas must be broken. And if these conditions are to be satisfied, not only must housing conditions be improved but educational facilities and the environment must be brought up to a level at least equivalent to that of suburbia. Parity of esteem being guaranteed, a degree of concentration can be acceptable.

TOWARDS A CO-ORDINATED APPROACH

Voluntary dispersal is inevitably a long-term proposition:
the immediate problems facing policy-makers – and those
more personally affected – are likely to be those characteristic of the run-down inner areas of major cities. Since
1968 the Government has been attempting a co-ordinated
approach to some of the problems arising from the multi-
plicity of pressure on the inhabitants of these areas. As Lady
Serota put it in the House of Lords debate of December
1969: 'It is indeed a measure of positive discrimination,
which is intended generally to help those people in areas,
particularly urban areas, of special social need who are
suffering from a concentration of social handicap and
difficulty, a concentration of bad housing, poor schools and
all the [other] problems.'[9]

The urban programme, as we have indicated in the text, is
operated under the general supervision of the Home Office
and involves an expenditure of from £20–25 million of local
authority money by 1972. This expenditure is reimbursed at
the rate of 75% by central Government. The first phase of
the programme was devoted principally to the provision of
day nurseries, nursery classes and children's homes; the
Government has given approval to over 400 new classes providing some 10,000 nursery school and class places for the
under-fives. The second stage of the programme is on a
broader basis and involves 89 local authorities in a series of
projects covering such fields as neighbourhood advice
centres, unattached youth workers, in addition to further aid
to play groups for the under-fives – one of the instances in
which there has been a co-ordination of voluntary and statutory effort. This main component in the programme is supplemented by grants under Section 11 of the 1966 Local
Government Act, amounting to £4 million in 1968–69, in
respect of the employment by local authorities of staff whose
work is directly related to special needs of immigrants.

To the extent that it represents the beginnings of a co-
ordinated attempt to deal with the problems of major cities
on a basis of need, the programme deserves the warm welcome which it has received. As a potentiality, at least. But
the funds so far made available are not sufficient to open up

any realistic prospect of making fundamental and lasting changes in the environment and services in the twilight zones. Moreover, it is legitimate to wonder whether in the selection of priorities for the programme some of the most serious of the problems facing the inhabitants of those areas have not been evaded. It is true that the programme needs to be seen against the background of the additional provision now being made for housing in these areas, and the educational priority areas programme involving the expenditure of £16 million on a new school building programme launched after the publication of the Plowden Report. Nevertheless, the broad attack on the problem of under-privilege undertaken in operations like the Model Cities programme in the United States has not yet been attempted in this country. There is an argument for considering such an assault on these problems. As it is, the programme has fulfilled a useful function in bringing official resources on problems for which it has not previously been available – notably provision for the under-fives. Section 11 funds have also helped to ameliorate the staffing difficulties of local authorities in districts with sub-stantial immigrant population. These are useful achieve-ments but they do not altogether justify the high praise with which the Government spokesmen refer to the programme, which is sometimes uncomfortably reminiscent of the exag-gerated claims made by administration spokesmen for com-munity action programmes in the United States. The discrediting of these claims has helped in turn to discredit much of the constructive work done in the course of the poverty programme – and eventually contributed to its par-tial dismantling at the hands of the incoming Nixon Admin-istration.

PERSPECTIVES

Outside this one area in which a policy specifically designed to cater for the needs of minorities has been evolved, there are a number of other policy areas in which detailed rec-ommendations were made in *Colour and Citizenship*. As we have stated earlier, we do not believe a detailed programme for action in a rapidly changing situation is appropriate here. However, we do feel it right to state an order of priorities. In our view, none of the problems in this field is soluble unless the principal problems of housing and employment are first solved. In both these fields there are a number of lines of approach which in our view need to be followed in any programme that is devised and we state them below, together with the priorities (as we see them) in a number of other subject areas.

Housing

As we have tried to show in our analysis of the evolution of the housing policy, various approaches adopted by successive governments since the war have failed to resolve the problems of inner urban areas of multi-occupation and poor environment and services. As the private rented sector continues to shrink and the local authority sector grows, these residual but deep-rooted problems may in many cases be aggravated. Change is often achieved at the expense of the poorer tenant who sees the stock of accommodation available to him at a reasonable rent diminishing rapidly and cannot rely upon obtaining a council tenancy.

The new approach to these areas signalled by the White Paper *Old Houses into New Homes* and the subsequent legislation, the Housing Act of 1969, will go some way towards resolving these difficulties in its proposals for co-ordinated action in areas of poor housing facilities and the re-habilitation of property. Nevertheless, it seems to us that there are a number of further steps that need to be taken. First, the provisions of the Rent Act need to be more widely publicized. Serious consideration should be given to tackling the increasing evasion of its provisions through the transfer of property to the furnished sector by the extension of the Rent Acts to these tenancies. Second, we endorse the recommendations by the Cullingworth Committee in relation to local authority housing and the responsibility which should be assumed by authorities for the rehousing of those in need in their areas. Third, we attach great importance to the provision of mortgage funds for those attempting to break out of under-privileged conditions and purchase their own housing. Fourth, it is essential that the provisions against discrimination in housing contained in the Race Relations Act of 1968 should be kept under closest review in order to ensure that they are and continue to be effective. Fifth, the staff of local authorities who have the responsibility for dealing with the problems of minorities – and indeed the inhabitants of twilight zones generally – should receive adequate training to equip them for the very complex tasks involved. Alongside this reform in training procedures should go consideration of a re-structuring of the machinery of local government with the emphasis on providing a co-ordinated service. There should be further exploration of the part that housing associations can play, in association with local authorities, in providing for those inhabitants of these urban areas who cannot find accommodation through existing channels. Finally, we warmly agree with the Cullingworth Committee's recommendations on the more effective dissemination of information by local authorities and welcome the initiative already taken by Lambeth Borough Council in setting up a housing advisory centre.

In general, it seems to us that although in existing circumstances local authorities are likely to play a continually increasing part in resolving the problems of the central city, it is essential that the central government should be prepared to assist – or even intervene directly – in those cases where local authorities are unable or unwilling to discharge their responsibilities. The urban programme provides the precedent – if only as a potentiality.

Employment

The passing into law of the Race Relations Act of 1968 introduced a new element into the field of industrial relations. It is too early to say whether the Act has, in fact, proved successful in outlawing discrimination in employment but it is of the greatest importance to ensure that its provisions should be effective and our first priority would be to reinforce the effectiveness of the Act. With this in mind, we suggest that the Board should make full use of their powers to undertake 'pattern' inquiries into practices in various sectors of industry. We also hope that other organizations will involve themselves in the continuing task of testing the extent of discrimination. In this context we attach considerable importance to the keeping of records by employers of all kinds which distinguish employees by ethnic origin at all levels of employment. This should apply to

Government agencies and local authorities as much as to the private sector. Second, we attach considerable significance to the exemplary role of Government. This involves (among other things) taking an active role in seeking out recruits from minority groups, and providing opportunities for promotion for them. We welcome the belated introduction of a non-discrimination clause in Government contracts and we hope that this example will be followed by local authorities. 'The Government should also ensure that its own employees are adequately equipped for the tasks that they have to perform in this field. It is of particular importance that youth employment officers should receive additional training which would equip them to function more effectively.'

We agree with Lord Shepherd's comment in the Lords debate that 'affirmative action to provide opportunities regardless of colour is likely in the long run to prove more effective than simply taking action as the occasion arises to deal with individual examples of discrimination'.[10] . . . 'The Government,' he added, 'see the provision of equal employment opportunities for all as part of an overall improvement in all labour relations and efficiency of industry.' We hope that the Government itself, as an employer, will set an example for the private sector.

The role of Government in this field can be supplemented by both sides of industry. Companies wherever possible should commit themselves to specifically planned policies with targets where possible which are the responsibility of a senior member of management. These policies should be communicated to the employees, the community at large, and the official race relations agencies. Wherever possible, steps should be taken to ensure that such professions of faith are not merely empty declarations but are followed through with the full weight of managerial authority. Similarly, trade unions should be prepared to issue declarations that they are committed to a policy of equal employment opportunity and follow this through by appointing senior officials to ensure that the policy is translated into action.

Finally, and in many ways, the most important of all, is the whole question of training. With the increased pace of technological change and the spread of industrial mergers, new jobs are appearing and old ones disappearing continuously. In order to meet the needs of the situation and capitalize on the potential that such changes hold for the country there is a growing demand for retraining which can be of particular benefit to coloured workers. The scope and scale and organization of training in this country has been and is inadequate. There is a need for a large-scale expansion of training facilities and greater inducements to encourage workers, management and unions to utilize these facilities. We also believe that there is considerable scope for a more imaginative use of the Industrial Training Act for the benefit of all workers to acquire skills in their widest sense. Additionally, the Industrial Training Act should be operated in a way that ensures that employees have an equal opportunity to acquire skills and that in order to qualify for training grants under the Act employers should be required to show they are not discriminating in any way. Companies who employ non-English speaking workers should provide them with an opportunity to learn English either by organized instruction, or through day release, paid for by the Industrial Training Board.

Education

As we indicated in the introduction to this section, the problems facing local authorities in areas of potential immigrant settlement are often such as not to be within the scope of the local education authorities' capacity to resolve. Nor has the Department of Education and Science been in a position to assist. As Lady Serota told the House of Lords, 'the role of the Department has been to give them (the local education authorities) support by making available extra resources, by providing buildings and teachers; by stimulating curriculum development and research, in consultation with other bodies, and by collecting and disseminating statistics on which policies are based. And above all, and perhaps most important of all for the future, by encouraging new approaches to teacher training with immigrant needs in mind.'[11]

As we have tried to show in our chapter on the evolution of policy, this interpretation of the D.E.S.'s past role is a flattering one. Although progress has been made in some of the areas mentioned by Lady Serota there are other areas in which further action is still urgently required. For example, it is essential to clarify official thinking of the question of dispersal. Lady Serota told the House of Lords that the department recognized that 'this field of policy "must be kept" under review in the light of the progress that is being made in the schools, by meeting the linguistic problems of our immigrant children'.[12] In the light of past events this is not an encouraging statement and it reinforces our desire to see a full-scale inquiry into the effect of the dispersal. D.E.S. witnesses before the House of Commons Select Committee made it clear that the existing policy had developed on a rule of thumb basis; it is long since time that policy in such an important area were evolved on a more systematic basis. In addition, it is essential that the inspectorate which advises the minister should be better equipped to fulfil its functions in this particular area. A special branch assembling and disseminating expertise not only on language teaching but also on race relations and other problems facing the typical urban multi-racial school could also prove valuable. Similarly, local authorities should be equipped to meet the new needs arising from the present immigrants by changes in their internal structure – a special advisor for immigrant children would seem in most instances to be a justifiable appointment. Such an advisor should have as part of his terms of reference the supervision of various innovations – teaching centres, part-time courses, nursery and infant teachers and crash induction courses for new teachers. Such courses need to be backed up by the introduction into the syllabuses of colleges and universities departments of education of courses that will equip teachers to teach in multiracial areas. Additional provision should also be made to help teachers in primary schools through the provision of new teaching material and, wherever possible, full-time assistants in the classroom. There should also be added attention to the question of the relationship between immigrant parents and their children in schools and care should be taken to ensure that educational psychologists and others who are involved in the child guidance services are equipped to cope with the special problems that may face the children.

Some of the problems facing West Indian children will persist when the immediate difficulties arising from language differences have been resolved. We urge that continued attention should be given to resolving these problems, both by the D.E.S. and local education authorities.

Police–Community Relations

The problems that confront the police and coloured immigrants in their mutual relations are frequently the problems of the areas in which they meet. Many of our proposals would apply to police work in cities generally but there are others that arise from the nature of race relations as such. We attach particular importance to the work of the police in this field since any deterioration in the relationship between police and minorities would have far-reaching consequences.

Our first concern is with the question of the training of the police and we recommend that a committee of inquiry should be set up to assess the adequacy of current methods. In-service training is as important as recruit training, and the experience of the new recruit fresh from training school should be regarded as a critical stage in any training scheme. Training officers at local level play a vitally important part in this respect. Almost equally important is the question of recruitment. Not only should there be a firm declaration of policy on the recruitment of police officers from among all the minority groups but there should also be a special attempt to recruit from those groups among which there has not so far been a response, extending where necessary special pre-recruitment programmes. We endorse the efforts already made by various police forces to introduce a local liaison scheme and we suggest that to support the work of liaison officers a special appointment should be made to the staff of H.M. Inspectorate, with this responsibility. We endorse criticism that had already been made of the existing machinery for adjudicating complaints against the police and consider that some form of new procedure for handling such complaints, involving the principle of external review, should now be introduced. We also recommend that the Home Secretary should revert to his original decision to include in police discipline regulations a special category of offence: racial discrimination. Both these proposals are designed to ensure that the confidence of minority groups – and others – in the fairness of the police should be maintained, and strengthened.

Finally, we feel that there should be a systematic attempt to circulate information on the rights and obligations of the citizen vis-à-vis the police and that there should be further research into the development of the community relations function in the police service.

Community Relations Commission

The new Community Relations Commission, which was set up under the Race Relations Act of 1968, has taken over the function of the old National Committee for Commonwealth Immigrants. On the basis of the first year's work it is probably still too early to judge the success of the Commission's operation, although considerable criticism has been voiced in Parliament and elsewhere of its performance. For example, it cannot be said that the difficulties that arose in the case of the N.C.C.I. between the liaison officers on the one hand and the national body on the other have been satisfactorily resolved. Nor is the question of their activities from liaison officers and the supervision of their activities from the centre yet placed on a proper footing. However, problems have continued to arise in local situations with which liaison officers operating within the existing machinery find it difficult to cope. A large section of the local committee is very often concerned to block controversial action and many of them have been dominated by political representatives who do not wish to have their policies questioned. In some areas the weakness of immigrant organizations and the lack of effective leadership has also been a serious handicap; too often the immigrant communities have been represented by prestige leaders who have no roots in the community.

The problems that result from this complex of difficulties do not admit of a single simple solution. We would urge that the various proposals for reform that have been put forward should now be recognized – among them the recommendation in the original report for the centralized recruitment and training of liaison officers.

Civil Rights and Immigrant Leadership

The likelihood of a civil rights organization emerging that would embrace all the immigrant communities seems to us still remote. The rank and file of immigrants are still concerned with establishing themselves in this country and the different communities have little in common except the fact of migration and the shared experience of discrimination. The diplomatic and consular role of the High Commissions perpetuates uncertainty in the minds of immigrants about their status and has mixed consequences for the evolution of immigrant organizations.

No one from outside the immigrant communities can create a civil rights organization and it is not for us to recommend what can only occur spontaneously. In view of the misunderstanding that has risen over the form in which our comments in the original report were cast, we would like to state quite emphatically that we would welcome the emergence of such an organization. If the recently-established Martin Luther King Foundation proves to be such an organization, that will be a significant step forward. We also hope that there will be serious consideration of the proposal in the report about consulting immigrant leaders and their co-option on to various advisory bodies. We would add that if an emergent body should happen to bear the label 'Black Power' it should not, on that score alone, be rejected by central and local government. At this stage, Black Power still represents a minority tendency within the broad range of immigrant organizations, but on the evidence available to us it seems to have advanced in importance since *Colour and Citizenship* was drafted. The aspirations that it represents are a reflection of the progressive disillusionment which has been so strongly felt by minorities over the past few years. Black Power enshrines a real emotion based on real grievances and needs to be treated seriously.

The Churches

In our analysis we noted the decline in the hold of nearly all the major denominations in the central areas of the major cities and the inadequate preparation of many ministers for the situation with which they are confronted. Some form of provision in the training of priests and ministers that would enable them to cope with these problems would be desirable; equally, they should be made familiar with the range of social services available in such areas. We would also like to see churches of all denominations prepared to release buildings for community activities. So many community projects are frustrated for lack of premises at the same time as church buildings are under-used. Church buildings should, in our view, also be made available to West Indian sects and members of other faiths for the holding of religious services.

We also urge that the Church should make a more substantial use of their mediating role between the minorities and the majorities. This could be particularly important in relation to the local press and the local police. Churchmen may often find that their most effective contribution may be made in conjunction with others who are working for the same ends, but that they have special opportunities should not be overlooked.

Public Education

In our view, there is a need for an extensive, varied, and authoritative effort to publicize the actual facts concerning immigration, in particular the real characteristics of the coloured population. We welcome the work of the Runnymede Trust in this direction and hope that it can be extended. Second, there seems to be a need to define expressively what our national values are and their implications for issues of race and colour. The fluidity of the situation and the persistence of a degree of tolerance suggests that forthright unequivocating leadership could go some way towards allaying anxieties. Such leadership should be expected not only of the heads of the major political parties but also from those in authority in other institutions.

Public education should also be directed towards informing people of all ages about cultural variety, the contribution that immigrant groups have made and the importance of diversity that they have produced in this country for the health of our society.

But perhaps more important still are those constructive programmes of community action which involve citizen participation and which focus on the real problems of the community. The feeling of impotence in the face of what is seen as a natural disaster lies at the root of much of the resentment against the coloured immigrants, who are often held responsible for the decline of the amenities and environment of inner city areas. The old-established residents are potentially valuable allies. They are not likely to be interested in programmes which have the express aim of integrating the immigrants, but their energies can be enlisted for projects designed to improve the neighbourhood as a whole. Such local organizations are effective if they can create a sense of purpose and make people believe that it is possible to get things done to improve the conditions in which people are living.

The Mass Media

The role of the press and of broadcasting authorities can in many ways be crucial. In the last five years immigration and race relations have had an irresistible appeal for news and features editors and those who produce discussion programmes. Whenever a politician speaks on this subject he knows he is likely to be reported and the emphasis given to his statements varies in proportion to the extremism of the views he professes. We are not questioning the judgment of those who decide on news values but there are certain matters of procedure which we feel are of importance. Editors who have a sense of responsibility to the public will not wish to incite the prejudices which are latent in most of us, yet some of the practices in newspapers have this effect. For example, the ethnic identification of defendants in criminal proceedings, or the printing of letters which are hostile to coloured immigrants. Then there is the headline treatment and play on stories involving coloured immigrants. There is a tendency to sensationalize, pick out the most prejudicial elements in the stories and to print scare headlines.

In the fifteen years of its existence, the Press Council has had something to say on these practices. Their policy seems, on balance, to have been a rather contradictory one; for example, in two cases, one in 1965 and one in 1968, the council took a rather different position. In the first, the 'harmful social effects' of a story in a local evening newspaper was deprecated. But in the latter case, it was ruled that a cartoon which might be offensive to coloured immigrants could not be censored since the fact that a publication might be 'offensive to a part or even a majority of the population would be quite inconsistent with the freedom of the Press'. This seems to us to be confusing the council's duty to censor bad taste with its obligation not to censure opinion.

Our view is that it would be advantageous to have frequent discussions between the press and broadcasting authorities and in particular those in responsible positions in the major institutions (perhaps through their professional associations) and that the Press Council should address itself to these questions and lay down certain guide-lines for professional practice. And in the field of television, where both the B.B.C. and the commercial television companies have carried large numbers of discussion programmes on this topic, there should be some attempt to consider whether the techniques currently employed may not risk having an adverse effect on race relations.

Immigration Policy

In introducing the annual debate on the renewal of the Commonwealth Immigrants Act, Baroness Serota told the House of Lords that 'it has been customary ... to tax the Government on these annual occasions with the fact that immigration control continues, year after year, to be renewed on this annual basis. [Members] take the view, as indeed do the Government, that legislation of such continuing importance should be placed on a permanent footing. ... This is the first occasion when I, myself, have taken part in one of these debates and I do not propose to spend time apologizing for the fact that once again we are seeking an annual renewal of legislation governing the immigration of aliens and Commonwealth citizens. The Government are on record as agreeing that permanent legislation is desirable, but we have been, I think the House will agree, far from inactive in the field of legislation in the immigration area in these last few years. ... My Right Honourable Friend, the

Home Secretary, thinks it right that we should gain experience of the workings of the appeals system before consolidating the immigration laws on a permanent basis.'[13]

It therefore seems clear that any comprehensive review of the current system of immigration control is likely to be put off for a further period. In the circumstances, we do not think it necessary to restate the detailed proposals that are incorporated in the original version of *Colour and Citizenship*.[14] Nevertheless, it may be of some value to outline the general principles that we consider should underlie any system of immigration control and which should be taken into account, in any review of the existing system. We feel that four broad considerations need to be kept in mind in framing a policy. First, the view that in the case of the movement of population to the United Kingdom the national interest should ultimately take first place is reasonable under present circumstances – as long as population policy is the responsibility of nation states and while effective machinery for co-ordination on an international basis does not exist. Secondly, there must be recognition that migration is a process that does not solely affect the country of reception. It also involves the sending society, and sometimes third parties – as in the case of the Kenya Asian episode. Policy must therefore be devised not solely on the basis of the interest of the receiving country, but take into account the legitimate concerns of the other parties to the process. Thirdly, it is important to devise an efficient structure for operating an immigration policy which will serve these ends – and one that operates fairly and efficiently and is seen to operate fairly and efficiently. Finally, policy must be linked with a fair and coherent system of citizenship. At present, the system of U.K. citizenship deriving from the British Nationality Act of 1948, is in a state of disrepair as a result of legislation passed in 1962 and 1968.

Within these broad outlines, we feel that there are other objectives which should if possible be met. First of all, we attach great importance to the principle that families should, wherever possible, not be divided. Second, we feel it important that there should be scope for the ambitious unskilled worker to obtain entry into this country, where he may often be able to make a substantial contribution. Third, we attach importance to the fairness of the system as between different immigrant groups; any suggestion of a more favoured status deriving from the ethnic composition of the population of one country or another must be avoided. At the same time, it should be recognized that there are cases where individual countries may well have a good case for special treatment. Political pressure in the case of Gibraltar and economic pressure in the case of some West Indian islands are an obvious example. Finally, in our view there is no longer any overwhelmingly strong reason why any system of immigration control should not be made uniform – *provided* that it will be susceptible of modification in the event of entry into the European community, conferring a more favourable status on European workers.

The task of putting flesh on these bare bones is a complex one which would certainly include a great deal of labour and Parliamentary time. Nevertheless, we are convinced that it is justifiable and that the Government are right in principle to accept that reform is overdue. The present patchwork system is a standing invitation to exploitation by the unscrupulous of all shades of skin colour. Whether the Government's activities in the field, to which Lady Serota refers, have been altogether constructive in this consequence is more doubtful. But we have no doubt at all that one important way of recapturing the confidence lost by some of these measures would be to get the whole system of control on a just, logical and humane footing. We hope that this will not be much longer delayed: the scrutiny of control procedures now being undertaken by the House of Commons Select Committee could provide a useful stimulus to action.

CONCLUSIONS

Even if all the proposals we have outlined were adopted overnight, they would not produce the multi-racial millennium. Advance in this field involves slow and painful effort: there are no simple solutions to such complex problems. And, as the bulk of the evidence that we have presented indicates, time is no longer on the side of those who believe in peaceful change as a real possibility. The best that can be said of the situation of minorities in our society is that it is not getting any worse: and this at a time when the standards by which these minorities will judge the performance of our society are becoming steadily more rigorous. Rightly, our coloured fellow citizens are coming to demand equality and nothing short of equality.

The Government has recognized the need for action and grasped – after exasperating delays – the basis on which constructive policies can be launched. But there is still too great a willingness to mistake gestures for action and the notion is still too commonly found that strategically applied patches will prevent the underlying structural problems from bursting out. The complex of problems affecting the inner city, of which race relations form a key part, demands fundamental reforms for their resolution.

But fundamental reforms cost money (there is no escaping that) and spending money on a scale sufficient to make significant progress will demand, in turn, a commitment to change which can only be made if it commands broad consent. If we are right in our analysis and the 'liberal hour' is passed, such consent seems impossibly far away. The water has been too muddied by the acrimonious exchange of accusations and counter-accusations between those of all kinds of views and skin colours who should be the consenting parties to change. Perhaps Pogo (of the comic strip) is right: 'We have seen the enemy and he is us.' Not out of 'racialism' (another of the infinitely elastic terms, like integration) or malice or blind selfishness. These are simpler failings; from exhaustion, lack of direct involvement, boredom with a topic over-exposed to public view. Because our situation is not dramatic, the temptation is all the stronger to relegate the whole subject to the mental lumber room with last year's other headline stories. But the lack of drama that justifies such action also conceals the deep-seated faults which will eventually divide our society irreparably, like other societies, if the gaps cannot now be bridged.

Deep-seated the problems may be, but not incurable. The first and longer version of this report was compared by one reviewer in its shape, colour and weight – to a domestic brick. This abridged volume, its successor, may be only a half brick, but half bricks may prove handier missiles with which to break the windows of the rooms where Auden's 'quiet men, working too hard' are taking the vital decisions – and let in a sense of urgency.

REFERENCES

1. House of Lords Debate, 16th December, 1969 (Vol. 306, Col. 1007).
2. *Jewish Chronicle*, 28th November, 1969.
3. House of Lords Debate, op. cit. (Vol. 306. Cols. 1087–8).
4. *The Problems of Coloured School Leavers: Observations on the Report of the Select Committee on Race Relations and Immigration* (London, H.M.S.O. 1970), Cmnd. 4268. This White Paper was issued after this book had gone to the printers and confirms the impression discussed on page 353 that Government has been and is too complacent. Apart from admitting that the Department of Education and Science could have taken action sooner (p. 2) little sense of urgency or of a critical re-evaluation of past policy is apparent. The main method of action proposed by the Government is to encourage and discuss with the appropriate authorities methods of bringing certain additional resources to bear on particular problems. Apart from the familiar difficulty of persuading recalcitrant local authorities, employers, trade unions and others to take action there is the more fundamental objection that the resources available can do no more than gild a crumbling façade.
5. *Colour and Citizenship*, p. 755.
6. House of Lords Debate (Vol. 306, Col. 1007).
7. House of Lords Debate (Vol. 306, Col. 997).
8. *Council Housing: Purposes, Procedures and Priorities* (London, H.M.S.O., 1969).
9. House of Lords Debate (Vol. 306, Col. 1083).
10. House of Lords Debate (Vol. 306, Col. 1001).
11. House of Lords Debate (Vol. 306, Col. 1086).
12. Ibid.
13. House of Lords Debate, 25th November, 1969 (Vol. 306, Col. 1191).
14. *Colour and Citizenship*, pp. 744–53.

Sources

Abrams, M., *The Newspaper Reading Public of Tomorrow* (London, Odhams Press, 1964).

Acton Society, 'Study of Immigrant Workers in London Transport' (unpublished material for I.R.R.).

Alderson, S., *Britain in the Sixties, Housing* (Harmondsworth, Penguin Books, 1962).

Allen, S., 'Study of Pakistanis in Employment, Bradford' (unpublished material for I.R.R.).

Aurora, G. S., *The New Frontiersmen* (Bombay, Popular Prakashan, 1967).

Bagley, C., 'The Educational Performance of Immigrant Childrens', *Race* (Vol. X, No. 1, July, 1968).
— 'Relative Deprivation and the Working-Class Racialist', *I.R.R. Newsletter* (June, 1968).

Banton, M., *The Coloured Quarter* (London, Cape, 1955).
— *The Police and the Community* (London, Tavistock, 1967).
— *Race Relations* (London, Tavistock, 1967).
— *White and Coloured* (London, Cape, 1959).

Barker, E., *Commonwealth Immigrants; the Work and Attitude of the Church of England* (London, Board for Social Responsibility, 1963).

Barr, J., 'New Towns as Anti-Ghettoes?', *New Society* (No. 131, 1st April, 1965).

Bayliss, F. J., and Coates, J. B., 'West Indians at Work in Nottingham', *Race* (Vol. VII, No. 2, October, 1965).

Beetham, D., *Immigrant School Leavers and the Youth Employment Service in Birmingham* (London, I.R.R., Special Series, 1968).

Bell, R. R., 'The Lower Class Negro Family in the United States and Great Britain', *Race* (October, 1969).

Bennett, A. G., *Because They Know Not* (London, Phoenix Press, n.d.).

Bettelheim, B. and Janowitz, M., *Social Change and Prejudice, including dynamics of prejudice* (1st edn.) (New York, Free Press of Glencoe, 1950).

Blake, Judith, *Family Structure in Jamaica* (New York, Free Press of Glencoe, 1961).

Bloom, Leonard, 'Study of Butetown, Cardiff' (unpublished material for I.R.R.).

Bonham, J., *The Middle-Class Vote* (London, Faber and Faber, 1954).

Borrie, W. D. (ed.), *The Cultural Integration of Immigrants* (Paris, U.N.E.S.C.O., 1959).

British Medical Association, *Medical Examination of Immigrants: report of the working party* (London, B.M.A., 1965).

Brookes, Dennis, 'Study of Immigrant Workers in London Transport' (unpublished material for I.R.R.).

Bulla, H. M., 'Immigration – Past, Present and Future: attitudes and official policies of local officials in West Bromwich to coloured Commonwealth immigrants' (Dissertation for B.A. degree, University of Bradford, 1966).

Burgess, T., *et al.*, *In Matters of Principle: Labour's Last Chance* (Harmondsworth, Penguin Books, 1968).

Burgin T. and Edson, P., *Spring Grove: the education of immigrant children* (London, O.U.P., for I.R.R., 1967).

Burney, Elizabeth, *Housing on Trial* (London, O.U.P., for I.R.R., 1967).

Burt, R. A., 'Colour Prejudice in Great Britain' (B.A. thesis, Princeton, 1960).

Butler, D. E. and Rose, R., *The British General Election of 1959* (London, Macmillan, 1960).

Butterworth, E. (ed.), *Immigrants in West Yorkshire* (London, I.R.R. Special Series, 1967).

— 'Policies for Integration: a study of Bradford' (unpublished material for I.R.R.).

Callaghan, Rt. Hon. James, M.P., Speech to Institute of Race Relations, 8th February, 1968, in I.R.R. *Newsletter* (February, 1968).

Calley, M. J. C., *God's People* (London, O.U.P., for I.R.R., 1965).

Campaign Against Racial Discrimination, *The White Paper: A Spur to Racialism* (London, C.A.R.D., 1965).

Central Housing Advisory Committee Housing Management Sub-Committee, *Council Housing: Purposes, Procedures, and Priorities 1969* (Chairman: J. B. Cullingworth).

Children and their Primary Schools, A Report of the Central Advisory Council for Education (Plowden Report) (London, H.M.S.O., 1967).

SOURCES

Ciba Foundation, *Immigration, Medical and Social Aspects*, edited by Wolstenholm, G. E. W. and O'Connor, M. (London, Churchill, 1966).

Clarke, Edith, *My Mother who Fathered Me* (2nd edn, London, Allen & Unwin, 1966).

Cohen, B. and Jenner, P., 'The Employment of Immigrants: a case study within the wool industry', *Race* (Vol. X, No. 1, July, 1968).

Collins, Sidney, *Coloured Minorities in Britain* (London, Lutterworth Press, 1957).

Collins, W., *Jamaican Migrant* (London, Routledge & Kegan Paul, 1965).

Commonwealth Immigrants, Circular No. 15/67 (London, Home Office, February, 1967).

Commonwealth Immigrants Act 1962: control of immigration statistics 1962/3–1966, Home Office (Cmnd. 2151, 2379, 2658, 2979, 3258) (London, H.M.S.O., 1962–67).

Commonwealth Immigrants Advisory Council, *Report* (Cmnd. 2119) (London, H.M.S.O, July, 1963).

— *Second Report* (Cmnd. 2266) (London, H.M.S.O., February, 1964).

— *Third Report* (Cmnd. 2458) (London, H.M.S.O., September, 1964).

— *Fourth Report* (Cmnd. 2796) (London, H.M.S.O., October, 1965).

Community Relations Commission, *Annual Report* (London, H.M.S.O., 1969).

Conference on Racial Equality in Employment, London, February 1967, *Report* (London, National Committee for Commonwealth Immigrants, 1967).

Craven, Anna, *West Africans in London* (I.R.R. Special Series, 1968).

Cumper, G. E. 'Employment in Barbados', *Social and Economic Studies* (Vol. VIII, No. 2, 1959).

— 'Working Class Emigration from Barbados to the U.K., October, 1955', *Social and Economic Studies* (Vol. VI, No. 1, 1957).

Dahya, B., 'Study of Pakistanis in Bradford' (unpublished material for I.R.R.).

— 'Study of Yemenis in Birmingham' (unpublished material for I.R.R.).

Dahya, Z., 'Pakistani Wives in Britain', *Race* (Vol VI, No. 3, January 1965).

Daniel, W. W., *Racial Discrimination in England* (Harmondsworth, Penguin Books, 1968).

Davison, Betty, 'No Place Back Home: a study of Jamaicans returning to Kingston, Jamaica', *Race* (Vol. IX, No. 4, April, 1968).

Davison, R. B., *Black British* (London, O.U.P., for I.R.R., 1966).

— *West Indian Migrants* (London, O.U.P. for I.R.R., 1962).

Deakin, Nicholas (ed.), *Colour and the British Electorate 1964* (London, Pall Mall Press, 1965).

— 'The Politics of the Commonwealth Immigrants Bill', *Political Quarterly* (Vol. 39, No. 1, January–March, 1968).

Deedes, W., *Race Without Rancour* (London, Conservative Research Department, 1968).

Department of Education and Science, *Statistics of Education* (Vol. 1) (London, H.M.S.O., 1966).

Department of Health and Social Security, *Digest of Health Statistics 1969* (London, H.M.S.O., 1969).

Desai, R., *Indian Immigrants in Britain* (London, O.U.P., for I.R.R., 1963).

Dines, M. (London Council of Social Service) The West Indian Family', *Race* (Vol. IX, No. 4, April 1968).

Donnelly, L. (ed.), *Justice First* (London, Sheed & Ward, 1969).

Donnison, D. V., *The Government of Housing* (Harmondsworth, Penguin Books, 1967).

Dummet, A., 'What to do', *Race Today* (July 1969).

Economist Intelligence Unit, *The Immigrant Community in Southall* (London, E.I.U., 1965).

Economist Intelligence Unit, *Studies on Immigration from the Commonwealth, 1. Basic statistics* (London, E.I.U., 1961).

The Education of Immigrant Pupils in Primary Schools, Report of the Working Party of Members of the Inspectorate and School Psychological Service (London, Inner London Education Authority, 1967).

The Education of Immigrants, Department of Education and Science, Circular No. 7/65 (London, D.E.S., June, 1965).

Elahi, Karem, 'Some aspects of Social Adaptation of Pakistani Immigrants in Glasgow' (M.A. thesis, Edinburgh University, 1967).

English for Immigrants, Ministry of Education (London, H.M.S.O.).

English for the Children of Immigrants, Schools Council, Working Paper, No. 13 (London, H.M.S.O., 1967).

Eversley, D. and Sukdeo, F., *The Dependants of the Coloured Commonwealth Population of England and Wales* (London, I.R.R. Special Series, 1969).

Figueroa, Peter, 'West Indian School Leavers in North London' (unpublished material for I.R.R.).

Fitzherbert, K., *West Indian Children in London* (London, G. Bell, 1967).

Foley, Maurice, speech given at Leicester, 12th September, 1965, reprinted in *Plebs* (December, 1965).

Foot, Paul, *Immigration and Race in British Politics* (Harmondsworth, Penguin Books, 1965).

— 'The Strike at Courtaulds, Preston', I.R.R. *Newsletter* (July, 1965 Supplement).

Francis, O. C., 'The Characteristics of Emigrants just prior to Changes in British Commonwealth Immigration Policies', in *The Caribbean in Transition* (University of Puerto Rico, Institute of Caribbean Studies, 1965).

— *The People of Modern Jamaica* (Kingston, Department of Statistics, 1963).

Gardiner, R., *A World of Peoples* (London, B.B.C. Publications, 1966).

General Register Office, Census 1961 England and Wales (London, H.M.S.O.).

— Sample Census, 1966 Great Britain (London, H.M.S.O.).

Gish, O. and Robertson, A., 'Where Immigrant Doctors Go and Why', *New Statesman* (14th March, 1969).

Gish, Oscar, 'Training and Advancement of Non-British Nurses', I.R.R. *Newsletter* (November–December, 1968).

Glass, Ruth, *Newcomers* (London, Allen & Unwin, for Centre for Urban Studies, 1960).

Glass, R. and Westergaard, J., *London's Housing Needs* (London, Centre for Urban Studies, 1965).

Goodall, John, 'Huddersfield', I.R.R. *Newsletter* Supplement (October, 1966).

Gorer, G., *Exploring English Character* (London, Cresset Press, 1955).

Griffith, J. A. G., *Central Departments and Local Authorities* (London, Allen & Unwin, 1966).

Grigg, Mary, *The White Question* (London, Secker & Warburg, 1967).

Half Our Future, A Report of the Central Advisory Committee for Education, England (Newson Report) (London, H.M.S.O, 1963).

Hall, Stuart, *The Young Englanders* (London, N.C.C.I., 1967).

Hawkes, N., *Immigrant Children in British Schools* (London, Pall Mall Press, for I.R.R., 1966).

Heineman, Jr, B. W., 'The Policies of Race: a study of the Campaign against Racial Discrimination' (unpublished B.Litt. thesis, Oxford, 1967).

Henriques, Fernando, *Family and Colour in Jamaica* (London, Eyre & Spottiswoode, 1953).

Hepple, Bob, *Race, Jobs and the Law* (London, Allen Lane, the Penguin Press, 1968).

Hill Clifford S., *West Indian Migrants and the London Churches* (London, O.U.P. for I.R.R., 1963).

Hill, C. S. and Matthew, D. (eds.), *Race: A Christian Symposium* (London, Gollancz, 1968).

Hindell, K., 'The Genesis of the Race Relations Bill, *Political Quarterly* (Vol. 36, No. 4, October–December, 1965).

Hinds, Donald, *Journey to an Illusion* (London, Heinemann, 1966).

Houghton, D., *Paying for the Social Services* (London, Institute of Economic Affairs, 1967).

House of Commons Select Committee on Race Relations and Immigration: The Problems of Coloured School Leavers. Vol. 1 – Report, Vols. 2, 3 and 4 – Minutes of Evidence (London, H.M.S.O., 1969).

The Housing Programme 1965 to 1970, Minister of Housing and Local Government, White Paper (Cmnd. 2838) (London, H.M.S.O., 1965).

Hunte, J. A., *Nigger Hunting in England?* (London, West Indian Standing Conference, London Branch, 1966).

Immigrants and the Youth Service, Report of a Committee of the Youth Service Development Council (Hunt Report) (H.M.S.O., 1967).

Immigration Appeals Bill 1968, Aliens: Draft Instruction to Immigration Officers, Home Office, White Paper (Cmnd. 3830) (London, H.M.S.O., 1968).

Immigration from the Commonwealth, The Prime Minister, White Paper (Cmnd. 2739) (London, H.M.S.O., August 1965).

Interim Housing Survey, Notting Hill Summer Project 1967 (Notting Hill Housing Service, 1969).

International Social Service, *Immigrants at London Airport and their Settlement in the Community* (London, I.S.S., June, 1967).

Israel, W. H., *Colour and Community* (Slough, Council of Social Service, 1964).

James, J., in Campaign Against Racial Discrimination *News Letter* (No. 2, July, 1967).

Jenkins, Rt. Hon. Roy, M.P., Address given by the Home Secretary to a meeting of Voluntary Liaison Committees, 23rd. May, 1966 (London, N.C.C.I., 1966).

— *The Labour Case* (Harmondsworth, Penguin Books, 1959).

— 'Speech to Institute of Race Relations', reprinted in *Race* (Vol. VIII, No. 3, January 1967).

SOURCES

John, DeWitt, *Indian Workers' Associations in Britain* (London, O.U.P. for I.R.R., 1969).

Jones, K., 'Immigrants and the Social Services', *National Institute Economic Review* (No. 41, August, 1967).

Jones, M., 'The Police and the Citizen', for the N.C.C.I. (London, October, 1969).

Katznelson, I., *The Policies of Race Under the Impact of Migration: the United States (1900–1930) and the United Kingdom (1948–68)*: unpublished thesis.

Kent, B., 'The Social Worker's Cultural Pattern as it Affects Casework with Immigrants', *Social Work* (October, 1965).

Kiev, A., 'Psychiatric Illness among West Indians in London', *Race* (Vol. 5, No. 3, January, 1964).

Kinder, Clive, 'Study of Moss Side' (unpublished material for I.R.R.).

Lambert, John, 'Study of Immigrant Crime and the Relations of the Police and Immigrants in a Division of Birmingham' (to be published by I.R.R. as 'Crime, Police and Race Relations').

Lester, A. (ed.), *Essays and Speeches by Roy Jenkins* (London, Collins, 1967).

Lester, A., 'The Race Relations Bill', *Venture* (Vol. XX, No. 5, May, 1968).

Lester, A. and Deakin, N. (eds.), *Policies for Racial Equality* (London, Fabian Society, 1969).

Levitan, S, *The Great Society's Poor Law* (Baltimore: The Johns Hopkins Press, 1969).

Lewis, G., 'Race Relations in Britain: a view from the Caribbean', *Race Today* (July, 1969).

— 'Protest Among the Immigrants – The Dilemma of Minority Culture', *Political Quarterly* (October–December, 1969).

Little, K. L., *Negroes in Britain: a study of race relations in English society* (London, Kegan Paul, 1947).

Lowenthal, David, 'Race and Colour in the West Indies', in *Daedalus* (Spring, 1967).

Lyon, Michael, 'Study of Settlement Patterns' (unpublished material for I.R.R.).

Manchester University Liberal Society, Study Group, *Anti-immigrant Organisations* (London, Union of Liberal Students, 1966).

Marris, P., 'The British Asians in Kenya', *Venture* (Vol. XX, No. 4, April 1968).

Marsh, P., *The Anatomy of a Strike: Unions, Employers, and Punjabi Workers in a Southall Factory* (London, I.R.R. Special Series, 1967).

Maunders, W. F., 'The New Jamaican Emigration', *Social and Economic Studies* (Vol. IV, No. 1).

Maxwell, Neville A., *The Power of Negro Action* (London, The Author, 1965).

McPherson, K. and Gaitskell, J., *Immigrants and Employment: two case studies in East London and Croydon* (London, I.R.R. Special Series, 1969).

Milner, D., 'The Effects of Prejudice', *Race Today* (August, 1969).

Milson, F., *Operation Integration Two: The Coloured Teenager in Birmingham* (Birmingham, Westhill College of Education, September, 1966).

Mishan, E. J. and Needleman, L., 'Immigration, Excess Aggregate Removed and the Balance of Payments', *Economica* (May, 1966).

Morris, H. S., *The Indians in Uganda* (London, Weidenfeld & Nicolson, 1968).

Myrdal, G., *An American Dilemma* (New York: Harper, 1944).

Nandy, Dipak, *The National Committee for Commonwealth Immigrants* (C.A.R.D. discussion paper, July, 1967).

National Committee for Commonwealth Immigrants, *The First Six Months: a report of the National Committee for Commonwealth Immigrants* (London, N.C.C.I., 1966).

National Committee for Commonwealth Immigrants, *Areas of Special Housing Needs* (London, N.C.C.I., May, 1967).

—*The Housing of Commonwealth Immigrants* (London, N.C.C.I., April, 1967).

—*Practical Suggestions for Teachers of Immigrant Children* (London, N.C.C.I., 1967).

—*Report for 1966* (London, N.C.C.I., 1967).

—*Report for 1967* (London, N.C.C.I., 1968).

—*Training Procedures and the N.C.C.I. Role,* Chief Inspector K. L. Lee (Metropolitan Police) NC/TRG/68/5, appendix 2.

National Union of Teachers, *The N.U.T. view on the Education of Immigrants* (London, N.U.T. 1967).

Nevitt, Della, *Housing, Taxation and Subsidies* (London, Nelson, 1966).

Oakley, R., *New Backgrounds* (London, O.U.P., for I.R.R., 1968).

Oakley, Robin, 'Study of Cypriots' (unpublished material for I.R.R.).

Old Houses into New Homes, White Paper (Cmnd. 3602), (London, H.M.S.O., April, 1968).

Oppé, T. E., *et al., Children of West Indian Immigrants: A study of One-Year-Olds in Paddington* (London, I.R.R. Special Series, 1970).

SOURCES

Oppé, T. E., 'The Health of West Indian Children' in *Proceedings of the Royal Society of Medicine* (Vol. 57, No. 3, April, 1964).

Orwell, G., *England, Your England and other Essays* (London, Secker & Warburg, 1953).

Our Older Homes: A Call for Action, Report of the Sub-Committee on Standards of Housing Fitness (Denington Report) (London, H.M.S.O., 1966).

Patnaik, Anjali, 'Study of Sikhs in Southall' (unpublished material for I.R.R.).

Patterson, Orlando, *The Children of Sisyphus* (London, Hutchinson, 1964).

Patterson, S., *Dark Strangers* (London, Tavistock Publications, 1963, and Harmondsworth, Penguin Books 1965).

— *Immigrants in Industry* (London, O.U.P. for I.R.R., 1968).

— *Immigration and Race Relations in Britain 1960–67* (London, O.U.P., for I.R.R., 1969).

Peach, G. C. K., 'Factors affecting the Distribution of West Indians in Britain', *Transactions and Papers 1966* (No. 38, Institute of British Geographers, 1966).

— 'West Indian Migration to Britain: the Economic Factors', in *Race* (Vol. VII, No. 1, July 1965).

— *West Indian Migration to Britain* (London, O.U.P. for I.R.R., 1968).

Political and Economic Planning and Research Services Ltd., *Racial Discrimination*, London, P.E.P., 1967).

Powell, Rt. Hon. J. Enoch, M.P., text of speech delivered on 20th April, 1968, in Birmingham, *Race* (Vol. X, No. 1, July, 1968).

Power, J., *Immigrants in School: a survey of administrative policies* (London, Councils and Education Press, 1967).

Price, C. A., *The Cultural Integration of Immigrants* (Paris, U.N.E.S.C.O., 1959).

— *Southern Europeans in Australia* (Melbourne, Oxford University Press, 1963).

Race Relations Board, *Report of the Race Relations Board 1966–7* (London, H.M.S.O., 1967).

Radburn, Robert, 'Investigation of Household Budgets among a Sample of Indians, Pakistanis, and West Indians in the Midlands' (unpublished material for I.R.R.).

Radin, B., 'Coloured Workers and British Trade Unions', *Race* (Vol. VIII, No. 2, October, 1966).

Report of the Commissioner of Police of the Metropolis 1967 (Cmnd. 3659).

Report of the Committee on Housing in Greater London

(Milner Holland Report) (Cmnd. 2605) (London, H.M.S.O., 1965).

Report of the Committee on Immigration Appeals (Wilson Committee) (Cmnd. 3387) (London, H.M.S.O., 1967).

Report of the Committee on Local Authority and Allied Personal Social Services (Seebohm Report) (Cmnd. 3703) (London, H.M.S.O., 1968).

Report of the National Executive Committee Working Party on Race Relations (Labour Party) (July, 1967).

Report of Her Majesty's Chief Inspector of Constabulary for the year 1965 (H.C. 251) *(for the year 1966 — H.C. 544)*.

Report of the National Advisory Commission on Civil Disorders (Kerner Report) (New York, Bantam Books, 1968).

Rex, J., 'The Race Relations Catastrophe', in *Matters of Principle: Labour's Last Chance* (Harmondsworth, Penguin Books, 1968).

Rex, J. and Moore, R., *Race, Community and Conflict: a study of Sparkbrook* (London, O.U.P., for I.R.R., 1967).

Richmond, A. H., *Colour Prejudice in Britain: a study of West Indian workers in Liverpool, 1942-51* (London, Routledge, 1954).

— *The Colour Problem* (Harmondsworth, Penguin Books, 1955).

Richmond, Anthony and Lyon, Michael, 'Race Relations in Bristol' (unpublished material for I.R.R.).

Roberts, G. W. and Abdulah N., 'Some Observations on the Educational Position of the Caribbean', *Social and Economic Studies* (Vol. XIV, No. 1, March, 1965).

Roberts, G. W. and Mills, D. O., 'Study of External Migration affecting Jamaica 1953-55', *Social and Economic Studies* (Vol. VII, No. 2, Supplement, 1958).

Rose, Hilary, *The Housing Problem* (London, Heinemann, 1968).

Royal Commission on Police: Minutes of Evidence 1960-2 (Chairman Sir Henry Willink), (London, H.M.S.O., 1963).

Royal Commission on Trade Unions and Employers' Associations 1965-1968, *Report* (Donovan Commission) (Cmnd. 3623) (London, H.M.S.O., 1968).

Senior, C. and Manley, D., *A Report on Jamaican Migration to Great Britain* (Kingston, Government Printers, 1955).

Silver, Eric, 'Maurice Foley', in *I.R.R. Newsletter* (February, 1967).

Simpson, G. W. and Yinger, J. M., *Racial and Cultural Minorities: an analysis of prejudice and discrimination* (3rd edn.) (New York, Harper and Row, 1955).

Simpson, R. E. D., 'Study of a General Practice with a large proportion of Immigrants' (research commissioned by the

SOURCES

Institute's Survey of Race Relations in Britain).
Singh, Khushwant, *A History of the Sikhs 1839–1964*, Vol. 2 (Princeton, Princeton University Press, 1966).
Sington, Derrick, 'Race Relations and the Police' (unpublished material for I.R.R.).
Skone, Dr. J. F. and Simpson, Dr. R. E. D., 'Socio-medical Study, Bristol' (unpublished material for I.R.R.).
Special But Not Separate, a Report on the Situation of Young Coloured People in Liverpool (Liverpool, Liverpool Youth Organisations Committee, 1968).
Steel, D., *No Entry* (Hurst, 1969).
Stroud, C. E., 'The New Environment', *Postgraduate Medical Journal* (October, 1965).
Tajfel, H. and Davison, J. L. (eds), *Disappointed Guests* (London, O.U.P., for I.R.R. 1965).
Thompson, J., 'Differential fertility among immigrants to England and Wales and some implications for population projections' in *The Journal of Biosocial Science* (Supplement, No. 1, July, 1969).
Times News Team, *Black Man in Search of Power* (London, Nelson, 1968).
Titmuss, R. H., *Commitment to Welfare* (London, Allen & Unwin, 1968).
Townsend, P., *Social Services for All*, Parts one and four, Fabian Tracts 382 and 385 (London, Fabian Society, 1968).
Trades Union Congress, *99th Annual Report, 1967* (Cooperative Printing Society, n.d.).
Uberoi, Narindar, 'Sikh Women in Southall', *Race* (Vol. VI, No. 1, July, 1965).
U.N.E.S.C.O., *The Positive Contribution by Immigrants* (Paris, U.N.E.S.C.O., 1955).
Waterhouse, J. A. H. and Brabban, D. H., 'Inquiry into fertility of immigrants: preliminary report', *Eugenics Review* (Vol. 56, No. 1, April, 1964).
West Indian Standing Conference, *The Unsquare Deal* (London, W.I.S.C., 1967).
Whitaker, B., *The Police* (Harmondsworth, Penguin Books, 1964).
Wiles, S., 'Children from Overseas' (1) and (2) in I.R.R. *News-letter* (February and June 1968).
Williams, L. F. Rushbrook, *The State of Pakistan* (rev. edn.) (London, Faber, 1966).
Williams, R. M., *Strangers Next Door: ethnic relations in American communities* (Englewood Cliffs, Prentice Hall, 1964).
Willmott, P. and Young, M., *Family and Kinship in East London*

(London, Routledge & Kegan Paul, 1957).

Wood, W. and Downing, J., *Vicious Circle* (London, S.P.C.K., 1968).

The Work of the Youth Employment Service 1965–8, Central Youth Employment Executive (London, H.M.S.O., 1968).

Wright, P., *The Coloured Worker in British Industry* (London, O.U.P., for I.R.R. 1968).

Yudkin, S., *The Health and Welfare of the Immigrant Child* (London, N.C.C.I., 1965).

Zander, M., 'The Unused Rent Acts', *New Society* (Vol. 12, No. 311, 12th September, 1968).

Panther Science

The Environment Game
Nigel Calder 8/6

The author, until recently editor of *New Scientist*, argues that the agricultural method of producing food has become too wasteful of the world's land areas. We must plan to produce our food as we produce motor cars or clothing – in factories. An abundance of food photo-synthetically produced – and, hand in hand, an abundance of reverted land to play with. Present agricultural areas will return to their pristine condition; vast tracts of a splendidly re-invigorated Mother Earth will become our playground. Not, as today, faraway, exclusive, expensive playgrounds for a small minority – but a world for all of us.

'Any solution to the problems posed by the present expansion of the world's population and the still accelerating productive capacity of technology in other directions must be to some extent Utopian. Mr. Calder's Utopia is curious, original and logical'
Times Educational Supplement

Panther Science

The Language of Life
An Introduction to the Science of
Genetics

George and Muriel Beadle   8/6

Genetics, a relatively new science, is concerned
with heredity and variations from it, and its
significance is that for good or for ill it may soon
be in a position to modify the biology of the
human being. Because it is a new discipline its
way of thought and its language have tended to
baffle most readers. This present book is one of
the first to deal with the vital problem of
communication.

'Dr. Beadle, a geneticist whose work earned
him the Nobel Prize in 1958, explained each part
of the subject to his wife who had no scientific
training, and it was she who actually wrote the
book. This has removed the major barrier of
language that exists between scientist and
laymen. The terms used are clearly explained,
helped by a free use of metaphor and a
simple style'
Times Educational Supplement

Panther Science

The Biological Time-Bomb
Gordon Rattray Taylor 8/6

'The first major exposition addressed to the general public of issues which are going to be very much with us in the next few decades . . . The point at issue is simple to state, very difficult to deal with.

The pursuit of knowledge eventually brings the power to control the subjects that knowledge is about; and power can be used for many purposes. In the physical sciences mankind has already been brought face to face with this. Knowledge of the atom has given him the power to devastate the Earth with nuclear bombs. Taylor's aim is to show us that biological knowledge is on the point of presenting us with powers that are equally double edged'
C.H.Waddington in *Science Journal*

'Taylor's book with its remorseless assembly of the components of the biological time-bomb, already dangerously near the critical mass, should alarm us'
Ritchie Calder in *New Scientist*